General Editor's Introduction

Asbury Theological Seminary Series in World Christian Revitalization Movements

This volume is published in collaboration with the Center for the Study of World Christian Revitalization Movements, a cooperative initiative of Asbury Theological Seminary faculty. Building on the work of the previous Wesleyan/Holiness Studies Center at the Seminary, the Center provides a focus for research in the Wesleyan Holiness and other related Christian renewal movements, including Pietism and Pentecostal movements, which have had a world impact. The research seeks to develop analytical models of these movements, including their biblical and theological assessment. Using an interdisciplinary approach, the Center bridges relevant discourses in several areas in order to gain insights for effective Christian mission globally. It recognizes the need for conducting research that combines insights from the history of evangelical renewal and revival movements with anthropological and religious studies literature on revitalization movements. It also networks with similar or related research and study centers around the world, in addition to sponsoring its own research projects.

Viv Grigg's extensive work among the poor in third world megacities informs his research on the revitalization of this population. His focus on "citywide transformative revival", embracing a concept of synergistic revivals in multiple sectors of a mega-city, envisions the long-term change of urban communities to reflect apostolic themes that are outcomes of gifts released in revival. These initiatives have already evidenced the emergence of new transformative structures which engage the postmodern "city soul". Hence, the focus of this volume demonstrates congruence with the mission of the Center and serves to advance its research objectives.

J. Steven O'Malley, PhD, Director
The Center for the Study of World Christian Revitalization Movements
Asbury Theological Seminary

Sub-Series Foreword

Intercultural Studies

The behavioral science approach to the study of revitalization movements has a long history that has developed several models. Anthropologists, among others, observed that people responded to colonialism and the expansion of the West in various ways including armed resistance, selective acceptance, and passive resistance. The problems of the colonial frontier led to a memorandum on acculturation written by Robert Redfield, Ralph Linton and Melville Herskovits in 1936. Elsewhere in the world, anthropologists observed "nativistic" or "cultural renewal" movements as well: cargo cults in Melanesia, messianic movements in South Africa, and politial revolutions in Latin America.

Anthony F. C. Wallace brought some order to this area of study with his 1956 article where he named the stages and subsumed the movements under the name of "revitalization movements." Harold Turner contributed the notion of New Religious Movements to focus on the indigenous responses to mission work seen on every continent. This can be seen as part of a larger development, from the 1960s on, to develop Social Movement Theory where people are seen as agents intentionally acting to renew and reform society by organizing others to resist or dethrone the powers that be. Such movements develop a culture and social organization that give meaning and impetus to action on behalf of the movement's aims. Meanwhile Church Growth theory continued to develop as a specific discipline in its own right, including some elements of these sociological theories.

In this book, Viv Grigg reflects on a lifetime in urban missions while encouraging the church to recover its undivided ministry of proclamation and social transformation. By using an action-reflection model, Grigg has documented the New Zealand church's process of renewal that is moving toward a new theology and practice of urban transformation. Beginning with people's stories means dealing with a variety of narratives that reflect the chaos of cities. Yet God works, the Kingdom comes, and the 'transforming revival' continues.

Michael A. Rynkiewich, PhD
Editor for the sub-series on Intercultural Studies

THE SPIRIT OF CHRIST AND THE POSTMODERN CITY

Transforming Revival Among Auckland's Evangelicals and Pentecostals

Viv Grigg

Published by
EMETH PRESS
www.emethpress.com
in Collaboration with the
Asbury Theological Seminary Center for the
Study of World Christian Revitalization Movements
and the Urban Leadership Foundation
www.urbanleaders.org

The Spirit of Christ and the Postmodern City,
Transforming Revival among Auckland's Evangelicals and Pentecostals

Copyright © 2009 Viv Grigg
Printed in the United States of America on acid-free paper

All rights reserved. No part of this book may be reproduced, or stored in a retrieval system or transmitted in any form or by any means, electronic, mechanical, photocopying, recording, scanning or otherwise, except as permitted by the 1976 United States Copyright Act, or with the prior written permission of Emeth Press. Requests for permission should be addressed to: Emeth Press, P. O. Box 23961, Lexington, KY 40523-3961.
http://www.emethpress.com.

Library of Congress Cataloging-in-Publication Data
Grigg, Viv.
  The spirit of Christ and the postmodern city : transforming revival among Auckland's evangelicals and pentecostals / Viv Grigg.
    p. cm. -- (The Asbury Theological Seminary series) (Intercultural studies, No.2)
  Includes bibliographical references and index.
  ISBN 978-0-9819582-4-8 (alk. paper)
  1. Revivals--New Zealand--Auckland. 2. Evangelicalism--New Zealand--Auckland. 3. Pentecostalism--New Zealand--Auckland. I. Title.
  BV3793.G75 2009
  269.0993'24--dc22   2009027166

Graphics and typesetting by Renée Lam, www.reneelam.com
Cover design by Jess Smith

Scripture taken from the Holy Bible, New International Version © 1973, 1978, 1984 by The International Bible Society. Used by permission of Zondervan Publishing House.

Sections of this book previously published as parts of chapters in:
1997. Transforming the Soul of Kiwi Cities. In Bruce Patrick (Ed.), *New Vision New Zealand* (Vol. II, pp. 106-126). Auckland: Vision New Zealand.
1997. Transforming the Soul of the Nation. In Bruce Patrick (Ed.), *Vision New Zealand Congress (1997).* Auckland: Vision New Zealand.
2000. *Creating an Auckland Business Theology.* P.O. Box 20-524, Auckland: Urban Leadership Foundation.

Introducing a Conversation

Here is a path-finding book of global significance. Though the research focus is New Zealand, the theological and historical insights have much broader applicability.

Viv Grigg is known for his compassionate ministry among the urban poor—Manila, Calcutta (Kolkata), and other great cities. For the past several years he has networked and trained urban church planters globally. He previously authored *Companion to the Poor* (1984, 2004) and *Cry of the Urban Poor* (1992, 2004).

Long interested in the dynamics of authentic revival, Viv Grigg now offers this book as the fruit of his doctoral research. It is a theological and theoretical case study of revival in New Zealand in the light of emerging urban postmodernism.

What emerges here is a holistic missional theology of revival. I appreciate his emphasis on "the link between preaching the Kingdom and socio-economic transformation," which too often goes missing in discussions of revival. The book reaches beyond "largely 'spiritual' Western formulations" to a "holistic Kingdom vision of the spiritual, communal and material aspects of the postmodern city." The author traces revival and renewal dynamics throughout history, noting for example in the 20th century the prophetic work of Kagawa in Japan.

The book is theoretically rich, drawing on the likes of Paul Pierson, J. Edwin Orr, Rodney Stark, Donald McGavran, Ralph Winter, Anthony Wallace, H. Richard Niebuhr, Walter Rauschenbusch, Jürgen Moltmann, and Miroslav Volf (among others). Good missiology is by definition interdisciplinary; here is what that means.

He gives us global, urban, postmodern, thoroughly Christian missiology that springs from on-the-ground, in-the-slums experience.

-- Howard A. Snyder, Professor of Wesley Studies
Tyndale Seminary, Toronto
26 March, 2009

Viv Grigg by Hugh Todd, 1982

Come on in, Sit Down, and Converse...

This book is part of an ongoing conversation about God and cities. It builds on former works that in urban missions have created new paradigms of following Jesus among the urban poor, apostolic orders, and citywide leadership. It extends the search for movements of spiritual transformation. It is part of my ongoing contribution, in the midst of a global prophetic call, to my home, New Zealand - Aotearoa.

Thanks are due to those who have mentored me in revival: Paul Pierson, Geoff & Gayle Stevens, Bob & Prue Wakelin, Howard Snyder, Edwin Orr, John Wimber, the godly pioneers among the poor of Manila, São Paulo and Kolkuta and city leaders of the AD2000 movement; Rev Dr Neil Darragh, as supervisor of this as a PhD thesis, as a pioneer of contextual theological reflection in New Zealand with his patient incisive questions at many points in its development. Dr Rob Bellingham and Dr Kevin Ward contributed germaine elements. Russell Greenwood several times painstakingly refined the English. My wife, Iêda and family paid a heavy price for many late nights and early mornings.. My board and Hillsborough Baptist Church were gracious to give me the freedom to study; Auckland University wise to fund some living costs to free a person to philosophise about 30 years of experience.

May this be seminal in releasing a new wave of reflective-practitioner across our nation who lead clusters of movements both within the church and in the public domain. To the global evangelical community, may this indicate pathways forward into the work of the Spirit in transforming the urban millennium.

Viv Grigg
Auckland
31 March, 2009

TABLE OF CONTENTS

PART 1: FRAMING THE CONVERSATION 7

1. Structuring the Conversation 7
2. Transformational Conversations 19
3. A Short History of Conversations about Transformation 31
4. The Conversationalists of Auckland 41

PART 2: GOALS OF POSTMODERN CITY TRANSFORMATION 58

5. City of God: Ideal City 59
6. The Soul of Auckland 69
7. Conversational Complexity: The Postmodern City 81
8. Spirit, Kingdom and Postmodern City 100

PART 3: PROCESSES OF CITYWIDE TRANSFORMING REVIVAL 121

9. Tides of National Revival 123
10. The Nature of Revival 144
11. Revival & Enraged Engagement 163
12. Citywide Transforming Revival 175
13. Prophetic Sources of Transformation in Urban Cultures 185
14. Apostolic Structures as Transforming Voices 194
15. Transforming Business Culture 211

Finishing a Conversation – Extending the Dreaming 217

CONVERSATIONAL SOURCES 221

INDEX 243

FIGURES

Fig. 1: Urban Theology as Transformational Conversation 20
Fig. 2: Processes in a Conversation about Transforming Revival 24
Fig. 3: Elements of a Web of Belief Analysis 27
Fig. 4: Denominational Distribution of Congregations in Auckland 43
Fig. 5: Weekly Attendances by Denomination 45
Fig. 6: Ethnic Congregation Explosion in Auckland 54
Fig. 7: The Nature of God as Reflected in the Good City 68
Fig. 8: Auckland Ethnicity by Region of Birth (1996 Census) 72
Fig. 9: Auckland Social Marital Status 77
Fig. 10: Conversational Spaces: Auckland Urbanism and the Good City ... 80
Fig. 11: Internal and External Forces Defining Kiwi Society 83
Fig. 12: Postmodernisation: Structural Change from Modern
    to Global Culture 85
Fig. 13: Postmodernism: Collapsing Modernism,
    Emergence of Global Culture 92
Fig. 14: The Kingdom of God as Integrating Biblical Theme 104
Fig. 15: Discipleship: Response to a
    Spiritual-Economic-Socio-Political Kingdom 106
Fig. 16: Kingdom Discipleship Beyond Modernism 118
Fig. 17: Elements in the Conversation: Kingdom Integration in and
    Beyond Postmodernism 120
Fig. 18: Chapters in Part 3 - Faith Community Conversation
    On Transforming Revival 122
Fig. 19: Baptist National Annual Baptisms and Membership 127
Fig. 20: Expanding Phases in the New Zealand Revival 129
Fig. 21: Common Web of Belief about Phases of Revival Movements .. 160
Fig. 22: Processes Common to All Levels of Revival Movements 161
Fig. 23: Proposed Web of Belief: Phases of Transforming Revival 180
Fig. 24: Transforming Revival: Generating Kingdom
    Movements in Society 202
Fig. 25: Estimating Transformational Engagement of
    Evangelicals in Auckland 204
Fig. 26: Conversational Sources of Auckland Business Theology 213
Fig. 27: Auckland Business Theology and the Kingdom of God 216

CAMEOS

Preaching Socio-economic Revival 8
Shifting the Global Evangelical Mindset 8
Building an Apostolic Network 9
From Theology to Prophetic Call in Auckland 9
The Kingdom as Integrating Vision 10
Storytelling Consultation Process 21
From Stories to Global Theology 22
Lawyers in Christ 29
Dancing Into City Transformation at Victory Christian Centre 59
A People without Vision? 69
The City Council's Community Vision — Auckland 2020 70
Ethnic Leaders' Hui 74
Postmodern Child-raising 82
Discipleship as Methodology or the Fruit of the Spirit? 107
Changing the Mindset of a Nation 108
Liberty Trust: A Vision of Escaping Economic Bondage 112
DNA Determinism 113
The Source of Psychology 113
The Search for the Spirit 124
Early Public Expression of Revival 125
Small Group Healing 131
Small Group Multiplication 132
Collective Prayer — Predictor of Social Activism 135
Cell Groups At the Edges of Revival 137
Migrant Evaluations of NZ Evangelical Spirituality 138
"Successful" Postmodern Globalized Church 138
Limitations of Spiritual Authority and Control 141
The Presence of God, Healing and Spiritual Encounter 152
Initiating a "People Movement" Revival 156
Polarising National Leadership 169
Failed Censorship Laws 169

John Skeates: Manager of Corporate Culture Change	173
NZ Prophet of Revival	176
Dick Hubbard: Social Entrepreneur	178
Called to Reconcile	178
Two Prophets from the South	188
Values Education	191
Non-Church Apostolic Movement	198
Apostolic and Pastoral City Leadership Styles	198
Small Group Struggles	199
Navigators: Non-Church Church	200
Developing the Apostolic From Within the Mega-Church	200
Wyn Fountain and the Business Roundtable	205
Environmental Network	207
Bev Norsworthy: Christian Teachers Training College of Aotearoa	207
Bruce Logan: Prophet of Educational Values	207
John Heenan: Values Education	208
Responses to Anti-Christian Media Bias	208
Trevor Yaxley: Media Dream	208
Postmodern Music Culture: Parachute Festival Extreme	209
Marriage and Family Retreats	209
Petitions Against Expanded Abortion Legalisation	209
Promisekeepers: Alternative Communities of Purity	210
New Sounds of Revival	218

PART - ONE -
FRAMING THE CONVERSATION

- 1 -
STRUCTURING THE CONVERSATION

Filling a Gap in Evangelical Theology

During the 1980's and 1990's, increasing numbers of spiritually gifted New Zealand believers have moved beyond the charismatic renewal, searching for a greater connection between faith and their leadership roles in society. Our faith has been born and nurtured in the midst of revival, with the work of the Spirit central to our spirituality. We are searching for significant theologies by which to transform secular society, provide informed leadership and revitalize the national soul and vision.

The personal cameos[1] introducing this study reflect my thirty years of involvement in developing communal theologies. For the roots of theology are autobiographical, though theology is not a personal story. The autobiographical is also rooted in community.

---

1   Throughout, I use illustrative cameos to anchor the study to the local realities.

- Preaching Socio-Economic Revival -

> At times between 1976 to 1984, I was back in New Zealand after living in various Manila slums. I spoke across the New Zealand charismatic renewal movement and called many renewed churches to commitment to the poor. Many evangelical churches in both mainline and evangelical denominations were directly experiencing encounters with what evangelical theology defines as the Holy Spirit. Waves of small confessional groups, prayer movements and signs and wonders occurred up and down the country.
>
> I spoke about the progress of renewal to revival, teaching from Luke 4: 18: *The Spirit of the Lord is on me, because the Lord has anointed me to preach good news to the poor.* This verse declares that the anointing of the Spirit always occurs for the purpose of preaching the good news of the Kingdom of God among the poor. Jesus then expands on the context of that proclamation — a context of healing and deliverance, social involvement and an understanding that an eternal Jubilee has come where economic issues are addressed. I used the Acts 2 story to demonstrate how the newly empowered first church caused new economics and new social structures of the Kingdom (1985/2004:152).

This Kingdom of God theme became popular among national leaders in the Evagelical and Pentecostal churches, who were further influenced by sources in the wider charismatic Evangelical and Pentecostal world. Embryonic teaching on socio-economic aspects of the Kingdom began to emerge. The story became communal. In today's world, the communal is globalised.

- Shifting The Global Evangelical Mindset -

> Ten years on, moving on from pioneering in Calcutta in 1991, I found myself drafting the goals for the global AD2000 city leaders' network around the theme of city evangelisation and transformation. My presentation of this to a grouping of Evangelical and Pentecostal global mission leaders, was quietly rejected. How does transformation help evangelisation? The link between preaching the Kingdom and socio-economic transformation was distant from the mainstream evangelical mindset at that time.
>
> This had changed radically by the end of the century. In giving guidance to two global city leadership networks around these themes, I have seen such ideas and concepts multiplied in a number of cities. By 2001, urban mission leaders were writing articles like *Ten Paradigm Shifts Towards Transformation* (Swanson, 2003). George Otis Jr., leader of the Sentinel Group which researches spiritual phenomena in cities and countries and who was part of the AD2000 leadership, subsequently developed a video demonstrating the theme, simply called "Transformations" (1999). Over 8000 sold within a few months.

- BUILDING AN APOSTOLIC NETWORK -

> To model this in the local context, in January 1996, I invited an *ad hoc* group of fifteen Auckland charismatic and Pentecostal leaders to the home of the then deputy mayor to discuss issues of citywide leadership. This group, meeting monthly for the next six years, became the Action Group then the *Vision for Auckland* forum.

These leaders had emerged during the charismatic renewal sweeping through most churches in New Zealand in the 1960's - 1980's. It expanded the Evangelical/Pentecostal wing of the Christian churches to approximately 6% of New Zealand's population among the 10-15%% of Kiwis who seek to attend church weekly, and the 17-19% attending 2-3 times per month or more.[2] Results from this fruitful period, included a culturally adaptive entrepreneurial Christianity, several significant Pentecostal denominations, renewal movements within traditional denominations, structural changes in some denominations and inner personal character and vision formed by revival dynamics in many lives. However, the penetration of this renewal into society, with significant social movement towards the values of the Kingdom of God, seemed frustratingly distant.

- FROM THEOLOGY TO PROPHETIC CALL IN AUCKLAND -

> At a *hui*[3] following two years reflecting with the *Vision for Auckland* Action Group, the following challenges were made to seventy leaders of the church of Auckland (Grigg, 1999b).
>
> The call to unity: networked leadership infrastructure with common visions.
>
> The call to redefine the soul of the city from bicultural reconciliation to a multicultural church and city.
>
> The call to Kingdom transformation of values and institutional directions of major sectors of society in the midst of decline of Western (Pakeha) civilisation.
>
> The call to a progression of public events that transform public perception of Christianity.
>
> The call to prepare for the emergence of a multicultural youth revival and integrate it into sustaining movement structures.
>
> The call to waves of repentant, broken holiness that release evangelisation of the unchurched 80% and lift church attendance from 16% to 20% to 25%.

---

2   Figures explained in Chapter 4.
3   A hui is a gathering for debate of an issue on a Maori *marae* (meeting house), often lasting 2-3 days.

This book reflects on these six calls but is focussed on the theological elements of the call to transformation of values in sectors of Auckland city.[4] I will develop this study around two themes related to transformation – revival and the Kingdom of God. In the New Zealand revival a certain level of clarity developed in relation to these two themes, collectively owned across the renewal leadership.

- THE KINGDOM AS INTEGRATING VISION -

> In 1982, when founding Servants to Asia's Urban Poor, I brought "Kingdom of God and the Poor" seminars to many charismatic churches. Then a group including Wyn Fountain, Bernie Ogilvie, Brian Hathaway, Tom Marshall and others took teaching about the Kingdom to churches in towns across the nation. They published a *Kingdom Manifesto* and later Brian Hathaway integrated this into a book (1990) about his Brethren assembly, which had applied these principles in Te Atatu Peninsula. Tom Marshall, a businessman and pastor, published a magazine, *Saltshaker*, for several years. This expanded on these issues. After his death, the Bible College of New Zealand integrated it into *Reality* magazine which continued to emphasize the themes of the Kingdom in every sector of society.

The Focus of this Book

The outcome of this study is a missions theology underlying both process and goals of "Citywide Transforming Revival." This has been grounded in local realities of Auckland as a representative modern/ postmodern city.

Global processes among urban missions strategists and theologians have provoked the question, *"What is the relationship of the Spirit of Christ to the transformation of a postmodern city?"* I have examined this in a limited manner by using two local indicators, the NZ revival (for the work of the Holy Spirit) and Auckland city (for emergent modern/ postmodern megacities). This has resulted in an exploration of *revival theology and its limitations among Auckland's Pentecostals and Evangelicals* and a *proposal for a theology of Transforming Revival that engages the postmodern city*. Thus, the study oscillates between local analysis and global theologies.

To accomplish this within an evangelical perspective I propose a new hermeneutic (the processes of studying, interpreting and applying the scriptures) of *"transformational conversations"*, an interfacing of *faith community conversations* and *urban conversations*.

Consequently, I develop a new theory of *"citywide transforming revival"* as an expansion of revival theories, a field within pneumatology. Citywide Transforming Revival is a concept of synergistic revivals in multiple sectors of a mega-city. This results in long-term change of urban vision and values towards the principles of the Kingdom of God.

I develop a theology of *transforming process* from the apostolic and prophetic themes that occur when spiritual gifts are released in revival. Transforming Revival results in new transformative *apostolic and prophetic structures* that engage the postmodern city soul.

---

4   Summary discussions may be found in Grigg (2000d). I have developed reflections on the others in papers from the hui and in *VisionNZ* publications.

Transformation implies *goals*. I explore the results of revival, the *transforming visions* for the city, by reflecting on themes of the City of God and the Kingdom of God. These expand largely "spiritual" Western formulations of the Kingdom to a holistic Kingdom vision of the spiritual, communal and material aspects of the postmodern city.

Definitions

I define *revival* as the experience of the person of the Holy Spirit falling on groups resulting in a dramatic transformation of their Christianity, caused by or resulting in repentance, accompanied by boldness in evangelism, power, love and unity.

A *revival movement* occurs when the Holy Spirit falls on multiple groups, as those initially touched by the Spirit, go in power and take his presence into related social groups.

Transformation, in the text on Social Transformation of the Wheaton 83 Consultation is:

> *The change from the condition of human existence contrary to God's purposes to one in which people are able to enjoy fullness of life in harmony with God*

(World Evangelical Fellowship, 1983: section 11).

I use *transforming revival* for a consummated revival movement fully *engaged* in transforming the core and the nooks and crannies of society and culture. It may cause a *cultural revitalisation*, beginning with engagement in the public domain.[5] Then as major paradigm shifts occur within a generation or so, progressively *transforming the values and vision* of major cultural sectors with the values of the Kingdom.

The public domain is that *space of conversation* about vision, values and structure between diverse ethnicities, interest groups and corporate structures in sectors of the city.

Evangelicalism includes traditionally orthodox[6] Protestants from many denominations and includes Pentecostals, charismatics, conservatives and fundamentalists. The term was popularised during the Great Awakening in Britain and the US, dramatic periods of revival resulting in conversion of hundreds of thousands. Three global networks currently link these: World Evangelical Fellowship, the Lausanne Movement and, during the 1990's the AD2000 movement (now morphed into the Transformation Movement). Central to Evangelicalism is belief in the atoning work of Christ for salvation, the necessary proclamation of the gospel and the authority of the written Word of God "in faith and practice."[7] The term came to represent a historic conflict with "*liberal*"[8] Protes-

---

5   This study presumes the existence of such public space in Auckland, hence "transformation" focuses not on the development of such a space, but how to utilize it. Neuhaus has analysed this in *The Naked Public Square* for America (1984). Mouw, has sought to do so for Evangelicals (1973; 1976).

6   "Orthodox" in their commitment to the historic creeds and the authority of the Scriptures Evangelicals would prefer to be simply known as those who follow the beliefs of the first Christians. "Orthodoxy is that sustained tradition that has steadily centered the consenting church in the primordially received interpretation of the apostolic witness" (Oden, 1995:398).

7   Historian Bebbington (1989:3) speaks of conversionism, activism, Biblicism, and crucicentrism as the four priorities of evangelicalism. New Zealand definitions may be found in Ahdar (2000:40).

8   Liberal Protestant is utilised in this study not from within the self-definition of those at the fore-

tants who are defined as those who would not necessarily centralise verbal evangelism or historic Christian commitments to the authority of the canon as the Word of God.

The *Pentecostal* movements grew in multiple indigenous movements parallel to Evangelicalism, involving those who by their own definition, have passed through two determining experiences in their relationship to the God of the Bible.[9] The first experience is conversion based on repentance and receipt of forgiveness through the atoning work of Christ on the cross. The second is a concomitant or subsequent experience of the "baptism of the Spirit" which may signify receipt of the Holy Spirit, extra empowering, anointing or a host of other existential experiences.[10] Global researcher, David Barrett defines,

> Christians who are members of Pentecostal denominations... whose major characteristic is a rediscovery of and a new experience of the supernatural with a powerful and energising ministry of the Holy Spirit in the realm of the miraculous that most other Christians have considered to be highly unusual (1988:124).

Generally, Pentecostals identify these experiences as the release of spiritual gifts and in particular, the gift of speaking in tongues (*glossolalia*). In practice, only half of Pentecostals actually speak in tongues.[11] The specificity of these doctrines results in the establishing of independent Pentecostal churches although these rapidly form into some form of denominational structures.

In comparison, *charismatics* tend to have had similar experiences of the Holy Spirit but to have chosen to remain within their older denominational structures, forming organised renewal groups. As a result, their interpretations of cause and effect tend to be different. Catholics, Anglicans and Lutherans, for example, do not necessarily see the need for a "conversion" experience prior to a "baptism of the Spirit" experience, but rather view baptism as an affirmation of their being part of the faithful, born into the church and confirmed into their faith.

Many charismatics do not see "speaking in tongues" as the necessary sign of the "baptism of the Spirit",[12] recognizing that the Scriptures teach of multiple giftings for individuals. The "baptism of the Spirit" as a sign of conversion is not highly differentiated from the "baptism

---

front of Protestant liberalism, but as the 'other' for evangelicals. Those who are not evangelicals because they do not accept that all written scripture is inspired, or essentially accurate, and do not centralise evangelism etc.

9 At times in this study, 'Pentecostals' are subsumed with fundamentalists and Evangelicals under the generic word, "Evangelical".

10 Throughout the study, the Holy Spirit will be identified with feminine pronouns, in line with Wesley's usage and the feminine use of the word in the Scriptures, whereas God the Father is identified in the masculine, following classic use, while recognising that he is source of both male and female. This is not a developed theological statement, just a convention to remind ourselves of the complementariness of the godhead.

11 Smidt et al. indicate, from a US study, though with reasonably small sample, that 55% of White Pentecostals and 33% of Black Pentecostals speak in tongues, while 74% of nondenominational charismatics speak in tongues (1999: 116). One is presuming similarities in NZ Pentecostalism.

12 However, a higher percentage of nondenominational charismatics speak in tongues (Smidt, 1999: 116).

of the Spirit" as a sign of spiritual power and anointing.

Evangelicals also include *Fundamentalists*,[13] who tend to be more literal in their understanding of the genesis and use of the Scriptures, and strongly emphasize end-time scenarios. They reject many charismatic and Pentecostal experiences of the Holy Spirit. (However, many Pentecostals are fundamentalistic in their view of the Scriptures and attitude to truth). Important within this stream is the century-old teaching of dispensationalism which divides history into seven dispensations, each possessing different God-human-state-creation relationships. Significant for this study is their rejection of the "sign gifts." Many believe these "ceased with the early church." Thus, they reject renewal, revival and associated phenomena, while working in uneasy alliance with Evangelicals, Pentecostals and charismatics. The Brethren assemblies, Salvation Army and Churches of Christ, among others, tend to be fundamentalist in New Zealand. Many interdenominational evangelistic groups such as Scripture Union, the Navigators and Open Air Campaigners developed from earlier phases of fundamentalism (Gilling, 1989:43-53).

The Genre of Urban Missiology

This is an urban missions' theological study. Missiology is well defined as a relatively new[14] but eclectic discipline,[15] accepted across the spectrum of Christian denominations (as best shown perhaps, in the diversity of one of its major journals, *The International Review of Missions*). It is eclectic, integrating perspectives from four major fields: theology of mission, cultural studies and linguistics, aspects of sociology of religion (particularly movement growth, leadership and church growth) and mission history (related to, but distinct from, church history). A theology of mission cannot be developed independent of these fields.

Within missiology, the field of Urban Missions is well defined. It expands the evangelical mindset into handling heterogeneity, spirituality within the urban environment and a holistic integration of evangelism with response to structural evils (Conn, 1993:96-104). Urban Mission is grounded in urban anthropology (Shipp, 1992:3). In past research, I have found anthropological case study and participant-observer processes to be compatible with involvement in the leadership and movement dynamics that I have been investigating. In terms of urban missions theology, this participatory approach begins with a "theology of the people."

This kind of research on the development of mission theologies must refer to their structural outworking. This, however, differs from development of a comprehensive strategic study, but is an analysis of the theology underlying such strategies. Thus analysis of theology-based actions is included as illustrative of the theology.

---

13 Term developed in a 1910 General Assembly of the American Presbyterian Church, a statement of "Five Fundamentals" considered nonnegotiable: the miracles, virgin birth, atoning death and resurrection of Christ and the authority of Scripture.
14 As late as 1973, Tippett was writing *Missiology, a New Discipline* (1973).
15 See Luzbetak (1989:12-15) and Bosch (1991:8-11) for definitions.

Steps in the Research Process
The next chapter outlines the hermeneutic and theological research methodology. In this section, I identify research steps taken and identify issues in participant-observer methodology.

Step 1: Literature Search
Throughout, I have searched for literature in urban missions, focussing on theological issues related to transforming revival. This research covered historic transformational, NZ church-state, urban and revival theologies. As no comprehensive data was available on the transformational workforce or growth of the movements, I collated analyses of the recent growth of the charismatic Evangelical movement.

Step 2: Networking Analysis of Movement Leaders in Auckland
I developed a database of significant charismatic and Pentecostal leaders. This involved identifying 736 leaders and 729 mission organisations nationally. These were identified through networking from leader to leader and included my personal interaction with 150 emergent Christian leaders in some secular roles in major social sectors of Auckland. I complemented this with a database of 1084 Auckland congregations and their leaders, including 350 ethnic congregations and leaders. These had to be identified through networks in each ethnic grouping as many are independent and do not meet in a "church" building but warehouses, school halls and large homes. They included major streams of church life (some mainstream Protestant, many conservative evangelical, majority charismatic evangelical and Pentecostal, a few Catholic). I analysed these in terms of denomination, 15 social sectors, or 18 ethnic sectors, and their level of leadership (local, city sector, citywide, national, international) and type of Christianity (evangelical, charismatic, fundamentalist, liberal, Catholic).

Step 3: A Spiral of Action-Reflection
I have used four cycles of action-reflection, following the transformational conversations approach developed in the next chapter.

Cycle 1: Looking Back — Anger at the Loss of a Culture
While the primary cycle of research was in the city leadership group, I had to go back one cycle to locate their issues in the context of social disempowerment during the expansion of the revival. From the action group discussions came a growing understanding of what had forced Evangelicals into social issues – their sense of disempowerment as New Zealand culture diverged from its Christian foundations. The energy for change however, could frequently be related back to experiences of the Holy Spirit in the renewal. Expansion of these themes required research in the published literature on involvement in public issues.

Cycle 2: Participant-Observation in Theological Action-Reflection
I have been participant-observer in a cycle of action-reflection with the Vision for Auckland leadership. This included think tanks with groups of Christian leaders in each of several social sectors. In these, I sought to document emerging theologies and to test the viability of elements of teaching on transforming revival. Among the groups were:

- The national VisionNZ city leadership network and theology working groups in their reflection process, with leadership and theology working group documents outlining vision, strategy and theology (participant-observer).
- The Vision for Auckland leadership team in strategies, ethnic and transformation task forces, public meetings and four consultative hui produced shared visions and fifty-five vision summaries. I was involved in and reviewed the minutes of discussions of over fifty ongoing monthly forums of Vision for Auckland. This was the primary context for continual integration of the broadest level of transformational conversations between Evangelicals and the city (initiator and leader of process for two years, then participant-observer).

Cycle 3: Redefinition of Themes at City Sectoral Level

This open-ended approach, with initial consultations at national and city leadership levels, resulted in re-examination of themes of social justice, the common good, the city of God as themes defining the end goals of revival, with a final preference for the expansion of the theme of the Kingdom of God. In a cyclical dynamic, initial leadership gatherings set the ongoing research agendas for my encouraging smaller work groups, developing a web of research studies. I analysed seven factors including theology, vision, leadership progressions, etc., in twelve social sectors.

The networks and my roles were:

1. An ethnic leaders' network drawn together in *hui* (as catalyst, participant-leader).
2. A network of intercessors across Auckland (as occasional participant, observer).
3. A business leaders' network, sports network, legal network, medical network, etc. (as observer, at times theological integrator).

Cycle 4: The Kingdom in the Business Sector

I created a business leaders' storytelling process and publication which resulted in a more detailed analysis of the theological nuances in that sector and their relationship to the Kingdom of God as an integrative theme for transformation (as research designer, editor and theologian).

Step 4: Developing the Theory of Transforming Revival

Reflection on the above four cycles enabled me to first develop a model of revival movement processes, then the transforming revival theory. I had to anchor it in the context of Auckland as urban and postmodern environment, identifying *conversation spaces* between the Kingdom and postmodernism which enable definition of the goals of transforming revival.

Limitations to the Research

I set the following limits to the study:

1. *Representative City*: The study is based on Auckland as representative postmodern mega-city. This is not unreasonable as definitions of a modern mega-city include recent rapid growth due to migration, multi-ethnicity, multiple cities within a city and a population of over

1 million. At 1.3 million, it is the 433rd city in terms of population in the world.[16] Comprising several cities, it is the centre of northern New Zealand and a centre for the Pacific Islands. Relatively new as a city, at only 150 years old, it contains tribal, modern and postmodern elements. Studying multiple cities would have widened the theoretical base but allowed less depth to the research. I have used that approach in two previous books, but learned in the last that communal theologising and global analysis can result in idealized theology that is not always accurately reflecting realities.

2. *Participant-observation*: This study is not a statistical, sociological survey approach to vision change within a city but a participant-observer's analysis. The observational nature of participant research must also be integrated with the predictive nature of the prophet and strategist in an urban missiology. This requires care to avoid predetermined biases. Fortunately, I have been somewhat blessed to be an 'exile' for long periods, so write from a liminal position within New Zealand Evangelicalism, living in several worlds concurrently and thus free to compare the present context under study with parallel universes (Bauman, 2000: 203).

3. *A theological focus rather than strategy*: Theology does not predict future effectiveness independent of the social structure of movements. These issues are too broad to cover in one study so I have chosen to focus on the theological. In doing so, I recognise the complex interplay between the social structure of movements and their underlying theology, each being determinative at certain points. Issues of group mobilisation, charismatic or transformational leadership emergence, the turning of theology into slogans for the masses, popular appeal, appropriateness of theological response for the given time and so on, are touched on in this study. Full development requires a parallel study.

Issues of Style

Seeking the derivation of theology from the people, I have utilised elements of ethnographic research. Definitions of cultural research, identify particular methodological aspects:

> *ethnographies generate hypotheses, focus on context, are written up using thick description, require participant-observation and use multiple measures for data collection, that is, triangulation... More recently, definitions explore case-study reporting and the dual roles of ethnographers in composition...*(Bishop, 1999: 18).

This study carries all these elements. The diversity of disciplines in urban missiology results in a thick description and a diversity of styles. Oscillations between biblical thematic studies to theological concepts to cultural analysis to case study and strategic thinking, at times represent marked departures from classical historical/biblical theological studies. are common in missiological studies globally (Elliston, 1997).

Role of participant-observer: In the research I have been observer and, at times, also involved relationally and emotionally and deliberately active in determining the directions of theological change, particularly in the second research cycle. Dewalt, Dewalt and Wayland talk of the tensions:

---

16 Based on the AD2000 Cities Network database of 6600 cities (Grigg, 1996).

Participation involves emotional involvement, observation requires detachment. Pure observation requires removal from the object. Pure participation involves "becoming the phenomenon." In examining participation, we need to identify both the level of participation and the level of emotional involvement (1998: 263-4).

I prefer to see these as integrative aspects of truth seeking. This is something I have developed in missiological research over the last two decades. While seeking full engagement with the processes under study; in my analysis I have sought to be objectively detached. This involved defining my biases without necessarily rejecting them and identifying emotional and volitional elements that affect my evaluations. In wanting Evangelicals to move in the directions proposed by the study, I have had to also evaluate hindrances to those progressions. In proposing a certain theological path ahead, I have had to deduce why other possible theological configurations (some held aggressively by those studied), will not achieve the ends proposed. In part, I also modified my relationships to the core group of leaders in the study, moving back from being instigator to observer, after an initial period as catalyst.

Presuppositions

The Locus of Authority

This study is within an Evangelical and canonical tradition, which would understand that the knowledge of Christ, the living Word, is through the Scriptures as "the Word of God."[17] They are seen in total as "truth," or as the Westminster Catechism puts it, "the only rule for faith and practice." This tradition holds that "all Scripture is inspired by God" (II Tim 3:16), including the sum total of Old and New Testament canon, as defined by the early church.

Reality of the Person of the Holy Spirit

The rationalist analysis of religion commonly relegates religious experience to psychological realms. However, this study begins with evangelical *a priori* assumptions of the Bible as authority and thus, secondly of an external God revealed in the Scriptures as supernatural and personal. The Scriptures show development as to the personality of the Holy Spirit. This begins with the wind of God (*ruach*), the Spirit, involved in a three-way conversation within the Godhead, in the work of creation. It extends to the teaching of Jesus about the personality of the Spirit as guide (Rom. 8:14), counsellor, teacher and the one who speaks, convicts and bears witness to truth (John 14:15,26; 16:8,9). This contrasts with the understanding by over a third of those identifying themselves as Christians in New Zealand, that the Spirit is an impersonal life force (Webster & Perry, 1989:83)[18]. Given the scriptures as source of authority, the logical extension of these

---

17 This contrasts with Karl Barth's Christocentric Word as the only source of knowledge of God. "Christ is God's word incarnate; the Word is in Scripture but the Scripture is not necessarily the Word. The word is God's communication to humans; his self-disclosure in Jesus Christ." Despite respect for Barth in his prophetic corrective within European liberalism, Evangelicals reject this view because of their doctrine of verbal inspiration as the basis of scriptural authority, understanding that the Scriptures have authority in and of themselves.

18 43% of those who identify as Anglicans, 40% of Presbyterians, 33% of Methodists, 29% of Catholics, 25% of Other Christians and 13% of Baptists were identified as preferring a belief in

statements is to presume that when people speak of personal encounters with God the Holy Spirit, they may reasonably be speaking truth (i.e., they are not deluded). Alternatively, these experiences can be logically tested against the biblical data concerning the nature of God and his encounters with men and women in redemptive history and the nature of the Holy Spirit. The Scriptures themselves give guidelines for judgement of the validity of prophecy and other supernatural phenomena.

The study presumes some missiological background in the literature of pneumatology and phenomenology of religion. For those from another faith community, helpful foundations may be found in anthropologist Paul Hiebert's "Flaw of the Excluded Middle" (1982), or the sympathetic analyses of the Pentecostal movement in liberal theologian, Harvey Cox's *Fire from Heaven* (1995). Or within charismatic evangelical literature, John Wimber's exegeses (1985) on the miraculous in the life of Jesus and church history and its implications in terms of theological interpretation of phenomenology are useful.

"some sort of spirit or life force" over against belief in a "personal God". Webster and Perry do not analyse the correlation but one can observe a correlation with the percentage of attendance by adherents in each denomination. The greater the attendance, the higher the belief in a personal God (Webster & Perry, 1989:38).

- 2 -

Transformational Conversations

Revolutions in human thinking are not created by new information but by new paradigms that allow more information to be fitted more fully and adequately. And revolutions in scientific paradigms can be awesome moments of cognitive dissonance.

Harvey Conn[1]

Theology begins in the truth of story — God's story, my story, our story. Over the last fifteen years my involvement in leadership of the global AD2000 cities network mentoring city leadership teams and the Encarnação network of urban poor mission leaders has prompted the evolution of a new hermeneutic – new at least for Evangelicals. This study develops the concept of a "transformational conversation hermeneutic."[2]

---

1 (1984:54) on Kuhn's (1962/1970) idea of paradigm and Festinger's (1959) cognitive dissonance.
2 Throughout this study, I utilise the word "frameworks" for meta-narratives that include multiple themes —the hermeneutic framework, the framework of the Kingdom of God, or postmodernism as a framework.

Fig. 1: Urban Theology as Transformational Conversation

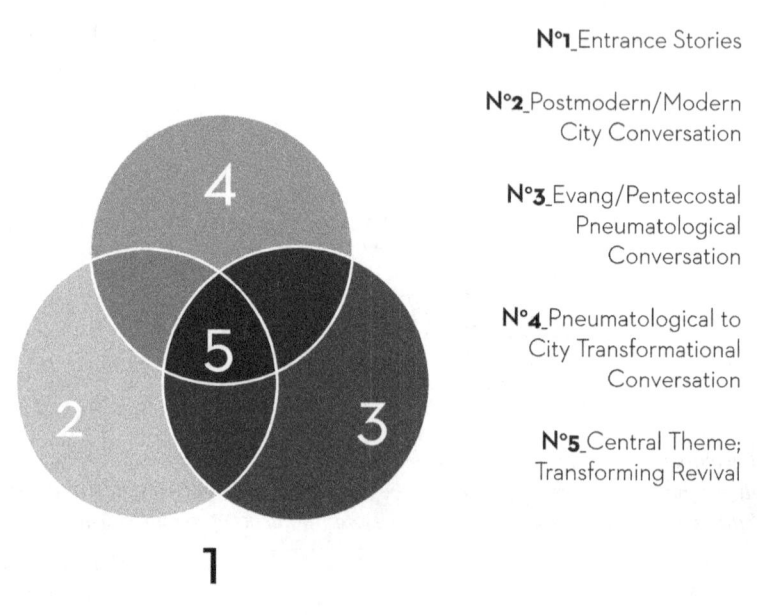

Nº1 Entrance Stories

Nº2 Postmodern/Modern City Conversation

Nº3 Evang/Pentecostal Pneumatological Conversation

Nº4 Pneumatological to City Transformational Conversation

Nº5 Central Theme; Transforming Revival

Fig. 1 shows a process for developing urban theology about Transforming Revival. It begins with an entrance story (Nº 1) and involves three components: the in-city conversation(Nº 2), internal Christian conversation on pneumatology (Nº 3), and interfacing of these in a transformational conversation (Nº 4). These contribute to central theme (Nº 5).

I discovered urban Christian workers constantly struggling with the sense of "irrelevance" of their training in systematic theology and its dissonance from the nature of the God of action they followed. In contrast they loved *building* collective theologies from their stories. I build the theory from such tensions by defining my terms and relating these tensions to four polarities in our perception of the godhead: his structuring and creativity, his relationship to the present and to history, his existing and acting and his transcendence and immanence. I consider the relationship of this hermeneutic with Postmodernity in an excursus at the end of chapter 8, exploring to what extent evangelical theology can engage with or become postmodern in style.

Transformational Conversations

The phrase "transformational conversations" was sparked by Brueggeman's comments about intertextuality as "an ongoing conversation that is as urgent and contemporary as the present moment, but it is also a conversation that stretches over the generations" (1997:78-79). This study regards theology as both diachronic "conversations" (over the generations) and synchronic conversations (one time, across cultures). It defines urban theology as communal conversations with the potential for social transformation.

The three circles in Fig. 1 link three conversations in a total process which I am calling a "transformational conversation": firstly, the conversation within the faith communities, secondly, the community conversation within the city and thirdly, the transformational conversation between these two.

The transformational conversation hermeneutic is fed by the metaphors and symbols, imagery and grammar, dialect and cadence of both the city and the faith community. The hermeneutic results in defining public space for open conversations about complex issues (I will use the term "conversation spaces"), in contrast to some approaches that reduce the scriptures to singular meanings or to absolutist slogans.

Personality of God in Theological Style

Theology may be considered as human reflections on the nature of God. In grappling with story-telling theological processes in urban poor pastors' and city leaders' consultations we stumbled onto an understanding of doing theology as conversation. Doing theology this way consistently resolved four polarities about our perception of God better than the systematic rationalist approaches common among Evangelicals:

- Is God a rationalist philosopher or creative storyteller?
- Is God or was God? Do we know God primarily in his present actions around the globe or through his involvement in history?
- Is God incarnate or cosmic? Immanent or transcendent? Local or global?
- Is God or does God? Is God the God of being or the God of action?

God of Story or Rationalist Philosopher?

From many of the last 30 years in and out of slum areas in cities around the world I have concluded that Jesus' storytelling style embodied the primary style of teaching used among the poor. We think story, communicate story to story.

- STORYTELLING CONSULTATION PROCESS -

> In 1996, we held a typical storytelling consultation in Mumbai with 80 leaders of urban poor ministries. Each day we would introduce the day's theme. Each worker then had ten minutes to tell his or her story. At the end of each day, we would integrate the theology and strategies that had been shared. Many worked for Western funded missions to the poor. On the side, they did what they knew really worked. It was these Indian stories of how Indians were finding solutions in their context that were crucial. At the end of the week, the whole group knew we had developed a genuine Indian theology and praxis of working with the poor.

In integrating urban poor theologies[3] we extended this methodology of developing grassroots theology, simply labelled as "storytelling theologies."

This requires a theological facilitator trained in ethnotheological perspectives and able to work with leadership in designing insider-outsider reflection processes. The role of the trained theologian is thus not that of the expert coming with truth, but as:

> *The reflector and thematizer, the one who is able to provide the biblical and traditional background that will enable the people to develop their own theology*
>
> (Bevans, 1996:51).

I would add that the theologian must come as revivalist, bringing the presence of God, for such theologies have been developed much on our knees. These gatherings are often filled with a sense of the presence of God, so that the theology evolved is not simply cognitive and communal but experiential, healing, creating unity and love. At a leadership level, the process becomes more refined, systematic and rationalised.

- From Stories To Global Theology -

> From 1991-1997, as part of the AD2000 city network, a global team of city leaders from most continents extended the "storytelling" method to city leadership consultations in other regions and cities.[4] From these were developed urban theologies and urban strategies (Grigg, 1997b). At this level, the complexity increases. We drew from stories given in multiple city contexts. I remember sitting with the leadership team for five days in 1993, identifying strands that seemed to keep twisting with other strands, becoming braids that eventually linked to major themes. The themes became paramount in the final written theology. The outcome was a *globalised theology and strategy* reproduced now in a number of cities.

The theologies are not developed in a vacuum. The synchronic are based on the diachronic. Participants come with previous formal or informal theological training that draws on systematic and biblical theologies, for these remain foundational. What they had never been able to express was the outworking of that theology into new indigenous theologies for their decade (thus answering the second query, "Is God or does God?" by a transition to the present and synchronic,). These new theologies are not grounded in a single denominational view imported from another continent, but from indigenous expressions within the workers' own people and land. They often contradict their own views developed from imported formal training. Thus *communal ownership occurs.*

Such theologies develop comprehensive themes of city leadership, holistic ministry among the poor, urban poor church life, etc. This *comprehensiveness* is not because the

---

3   In, India ('93,'96,'03), Hong Kong ('96), Manila('99, '04), Sao Paulo ('02), Nairobi ('03), Addis ('03) Bangkok ('04) and other cities.

4   I led a number of global and regional consultations yearly, among them: Calcutta ('92), Chicago ('91), Los Angeles ('92), Seoul ('95), Hong Kong ('96), Mumbai ('93), Delhi ('93) with these coordinators . They extended these at national and city levels. A New Zealand leadership team developed a city leaders' consultation in Wanganui in 1996 (Grigg, 1997d).

theologies are developed with systematic logic, from a foundational web of belief, but because the stories cover the essential range of current issues, related to a given theme, identifying a new web of belief. Stories also gave a warm human sense of truth, honed from both Scripture and involvement. "Systematic theology engages the intellect; storytelling engages the heart and indeed the whole person" (Bausch, 1984:6).

Struggles with "storytelling theology" led me to "transformational conversations" as a more encompassing description. Stories are part of wider urban conversations.

Stories, Chaos and the Multivariate Urban Context
This illustrated a major shift in urban theology from the stability and continuity of rural theologies (emphasis on God is, the God of being and stability) that have been the context of the historic church, to the ongoing discontinuities and chaos of the mega-city (emphasis on God does, the God of action and change). Ariovaldo Ramos, Brazilian Evangelical leader, commented once to me, "since the city is always somewhat chaotic, an urban theological response should also be somewhat chaotic."

My father, a scientist, left a book around on chaos theory in mathematics. Chaos theory developed because of the nature of multivariate analysis — small perturbations in starting conditions lead to extensive divergences in ending conditions, apparently random, but actually following clear mathematical rules, such as in predicting weather conditions across the earth (Gleick, 1987). Cities are multivariate. Indeed, urban planning contains a whole science of fractal geometry based on multivariate analysis, that when applied to the apparently chaotic emergence of city forms enables planning predictions (Batty & Longley, 1994). The parallel concept is multivariate theologies.

In Brazil during this study, I discovered that some Latin theological methodology has also progressed from the intrusion of Marxist analysis into Catholic theology through liberation theology. Fr. João Batista Libanio in a Brazilian Catholic theology of the city, *As Lógicas da Cidade* (The Philosophic Structures of the City (2001)), affirms the approach of beginning from stories. He expands on Foucault's idea (1972:10) about seeking discontinuities beneath grand themes and relating them back to the continuity of historic theologies:

> *We opt for a reading (of theology, of the city) that creates discontinuity before we create order. This is in contrast to two very different ideological options of our time... One traditional reading prefers order, continuity... The other posture, with a modern tinge, specializes in the unity of thought of neo-liberalism. This also announces changes but at their heart, these changes only maintain continuity. It fixes on a unified structural model of the city...* (2001: 23 tr. from Portuguese mine).

This concept of multiple discontinuities, multiple variables, causing us to stop in our tracks because they are different or perplexing, distinguishes urban theology.

Fig. 2: Processes in a Conversation about Transforming Revival

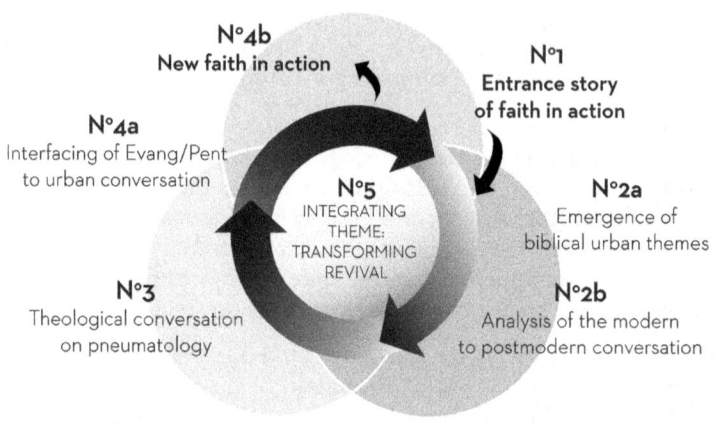

Fig. 2 expands the steps for developing a transformational conversation on the relationship of Holy Spirit and city. It begins in an action story (1). From reflection on the action, biblical urban themes develop (2a). This leads to an interface between the urban conversation (2b), the communal context and Scripture. A faith community conversation on pneumatology (3) develops from that entrance story. In turn, this leads to an interface between these two conversations on the Spirit and the city — the transformational conversation (4a). This creates a new praxis (4b).

Multiple Story Conversations

However, if multivariate analysis in chaos theory produces beautiful art out of apparent discontinuities, can an overarching pattern be seen in the Scriptures? This highlights a historic hermeneutic problem of the search for a unifying centre. Osborne states,

> As the interlocking principles between strata of the biblical period become visible, the patterns coalesce around certain ideas that bridge the gaps between the individual witnesses. However, it is very uncertain whether any single theme or concept stands at the apex of biblical theology. Many believe that the complete lack of consensus demonstrates that a cluster of ideas, rather than a single theme, unites all others (1991: 282).

If there is no single theme, can multivariate theologies be patterned? William Temple utilised a concept of drama:

> What we must completely get away from is the notion that the world as it now exists is a rational whole: we must think of its unity not by the analogy of a picture, of which all the parts exist at once, but by the analogy of a drama where, if it is good enough the full

meaning of the first scene only becomes apparent with the final curtain: and we are in the middle of this.[5]

Another perspective was to examine stories within multiple contextual theologies in both Scriptures and everyday contexts. This theological *storytelling* or conversational approach led us to a more fruitful practical approach, since most Evangelical/Pentecostal preaching is populist, from contextual story to biblical story, rather than systematic.

The pattern of transformational theology thus becomes a dancing, multifaceted conversations, rising from the lowest classes into multiple sectors of society. It is like a series of candles that flame into life in ten thousand corners of the city. The mapping of this urban conversation cannot simply be a search for a grand theme but for multiple simultaneous interwoven themes and within them tens of thousands of vignettes.

But what should the dance, the drama, the conversation, be called? Brueggeman's concept of the unifying substance of the Old Testament as a *plurality of voices* led to an expanded hermeneutic for *transformational conversation* as the interface of that biblical plurality of story with the plurality of urban conversations.

In this study, themes of revival, the Kingdom and city of God will be viewed as frameworks for such conversation spaces. However, no one theme can be elevated to a single integrating theme subsuming all others.

Similarities to Narrative Theology

Narrative theologies give us some exegetical tools for step 2 in Fig. 2. Narrative theology in the second half of the twentieth century developed as a crossover of ideas from literary theory to become popular as an interpretative approach to the biblical stories.[6]

> *In the plot, coherence, movement and climax that characterize a story, narrative theology sees a way to overcome the problems theology creates for itself through its subservience to discursive reasoning* (Fackre, 1983:340).

Evangelical theologians have recently been more receptive to a liberal exegetical concept of "narrative" (Van Engen, 1996:44-70). However, problems exist. Only parts (admittedly large) of the Hebrew Old Testament, the Gospels and Acts are narrative in style. Pauline and Johannine theology are both conceptual. The Wisdom literature is of a very different genre. Thus a purely narrative focus reduces the range of the God-side of a transformational conversation purely to story. The Proverbs and poetry (of David), the rhetorical questions (of Job), the pathos (of Jeremiah) and rationality (of Paul) must all be aspects of the conversation.

Thus, in seeking a better phrase than "storytelling" I have chosen not to use "narrative theology." It is too emotionally loaded for Evangelicals and too limited in its biblical compass.

---

5   In a letter towards the end of his life (Iremonger, 1948).

6   Brevard Childs (1970) traces it from the early 1940's to its decline in the 1960's. Because the crossover from literary analysis occurred at multiple points globally, the emergence of narrative theology occurred through multiple sources. Van Engen comments, "One realise(s) it is practically a misnomer to speak of a narrative theology "movement." The presuppositions, methodologies, agendas and styles of the players in narrative theology are too diverse to be lumped into a single cohesive movement" (1996). Yet it infuses theological thinking.

Is God or was God?

In answering the second question, "Is God or was God?" I recognise that philosophic and systematic theologies tend to be *diachronic*, testing for validity against historical patterns of theology back to the Scriptures. All theology must pass this test to some extent. In theology within a context of historic roots in traditional Western Europe, diachronic approaches are appropriate.

In contrast, *practical, pastoral, contextual and mission theologies* prefer to start with contemporary stories of the day (real stories = truth) and then find biblical truths and stories responding to these. As the global village of the 20th century shifts into the urban millennium, the verification of theology has moved from the above diachronic perspective to a synchronic perspective where we contrast theology across cultures in a single timeframe. When operating globally, those of us doing theology largely share e-mail networks enjoying collective paradigms. This process often moves too rapidly for formal publishing.

Recently, Biblical theologians have responded to social change by increasingly speaking about the active "God of redemption history" in contrast to categories of the "God of being" of classic theology. This raises the question about whether foundationalism (building rationally from some foundational truth) has failed[7] as the basis for theological study. In a postmodern world, history as a rational construct has been found wanting by some (see discussion in Hagner, 1998; Perdue, 1994), so ceases for many to be a valid basis for testing truth — but both rationalist liberal and evangelical theological study are deeply rooted in historical paradigms.[8] However, there are other routes to rationality than Cartesian foundationalism, which requires beliefs to rest on verifiable evidence and deductions from inarguable foundations (Vanhoozer, 1995:11).

A Web or a Building?

A helpful model is that of "knowledge as a web or net"[9] with neither foundation nor starting point (Quine & Ullian, 1978). Quine argues that nonfoundational theology fits the way Christian faith and practice generally operates. This requires attention to patterns inherent in beliefs and practices rather than a general theory of rationality. Since knowledge is seen as a web, there is not the question of the building collapsing if one piece of knowledge is found wanting. The stories must mesh, but need not necessarily do so in a rationalistic linear manner from a foundational point.

---

7   Both liberal and evangelical theologies are rationalist in style and foundational in approach. Where they differ is the basis of that foundationalism. Liberal theologians view the ability of the human intellect as able to discern the foundations. For evangelical theologians the foundation is the Scriptures as revealed truth (Marsden, 1997:98).

8   Brueggemann seeks to develop a post-liberal or nonfoundational approach to Old Testament studies, while recognising the collapse of trust in historical foundationalism (1997:84-87).

9   "Just as modern epistemology was dominated by an image, that of a building needing to be supported, so postmodern epistemology is dominated by a picture: W.V.O. Quines's image of knowledge as a web or net" (Murphy, 1997:27).

Fig. 3: Elements of a Web of Belief Analysis

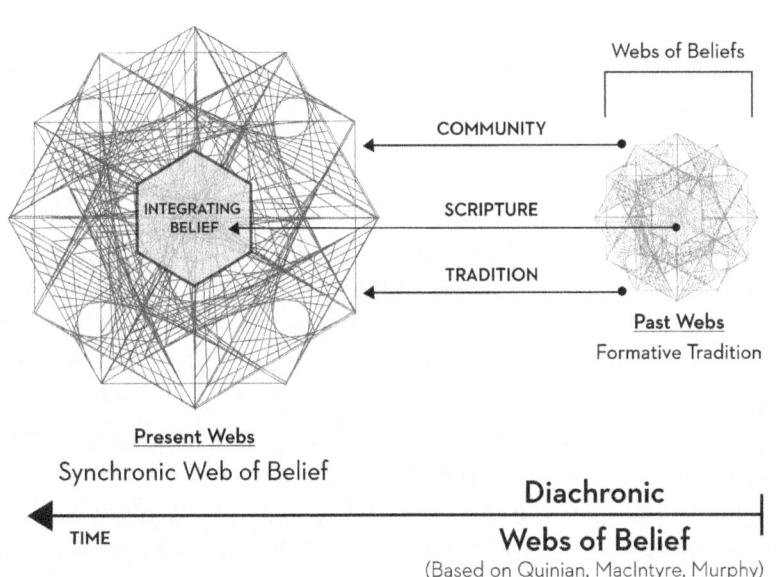

Fig. 3: The elements of a web of belief analysis. In synchronic (present time, global) analysis, the integrating truth is validated by comparison of theologies across cultures. Multiple historic Christian communities and traditions feed these. In contrast, validation in traditional diachronic analysis is against past traditions derived from a formative tradition. The particular community of faith, reflecting on both Scriptures and traditions informs and validates each web of belief.

This web approach better describes global thought processes. Filipino or Maori cultures like most band, tribal or peasant societies are story-based, holistic in discerning truth. The aberration has been the Western nations' loss of story as primary vehicle for truth.[10] As Newbigin says about Western imposition of principles on biblical interpretation:

> *Our European culture (with its large non-biblical component) predisposes us to think of the biblical stories primarily as illustrative of principles which can be grasped conceptually and which enable us to remain in orbit after the supporting illustrations have been*

---

10 Berger, Berger and Kellner's, *The Homeless Mind* (1973) demonstrates the development of linear rationalism as a primary cultural mode of thought within modernism. This contrasts with holistic categories of lowland Filipino thought, (Lynch, c1979), representative of many peasant cultures. See an expansion of these ideas in the psychology of slum-dwellers in *Cry of the Urban Poor* (Grigg, 1992/2004 ch. 15,16).

> *jettisoned. To live with the Bible, however, means to recognize that it is the story which is primary and irreplaceable, a story of which we and our contemporaries are a part and that the "principles" are not the enduring realities behind the story but rather the time conditioned attempts of a people at particular moments in the story to grasp its meaning* (1981:357).

This is not a rejection of rationality. However, it is an understanding that rationality need not be linear and foundational, but can be holistic.

Nancey Murphy (1997:120) develops MacIntyre's (1988) description of tradition, to give a three dimensional, (what I call a "helical") model linking the diachronic and synchronic components. In transformational conversations, we mesh synchronic Quinian web analysis with diachronic analysis, interfacing the historic conversations with the present web (see my summary diagram in Fig. 3). The storytelling consultations involve people trained in diachronic theologies, yet immersed in urban contexts, providing a multi-traditional background to the synchronic processes.

Incarnate or Cosmic?

This helps answer the third question, the dialectic of cosmic Christ and incarnate Son. Urban missiologists generally insist that transcendence is rooted in incarnational living. We share a strongly held value that following Jesus demands this.

But some of us while living in the story-telling environment of the poor, also gravitate to linking the stories to global systematic theologies based on principles and philosophy. This reflects not just Western rationalism accentuated by rationalist modernisation but the mind of Christ who structures and organizes the universe. In his image, we intuitively search beyond the stories for supra-theological truths to connect our contextual theologies to one another.

> *The final stage of development of a biblical theology is the identification of an archetypal concept(s) or unifying themes behind the diverse documents.... Many believe that the complete lack of consensus demonstrates that a cluster of ideas, rather than a single theme, unites all the others* (Osborne, 1991:282).

Thus in answer to the third question, "Is God cosmic or local God? Transcendent or immanent?" we recognize the necessity of both poles, but among urban workers keep the emphasis on story for we find the storytelling carries living theology better than global rationalism.

Bottom-up Contextual Theologies

This leads to the next concept. Transformational conversations exist within a genre of contextual theology. Urban missions theology is by its very label contextual theology. In reality, all theologies are in essence contextual:

> *The Bible is a library of books and consequently of theologies. The Hebrew Scriptures are made up of Yahwist theology, Elohist theology, Priestly theology, Deuteronomic theology and Wisdom theologies, prophetic theology, exilic theology... the New Testament includes Pauline theology, Johannine theology — to name but a few* (Bevans, 1996: 3).

Systematic theology itself is a contextual theological genre, with its Western, Aristotelian roots, philosophic context, establishment environment and so on.

Is God or Does God? Conversations as Action Theologies

The fourth question in establishing this hermeneutic theory is, "Is God or does God?" This is at the heart of praxis theologies. City transformational conversations begin in missional action where we seek to respond in godly manner to a need or an issue in the city. That is biblical. Theology, the knowledge of God, flows from obedience. This is part of the unspoken hermeneutic of Pentecostal theology, part of the "but does it work?" syndrome.

Like the incarnate Word, we live out conversations. Moreover, the incarnation is communal, hence structural. Structures are indicators of the realities of our theology, an anchoring into earthiness, demonstrating the God-humanity-creation linkages of a full-orbed theology.

- Lawyers In Christ -

> As an example of discerning or creating a charismatic/ Pentecostal transformational theology, we could take the legal sector of New Zealand. I first asked several Christian lawyers for stories of how the Holy Spirit has led them into the public arena as Christians in an anti-Christian environment. Doing this collectively helped identify the first themes of a transformational conversation in the legal sector — themes that in their professional isolation they have been unable to identify. For lawyers work alone much of the time.
>
> However, from the entrance stories we must press on through the conversational process to new action stories, for God is a God of action. That means enabling the lawyers to engage fully in conversation between the Scriptures and the legal sector of the city. Part of that conversation is conversation as structure. Two evangelical Christian law firms have become the core of that structure and worked with Australian counterparts to put together consultations of Christian lawyers every second year, though mainly focused on the details of Christians in the legal environment.[11]

This study explores the idea that major urban conversations are conversations of ideas embodied in structures. Sustaining and expanding the structural base numerically and in quality is essential for ongoing social influence. The perception of entrepreneurial success, momentum and structural expansion is part of gaining credibility in the postmodern cultural milieux. Those who lead larger structures often gain necessary credibility to speak to higher levels of city leadership. More than image, the reality of numbers of people on the ground, with capacity to speak, expands the potential of meaningful conversation at critical social junctures.

This study proposes that should that be the case, conversation may ensue — if the theological hermeneutics enable the conversationalists to impart significant meaning in their conversation. A discussion with a battered mother about the dignity of personhood from Genesis 1 and Psalm 139 while watching our kids score goals at Saturday

---

11 Details from discussion with Les Allen, partner in Gaze Burt, May 2005.

soccer is only possible if I understand the theology of the meaning of personhood. The same principle is true at a structural level in the city.

Conclusion and Implications for this Study

"Transformational Conversation Hermeneutics", a paradigm for creating new postmodern theologies, is rooted in the nature of God. Bringing together the stories, then identifying and reflecting on themes enables conversations within the community of faith, within the postmodern urban context and between the two. (If the reader wishes to evaluate this hermeneutic as a postmodern approach, they may turn to the excursus after Chapter 8 on postmodernism).

I have introduced the study with action stories (#1 in Fig 2) in chapter 1. In this chapter I have developed a hermeneutic theory supporting the investigative process. Chapter 3 reviews literature that reflects transformational conversations of the modern period. Part 2 develops the *urban conversation spaces* about transformational vision. This lays the basis for Part 3 where I trace the *pneumatological conversation*. *Transformational conversations* are developed contextually within both part 2 and 3.

- 3 -
A Short History of Conversations about Transformation

The earth was formless and void, darkness was over the surface of the deep and the Spirit of God was hovering over the waters... and God said, "Let there be light" (Gen 1:2).

This is the first image of transformation.

Are there conversations within history that are essentially pneumatological, but feed into a theology of transforming revival? I now examine transformational themes during the modern period, demonstrating the drift over the last half century towards the emphasis on the Holy Spirit and cultural transformation.

Radical History of Pneumatology and Transforming Vision

Three decades ago, I recall an old saint from among the Brethren, Milton Smith (Steel, 2003), laying out a fascinating scenario of church history from the Anabaptist point of view. The central motif was that the primary work of the Spirit of freedom has always been external to the institutional church (the stuff of church histories). He expressed a popularly held belief among Evangelicals and Pentecostals that power and institutionalisation corrupt and hinder the work of the Holy Spirit. Such a view affirms apostolic succession not through the bishops but through the apostles (how many bishops are apostles?).

Within the flow of this strand of history, Joachim Fiore (ca. 1130-1202) predicted a new utopian "Age of the Holy Spirit" replacing existing Christian institutions and practices as the world is evangelised and the church perfected. This idea affected many subsequent movements such as the Franciscans, Cistercians and Dominicans who understood their mission in terms of her *renovatio mundi* (Burgess, 1997a:131). During this period the Albigensians linked the "Baptism of the Spirit" with a moment of cleansing or perfecting — a doctrine that resurfaces (a little mutated) today.

My saintly friend Milton traced these themes as they migrated up into the Anabapist movements of Southern Germany resurfacing in Zwingli, Spener, Zinzendorf and the Moravians and from there into the teaching of Wesley, the Holiness movement, then the explosion of Pentecostalism. These radical reformers understood the relationship between the work of the Holy Spirit and the social reformation, emphasizing the creation of alternative societies.

I was fascinated a few years later to hear a learned Presbyterian, professor of missions history at Fuller Seminary, Paul Pierson, tell the same story (1985; 1998). Then to find a Wesleyan professor, Howard Snyder (1989/1997; 1996a; 1996c), write yet again of the same themes.[1]

Wesleyan Revival Roots to Transforming Actions

We can briefly trace much English-speaking evangelical understanding of revival to Wesley's influence at the beginnings of the industrial revolution.[2] Whitefield and the Wesley's experiences were profoundly affected by encounters with the outpouring of the Holy Spirit as they preached. Their conversion theology involving a personal relationship with God manifested by an experiential knowledge of God's presence was essentially Moravian. David Smith (1998:x) asserts that this was coupled with aspects of Calvinistic world-transforming commitment to social responsibility, inheriting a Reformed doctrine of the Christian calling in the world and anticipating the spread of a gospel with significant social consequences.

The aristocratic evangelical, William Wilberforce and *the Clapham sect* (a group of wealthy and influential men from Clapham parish church) were direct spiritual descendants of Wesley's emphases on conversion and the necessity of revival power. They brought Wesley's experiences and theology among the common people into upper levels of nineteenth century society. Wilberforce and this group of wealthy leaders initiated scores of legislative reforms for the poor, for factory workers, child labour and so on. His motivation was not so much structural change as revival among the elites and ethical change within existing social structures.

> ...*softening the glare of wealth and moderating the insolence of power, (it) renders the inequalities of the social state less galling to the lower orders, whom she instructs in their turn, to be diligent, humble, patient; reminding them that their more lowly path has been allotted to them by the hand of God* (Wilberforce, 1797:405).

---

1   Knox gives an alternative and in-depth Catholic critique and largely rejection of these and related charismatic movements throughout history in his *Enthusiasm* (1962). The rejection is built around themes of ecclesiastical authority and control. Pietists and their descendants emphasise freedom and the ability of the Spirit to guide into all truth based.

2   Marquardt (1992) summarizes his social work, contributions to economic ethics, educational work, battle against slavery and concern for prisoners. The inception of the Methodist awakening was 1739.

The Second Evangelical Awakening of 1858-9 produced over a million conversions in Great Britain and similar numbers in the US (Orr, 1955:76-78, 83). Its fruits included great evangelical unity across denominations, leading to the Evangelical - the direct ancestor of the global WCC, World Evangelical Fellowship (WEF), and Lausanne networks today; the emergence of a lay leadership movement; the expansion of a global missions movement and dramatic social and ethical changes (Orr documents the drop in criminal convictions in six counties during the time of revival (1955:92)). From it came the YMCA, the Barnardo homes, the rescue of prostitutes (over 1000 a year, which resulted in a petition of over two million signatures in 1887 to repeal government patronage of prostitution), Sunday schools for uneducated youth and thousands of other organisations.

Central in this was a response to the Dickensian evils of urban England, the spawning of a home missions movement and inner city missions. With the blessing of others, a major denomination was created, the Salvation Army. General Booth's grand schema for transforming London is documented in *In Darkest England and the Way Out* (1890). The revival created new and intense sympathy with the poor that went straight to the heart of the slums with practical responses.

I had the privilege of attending the last classes of Dr Edwin Orr, author of over 50 books on revival. His conclusion in this class about the First and Second Great (1858-9) Awakenings were that they gave birth to a litter of active religious and philanthropic societies, which accomplished much in human uplift, the welfare of children, reclamation of prostitutes, reform of alcoholics and criminals and the development of social virtues. He reflected on the political changes these wrought, in that they prepared America for a theistic republic and saved Britain from a bloody Revolution, such as occurred in France. Revival changed the social order by stages, spectacularly in the abolition of slavery. The Evangelical Revival of the eighteenth Century, instead of producing a revolutionary development, made possible an evolutionary development.

Orr identified these two major revivals and their centennial predecessors, the sixteenth century Reformation and the seventeenth century Puritanism, as primarily religious and social in manifestation — the "political factors" being treated as important accidentals. They were, "radical in their liberating power, unleashing forces for the greater emancipation of mankind... spiritual freedom seems to develop unendingly."

Middle Axioms Derived from the American Social Gospel

A generation later, in an opposite camp, the Christian *social gospel* at the turn of the century was integrated around two major works. Ernst Troeltsh in *The Social Teaching of the Christian Churches* (1911/1960) wrote of the "modern social problem" of making "Christianity relevant to a nationalistic, capitalist, technological and increasingly secular order". This was published five years after the manifesto of a burgeoning Christian social movement appeared from the pen of Walter Rauschenbusch in *Christianity and the Social Crisis* (1907/1991).

Crucially, the 1937 *Oxford Conference on Church, Community and State* was pivotal in created a new global consensus for ecumenical social ethics for the next 25 years. It was pivotal in leading to the World Council. This lasting influence was possible because of the number and quality of the Conference's reports and other related publications which it inspired (Evans, 1992:51-52).

Integral in the conference deliberations were the issues of increasing de-Christianisation and growing totalitarianism of Western societies. The resolution was to call on the laity to institute change. But on what matters can the church advise the State, particularly where technical and expert knowledge is required? The solution here followed the arguments of the "middle axioms," of John Bennett, an American social ethicist (1941:77) and William Temple. The State should adhere to certain Christian principles, but the church should not comment at the level of specific programmes, including legislation and political strategy. A middle axiom is more concrete than a principle but less specific than a political programme or legislation. To arrive at a middle axiom it is necessary to move from general principle to consultations, drawing on relevant expertise and practical experience as well as theological reflection. Consensus may or may not develop as committed Christian technical experts may disagree. If agreement is reached the church may make pronouncements. If not, the areas of disagreement can be defined and the process assists the practitioners to reflect on finding middle ground from within an ethical framework. Preston's comments about alternatives are valid for the movements under discussion in this study:

> *The alternatives on offer usually want to move from some biblical text or doctrinal statement directly to a detailed policy conclusion in the modern world, which is inescapably arbitrary, or to take over some secular analysis of that world without a sufficient theological critique of it. Against these, Temple's procedure is better* (1981).

The delegates from 120 countries at the Oxford Conference gave leadership and published extensively across the globe. Kagawa of Japan (Davey, 2000), stands out as the theologian of last century in the application of these theologies. After 15 years in the slums he took his understanding of the social gospel, learned from a stint in the US, into reconstruction of the very centre of Japanese society. While he evangelised Japan, converting more Japanese than any other, he established trade unions, agricultural cooperatives, reconstructed Tokyo after an earthquake, preached to the emperor and wrote 50 novels and other books on these themes.

The globalisation of Christianity has created a plethora of theological issues embracing religious, cultural and ideological perspectives unknown to the early social gospellers. By the 1960's, the consensus of liberal Christianity had broken down. The integrating theme of the responsible society with its emphasis on Christian order had failed. Central themes such as managing class conflict, democratising of economic power in a new socio-economic order, issues of equality of opportunity and so on, remained. The collapse of American liberal theological consensus in the middle of last century, is analyzed in *Soul in Society* (Dorrien, 1995).

These liberal theologies make little mention of the Holy Spirit. David Bosch in his exhaustive mission treatise, *Transforming Mission*, picks up on this theme of the Spirit occasionally (1991:40, 113-115), but there remains a sense that the Spirit is an afterthought to the activity of the church in connection with Jesus (Kim, 2000: 173).

That was to change dramatically with the seventh assembly of the World Council of Churches in Canberra in 1991. The assembly, with growing representation of Pentecostal and indigenous churches, was based on a missionary pneumatological and creational theme, *Come Holy Spirit — Renew the Whole Creation*, influenced by the "Spirit of Life" theology of Jurgen Moltmann (1991; 1993; 1997).

Evangelical Social Theologies

While liberal Protestant churches were grappling with these issues, Evangelicals, retreating from the social gospel since the turn of last century, had emphasised inner holiness.

But such reductionism was unsustainable. Francis Schaeffer in *The God Who Is There* (1968a; 1968b), became a popular leading Calvinistic spokesman for Evangelical intellectuals seeking a faith that dealt with the social agendas of modernism. Jim Wallis edited *Sojourners* as a focal journal of this movement in the US, sparked by the questioning of a generation locked into the Vietnam War. People such as Charles Colson, converted aide to President Nixon and President of Prison Fellowship, became popular. Two of his popular but intellectually significant books on evangelical political engagement, *Against the Night* (1989) and *Kingdoms in Conflict* (1987), develop political applications of the Kingdom.

The Lausanne Covenant

The Lausanne Covenant (Lausanne Committee for World Evangelization, 1974), marked a watershed for Evangelicals globally. The Lausanne Congress was, for the world's millions of Evangelicals, equivalent to Vatican II for Catholics, though lacking in its decorum. The Lausanne movement was for 15 years, until 1989, the international forum for global evangelical debate, involving over 80 consultations and scores of publications. The *Lausanne Covenant* justified a paralleling of evangelism and social involvement. It has become a recognised doctrinal statement across the Evangelical world.

In 1983, the *Wheaton Declaration* further strengthened the theological basis of holism and chose what had become a popular term in international development circles around 1980 — the term of "transformation." Among Evangelicals involved in third world development during the 1980's, "transformation" became the preferred term. This includes as definition:

> *According to the biblical view of human life, then, transformation is the change from a human existence contrary to God's purposes to one in which people are able to enjoy fullness of life in harmony with God (John 10:10; Col 3:8-15; Eph 4:13)*

(World Evangelical Fellowship, 1983).

Subsequently *Transformation* magazine from three centres — a group at the Oxford Centre in England, from Ron Sider and *Evangelicals for Social Action* based at Eastern Baptist Seminary, Philadelphia, and from Tokunboh Adeyemo of the *World Evangelical Fellowship* — has disseminated these ideas.

1989 was the year of collapsing command economies. It signalled a death-knell for the social Christian consensus which pitted biblical commitments to cooperative economics against the competitive spirit behind *laissez faire* capitalism. The Christian social gospel movement had fractured and lost its momentum in the 1960's. However, although Evangelicals became a primary religious force in Britain and the USA, as well as globally, they have not generated a comprehensive theological momentum to become a voice on economic philosophies.

In contrast, from the 1980's onward, there has been a multiplication of right-wing, Calvinist justifications of American Republican (or British Thatcherist)[3] views on dismantling the socialised aspects of the modern capitalist state. Griffiths advocates severing the market economy from secular humanism and incorporating it within a distinctively Christian ideology (1984:112). These voices appear to be prophetic in attempting to downsize governmental economic controls, yet violate the biblical commitments to defend the poor against the powerful.

Right-wing Republican economics and political books[4] are now more readily available to New Zealand Evangelical leaders, who now travel more in the US than in Europe, than are writings from what appear to me to be more balanced European democratic traditions, such as British M.P., David Alton's *Faith in Britain* (1991). Even more extreme, are patterns of *reconstructionism*.[5] The central tenet is to reconstruct American society as a Christian society of a previous era.

The Structural Question Becomes an Anthropological Question
In both liberal and evangelical streams, through people like E. Stanley Jones in India (1972); Kagawa of Japan in *Christ and Japan* (1934); Vishal Mangalwadi of India (*Truth and Social Reform* (1986)) or Bishop Lesslie Newbigin (*The Gospel in a Pluralist Society* (1989)), the discussion ceased to focus primarily on the historic structuralist question of church and state shifting to the anthropological question of the nature of the gospel and culture. It became a discussion about worldview change resulting in structural changes.

This outworking of the globalisation of the church represents the progression from Western Christendom to indigenisation. Indigenisation led to theologies of contextualisation, incarnation, social change, transformation and liberation as against reform. Cultural hermeneutics produces new patterns of biblical hermeneutics. The emergence of free nations from the colonial era led to issues of national identity, national church and national economic development. Local theologies arose to meet these needs.

---

3   A significantly positioned representative for these views in England has been Brian Griffith, formerly head of Margaret Thatcher's Downing Street policy unit. His *Morality and the Market Place: Christian Alternatives to Capitalism and Socialism* (1982), is an introduction to Christian conservatism; see also *The Creation of Wealth* (1984); *Monetarism and Morality: A Response to the Bishops* (1985).

4   For example, George Grant, *The Changing of the Guard: Biblical Blueprints for Political* (1987b); *Bringing in the Sheaves: Transforming Poverty into Productivity* (1987a); Dennis Peacocke, *Winning the Battle for the Minds of Men* (1989); or John Whitehead, *Christians Involved in the Political Process* (1994)

5   For example, the comprehensive definitions of social objectives in many spheres of public life in *The Christian Worldview Documents* (Grimstead, 1990). These include the complete closure of the Internal Revenue Service and minimalist government (Grimstead, 2005).

The progression has been aided by the cross-fertilisation of ideas through journals such as *Missiology* (read by Catholic, liberal and evangelical missionaries alike). Fuller Theological Seminary School of World Mission professors developed models of the gospel and culture and church impacting culture, growing out of an evangelistic commitment.[6] These models multiplying through evangelical seminaries worldwide, have a ring of truth to Evangelicals. Liberal German theologians such as Tillich, in his distinctive method of "correlation" (Stenger & Stone, 2002), or Pannenberg in his anthropological theology (1995), had also explored the anthropological question of Christ and culture, but are not as common reading for Evangelicals because of their source in a tradition with a different style of commitment to biblical authority.

Urban Missions

Within this progression urban missions developed. My categories in this study are informed by years of leading and teaching urban missions from a framework of urban anthropology. My foundations were laid under missionary anthropologist, Paul Hiebert. His teaching reflected in *Incarnational Ministry* (Hiebert & Meneses, 1995), relates urban studies to urban church.

One stream of urban missions developed among churchplanters on the frontlines of penetration of Buddhist, Hindu and animist cities. It aims at the incarnational and evangelistic formation of holistic churches as a primary goal. Roger Greenway with the Christian Reformed Mission (1978, 1979, 1989a) mapped the field and Harvey Conn in *Urban Missions* magazine at Westminster Theological Seminary, provided a ten year forum. Since these deal with poverty as a primary context, they draw on urban economic theories (de Soto, 1989; Jacobs, 1984; Santos, 1979) and the holistic church among the poor (Grigg, 1984/2004, 1992/2004).

The second stream is essentially American deriving from Chicago, where the church already exists as a significant player in a highly government funded context of meeting social needs. Eastern Seminary urban missiologist Ray Bakke, has advocated this school globally (1987; 1997), in his role as urban consultant with the Lausanne Committee. Both schools adhere to an evangelical view of the Scriptures, commitment to doing justice (Linthicum, 1991b; Lupton, 1993), structural transformation and to centralising ministry to the poor.

These schools drew on urban studies, derived from the comprehensive sociology of Weber in *The City* (1921/1958) and historical works of Mumford (1969). These were further developed by the "Chicago School". The index of Gmelch and Zenner's anthology, *Urban Life* (1996), show the emphasis of common urban anthropology on urbanism as a way of life, migration, family and kinship, class and ethnicity, urban places and spaces. Urban planners and geographers would emphasize other issues of infrastructure, transportation, or public services (e.g. Gale & Moore, 1975). Newer works related to the emergence of postmodern cities are being produced from the University of Southern California (Dear, 2000; Soja, 1989/1997).

---

6   These built on the diverse missionary anthropological works of Alan Tippet.

Progression to Theologies of Revival

Harvey Cox, author of a popular urban theology *The Secular City* (1965), derived from liberal English Bishop Robinson's "Death of God" theology, which in turn was based on a view of the triumph of secularism, twenty years later retracted much of it in *Religion in the Secular City* (1984). A decade later he analysed Pentecostalism in *Fire from Heaven: The Rise of Pentecostal Spirituality and the Reshaping of Religion in the Twenty-First Century* (1995). He begins with this humble retraction:

> Even before I started my journey through the world of Pentecostalism it had become obvious that instead of the "death of God" some theologians pronounced not many years ago, or some waning of religion that sociologists had extrapolated, something quite different had taken place... I had swallowed them all too easily and had tried to think about what their theological consequences might be. But it had now become clear that the predictions themselves had been wrong (1995: xvi).

Recognising the explosion of global Pentecostalism in one century to 400 million, he then analyses them as a response to the modern context.

By 1989, they were a dominant force at the second *Lausanne Congress* in Manila. This conference faced major tension between the pragmatic evangelistic Pentecostal growth of the Third World and the entrenched theological streams of the US and European Evangelicals. The subsequent AD2000 movement developed the *Global Congress on World Evangelism* (GCOWE) in 1995 in Korea, the first global congress funded primarily from non-Western sources and led by non-Western leaders, largely Pentecostal. This strategy conference focused on evangelism. The finer theological nuances of transformation were relegated to one of ten tracks — the urban track.[7] Partly because evangelical transformational theology leaders critiqued this conference as a step backwards, in 2000 they developed a consultation of 300 in England around the themes of discipleship leading to transformation.[8] These conferences expanded an environment of dialogue, opening up to Pentecostal leadership the possibilities of the social aspects of the gospel. (Thus through the last century, global consultations shifted from the English Anglican power centre, to an American evangelical/fundamentalist centre then to an increasing global Pentecostal influence).

Meanwhile, global contextual issues moved beyond the North-South Marxist-Capitalist development debates to postmodern cultural debates located in mega-cities. Monographs in the *Christian Mission and Modern Culture* series by the Mennonites, (including Shenk (1995); also Bosch (1991: 349-362)), sought to locate mission in postmodern culture.

While the context of mission has largely migrated to the global mega-city, I would propose that pneumatology has concurrently become the central theme of missions theology for the next decade. The logic is strategically inescapable.

Firstly, the Protestant church has become global and is predominantly a missionary church in the developing world, largely Pentecostal in style. This affects even the World

---

[7] The above paragraph represents the author's view of these two Congresses - six years of work as leader of the urban track at GCOWE.

[8] Personal conversations with leaders.

Council of Churches in its agendas and created major debate as to the nature of that Spirit at the seventh assembly in Canberra.[9] In 1976, Karl Barth was thinking of a "theology of the Spirit," written, unlike his own, not from the dominant perspective of Christology, but from that of pneumatology (Busch, 1976).

This task was completed by Jurgen Moltmann as the fourth book in his systematic theology, *The Spirit of Life* (1991). This comprehensive book, affirms the work of the Spirit in all life-giving, what Moltmann calls "holistic pneumatology".

Unfortunately, it is limited in value by the imposition of the WCC biases as to the activity of the Holy Spirit in the world (universalism, a focus on liberation, an optimistic non-apocalyptic futurology).[10]

Secondly, theology in the global missional church, reasonably moves to a focus on a theology of the Holy Spirit, for sentness is the essence of *missio*-n — the Spirit is the one sent from the Father, (or Father and Son) and is the one who convicts and converts.

Thirdly, in the West, the sweeping charismatic movements among both Catholics and Protestants have made the Holy Spirit and revival to become significant themes. As these Catholic charismatics and Protestant Pentecostals increase in influence, seeding leaders into the government bodies, they find former theologies inadequate to deal with issues of changing governmental systems.[11] Thus, paralleling the cry in New Zealand is a cry from Latin Pentecostalism (Berg & Pretiz, 1996; Petersen, 1996; Villafañe, 1993a) for transformational theologies to serve a new generation of Evangelicals.

A review of specific revival literature appears in Chapter 10.

Literature on Transforming New Zealand Social Vision

How did revivals affect the attempts of the New Zealand church to define a vision for the nation? In 1861-63 four ships of non-conformists from the Great Revival in England, arrived to found Port Albert as a non-conformist city. It failed. They returned to Auckland making a remarkable impact on the foundational values of that city. Despite this, revival is not seen as a significant factor in church life or social transformation by the historians. Allan Davidson in *Christianity in Aotearoa* (1991) includes several chapters on church and society. In an extensively annotated doctoral thesis on *Church-State Relationships in New Zealand: 1940-1990*, Evans (1992) has developed this more thoroughly.

When focusing on Christian social vision, a series of works from a group connected to the Joint Board of Education of the National Council of Churches are available, beginning with a comprehensive monograph, *Finding the Way: New Zealand Christians Look Forward* (Martin, 1983) and *Christians in Public Planning* (Nichol & Vietch, 1981).

Other mainline church analyses have been attempted. George Bryant, Methodist lay preacher and prolific author, brought together articles by sixteen leaders in social spheres and projecting a future from a mildly Christian perspective on *New Zealand*

---

9   Insider critiques of the debate are given in Castro (1993; 2000a) and in Kim (2000b; 1994).

10 For critiques from six continents, see the *Journal of Pentecostal Theology*, 1994 (4), particularly that of Stibbe (Johnstone & Mandryk, 2001; Stibbe, 1994).

11 For example, explorations of a theology for an urban faith in Sao Paulo (de Castro, 2000; Ramos, 1995).

2001 (1981). In 1990, the Catholic and Anglican Bishops gathered four hundred people for a Symposium on New Zealand's Future in Wellington, *Te Ara Tika — The Way Ahead*. This included workshops on fifty-two topics and a progression from theory to practical outcome in the discussions covering six themes — environment, education, economy, social equity, bicultural society and human rights (Roman Catholic and Anglican Bishops of New Zealand, 1990). Neither an integrated theology nor reflection on praxis emerged — perhaps it was too hastily brought together in only five months.[12] These themes are reflected however, in *Making Choices: Social Justice for Our Times* (Smithies & Wilson, 1993), 9000 of which were distributed across the churches for discussion (Lineham, 2004: 161-2). None of these indicate the work of the Holy Spirit as a significant factor.

Alternative analyses were produced in the late 1980's and 1990's by Evangelicals that give a different interpretation of the church of New Zealand. Four books from *VisionNZ* conferences (Bruce Patrick, 1993; 1997a; 1997b; 1993) collated visions from over fifty Evangelical leaders and include considerable church growth data, along with some embryonic social analysis.

Kevin Ward has, step by step, expanded sociological analysis of New Zealand church growth and its relationship to baby boomers and postmodernity (2000; 2001; 2004; 2004a). Steve Taylor represents a cluster of thinkers delving into the nature of the postmodern emergent church (2004; 2005a). My arguments partly focus on the expansion of that church into social roles. Rex Ahdar (2000) develops the idea of conflict with a "Wellington worldview", in a series of papers reflecting on relationships between Evangelicals and the State from a legal perspective.

Published near the completion of this study, recent perspectives in *The Future of Christianity* (Stenhouse & Knowles, 2004), have given opportunity to verify aspects of this book. Peter Lineham's article on "Social Policy and the Churches in the 1990's and Beyond", contextualises engagement of mainline church voices and recent governments. Brett Knowles' chapter on "The Future of Pentecostalism", follows a similar trajectory to my own interaction with the work of Harvey Cox, raising similar concerns about Pentecostal control structures and changes in spirituality.

---

12 Peter Lineham has a more positive view (2004:151-2).

- 4 -
THE CONVERSATIONALISTS OF AUCKLAND

A widespread national revival movement, the charismatic renewal, has touched most of New Zealand's churches and denominations[1] over thirty years, stimulating Pentecostalism and evangelical denominations, and sectors of mainline denominations. This revival built on earlier revival movements and the Pentecostal denominations spawned by them. I contend that a major agent for transformation in Auckland is the fruit of this revival. Thus, before expanding the theology of revival, it is necessary to examine the size of the committed core of the church in Auckland, diverse futures of the Auckland church, the significance of charismatic and Pentecostal growth and from these, the potential workforce for transformation.

The most dramatic revival in New Zealand was conversion of 90% of Maori within two decades in the mid 19th century, with revival gatherings of 5000+, (Evans & McKenzie, 1999:2-30; Tippett, 1971:44). The Albertlanders, spawned Wesleyan and Baptist revival movements, the latter based from the founding of the Auckland Baptist Tabernacle. Edwin Orr speaks of the extraordinary movement of power of the Torrey-Alexander crusades in Dunedin in 1902, the impact of the Welsh revival (1904) and the Chapman-Alexander crusades of 1912 (1973:110-112). His revival crusades (1930's) affected thousands (1936). Hugh Jackson hints at occasions of overwhelming empowerment of the Ngaruawahia conventions (1987:64-5). This holiness movement influenced thousands prior to the charismatic renewal.

---

1   Including the Catholic church, but I am not qualified to comment on this.

Worsfold (1974) documents the Catholic Apostolic Church (Irvingites, 1831 renewal in England) who were present in New Zealand in the latter half of last century, the Salvation Army emerging from the 2nd Great Awakening, the Keswick movement (1880's - 1940's), the intrusion of the fruits of the Welsh and Madagascar revivals (1904) and the major evolution of Pentecostalism from the Smith Wigglesworth crusades of 1922 and 1923 which spawned Apostolic, Elim and Assemblies of God denominations in New Zealand (The Times, 1922). The Queen Street Assembly of God in Auckland became a major Pentecostal centre of the work of the Spirit over some decades. Many from mainline churches would visit during evenings.

Colin Brown (1985) indicates the birth of the charismatic renewal was among Anglican clergy in 1965 and by 1974 for example, 40-50% of the clergy in Auckland and people within a third of its parishes claimed to be 'baptised in the Spirit' (Church of England of New Zealand, 1974). These were encouraged by the appointment of leadership to the Anglican Renewal Ministries. There were at that time, significant though lesser responses in Presbyterian and Baptist denominations, limited impact among Methodists and rejection by Brethren. There were also a significant number of charismatic groups within Catholicism. The story of Milton Smith (Steel, 2003), indicates a much more diverse process of initiation. Knowles identifies crossovers of theology and experience from some Pentecostal leaders (2000: 83-87).

The Size of the Committed Core

Assessing the impact of revival on the city of Auckland requires comparison between the Spirit-filled church and the size of the city. What is the size of the Christian community, which is the cradle of the charismatic Evangelical and Pentecostal sectors of the church? Over four years I collated statistics on the nature, and physical locations (photographing many and mapping them) of congregations in greater Auckland, significant at 1084 congregations,[2] including 297 separate ethnic congregations, (apart from ethnic fellowships in existing Pakeha congregations, bringing the total to 350+ ethnic fellowships and congregations, as of 1998 (Fig. 4)).

To examine commitment, I needed to consider two issues: the committed core and among them, the second commitment to be cultural change agents. Webster and Perry's study (1989), showed a high correlation between weekly attendance and a frequent sense of spiritual presence, concluding that weekly attendance was the best indicator of "religiosity" or as others call it, "the committed core", "those who are practising believers, not simply adherents". As Bryan Wilson intimates in a critique on the use of attendance figures, "Church attendance is, at least in the Christian West, the most conspicuous indicator of the extent of persisting, voluntary, unconstrained, religious commitment among the public at large" (Wilson, 2004: xvi). I have been in a research network on churches in cities globally that has included the global missions researchers, Patrick Johnstone (2001), David Barrett (2001) and Global Mapping International

---

2   A congregation is defined as a separate worshipping entity with recognised leadership. Some churches like Hillsborough Baptist have several congregations: Indian, youth, traditional, contemporary, each with their own pastors and worship.

Fig. 4: Denominational Distribution of Congregations in Auckland

Denominational Breakdown Of 1084 Congregations In Auckland [Grigg, Sept 1998]

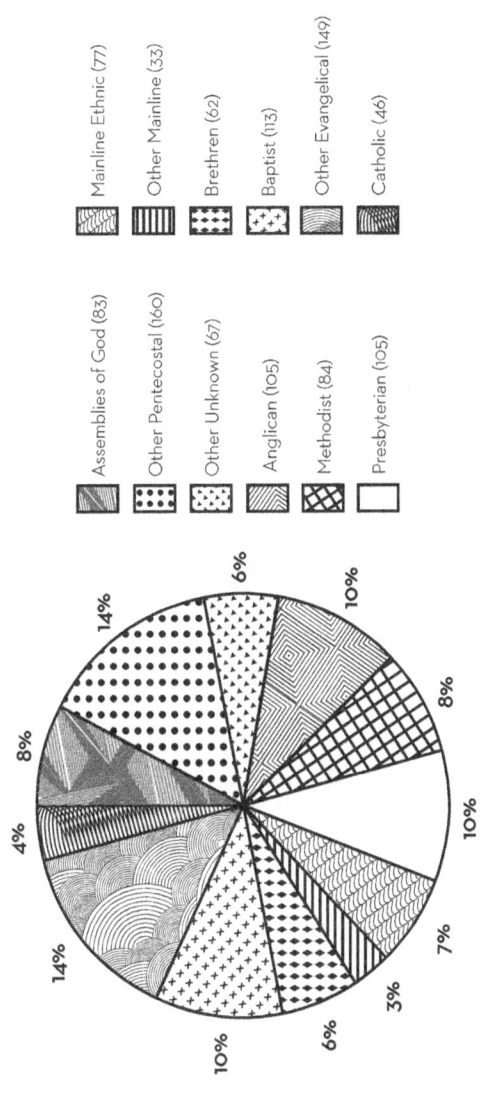

Fig 4: The breakdown by denominational grouping of congregations (some churches have multiple congregations) in Auckland based on the Vision for Auckland database. The percentages are numbers of congregations to total number of congregation.

(http://www.gmi.org/research/).[3] In the process, I have realised the level of estimation needed for strategic missional thinking. Often the data is not there, or half there. New Zealand is no exception. This is not a sociological study but in order to define the context of revival, in this chapter I have needed to bring together and make a few minor improvements on the statistical research that is available.

So how many Aucklanders attend church weekly? I became aware as I developed the above database that the commonly used figure of 10% of New Zealanders in church on Sunday was short of the reality in Auckland. Having sought to map the churches and photographed hundreds of buildings where they meet, I realised that almost every church had two, three or four congregations meeting in it, that new ethnic churches were mushrooming on a monthly basis, that several ethnic congregations had reached the 500+ level, that school halls were almost all being used, that each of the major city centres like Henderson had six to eight warehouse churches, – in fact there was a shortage of space for the church in Auckland. As I write, I have just preached to a thousand member Korean Assemblies of God in a converted TVNZ studio. The Auckland church is not in decline, it is bursting its seams.

I queried historian Peter Lineham, who sent me many of the polls taken by various news media, and by a marketing study group at Massey University and then I found the results of other polls. These numerous phone polls and estimated figures[4] that compare the percentage of total NZ population of "high participation" Christians, over the years from 1983 to 2005.[5] showed that:

- Those who say they attend church weekly fall consistently between 10 - 16% in New Zealand every Sunday.

- Those who attend 2-3 times per month, plus those attending weekly (the committed core for the purposes of this study) fall consistently between 17% and 19% throughout this period.

Those who attend at least monthly fall within a range of 20-24%. Actual participation is always lower than what polls identify (Ward, 2000: note 3). That is about 150,000 people in church in Auckland on a Sunday.

---

3   My AD2000 cities database of churches in the slums may be found integrated into each of these works.

4   These are largely phone interview research, with samples above 500 and usually nearer 1000 people.

5   Figures are included here simply to show that a thesis predicated on the expansion and size of the Evangelical and Pentecostal movements is valid. Calculations are based on the available studies (Signpost Communications, 1992; Webster & Perry, 1989, 1992; Withy, 1993), but indicate the need for further accurate sociological research beyond the scope of this paper. My figures may be compared among others with Lineham, 14.0% weekly, included Catholic at 6.14% of population, 43% of nominal Catholics (1982); (Correspondence from Peter Lineham, May, 2000). Alan Withy's (1993:123) summary, based on the 1991 census and church survey figures in 1993 showed an 11% weekly attendance (equivalent to 14.5% figure of those who seek to attend regularly.

Fig. 5: Weekly Attendances by Denomination

NZ & Auckland Baptist Weekly Attendance

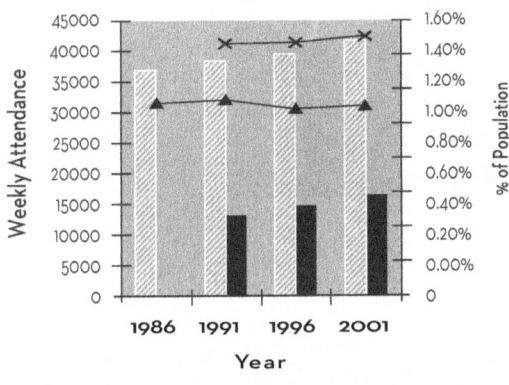
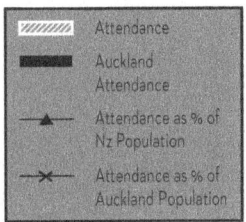

Greater Auckland Catholic Attendance
(22.8%, 2001; 21.5%, 1996 Of Affiliated Catholics In Census)

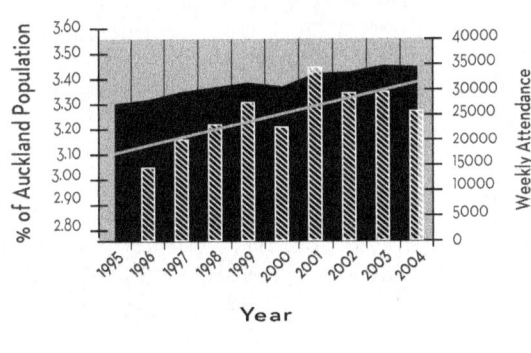
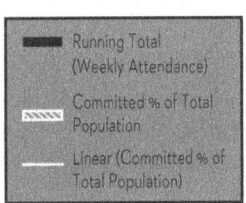

GREATER AUCKLAND ANGLICAN ATTENDANCE
(4.6%, 1991; 4.5%, 2001 OF AFFILIATED ANGLICANS IN CENSUS)

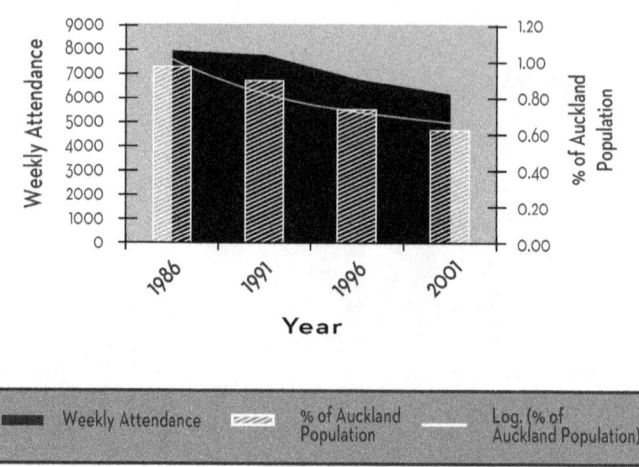

Fig. 5 shows some denominational trends, based on yearly denominational figures for weekly attendance. The above show both absolute numbers attending and percentage of Auckland or New Zealand population. Fig 5a: Auckland Baptist growth matches population and is higher than national averages, illustrating Evangelical and ethnic growth.[6] Fig 5b: Catholic Christianity has expanded in Auckland largely through ethnic growth in the last 10 years.[7] Fig 5c: Anglican decline has continued, illustrating strong liberal influences.[8] This has been ameliorated by growth of evangelical Anglican communions, largely due to Alpha courses.

Significance: Charismatic Evangelical / Pentecostal Growth

This analysis leads to three questions. Given the overall persistence of this wider Christian church, what is the size of the whole group under study — the Evangelical/Pentecostal movement within New Zealand? Is there the dynamism of an expanding movement? Is it significant in terms of internal strength?

Unlike my analysis of numbers of congregations and ethnic congregations, I not only worked from primary data for all this, but also had to make sense of the existing surveys mentioned above. I next compared them with denominational studies of attendance,

---

6 Based on Baptist Yearbooks for these years.

7 Based on yearly attendance figures collated by Pat Lythe, Catholic Pompalier Centre.

8 Based on figures for total attendance from Auckland Synod yearbooks for these years, averaged to weekly figures. Liberal Anglican decline is shown in many congregations of 10-30 people. There is significant growth in evangelical congregations (Discussion with Vicar Max Scott, about the Church Life Survey).

APOSTOLIC CHURCH PARTICIPANTS, 1988-2005

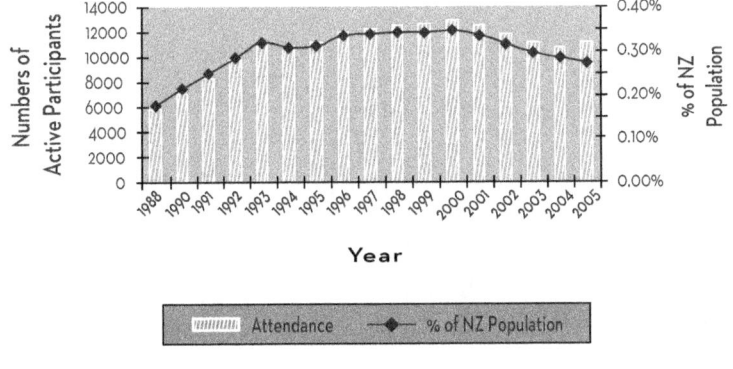

Fig 5d: Apostolic churches show decadal growth of 100%, then losses after the year 2000. This reflects anecdotal trends in other Pentecostal groups, though some of the losses have been secession of 3 congregations to Destiny churches since 1998, (which in effect demonstrates further growth through division, adding another graph on top of this one, around 5000 by 2005, indicating total sustained but slowing growth).

where they existed, and ferreting out the figures for some that did not exist, in a process of triangulation to see if they were indeed comparable. There were some indications (as shown in Fig. 5a and b) that figures for Auckland would be higher because of the large number of ethnic churches.

My conclusion was that significant growth in attendance had occurred in four areas of Evangelicalism. Firstly numbers of evangelicals in the mainline denominations have increased significantly. Evangelical Protestants can conservatively be rated as 40% and increasing of Anglican and Presbyterian denominations (or 60% and increasing of those who attend church regularly weekly),[9] and 40% of the Methodist bloc.[10] The evangelical Salvation Army, Church of Christ, Nazarene, Reformed, Baptist, and Brethren denominations have experienced small decline or some small increases, overall just keeping pace with population growth. Secondly, there has been significant

---

9 Conservative figures based on discussions with several church leaders. However Doug Lendrum, Presbyterian Co-Director of the Mission Resource team, in analysis of the 1997 Church Life Survey, documents 82% of Presbyterians holding traditional evangelical views on doctrines and 91% believing the Bible to be the word of God, indicating a large gap between members and clergy views (Brookes, 2000:73). Lineham, analysing the same data identifies 41.4% as Evangelical and charismatic (2000b:210).

10 The final shape of the evangelical Methodist church and the relationships with Pacific Island Methodists as it forms from the Methodist conference, makes it difficult to give a more definitive figure.

ethnic congregational growth both within these and in the emergence of new ethnic churches and denominations. Thirdly, Pentecostal growth in weekly attendance has grown from 1% to about 2.3% of the population.[11] After many iterations, juggling attendance figures from multiple sources, my personal estimate is that regular weekly church attendance of the charismatic, Evangelical and Pentecostal clustering has grown from about 4.5% to almost 6% of the population over the fifteen years from 1986 to 2001 (Grigg, 2005b).[12] This growth is linked by most leaders to revival and the charismatic movement over these last forty years.

This clustering of evangelicals and Pentecostals is now dramatically larger than the declining traditional liberal wing of the Protestant church. Catholic decrease is less rapid but significant, with an upturn in Auckland due to new ethnic congregations in the last eight years (3.2% regular attendance in 2001 in Auckland).[13]

Thus while some large sectors of society are being lost to Christianity and others are being gained, the overall percentage appears to be increasing from 1986 to 1996 and then slowing to 2001 and beyond.

Diverse Futures of the Auckland Church

Will these percentages increase or decrease? The expectation by mainline theologians and by secularist leaders is of decrease. The committed core of Christians has decreased from in the mid-20% ranges in the 19th century, with the maximum attendance 29.8% in 1894[14] to various estimates of between 10-15% attending weekly (and higher in Auckland (See Heylen poll, Richardson, 2004)). The anecdotal evidence, polls, and church attendance analysis that indicate overall gain up to 1996, is now being offset by post-revival plateauing and small decline. This was predicted by Hugh Dickie when he documented the rapid loss of children in Sunday Schools. In 1986, there were 200,000 children in mainline church Sunday Schools every week. By 1998, it was down to 19,000 (Dickie, 1997).

But what if revival synergies continue to reoccur? The ministry of Whitefield at a time of great moral depravity in England swung similar decline around. Synergistic revival movements fed by migration streams in the US led to decadally increasing percentages.[15] The Naga revival in a cohesive tribal people-movement led to over

---

11 I am basing this on the census figures, with comparisons with known data from denominations where possible. Withy and Knowles working from the DAWN figures concluded that Pentecostal attendance was 122% of census figures in 1992 (Withy, 1993:123), and Fernandez and Hall concluded 83.5% in 1986 and 102% in 1991 (Fernandez & Hall, 1987). Thus conservative use of the census figure, with adjustment for the change in the census question on religious affiliation in 2001, give these percentages.

12 The derivation of these figures, is based on both on some accurate data, and estimates of estimates, Even after perhaps 40 iterations over 6 years, it is better than previous information published. Some analysis is available on the web (Grigg, 2005b).

13 Based on yearly attendance figures (excluding Easters, Christmases and major events) from Pat Lythe, Catholic Pompalier Centre.

14 Calculations on census figures.

15 According to Littell (1962), America in its early years never was a Christian nation. In 1776 only 5 percent of the people belonged to the churches. By 1850 the figure was 15.5%. Revivalism dur-

90% conversion to Christianity, sustained until invasion by the Indian army in the last decades. Greeley (2004) documents the post-communist revival of religion in Eastern Europe.

We can interpret these dynamics by utilising four future streams of religiosity among New Zealand Christians, identified by Webster and Perry (1989:52) as possible categories, with the addition of a non-Christian religious category.

- A secular non-religious stream (expanding).
- A traditional religious stream relating to a personal God (1/3 of the population with about half of this experiencing the presence of God, declining).
- A mystical stream, relating to a non-personal life-force (expanding).
- A reactionary sect stream[16] (expanding), based on definite beliefs and convictions.
- Non-Christian religions among migrants (Hinduism, Jainism, Islam, etc., expanding).

For each of these streams there are both internal dynamics and external contextual factors affecting growth and decline.

A Secular Future?

Is the future secularist? While modernist liberal theology among Presbyterians in New Zealand, influenced by Prof Lloyd Geering, foresaw primarily a secular future, based on early secularisation theory, others see it as temporary state of affairs. Secularity has limited resources and provides no *raison d'être*, which religious belief does (Stark & Bainbridge, 1985:421). Sociologists, along with these theologians, predicted the loss of religion, only to be surprised by its resurgence in both fundamentalist and experiential modes (Berger, 1999).[17] On the other hand, the general sceptical attitude of sociologists like Bryan Wilson, a sociologist of religion in the Weberian tradition, sees such modern religion as being unable to challenge the dominant ethos, but rather as providing an enclave of meaning and significance to individuals in a world of machines, managers and bureaucrats. They "are not so much the progenitors of a counterculture, as random anti-cultural assertions" (1976:110).

Crucial as the secularisation debate is,[18] clearly the New Zealand and in general, Western secularisation of belief, has caused an exit from the institutional church. In terms of *internal dynamics* affecting decline, significant secularisation also exists in

---

ing western migration increased these figures to above 30%.

16 The term "sect" has continued to be used in sociology of religion and state church theologies, since Troelsch, to describe non-institutional (mainly evangelical) religious groups.

17 Berger recants on his commitment to the secularisation thesis. Bruce then speaks of it as an unnecessary recantation (2001). Both are dealing with the resurgence of evangelicalism and fundamentalism in the West, of Eastern European religion, and of Islam.

18 Bruce (2001: 90) argues that the tolerance and individualism at the heart of liberal ideology undermines the cohesion required for a shared belief system. Kevin Ward (2004a:3-5) summarizes the rise and fall of the secularisation debate, indicating the new sociological awareness of the persistence of religion and separating loss of belief from loss of belonging. Norris and Inglehart do not come to the same conclusion as to the loss of membership in voluntary organisations (2004: 183).

the committed core in the liberal sector of the Protestant church that has embraced modernist or secular theology, with concomitant loss of foundational beliefs, and consequently membership.[19]

For example, in the significantly liberal-led Presbyterian denomination in Auckland, attendance reduced by 27% from 7900 to 5800 in ten years (Holland, 1996). That involved a lot of pain.

Secularisation, Urbanisation and Loss of Faith
Secularisation is usually considered as an accompanying aspect of urbanisation. But the relationships are much more complex. Hugh Jackson in his articles on church attendance 1860-1930, denies this correlation (1987:64-5). The differences in church attendance within New Zealand denominations graphed in this chapter indicate a significantly higher Auckland urban attendance than rural over the last 15 years.

These large theoretical constructs of urbanisation and secularisation need to be broken down into constituent parts to make sense. For example, we can examine just one aspect of urbanisation in the present urban context of high mobility. Unless they are in an older suburban context, urban pastors must replace about a fifth to a quarter of their flock each year just to maintain their present size, as 20-35% migrate each year. Churches fixed in older structures and rituals generally cannot cope with the speed and level of change needed. They tend to retrench into older ways, particularly as congregations age. On the other hand Pentecost's (c1979) seminal research on receptivity to the gospel indicate that positive change in social, economic or political areas of life result in a responsiveness and receptivity to the gospel. The in-migration to Auckland involves such positive changes, so one would expect a greater responsiveness in Auckland than across New Zealand as a whole… provided the internal culture of a denomination affirms communication of the gospel to those responsive people.

Webster and Perry's early analysis predicted an ageing church: "This remnant is ageing and the congregation diminishing" (1989:49). This is certainly true of the mainline denominations analyzed by the Church Life Survey (Brookes & Curnow, 1998). For internal denominational factors also effect the emptying of churches, regardless of the receptivity of context. These include terminal illness of denominational structures through traditionalism; theologies denying biblical authority;[20] some training models of pastoral leadership based primarily on academics and ignoring skills and spiritual gifting criteria, or failure to internally structure for ethnic change in the community, among others. Christian Schwartz has identified eight quality characteristics and six biotic principles affecting growth of churches (see Natural Church Growth analyses in Shwartz, 1996). Lack of some of these factors

---

19 Catholic theologian, Darragh, concludes that the underlying secularist theological project begun in the 1960's will run its course within this generation (2004: 214). The difficulty is what becomes of the people left leaderless by loss of an integrated theological framework. Do these churches simply disappear, or is there transfer to newer denominations?

20 Greeley comments, after demonstrating the failure of secularisation theory to account for the revival of Eastern Europe, "Perhaps the decline in Britain, if there really is one, is the result of failure of the Church of England to hold onto the faith of its people, the way the Catholic Church has in Italy, Spain, Portugal, Poland and Ireland" (2004: 189).

contribute to the slow decline of Catholic Church attendance till 1996 (now reversed, at least in Auckland, by ethnic growth) and rapid decline of the liberal sector in mainline churches.

But the overall reality is much different to Webster and Perry's and Brookes and Curnow's "age and decline" opinions, so popular with journalists. Unfortunately, most Pentecostal, fundamentalist and ethnic churches were not on the list of churches contacted for the Church Life Survey — at least 50% of the Auckland churches. Thus the research sustained the myth that the church is declining.[21] More comprehensive statistics, which include these churches (Dickie, 1997, 1996), show reasonable consistency of sustained Christianity across ages. There are variations across denominations: fewer youth and increasing age in the mainline denominations; a loss of middle aged leadership in the Baptist denomination; large numbers of youth involved in Pentecostal and fundamentalist churches; significant numbers of migrant children in church; few Pakeha children in church. While there is gradual decline among Pakeha, it has been significantly offset by other urban phenomena into a shift to new styles of growing Christianity — Pentecostal, independent fundamentalist and ethnic. This is affirmed by Webster's revised views: "it remains uncertain whether there is an age-effect as such" (2001:169).

Kevin Ward (2004a:2-4) analysing the secularisation debate, concludes there is both declining religious authority and privatisation of religion, yet a persistence of religious faith, though a persistence whose content is morphing, with declining involvement, yet sustained religiosity. This chapter supports the persistence thesis and the morphing thesis. The indications are that until 1996, the charismatic revival prevented overall declining involvement, but that with the waning of revival from around 1989, another phase of national decline is probable (though with the expansion of ethnic churches in Auckland, may not occur in this city). However, his study of the disestablishment of rugby institutions as a parallel to the disestablishment of the church as institution (Ward, 2002), plus the figures above for loss of children in churches and the loss of revival dynamics, leaves one with grave concerns as to the future, even in Auckland.

Fundamentalism: Secure Haven in a Chaotic World
We now examine this morphing phenomenon. Harvey Cox's premise is that in the postmodern post-secular context, religions (whether Christianity, Hinduism, Islam, Buddhism) have all re-emerged in two forms, fundamentalism and experientialism. Both provide coherence where secularism has failed to provide a "culturally plausible response" (Cox, 1995:300-301).

Fundamentalism provides certainty in cultures that are increasingly incoherent mosaics of unconnected values, ideas and relationships (Ammerman, 1987: 192). It includes claims of absolute religious truth in the face of the social disintegration inherent in secularism. On the negative side:

---

21 The survey used denominational churches' databases. It also required significant payments by contributing churches. Consequently, newer church plants and most independent, ethnic and Pentecostal groups did not participate. In developing the Auckland churches database in 1996-9, I discovered only 400 of 1086 congregations were identified on the database for the survey. This was corrected to some extent in subsequent surveys.

> *Fundamentalism is not a retrieval of the religious tradition at all, but a distortion of it. The fundamentalist voice speaks to us not of the wisdom of the past but of a desperate attempt to fend off modernity by using modernity's weapons* (Cox, 1995:303).

In Auckland, fundamentalist groups have been increasing in numbers, providing a safe haven for those seeking a clear system of belief in a chaotic postmodern world. These include imported Calvinist churches from Holland (Dutch Reformed) and South Africa, descendants of fundamentalist missionary movements in Taiwan, Hong Kong and Korea, reinforced by traditionalist cultural tendencies and churches planted by missionaries directly sent to Auckland by fundamentalist US denominations. The Salvation Army, Churches of Christ, a significant percentage of the Brethren movement and a handful of Baptist churches have continued to sustain their fundamentalism, partly in reaction to the charismatic movement. This, in most cases involves decline, although there is growing openness to diversity and significant Brethren chapels have moved to pastor-led post-charismatic styles.

Expanding Experiential Religion

The alternative experiential, storytelling, mystical style of religion requires less defined boundaries. It can pull component truths from multiple sources, integrating and reintegrating them into new formulations. With their emphasis on the God who breaks in and on listening to the voice of that God, the charismatic movement and Pentecostalism place great emphasis on intuitive thinking. This leads to significant development of worship, music and creative arts, also stimulates highly adaptive leadership styles — an essential element in modern urban church leadership (Hall, c1985).

Paralleling the cultural shift from rationalist anti-supernaturalism to informal supernaturalism, the religious shift appears to be from rational systematic theology and formal religion of the mainline churches to the informal supernatural religion of the charismatics and Pentecostals. Some term it a third reformation, focusing on the move from formal religion to the relational small group experience of much charismatic and Pentecostal Christianity (Neighbour, 1988; 1995). Significant differences appear in the underlying assumptions of these two movements however. Pentecostalism perceives an abrupt break with past Christian tradition. Charismatic Evangelicalism affirms the history of the church. The difference is highlighted by Smidt and leads to one of the dynamics of renewal.

> *Renewal movements — that is movements that seek to make something old, new again — generally seek to re-appropriate their particular roots and traditions. Consequently, it would not be surprising if the Catholic renewal movement were to become more 'Catholic' than 'ecumenical'* (Smidt et al., 1999:125).

Charismatic renewal in many ways looks back. This ultimately diffuses its strength as a movement. Pentecostalism, emphasizing discontinuity with the past, can only look forward. It is not surprising, that 30 years after the birthing of the charismatic renewal in New Zealand, it has become diffuse and many of its beneficiaries who sought and failed to renew their older traditions, have eventually migrated into Pentecostal structures. That implies a possible future of Pentecostal growth.[22]

---

22   Many leaders feel intuitively, that attendance for Evangelicals is growing but at a less rapid rate

But this growth has leveled off. Robin Gill, analyzing 20 years of church attendances in the UK, examined the growth of evangelical groups there.

He concludes that for these groups:

> The historical data showed a persistent pattern... of only short term growth in newer/smaller Free Church denominations. Secondly, one reason why newer/smaller groups seemed to find growth difficult to sustain was that their initial growth typically depended, at least in part, upon transfers from other denominations. And thirdly, newer/smaller groups tend to expand to the point of collapse" (2003: 163).

These comments seem applicable to emergent Pentecostal denominations in New Zealand in their growth by transfer from the charismatic renewal. For example, David Allis, national administrator for the Apostolics comments about this Pentecostal denomination:

> Our 'kingdom growth' typically runs at 8-10% - this is the number of people added to our churches each year through salvation/baptism etc. Since 1998 (when we first started recording it), it has ranged between 7.2% & 10.6%.

But the backdoor is also significant for these newer churches:

> Overall, we typically see 20-30% join/leave our churches each year. (In good years a greater percentage remain. In bad years those joining and those leaving are about the same percentage).

Apostolic Mega-Churches

Church growth expert Peter Wagner, speaks of the necessity of new wineskins as an outgrowth of charismatic experientialism, viewing new apostolic-led mega-churches as the probable post-denominational future (1999). These relate more to each other than to their own denominations (often being as large as their denomination). His definition of apostolic is problematic,[23] but identifies the evangelising focus of these churches.

On the other hand, while such churches provide excellent structure, affirming and marketing revival, I suggest that this style of church violates many aspects of revival discussed in the following chapters. The centralising of human power and control, the emphasis on success and prosperity as against brokenness, confession and servanthood that mark revival, indicate that their growth[24] is not necessarily a sign of ongoing revival, but of social change and at times of post-revival control structures.[25] Peter Wagner and the

---

as: (1) the charismatic renewal largely died (1989?); (2) despite the new growth of some funda mentalist groups; (3) the fruit has largely finished the 7?? year migration to Pentecostalism. (4) Liberal leadership sustains control of much of Anglicanism, Methodism and Presbyterianism. (4) Pentecostalism has recruited from younger generations and has largely bought into postmodern styles. These do not necessarily provide long-term theologies that sustain people through the ongoing crises of life.

23 See discussion on the apostolic in Chapter 10.

24 There are a number of churches in Auckland that have grown to a reasonable size of several hun dred and are experimenting with larger church models of over 1000 members, notably Takapuna AOG, Central City Elim, Central City Church (CCC), Christian Life Centre Auckland (CLCA), Victory Christian Church, and in other Auckland cities, Windsor Park Baptist, Westcity Church, and the Korean AOG in Browns Bay.

25 An article on *God's Millionaires*, the BRW magazine (26 May, 2005) has given some critiques

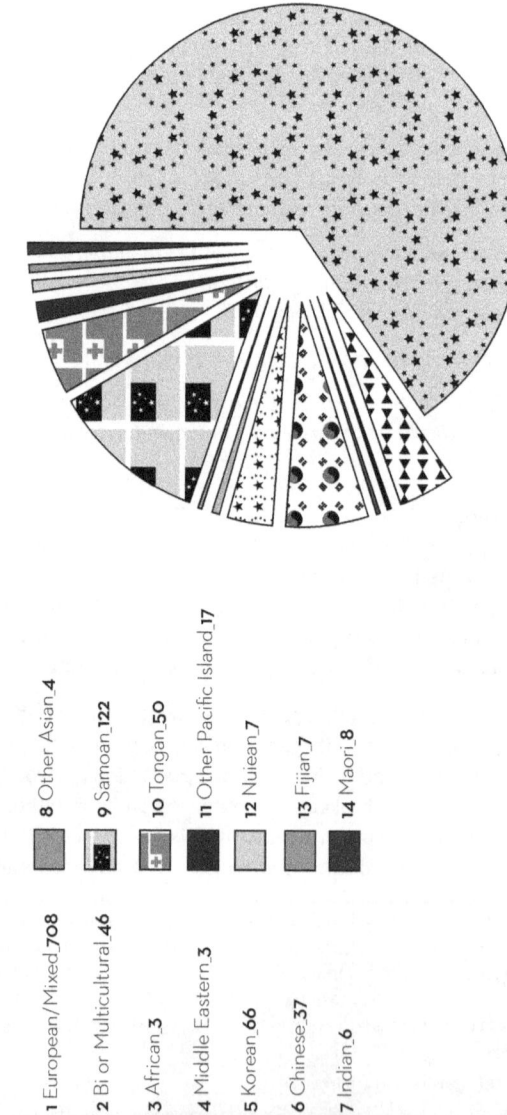

Fig. 6: Ethnic Congregation Explosion in Auckland

Ethnic Congregation Explosion In Auckland 1084 Congregations: [Grigg, Sept 1998]

1 European/Mixed_708
2 Bi or Multicultural_46
3 African_3
4 Middle Eastern_3
5 Korean_66
6 Chinese_37
7 Indian_6
8 Other Asian_4
9 Samoan_122
10 Tongan_50
11 Other Pacific Island_17
12 Niuean_7
13 Fijian_7
14 Maori_8

Fig. 6: A breakdown of congregations in Auckland by ethnicity. The European / mixed congregations are not generally defined by their ethnicity but also contain significant ethnic diversity.

church growth school believe that such centralised growth reflects God's blessing. German church growth expert, Christian Schwartz has combated this in the genesis of the natural church growth movement (1996).

Ethnic Churches: Wave of the Future
Another urban factor in revival dynamics follows the adage that the church follows population flows (Hitchcock, 1996: 26). Thus, growth in ethnic churches (see Fig. 6), will continue naturally, as the ethnic communities grow across the city. These figures (Sept. 98) are rapidly increasing. My estimate is of 500+ by 2005. The same figure from 20 years earlier, would have shown only a score of ethnic churches.

This represents the vigorous evangelical faith of most of these imported churches, which are often people from missionary churches in anti-Christian societies. I suspect analysis of numbers of churches vs. percentage of population that are migrant in Auckland would show a very close correlation. The extent of their growth, however, is limited by the size of their ethnic communities and their capacity to influence the English-speaking second generation children. Whether they are new Protestant or Catholic or Syrian Orthodox congregations, they tend to be culturally fundamentalist, in their retreat into cultural tradition. This is a survival strategy in a perceived unfriendly environment. From experience, I know that the period of responsiveness is within the first 18 months of migration, so growth may not be sustained.

Mysticism and Anti-Structuralism: The Non-Church Movement
We are also seeing non-structuralist groupings of Christians across the city, who reject formal church structures and doctrinal definitions but seek to maintain a vibrant faith (those who discuss this tend to be Pakeha).[26] Troelsch defined mysticism as one of his three categories of Christian structures that recur throughout history (1911/1960). Ward analyses debate that shows exit from formal religion is not the end of belief (2004a: 2-3). However, Webster indicates that such non-institutional belief evolves away from orthodoxy (2001: 168).

We do not know what percentage of committed Christians are non-institutional, nor how long they can sustain their commitments without the structure of a faith community. The nearest attempt has been Alan Jamieson's *A Churchless Faith*, where he indicates that 27% of 108 Evangelical and Pentecostal church leavers that he interviewed, developed an "integrated faith" outside the church (2000: 103). Thus, while in this study, I am exploring Christianity beyond the cloisters, I cannot analyse statistically the influence of this grouping as a source of agents for transformation. I suspect it is significant, as this group are often thinkers who have risen to social leadership and their "emergent church" structures indicate their entrepreneurial bent.

Theologically, I am working from presuppositions born of some years of establishing churches based on themes from the early church in Jerusalem, that connectedness to the body is essential to sustaining faith and that connectedness requires three structural elements: small group relationships, large group celebration and effective leadership that

---

26 I should include Maori Christian perhaps in this, where, before the emergence of Destiny Church, best estimates were of 3% in Auckland churches on Sunday. Yet there is a extensive living faith on the maraes. The discussion of emergent church by Pakeha has not referenced this dynamic.

includes significant levels of each of the five leadership gifts of Ephesians 4:11,12. Unless those who move from institutions find new institutional patterns that include each of the above, my experience is that faith is generally neither sustainable long-term, nor generationally (important for families). For the same conclusion from a sociological perspective, Steve Bruce in *The Social Organization of Diffuse Beliefs and the Future of Cultic Religion* (Bruce, 2004), extends his work on secularisation theory to address cults and new age religion, with relevance to non-structured churches or anti-structured churches. He argues that the social significance of the New Age movement is inevitably limited by its inherent relativism, individualism, eclecticism and anti-authority ethos, leading to a lack of commitment and consensus necessary to transmit the religion inter-generationally. I am arguing that some of these latter also lead to a limited lifespan for independent non-church groups.

The exceptions are where this search for a non-institutional spirituality has resulted in movements independent of church structures, yet with clear non-church structures with defined patterns of authority, commitment, and inter-group linkages. Precursors to these on the edges of historical revivals, are the Salvation Army and an institutionalisation of this anti-structuralism in the Brethren movement. The Navigators, *Renovare* movement, YWAM, Youth for Christ and Spiritual Growth Ministries are all nondenominational movements bringing small group structures, accountable leadership and theological structure to their non-establishment modus operandi.

There are voices that this is the way of the future , including discussions on emerging "Western" postmodern church structures (Riddell, 1998; Ward, 2004a). The lack of attention to apostolic leadership, the fivefold leadership gifts mix and necessities of structured local leadership in the discussions within, makes one skeptical as to sustainability. My own work has included the formation of apostolic orders of committed communities, living incarnationally among the poor – expressed initially in New Zealand through Servants to Asia's Urban Poor, where strong elements of anti-authoritarianism plagued the early work. I learned from this the necessity of clear definitions of apostolic and prophetic authority structures between communities as I catalysed the next couple of apostolic orders in the US and Brazil (Grigg, 1986).

Potential Workforce of Cultural Change Agents

I have discussed the extent, significance, commitment and missional relevance of Evangelical, charismatic, ethnic and Pentecostal congregations within the Auckland context. The significant expansion of a committed core up to the mid 1990's, supplies a potential workforce for transformation. While social factors have been examined, these cannot obscure what many identify as the cause of their expansion, the work of the Holy Spirit in revival and/or the preaching of the Scriptures.

But rather than church growth, this is a study of Evangelicalism, Pentecostalism and transformation. As the second part of the significance question, we need to evaluate the potential number and commitment levels of change agents in the public arena, towards the possibilities of developing a creative minority to catalyse major paradigm shifts within the culture. While deriving percentages of active churchgoers among Evangelicals and Pentecostals, one needs to remember, that those bold and gifted enough to stand in the public arena will be a minority of these, less than say 10% of more than 240,000 active churchgoers (in 2001) (Grigg, 2005b). Thus, there is a national pool of manpower and woman-power of perhaps 24,000 who could become publicly active in social transformation.

These people are already active in many spheres. For many the local church consumes their energies. For others, the drumbeat of evangelism that marks the movement requires a total commitment of time and energy. As believers, they sustain a high commitment to family and to education. Perhaps, we could justify half nationally (12,000) and a third of that in Auckland (4,000), who are bold, gifted and able to be motivated into public action. This is a large force in terms of the history of social change. (On social issues, they join an already active, theologically informed Catholic and mainline Protestant grouping of perhaps equivalent size).

What theologies will motivate and sustain these 12,000 into effective transformation equipping them theologically to utilize their technical and leadership skills? How can this prophetic nucleus be positioned to move the wider church into a transforming revival? In Part 2 of this study we enter the city conversation, and examine *goals of transformative revival*. In Part 3 of the study, I examine *revival processes* as they move towards transformation.

PART- TWO - GOALS OF POSTMODERN CITY TRANSFORMATION

No one has changed a great nation without appealing to its soul.

Robert Bellah in *The Broken Covenant* (1976:162).

The New Zealand landscape is littered with revived people *and* fuzziness. Few have questioned what a cultural revitalisation would look like, or asked the question, "a transformation into what?"[1] This vacuum of prophetic analysis allows for a multiplication of erratic prophetic statements. The revived people mill around like harassed and helpless sheep, unable to carry their secular friends forward into any promised land.

What if the culture is to respond to revival in a cultural revitalisation? In Part 2, I give reasons why postmodernism is a season for such hope. I develop the "city conversation" about a vision for Auckland. While such a question of "transformation into what?" is deceptively simple, we are dealing with transformation of a complex multivariate situation when examining the modern (Chapter 6) and postmodern (Chapter 7) urban context of Auckland.

We will utilise two major biblical themes, the city of God (Chapter 5) and the Kingdom of God (Chapter 8), anchoring both back in the work of the Spirit. My purpose is to identify critical *transformational conversation spaces* where these themes intersect with modernity and postmodernism.

---

1   Not that there are no visions for New Zealand. I have reviewed some literature in Chapter 3.

-5-

CITY OF GOD: IDEAL CITY

Utopia is a good place that is no place.

(Sargisson & Sargent, 2004: xiii)

The River of the City of God
- DANCING INTO CITY TRANSFORMATION AT VICTORY CHRISTIAN CENTRE -

> *A leader from the 'Toronto blessing'[1] preaches in a recently built Pentecostal auditorium for 2,500. Up front is a banner 'There is a stream that makes glad the city of God...' linking the work of the Spirit with the nature of the city. As we worship with a song of those words, women with banners dance around the auditorium. The whole gathering is laughing, singing, rejoicing!*
>
> *Down the mountains the river flows*
> *And brings refreshing wherever it goes ...*
> *The river of God sets my feet adancing,*
> *The river of God fills my heart with cheer,*
> *The river of God fills my heart with laughter,*
> *And we rejoice for the river is here.*

In speaking of Transforming Revival in Auckland, there has been a presumption of a better future, a spectrum of end goals that must be determined if transforming action is to be effective.

---

1 A recent revival movement from Canada, which a number of New Zealand leaders visited, returning with powerful impact on their churches. Other charismatic leaders publicly rejected it as extreme. It lacked an underlying teaching base for sustainable multiplication in New Zealand (Poloma, 1997).

Pentecostalism is a dancing religion. The above song captures its soul. It leads into the complex theological grid that meshes the visionary themes of the Spirit of God with the city of God. Other traditions describe it as a theology of the prevenient work of the Holy Spirit.[2] Revelations 22 interprets the underlying nature of the Spirit as the life-giving water of the ideal city of God.

The intersection of these two themes begins with a tantalising statement in the liturgical procession of Psalm 46, "There is a river whose streams make glad the city of God" (Ps 46:4). Tantalising, for it does not make known what that river is — Jerusalem of the day had no river.

A subsequent vision in Ezekiel (47:1-12) describes the river flowing from the temple. The stream begins in the inner temple and becomes a river that flows down to purify the Dead Sea, sustaining an abundance of life, indicating wonderful renewing power. Fruit trees will grow along the banks of the river, their unfailing leaves will become healing. The apostle John alludes to these verses in his vision of the Holy City, adding that these bring healing "to the nations" (Rev 22: 1, 2).

The theme grows in grandeur through the teaching of Jesus about streams of living water (John 7:38). It becomes the centre of attention in the great picture of that future city of God in Revelations. Jesus gives us a specific interpretative key as to what this meant when he (or the apostle John as interpreter) tells us, "By this he meant the Holy Spirit, whom those who believed in him were later to receive" (John 7:39).

This Spirit creates eternal life. It is this life that brings socio-economic-political life to the nations. The Spirit is the stream that brings life to the city of God. That stream-filled city is used in the Scriptures and has been used throughout history as a model against which the good city of each generation has been evaluated.

Thus, at the centre of the life of the city of Auckland is the sustaining Spirit of God. This is true, whether its citizens acknowledge the Holy Spirit or not. Revival, giving greater place to the Spirit's work, invoking his presence, ought to open up life-giving processes.

The extent to which that Spirit is free to bring life to the city can be evaluated[3] by contrasting the nature of its present urban realities with the ideal city of God.

The City of God: The Future Theme

What is the nature of that ideal city of God? With simple attention to the first chapters of the book of Genesis,[4] we can predict today's cities and the nature of those cities. For

---

2   In *Gaudium et Spes*, Vatican II's 'Pastoral Constitution on the Church in the Modern World', this wider understanding of mission is expounded pneumatologically rather than Christologically to a world in which God's salvation has already been operative secretly through his Spirit. 'This may, by the grace of God, issue in a more humane world.... the real author of this humanised history is the Holy Spirit' (Bosch, 1991: 391).

3   Measurable indicators can be derived from the thirty-five characteristics within seven theological themes in this chapter.

4   A more comprehensive theology of the city of God, covering the whole gamut of the Scriptures, based on the over 2000 references to cities in the Scriptures could be developed, but while it would refine the themes of Genesis 1 and Rev 21,22, it would not greatly affect their broad brushstrokes.

cities *grow out* of the collective nature of humankind. That human nature reflects the very nature of God, described thirty-five times in the Mosaic or priestly account of Genesis 1. Cities also *grow towards* the nature of God's city as expressed in the apocalyptic visions of Revelations.[5] For humanity, created in the image of God, projects God's nature into its communal structures. This defines an eternal basis for ideals for the transformation of a city, a vision of the "good" city. From Augustine's *City of God* (Dyson, 1998), to Ellul's *The Meaning of the City* (1997)[6], the theme of the city of God has always been one of viewing the future, defining the Christian dream and its utopias.

The (Jahwist)[7] narratives in Genesis 4 and 11 complement these optimistic themes of a city of God derived from the nature of God in the priestly account in Genesis 1, with a more sombre perspective on the city as a reflection of fallen humanity, for these first cities are built in rebellion against God. Cain, cursed to be a wanderer by God, builds a city, in defiance, for the security of his new-born child.[8] The descendants of his line later build Babel, a city where humankind is determined to reach God by their own patterns, to make a name for themselves, a city which God must step in to destroy. Redemption history has often been described as the history of struggle between these two cities, the city of humanity and the city of God.

The Scriptures continue this saga of two cities into Revelation. The two cities become symbolised by Jerusalem, the city of shalom, where God has set his presence and Babylon, the city of slavery, of oppression, the city against God.[9] The outcome is of the city of God triumphing, after the violent overthrow of Babylon by God himself (Rev 18). Then the bride of Christ, which is the city of God, is fully revealed in all its glory (Rev 21).

Hermeneutical Background

Using Genesis 1 to understand a position within the biblical tradition in order to deal with modern cities involves some hermeneutic problems. Yet these philosophic foundations from Genesis 1-11 are useful as a conversational framework for a multifaceted urban Christianity because of their acceptability across the theological spectrum. Whatever hermeneutic perspective one has of Genesis: literalists of fundamentalist background, or those Evangelicals committed to the inspiration of the

---

5   This chapter has developed from twelve years of reflection on the concept of Harvey Conn's *Genesis as an Urban Prologue* (1992). He queries whether Genesis was intended as a historical corrective to the literary traditions of mythic creation commonly known in the ancient world, where the city was the estate of the city-god. Nature is not deified and God is not urbanised into the god of a locality, but is seen as the cosmic sovereign with the whole of creation as his house-city.

6   I suggest this as the only fully comprehensive biblical theology of the city to date.

7   While recognizing the dramatic difference in style of Genesis 1 to subsequent chapters and the common acceptance of the J-P documentary hypothesis, Evangelicals generally remain skeptical of any theory that denies the traditional understanding of Moses as primary author of the Babylonic traditions (Hamilton, 1990:11-38).

8   "Cain has built a city. For God's Eden he substitutes his own, for the goal given to his life by God, he substitutes a goal chosen by himself - just as he substituted his own security for God's" (Ellul, 1997:5).

9   This becomes central to Robert Linthicum's urban theology, *City of God, City of Satan* (1991a) and underlies much Pentecostal spiritual warfare thinking.

canon but recognising the humanness of its formation, to those who view these early chapters as allegorical; there is universal affirmation of the metanarratives portrayed.

> *Regardless of terminology — whether myth, history, saga — the canonical shape of Genesis serves the community of faith and practice as a truthful witness to God's activity on its behalf...'* (Childs, 1979:158).[10]

Independent of our understanding of the sources or form of these passages, I would argue that to thus identify the primary philosophies inherent in the compressed symbols of Genesis 1 and track them through the Scriptures as a basis for present faith, is a normative manner of interpretative method. It is in line with the philosophic nature of the symbols in the source(s).

God of Creation
God of Time: Urban Development

"In the beginning..." defines a sense of time and process (for beginnings imply endings), as the opening statement in Genesis 1. It defines a directional historical process in contrast to Hinduistic or animistic thought, which are essentially cyclic, fate-defined or non-linear. Abraham Heschel describes the Hebrew faith "as a religion of time aiming at the sanctification of time" (1965(59):216). The biblical city will have a sense of time. The *fruitfulness* of Genesis 1 and multiplication of life indicate a process of growth and are foundational to themes of *urban development*. Without beginning there is no time and hence no development. The biblical idea of *rest* at the end of the chapter, indicates a seasonal process rather than a modernist perspective on purely linear growth, or an Eastern perspective on cyclic time. The periodic emergence of *new life forms and structures* in the Genesis account indicate the periodic quantum leaps of new growth which are woven into all life forms.

God of Creation: Cities of Creativity

"In the beginning God created," defines his subsequent rights to rule.[11] His creative activity defines ownership and authority. The prior rights, the beginnings, are matched at the end of the canon with final rights, the eternal. While that reign, that Kingdom, is first seen in a garden in Genesis, it is revealed in full in the final city of God of Revelation.

The trinity is here represented. Before the earth was formed, when all things were non-existent, *formless and void* (desert and wasteland),[12] and one could hear a pin drop in the

---

10   I am working from within an evangelical canonical perspective, that affirms a commitment to the superintending work of God in the process of formation hence the authority of these Scriptures. However I also recognise the human elements in the literary genre of the Genesis 1-11 sagas (cf.Westermann, 1980) and the Mesopotamian-style written accounts as debated in historical-critical research from the rise of the documentary thesis and its debates (Albright, 1940; North, 1986; Noth, 1957/1981; Van Seters, 1983, 1999; von Rad, 1962; Wellhausen, 1885).

11   There is grammatical debate over whether this should read, "in the beginning, when..", indicating the existence of matter before the creation of the heavens and the earth. Brevard Childs representing the consensus, concludes, 'we have seen the effort of the priestly writer to emphasize the absolute transcendence of God over the material" (1960:32). This is in line with Isa 45:18, "Yaweh... did not create it [the earth] a chaos".

12   See discussion in Hamilton on the translation of these words (1990: 108-9).

eternal silence, *the Spirit (rûah* = breath of God) *hovered*[13] *over the waters.*

The Spirit's presence pre-creation, as if brooding[14] over the birth and superintending (energising, giving life and vitality to (Hamilton, 1990:114)) creation, lends credence to the importance of the work of Spirit-filled believers in creating the city. If they are filled by this Spirit, that brooding and superintending of creation will be inherent in their being.

In the beginning God *created*... But this creation is only in this first instance of creation of light. "Everything else is created, or emerges in Genesis 1 by *fiat* plus some subsequent activity that is divinely instigated" (Hamilton, 1990:119). "God *made* the expanse and *gathered* the waters..." He speaks, then works to *separate* light from darkness, water from water.

In the beginning God *created*... This was the work of that Spirit, as in Job 33:4 *"The Spirit of God has made me; the breath of the Almighty gives me life"*, an ongoing work of creation, as Jesus says, "my Father is working still" (John 5:17).

Humankind, in his image, reflects that capacity to create something out of nothing, out of *desert* and *darkness*. Or, failing that, something out of something. Import-substitution is a theory that describes the heart of growth of cities. Cities that can innovatively copy and improve on items they import, then re-export them, are cities that will grow economically (Jacobs, 1984). For example, Silicon Valley lives off the creation of computer chips and their derivative products. A city filled with the Spirit will be a city of such creativity.

God the Communicator: Cities as Centres of Media and Learning
Father, Spirit and then the Word. For in the silence, suddenly there is a voice! Or as the physicists describe it, a perturbation creating waves in nothingness, leading in less than an instant to the big bang of an exploding, expansive universe. Immediately there is life and action simply by the voice. *"And God said...", "and God said..."* (vv. 3, 6, 9, 14, 20, 24, 26) — a recurrent voice, creating phrase by phrase, an ongoing creative process.

> *These eight specific commands, calling all things into being, leave no room for notions of a universe that is self-existent, or struggled for, or random, or a divine emanation* (Kidner, 1967:46).

The derived emphases, the foci on the presence of the incarnate Word, the church and the preached Word of God as source of creation of the city is inherent in these first verses of Scripture. For any city where the whole counsel of God is preached in every nook and cranny, will ideally become a creative and structured city.

And God said... God is also a communicating God. He is always speaking. The universe reverberates with his life-giving words and that conversation involves the Holy Spirit, who in turn continues within us, as a speaking being, speaking what is heard from Father and Son, speaking of the future, guiding into truth (John 16:12-15).

---

13 "Interestingly, in the Ugaritic texts, this verb is always associated with eagles... suggests the meaning "soar"" (Hamilton, 1990:115).
14 'Alateaba' (hovering) speaks of the fluttering of the wings of a brooding bird, portraying both protection and provision for its young (See Deut 32:11, Isa 31:5) (Villafañe, 1993b: 182).

All humanity in their image seeks to communicate so cities become the centre of the television channels, the Internet, the radio. Even when perverted, city dwellers still possess this inherent nature that reflects this communicating God. Thus a people and a city filled with the Spirit will find a liberation of good communication.

The Good City

And it was good. The goodness, the perfection of God is reflected into a good creation. That creation ultimately resulted in good cities where all people, structures and their interrelationships are infused with his Spirit and reflect and are subject to the values of the Kingdom of God. Should there have been no fall from God's grace, cities would have occurred that were all good. In the fall of humanity, the creation of cities instead reflected the lifelong internal conflict between the nature of God within collective humanness and the sinfulness of that collectiveness.

God of the Aesthetic: City as Environment

A second aspect of *and it was good...* is that the city, as communal reflection of the work of God, is to be aesthetically pleasing (Dyrness, 1983/1991:22), just as the garden was good and was perceived of as good. It is to be ecologically integrated and humanity is to manage it.

The godly city will also be seen to have spatial definitions that create humane environments[15] and enable the garden to flourish. For biblical history begins with a garden but ends with a garden in the centre of a cubic city. Alternatively, we may presume that demographics and urban expansion are deep within the Fatherhood of God, for fathers provide environments.

God's sovereignty in fixing "the boundaries of the habitation of the peoples" (Deut 32:8) is a recurrent complex theme that relates to land and land rights in cities.[16] How he does this in cities is a matter of wonder for geographers and mathematicians currently utilising fractal analysis in urban studies, for it is as if a hand outside humankind has generated patterns into which we fall. Urban demography is a great study of these processes of God's activity. The end of urban demography is predicted when the Scriptures speak of a cubic city, 1000 *stadia* high, 1000 *stadia* long, 1000 wide. We presume it is only symbolically complete, space-maximised, but what if it will actually be this shape? Certainly, the world's present population can fit one family per cubic *stadia*![17] Such theological questions lead us to a central godly relationship of people to space, community to geography.

In the mandate to *manage the earth*, he also holds the people of this city accountable for their spatial relationships and the contribution they make to this assigned task. A

---

15 Bakke (1997:60) asks the question, "Do we find a theology of place in the Bible?" indicating the failure of Evangelicalism to take this issue seriously when it cut itself off from the parish concept. He then seeks to develop the theme around corporate solidarity. It seems easier to develop it from the human-dust-garden motifs, as have Davies (1974) and Breuggemann (1977)

16 This is one element in theologies of land, land rights and housing for the poor (Grigg, 1985/2004).

17 If taken literally, 1 billion cubic *stadia* represents a cubic *stadia* for each family on the planet - fairly sizeable properties.

theology of urban planning flows from his Fatherhood and his delegation of managerial responsibility. The creation of Adam from dust requires our humanness to always be connected to the environment:

> *This interdependence with creation has another component... it is not possible for this solidarity to be broken. However much they may pride themselves on their independence, people are never "on their own" with respect to the physical environment... This is why...in rebelling against the order of things (forgetting we are dust) we not only ruin our lives, but in a sense destroy the earth as well* (Dyrness, 1983/1991:30).

The Auckland disconnection of Maori from their land, of migrants in transition from basic necessities of life, of youth from fathers or even extended family are part of the source of the dissonances leading to youth gangs, a neurotic society, teen suicide. Restoring healthy environments is an essential activity of the Godhead and hence of Spirit-filled believers. The gospel of salvation of soul cannot be heard independent of reconnection to the environment.

God as Community: City as Community

The city is also relational. God says *"let us make."* While there is the possibility of the "royal we" in the phraseology, the interpretive nature of John 1:1 indicates the presence of the Father, the Word and the Spirit. The Godhead is an "usness."

Made in his/her likeness, we reflect that communal nature, first in the village, then the town, then the city. In the garden there are clearly defined relationships of an infinite King with his subjects and of his subjects with the forms of life around them. Humankind is to rule in God's image, as his vice-regents and to be his brother's and sister's keeper. That image remains after the fall (Genesis 9:6; James 3:9), but it needs to be "renewed ... after the image of him who created them" (Col 3:10).

Inherent in creation are relational patterns that become the foundations of the relationships of the city. Within the Godhead itself is a *communication* and there are authority relationships. The Son does only what the Father does (John 5:19). The Father delegates and gives authority to the Son (John 5: 22, 27). The Spirit bears witness to the Son (John 16:14), who speaks of the Father. Godly cities reflect such *authority within equality.*

One relationship (the human management of creation) is to be a reflection of the vertical authority — an authority-submission caring-dependent nature of the God-human-earth relationship.[18] We are to *manage the created order* as vice-regents (variously understood as rule, be stewards of, or care for (Darragh, 2000)). "Thus the task of dominion does not have to do with exploitation and abuse. It has to do with securing the well-being of every other creature and bringing the promise of each to full fruition" (Brueggeman, 1982:32).

The other relationship in the cry, "Am I my brother's keeper?" (human-human) reflects the primarily horizontal relational nature of brotherhood and sisterhood, a relationship based primarily on equality and social responsibility.

---

18 This is in direct contrast to the notion of "subjugation" of the earth, popularly blamed for our current ecological crisis in environmental circles (White, 1967).

The creation of a companion for the man (from his ribs, not his feet nor his head) speaks of the *equality of being of male and female* in the dynamics of communication and working together. "The sexes are complementary: the true partnership is expounded by the terms that are used (a helper fit for him, 18,20 RSV; literally, a help as opposite him, i.e. corresponding to him)" (Kidner, 1967:65). This duality reflects the triune relationships in its unity. Its expansion into family reflects the triune nature of God. God's purpose was neither male nor female but the completeness of complementarity and family.

From these two patterns of communal relationships come our patterns of the city as community. As in the Godhead, there is headship and delegated authority, expressed in city councils and other leadership structures in the city. As in the Godhead, there is division of labour and equality of being. As in the Godhead, there is the companionship that outworks itself in the entertainment, the sports life, the media, the recreation of the city.

God Structures: Cities as Structure

In the first three days in Genesis, God *creates form out of a formlessness* and emptiness,[19] then he fills the form with life.[20] it becomes an integrated global and cosmic system, with an inherent goal. He commands humanity to manage it in his stead. As Claus Westermann points out, creation is "good or suited to the purpose for which it is being prepared" (1974: 61) –City planning and city management should be a reflection of that godly activity.

This *structuring nature of God* in us is the basis of predicting the emergence of cities as part of the goal of creation. For cities are centres of structures. For example, the agricultural system is based in rural cities; banking structures built off the production of the land are also based in cities. The structuring is inherent in the delegated roles. Human management involves the naming and categorising. The mandate to manage resources leads to issues of efficiency, patterns of decision-making, the spatial form and function of the city.

Let the land produce… let the waters teem… God creates things to be fruitful. Out of the fruitfulness comes the increase in wealth (not out of paper money). This principle enables life in the city to *be fruitful and to multiply*,[21] or in modern phraseology, the city is a centre of productive economic growth. Three times it is blessed (1:22,; 1:28; 2:3). "Blessing throughout Genesis is the conferring of beneficial power that produces fertility in humanity, in livestock and lands" (Dyrness, 1983/1991:23). The agricultural and banking systems are built on this fruitfulness. These are good. People are to manage that fruitfulness, to name it and order it. Justice, efficiency and form all reflect this God-given human task.

Our question is about the "goodness" of a city. Good and godly are not dissimilar. The garden is a place for the King to walk. Similarly, the city of Revelation centres on the King and his light-giving, watered by the river, symbol of the life-giving Holy Spirit.

---

19 Genesis 1:2 - Formless and void, 5 - evening and morning, day and night, 8 - sky, 9 - land, 10 - sea.

20 12 - land producing vegetation, 16 - filling the heavens, 20-23 - filling the seas and sky, 25 - filling the land.

21 28-30 - 'name' indicates taking authority over.

Thus one aim of developing a city in which the church is growing (as with its other healthy systems), is that its worshipping nature becomes centrally illuminating and life-giving to all other city systems. The church infused with the life of the Holy Spirit is the source of healing for the nations.

We may turn to the second creation account and 4:20-22 to see also the children of the first cities in the development of the orchestra, symbol of the city as centre of the arts and of toolmaking, the beginnings of technology and industry. These lead us to define the ideal city as a place of fulfilled artistry and creativity, alongside creative technology.

Inherent in this Genesis account is a later theme from the prophets, the theme of *justice*, aiming at a city that is both good and just — two overarching goals. Justice gives that sense of rightness and fairness that all humanity seeks, Christian or not. It is based on the structuring nature, clarity of authority and equality of being, defined in these early chapters. The theme of justice leads us to a definition of a city that at all of its incremental changes is just over time, in space and in its use of resources.[22] Justice is a balance of many principles, maximising different principles at different times. Justice is often related to a sense of fairness of distribution (Tonna, 1982). But it also must consider right management of resources in the context of managing the whole earth, in relationship to other ecosystems.

City as Delimited Evil

In envisioning an ideal, we need to consider the parallel theme in the Scriptures, the city of humanity in opposition to the city of God. Eventually the corrupted city of humanity is portrayed as that great city, Babylon in Revelations — a centre of world trade, immorality, greed and religiosity, to be shattered by the hand of God. Ellul (1997) outlines this, introducing us to Cain who in rebellion builds a city and of his line, "Nimrod, the verb form of whose name means 'let us revolt,' the world's first conqueror" (Conn, 1992:19).

Idealism must recognise the realities of the struggle between these two cities and create restraints to evil. In seeking to impart the vision of the city of God within this city, we must remember the globalisation of Babylon across the earth, purveyor of immorality and luxury. Proclaiming the ideal city of God invokes warfare by the human and spiritual forces arrayed against it in the Babylonic city that seeks to raise its head from our collective fallen nature.

> *Cities, the Genesis record seems to imply, are provisions of God's common grace; they play a remedial role in human life. Through them, God restrains the development of evil, blesses fallen creatures and works out his sovereign purpose in both judgement and grace* (Conn, 1992: 19).

---

22 First commented on in *Cry of the Urban Poor* as a 'Just Urbanisation Gradient' (Grigg, 1992/2004:91).

Fig. 7: The Nature of God as Reflected in the Good City

GOD AS RULER
>Fathering Cities
>Authority Structures

GOD WHO STRUCTURES
>City: Centre of Systems
>City: Managed Under God
>Efficient, Patterned, Productive
>Delimited Evil in Cities

GOD OF TIME
>City in Process of Incremental Development
>Growing City
>Seasonal Rhythm of Work and Rest

GOD AS CREATOR
>City as Centre of Creativity
>City of Good Work and Rest
>Artistic City
>Fruitful City

THE IDEAL CITY
God the Holy Spirit as Source of City Life

GOD AS COMMUNICATOR
>City as Centre of Knowledge
>Culture Affirming City
>City as Media Centre

GOD AS COMMUNITY
>Social Responsibility
>Just City
>City Diversity in Unity
>Equality in the City
>Male-Female Complementariness

GOD AS ENVIRONMENTALLY LIFE-GIVING
>Aesthetic City
>Garden in the City
>Humane Environments
>Planned Space
>Cities as Healing

Fig 7: Thirty-five elements of the character of God predicting the good, the ideal city, as his being is reflected in the collective humanity of cities.

Conclusion

The above themes give us conversational frameworks in which we can engage any city in envisioning ethical, cultural and strategic issues. The stream flowing through the city, the life-giving Spirit, is able to cleanse, heal and cause the city to become fruitful, productive, artistic, well managed – the good, the godly city.

-6-

THE SOUL OF AUCKLAND

- A People without Vision? -

> "What is the purpose of Auckland? What is its soul? What is its redemptive gifting?"
>
> The response is a pregnant silence. There are a few mumbles about a "city of sails." Then the request, "You tell us its purpose!"
>
> "Does it have a soul?" I counter and the discussion ranges over apathy, economic rapacity, the quality of the city in contrast to other cities globally, its role as centre of Polynesia.
>
> The scenario is repeated group after group. There is no apparent shared vision for a city of a million. People have a sense of general well-being and a vague sense of unease as to the ethics of those in authority — beyond that there seems little sense of direction.

What would happen if Transforming Revival resulted in cultural revitalisation in Auckland? This chapter develops dialogues between the seven themes of the ideal city of God from Chapter 4 with elements of vision for Auckland city. This part of the city conversation enables us to anchor the study locally. Such conversations are multivariate. They need to be broken down into subsets. I will identify these as *conversational spaces* – public spaces related to specific themes, where discussion of goals from reflection on the Scriptures and the city can occur.

Urban studies is an ecclectic set of disciplines with which to study the city. My selection of themes is reflective of the previous chapter, modified by some urban anthropology themes that I have found myself discussing with city leaders: definition of city soul, pluralism and ethnicity (related to the community of God), urban economics and technique (related to the mandate to manage the earth), urbanism including imploding families (related to biblical themes of equality, work and rest), and order in the city (related to God as Father, authority structures and managing creation).

To work from urban issues is new. A leader of the Green Party in an interview on Radio Rhema (March, 2005), commented that she did not expect Christians to have any input on the politics of the environment, as it was not one of their agendas. Similarly, Ahdar working from a legal perspective, identifies *engagement* by "Conservative" Christians to be self-defined by a range of morality and family issues where periodically they come into conflict with "The Wellington worldview" (2000:75-106). In contrast, I am postulating that Evangelicals are ready for a major paradigm shift into comprehensive cultural transformation, not just occasional conflictual engagement. The city of God enables such an engagement.

Conversations About Defining Soul

The question we are examining is, if the Spirit of God was freely accomplishing purposes in Auckland as a result of a series of synergistic revivals, what would Auckland become?

An attempt by the City Council in 1998 to define the soul of Auckland resulted in:

- THE CITY COUNCIL'S COMMUNITY VISION — AUCKLAND 2020 -

> *Auckland is Tamaki Makaurau, many peoples united in a proudly Pacific city. It moves ahead with confidence — constantly growing, creating opportunities and prosperity. It is New Zealand's first city of commerce and culture — sharing energy, growth and creativity. It is as unique as its volcanic cones, as sparkling as its waters and as beautiful and diverse as its islands. Auckland values its past, acts in the present and creates the future.*

This was distilled from multiple sectors of the community and reflects elements of the city of God in its productivity, creativity and community.

But perhaps seeking one definition for a city soul is unwise. Auckland has multiple souls. The *Entrepreneurial Business* soul is contrasted in New Zealand with Wellington, the governmental and cultural centre. Auckland is a *Multiethnic Regional Pacific City* centre for the Northern North Island and for the Pacific, also being the largest Tongan and Samoan city. Certainly, it is being seen as an *International Multicultural City*. With greater freedom for innovative education with the Education Act of 1989, it is increasingly becoming an *Educational City* for Asians. It is an *Industrial City*. While luxury yacht building is a rapidly expanding sector that could develop into a leading edge for industry, the phrase, "City of Sails" has represented a visionary direction. The name represents its role as a *Tourist City*, accentuated by the America's Cup and other sporting events.

Conversation space: What role will people full of the Spirit have in such definitions of city soul? How will they encourage that which reflects the image of God and reject that which violates the nature of the city of God? Are they alongside the city leaders in such a way that they can influence the definitions?

For example, the biblical denunciation of exploitation and oppression (the violation of themes of equality and brotherhood indicated in the theme of the city of God) would preclude the placing of a gambling casino with a high tower in the centre of the city of Auckland that currently destroys the family life of many people.

Or releasing creativity and productivity in humanity, a part of our reflection of the creative God, should result in proactive encouragement of industrial development into leading edge technologies, a certain kind of creative industrial soul.

Ethnic Conversation: From Bicultural to Multicultural Soul

Cities as Parties: Social Systems

I have described the cultural life of the city as generated from the image of a triune God when that image is integrated across a collective urban humanity.

In urban studies parlance that collectivity is broken into subsets.[1] *Social group* defines persons who find and feel themselves together with a common identity differentiating themselves from others. But the subsets — communities, neighbourhoods, ethnic groups — do not define the whole. The interrelationships between the communities and the whole are perhaps as important as the communities themselves. The formal and informal networks between people and groups end up as the *structures* of the city.

In ethnic neighbourhoods people need to be loyal members of a well defined group emotionally attached to some tribe, clan, or community. They feel lost when they cannot do so. As immigrants enter the city the very process of rejection by the residents who can not understand them, thrusts them together into their own supportive ethnic communities.

Another process occurs as communities of similar socio-economic values form, to some extent because the banks and developers cluster communities by the level of their bank accounts and to some extent by the inclination or necessities of the families. Poor families may not choose Otara — but economics may. Immigrant Indians with money choose Hillsborough because near here are the best schools and a primary motivation for their migration is education of their children.

These clusterings of the night erupt down the motorways early in the morning to reconfigure themselves in workplaces. Here race, ethnicity, social class and economic success are no longer the determining factors as to how relationships cluster. These are the contexts of social mobility. Generally these are secondary relationships, relationships of economic necessity rather than those of choice.

> *[The city] consists of a cluster of ethnically distinguished neighbourhoods whose members collaborate in staffing the firms, markets and other economic and political organizations of the city. Economic co-operation brings the members of the diverse ethnic communities into intimate and daily contact with each other. Social predilections separate them at the*

---

1   The city is a 'mosaic of social worlds'. In contrast to the early urbanologist, Wirth's theory of a 'culture of urbanism' (1966:4) defined by the total city, Oscar Lewis states, 'social life is not a mass phenomenon. It occurs for the most part in small groups, within the family, within neighbourhoods, within the church, formal and informal groups and so on. Consequently, the variables of number, density and heterogeneity are not crucial determinants of social life or personality' (1970: 34-37). This dialectic was synthesised into urban sub-cultural theories.

end of the day (Dorfman 1970:37).

Each ethnic migrant group for survival will need to find a niche in the city's economy (Dorfman, 1970:40) similar to the way the Fijian Indians now control Auckland's corner dairies and the Cambodians run the bakeries. Ultimately the community organisation of the ethnic communities into self-supporting economic and political power contexts within the wider diversity is a key to racial harmony.

What we can predict, based on trends in Los Angeles and other multinational cities, is that the ageing European population of Auckland will find themselves increasingly marginalised and disenfranchised. Their low birth rates coupled with the history of high out-migration rates in contrast to the immigrant birth rates will be one factor in this.

FIG. 8: AUCKLAND ETHNICITY BY REGION OF BIRTH (1996 CENSUS)

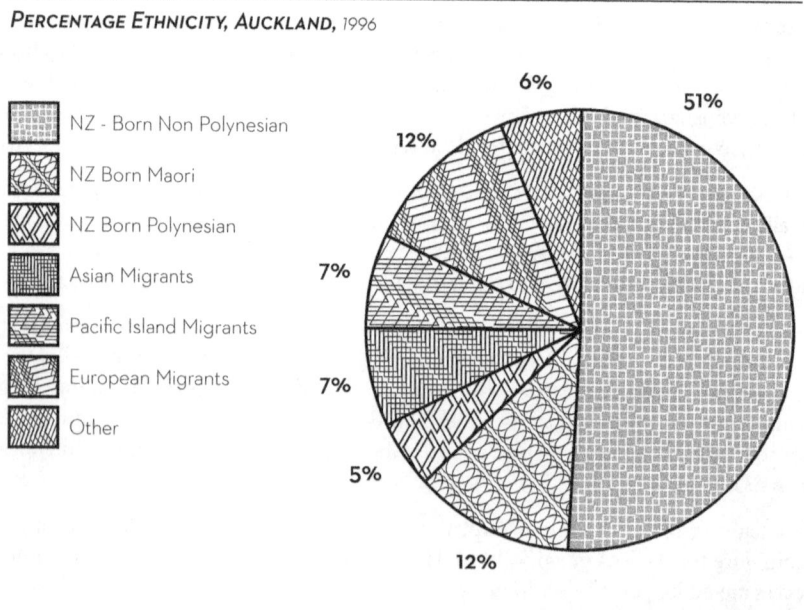

Fig. 8: Auckland Ethnicity of legal residents (1996) is made up of 33% migrants and 67% New Zealand born, of whom 12% are Maori and 5% Pacific Island background but born in New Zealand.

While English will remain the trade language and Hindi, Samoan, Tongan or Filipino probably will be rarely spoken except by the older migrants, there may possibly be sectors of the city speaking Cantonese, Korean and Japanese. For, while the former are adaptive cultures with a background of contact with English, these latter ethnic groups require several generations to integrate into other societies (Hiebert, 1993).

Chinese Howick, Indian Hillsborough and Samoan Otara may have consolidated their ethnicities.[2] Muslim suburbs will have developed around several multi-million dollar mosques begun from converted churches. More likely, given the small size of the ethnic communities and the significant impact of public schooling, the city will still contain clusters of ethnicity, but remain reasonably integrated.

Conversational Space: Beginning with the nature of God, who is diversity in unity, will spirit-filled believers facilitate the city in value systems, skills and mindset to cope with the increasing diversity and plurality of cultures? Will they create the environment of tolerance and communication, of respect and delight in the nature of God reflected in others' cultural systems?

People experiencing the brokenness of revival express the imperative of being their sisters' and brothers' keepers. In a city filled with the Spirit, the church will work with each subculture as it forms new associations in such a way that these reflect the values of the City of God. Reacting to an earlier article of mine (1997a) about the necessity of evangelisation among these new religious groups, Peter Donovan, professor of religious studies at Massey University, does an excellent analysis of civic responsibilities of the churches to peoples of other faiths, part of the answer to these questions (2000).

Pluralistic Religious Conversations
The emergence of these religious Asian and Pacific societies will bring religion back into the public arena. But it may be non-Christian religion which becomes politically correct, built on the 1990's anti-Christian secular culture. Islam will increasingly wield power, as political power is inherent within its religious worldview.[3] If new age spirituality over the last decade is a measure, politically correct, tolerant Hinduism will perhaps grow and be warmly received by a few pluralistic secularists seeking a form of spirituality. This will further open the door to the worship of various spirits and patterns of witchcraft, some deriving their roots from old English traditions and some from older pre-Christian Maori spiritualities, such as I found in a witchcraft shop in the old tram depot. A walk through Lynn Mall finds idols in several of the Chinese, Japanese and Thai food bars, where ten years ago they would never be seen.

The 2001 census (Statistics New Zealand, 2005) identified 39,798 Indian Hindus and 41,634 Buddhist, mostly Chinese, in New Zealand (more than 90% in Greater Auckland), along with 23,631 Muslims from Iran, Iraq, Pakistan and elsewhere (these figures exclude illegal migrants and non-residents and students (at least doubling these figures for Chinese).

Imagine it is 2040. The predicted new age of searching for spirituality is being outworked. The nation is now deeply spiritual, with daily incantations to multiple idols and major religious movements that ebb and flow every two or three years to worship of new spirits. Based on the 1989 changes to the education act, schools continually

---

2   See Dorfman, Harvard University economist, for the logic of this and its relationship to the ethics of homogeneity (1970: 34-37).

3   Norris and Inglehart summarize the debate around Huntington's "clash of civilizations" theory (1993) and from the global values study data confirm the support for greater religious leadership in active roles in public life in Muslim societies (Norris & Inglehart, 2004:133-155).

spring up based on teaching Christian fundamentalism, Catholic religion, Islam, Hinduism, Shintoism and traditional Maori religions.

Conversational Space: Who interprets this plurality to the second generation Pacific Island, Indian, Korean children of the churches of today? to the elderly of the Anglican, Brethren and Presbyterian remnants? How does the church expand the values of the city of God in this situation, no longer of secularism but of pluralism?[4]

- ETHNIC LEADERS' HUI -

> Yearly, lead by Bryan Johnson of New Covenant International Bible College, we have conducted ethnic leadership *hui*, where church leaders from eight to ten ethnicities, reflect together using conversational transformation approaches to discern theology and practice on issues related to the pain of migration, the problems of children of migrants etc. How do we expand this network and approach into effective development of comprehensive theologies and practice for these migrant communities?

Conversation With an Economic Soul

Cities house markets, which depend on numerous contacts and flows of information. Each city is the centre of a market of one sort or another: London as banking centre, Hollywood as movie production centre, New York as fashion centre, Kolkata as centre of Hindu philosophy. And Auckland???? Sailing? boat-building? IT? Biotechnology? Education?

Probably, but not inevitably, a second level informal economy will expand as in other major mega-cities, based on the failure of migration policies to sustain legality of a significant number of migrants and the failure of legal migrants to enter the workforce adequately. I have Indian migrant friends who are operating marginal businesses, acquaintance with a sector of Iranians who buy and sell second hand cars as an undocumented business, a Russian friend who is "self-employed." The WINZ (Work and Income Department) efforts to decrease the time between migration and entrance to the work force are significant and may preclude the formation of a significant informal sector, but as migration has accelerated this sector has been expanding.[5]

Successive governments have moved from egalitarian state to one with higher levels of wealth differentiation.[6] This, coupled with experience in mega-cities globally of the emergence of significant classes of street people leads me to expect such a class in Auckland. Yet, given the extent of the safety net and the commitment by all government parties to sustaining it, it is doubtful this will become significant.

---

4 Newbigin's classic, *The Gospel in Pluralist Society* (1989) develops Christian responses to pluralism. The original intention of this study was to address both these multicultural issues and the transformational issues. A choice was made to concentrate on only the transformational issues.

5 The government has used the same figure for some years of 20,000 overstayers but there is no published research on this. My estimate, based on experiences among migrants in L.A. and elsewhere, is of perhaps three times as many illegal - and if illegal, generally underemployed.

6 Brian Roper (2005) and Harvey Franklin (1985:46-55) analyse economic issues related to egalitarianism and alternatives to the loss of autonomy under globalisation.

Conversation space: To what extent do present economic options significantly reflect the God of justice and the God who creates structures to produce wealth? Teaching on simplicity vs. greed (Hofmans-Sheard, 2003), alternative communal economics reflected in co-operative housing (for example Liberty Trust, which has developed a loan cooperative process), economic sharing (Hathaway, 1990), support for the housing of these poor in transition and advocacy for governmental policies that reverse the class differentiations are but a few of the present Christian responses (Randerson, 1992). How does the Christian conversation engage the pervading economic conversation?

Conversation with a Technological Soul
If the Holy Spirit had great freedom in the city of Auckland, how would that affect its technological and economic aspects. People are not independent of the dust from which they come and to which they return. Ash Wednesday reminds us that we are defined by our connection to the earth and hence defined by technology that extends humanity's relationship to the land. Jacques Ellul (1964), the great Christian French urban philosopher, sees this as destructive.

The rapid expansion of cities over the last century has been closely related to the multiplication of technological innovation. Could you have New York as a mega-city prior to the invention of the elevator? Would Los Angeles exist independent of the invention of the freeway?

Technology also significantly defines the patterns of our humanness. Technology largely differentiates the characteristics of rural and urban persons. Similarly the nature of technology of any given city defines a person as against the technology in another city – the rickshas of Kolkata define a different mode of thinking to the high-speed trains of Tokyo. By the same tokens the levels of similarity of technology globally define universal modern urban personhood.

To survive, Auckland, as any future city, is moving from an agricultural and manufacturing base to a knowledge base, managing knowledge and its development, transmission and utilisation and promoting innovation. Auckland has both the educational centres and the high-technology industries to survive this challenge.

Conversation space: Based on the God-human-land relationships examined in the last chapter, it is reasonable to expect the Spirit of God to significantly separate her disciples from being technological machines into being people whose meaning is defined by inner spirituality and relational integrity. An alternative and an aberration is that the church will be a showplace for high tech super-dramas portraying a human Jesus in a non-human medium.

Paralleling technological development is the Spirit's work in an environmental ecology that seeks to bring into city structures the mandate to manage, to tend the resources of the earth. An environmental network has been developing as part of Vision Network to address such issues. Finlay (2004) and Darragh (2000) have written on environmental theology from a New Zealand perspective, but these issues remain largely undeveloped. Interaction with resource management planning are currently reasonably open. To what extent will the Spirit guide her people into teaching environmental theology as foundational to such processes?

Kiwi Culture of Urbanism
Urbanism[7] concerns the way of life of urban dwellers (as against urbanisation, the process). The study of socio-psychological characteristics of urbanism can be correlated with elements in the previous chapter of God as community, communicator, healer.

The rural migrant leaves the communal relationships of the village facing loss and grief and then finding overload. How does a person who related to 500 people in Paengaroa suddenly find the skills to relate to a million in Auckland? Wirth's original paper on (American) urbanism (1996) defines this as negative. The loss of a sense of identity, alienation and entrance into the "concrete jungle" produces competition and mutual exploitation rather than co-operation. Redfield (1969b(47)), developed a theory of folk-urban polar types of society defining the village as satisfying, peaceful and well integrated as against the impersonality and heterogeneity of the city, thus idealising the rural.

Later anthropological writers (e.g.Lewis, 1966) on the other hand, challenged these views, seeing urban life as a positive one of choice and freedom, of creative individuation as against forced communalism, of new co-operative structures. Thus the mutual support of the farming community of Stratford is left for the collective supportive working environment of the banking staff in an Auckland suburb. They developed theories of how new coping skills develop to handle this positive greater web of relationships and creation of new communities within the mega-city. Urban anthropologist, Gulick, integrated these opposing poles into a schemata examining disconnectedness and connectedness (1989:151-179).

Conversation space: Examination of emerging church movements, an expression of the community of the Godhead, must thus answer the question of how they are creating new patterns of connectedness in the city at two levels — creating the church to meet these social needs and helping create just communal structures for all peoples in the city. Though common grace in every culture enables a certain level of adaptation and integration, only the church has the integrating power of the cross to mediate the divisions between communities. But it must be present in each community to facilitate this. The failure of all the Auckland denominations (I have talked with a leader responsible in several of the major ones) to define a strategy for a church in every suburb prefigures increasing difficulties in accomplishing such a goal.

The Overworked Kiwi
The extended family, upon migration to cities, reduces to the nuclear family. But an increasing percentage of Auckland families exist without both parents (28% in 1996). Common lore is that this is a major contributor to neuroses, suicides and breakdowns.

One weakness of Evangelicals has been to view marriage breakdown purely as a failure of morality and not understand the external pressures of the urban environment that contribute. Consideration needs to be given not only to the psychological dynamics caused by the broken family structure but also to the increasing levels of stress.

---
7 Concept developed by Wirth (1966).

Fig. 9: Auckland Social Marital Status

	Partnered				Non-Partnered					
	Legal Spouse	Other Partnership	Not Further Defined	Total Partnered	Never Married	Separated	Divorced	Widowed	Total Non-Partnered	Not Specified	Total
Social Marital Status — For Usually Resident Population Auckland, Aged 15 Years and Over, Census 1996	382,407	71,631	2,988	457,029	202,545	19,788	31,794	39,870	293,994	72,867	823,887
	46%	9%	0%	55%	25%	2%	4%	5%	36%	9%	100%
					Extra-marital Relationship, Divorced or Separated =16%						

Fig. 9: Marital status in Auckland in the 1996 census, indicates 16% divorced, separated or living in an extra-marital relationship, with an additional 9% not specified.

Some see increased stress occurring because of the necessity of both spouses working in order to cope with family financial pressures. Thurow, an economic futurologist, in a chapter on the global economic viability of the family concludes:

> 'Competitive individualism' is growing at the expense of 'family solidarity.'... Patriarchal linear life is now economically over. Family values are under attack, not by government programs that discourage family formation (although there are some) and not by media presentations that disparage families (although there are some), but by the economic system itself. It simply won't allow families to exist in the old-fashioned way with a father who generates most of the earnings and a mother who does most of the nurturing. The one-earner middle-class family is extinct. Social arrangements are not determined by economics — there are many possibilities at any point in time — but whatever the arrangements, they have to be consistent with economic realities. Traditional family arrangements aren't. As a consequence the family is an institution both in flux and under pressure (Thurow, 1996:33).

The implications for New Zealand's future are significant. Women's work hours have increased dramatically. Family structures will increasingly struggle under this pressure. Psychological stress will exact a toll. Civic life is less and less staffed by volunteerism.

Conversational Space: From Genesis 1, we have observed that the city infused by the God of time will have clarity as to work and rest. Its incremental development will be paced to the needs of its people in seasons of work and rest. Can Christians generate modifications to an overarching economic philosophy, that move it towards these biblical principles? Randerson has attempted this in New Zealand from social gospel presuppositions (1987). Most business leaders among Evangelicalism I have talked to would find Griffith's (1982; 1984; 1985) emphasis on increasing productivity more acceptable. The prime minister's statements concerning the necessity of moving women into the workforce to increase productivity in February 2005, created significant debate in the media (see for example, Knight & Laugeson, 2005). Nowhere did Christian understandings of work/rest inform the discussion.

Conversations About Law and Order

The Spirit of God is involved in creating order and authority relationships. Cities and power are inseparable.[8] The economists and technocrats can increase productivity, but are often unable to order in a just way the configurations of economic relationships, so as to reduce mal-distribution, exploitation or the ongoing chaos of a continually changing city.

Auckland is moving from being a small city of a million to a full-fledged mega-city. Creation of regional planning authorities have been crucial at this stage in other cities with variable results as to their effectiveness in forward planning. The 2004 debates about failure of the Auckland Regional Council to adequately develop roading or the derision by urban planners of the Auckland council's decisions to create blocks of small sized apartments throughout the city are but two of many issues with roots in a biblical perspective of creating a humane environment.

---

8 Linthicum (1991a) and Jayakumar Christian (1999) have developed evangelical theologies of power and the city. Linthicum expresses his experience in Community Organisation by Alinsky; Christian is informed by his work in releasing poor communities in India.

The flip side of this is that cities are places of chaos and human depravity.

Conversational Space: Conversations about order correspond with theological elements of the God who rules as Father with authority and the God who structures. Catholic urban missiologist, Benjamin Tonna (1982: 58-77, 95-112), reflects theologically on legitimacy, order and disorder and urban planning in the city. These he bases on premises: that order belongs to the political domain, in our responsibility to function as God's vice-regents; that a God-filled city is a city where all is just; that the fallenness of humanity requires that the city constrain evil; and that the aesthetic beauty of the created order, is foundational to urban planning and governance. While there are Christians in civic roles and urban planning roles, there are no forums in the city where these meet to develop a framework of Christian ethics for order in the city.

In the government clinic in which my wife works, Christians have been instrumental in creating an effective rehabilitation process for prisoners that society considered refuse. Based on my database and anecdotal evidence, Christian involvement both in law enforcement and in restorative justice in New Zealand is significant, but where are the forums to identify the biblical frameworks for development of social ways of limiting evil?

Beyond Modernism

The modern context of urban studies and of Auckland of this chapter is now going through a major phase shift, a cultural turn into a transitional phase of cultural uncertainty known as postmodernism. This time of transition opens the door for greater opportunity for conversation about the reformulation of new cultural integrations, offering a season of opportunity for cultural revitalisation as response to expanding Evangelical and Pentecostal cultural engagement. We need now converseabout this season and its transformation.

Fig. 10: Conversational Spaces: Auckland Urbanism and the Good City

GOD AS RULER
›Conversations about Order

GOD WHO STRUCTURES
›Conversations about Order

GOD OF TIME, WORK AND REST
›Socio-Pschological Urbanism
›The Overworked Kiwi
›Imploding Families

GOD AS CREATOR
›Conversations about the Economic Soul
›Cities as Providers
›Technological Soul

VISION FOR AUCKLAND
The Ideal City of God
God the Holy Spirit as
Source of City Life

GOD AS COMMUNITY
›Ethnic Conversations
›Reconciliation
›Pluralism

GOD AS COMMUNICATOR
›Media Transformation

GOD AS ENVIRONMENTALLY LIFE-GIVING
›Urban Planning
›Maori Rennaissance
›Ethnic Integration and Cultural Affirmation

Fig. 10 summarizes the conversational spaces defined by interfacing the City of God with urban studies themes in the context of Auckland.

-7-
Conversational Complexity: The Postmodern City

> *In the past few decades, advanced industrial societies have moved through an inflection point, from the Modernisation phase into a Postmodernisation phase… With Postmodernisation, a new worldview is gradually replacing the outlook that has dominated industrializing societies since the Industrial Revolution…It is transforming basic norms governing politics, work, religion, family and sexual behaviour.*
>
> Modernization and Postmodernization (Inglehart, 1997:8).

I have sought to define modern Auckland in conversation with the ideal city of God. This chapter extends the conversation about goals of Transforming Revival by describing the context in elements of postmodernism, the lifestyle of the mega-city and identifying some conversation spaces within it. I will largely leave responses to the next chapter on the Kingdom of God.

Because the task of rational definition of postmodernism, an eclectic anti-foundational milieu with shifting boundaries, is impossible, I will simply describe some elements in its (non-existent?) metanarrative. The choice of elements reflects an extension of previous urban themes and an attempt to identify primary aspects of change in relationship to truth and authority, the material, the nature of humanness and the socio-political.

Postmodernism: Interpretative Key to Complex Cultural Change

- POSTMODERN CHILD-RAISING -

> My 11 year old Brazilian-Kiwi daughter comes home from an evangelical school, to sit before a computer designing 21st century cities, while messaging Pakeha friends who frequent a charismatic church and her Chinese friend whose father flies in from Hong Kong each month. At night, when she joins me to watch the news, I have to censor what she sees as she is bombarded by juxtaposed views of poverty, welfare, government interference, homosexuality and the regular update of police response to violence.
>
> In the midst of this plurality, sensuality, truth and sordidness, how do I interpret to her the cultural changes going on and the lack of public Christian response while expanding her understanding from evangelical retrenchment to the public engagement of the Spirit?

Unclear definition of the causes of social change and unclear theological and strategic processes to bring about actual engagement with structural causes of moral and social disintegration leaves many in a fog of failed dreams. Social analysis is an essential step in clearing away the fog. Such analysis must recognize the elements commonly lumped together under the nebulous term, "postmodernism."

To understand post-modernity, modernity in New Zealand needs defining. Auckland, representative of many emerging mega-cities, is a mixture of rural/tribal, modern and postmodern cultures and values. It grew from the rationalist modern period in which New Zealand was born. Five characteristics of that period are identified in Fig. 11.

This was a philosophic wave on which the leadership of New Zealand built momentum. Rationality created the drive for the efficient running of a capitalist economy, a bureaucratic or semi-socialist state and a highly valued scientific method (that supported my father's role as a soil research scientist in sustaining agricultural pre-eminence). These were all supported by a sense of economic and social progress and increasing control of the forces of nature. This technological modernity in which the New Zealand soul developed, has been characterised as *Descartes' autonomous, rational substance, encountering Newton's mechanistic world* (Grentz, 1996: 3).[1]

Conversation Space: For believers, such worldviews included a grieving of the Spirit, who created humanness in far greater complexity than rationality, to rule, and care for a world far more complex than mechanistic, and to do so not as autonomous agents but in dependence on Himself. Modernism denies the truth that in ourselves we have no existence — a worldview denial of God as the sustainer. Evangelicalism, growing in the modernist period and using its tools has always critiqued its foundations (Vanhoozer, 1995: 10-11).

---

[1] I would see it further characterised, since the 1980's, by *acceptance of plurality* begun at the Peace of Westphalia.

Rural Village to Modern City to Postmodern Megacity

FIG. 11: INTERNAL AND EXTERNAL FORCES DEFINING KIWI SOCIETY

EXTERNAL DETERMINANTS

A Nation Birthed >	An Emerging Modern Nation >	A Postmodern People in a Global Village
Two peoples defining themselves	Globalisation	Urbanism
	Urbanisation	Technicism
Colonial Dependency	Industrialisation	Pluralism/Tribalism
Rugged Survival	Modernisation	Hedonism
	Secularisation	Spiritualism

INTERNAL PILGRIMAGE

Maori Redefinition ⟶

Pakeha Redefinition ⟶ **The Millenial Kiwi** = *Global?* or = *Tribal?*

Migrant Community Expansion ⟶

Fig. 11 shows some external determinants in three phases of development of the Kiwi soul. These are paralleled by internal communal progressions. The early phase through till the second world war was one of survival and dependency. Aspects of modernism then became central. Issues of postmodernism in the 1980's and 1990's lead to both redefinition of the tribal and expansion of migrant communities as well as characteristics of the global postmodern city.

The Shift to Postmodernism

Twenty years beyond the failed responses of the Christian Heritage Party challenging "secular humanism" of modernism, a new cultural window has opened. For modernism, characterised by "the pervasive rationalisation of all spheres of society" (as Weber put it), has been fracturing at its centre as advanced industrial societies morph into postmodernism.

> ... modernization is not the final stage of history. The rise of advanced industrial society leads to another fundamentally different shift in basic values – one that deemphasizes the instrumental rationality that characterised industrial society. Postmodern values become prevalent (Inglehart, 1997:5-6).

This shift into postmodernism provides a window of time for new openness to transformational conversations.

Postmodernism describes a complex of social analyses of cultures beyond the expansion of modernity. Modernism has now moved into a new phase of global culture we might call *New Global/Tribal Culture*.[2] It is a global civilisation, embracing that sixth of the world not trapped by poverty and filtering down[3] to that other five-sixths, who are largely defined by tribal identities. It grew from a past Western Christendom and modern civilisation, based in Europe and was exported via the European empires. En route it was transmuted into a global civilisation, marked by jeans and McDonalds, Pepsi and computers, MTV and walkmans. Despite the prominence of some American cities, such as Los Angeles, in its emergence, it has no single base nor is it a politically defined civilisation. This kind of networked civilisation without central rule is something unknown in history.

Postmodernism Defined

There are multiple perspectives on postmodernism, not all compatible. Anderson describes a global paradigm shift in belief systems:

> *We still have the belief systems that gave form to the modern world and indeed we also have remnants of many of the belief systems of pre-modern societies... But we also have something else: a growing suspicion that all belief systems — all ideas about human reality — are social constructions... in which different groups have different beliefs about belief itself. A Postmodern culture based on a different sense of social reality is coming into being — and it is a painful birth* (1990:3,4).

The term *radicalised modernity*, used by Anthony Giddens in *The Consequences of Modernity* (1990) reflects thinking in economics and development studies. He argues that we are not so much living in a postmodern world as experiencing a fundamentally changed condition of modernity, where changing technology in late capitalism is increasing the scope and pace of change in cultural forms. This term better includes issues of continuity, in contrast to "post-" implying "against". British sociologist, Zygmunt Bauman (2000), also extends "heavy" or "solid" hardware modernity (the mass production factory society) to "liquid modernity," (the information society).

Postmodernisation

This Postmodernism as a description of *cultural values, beliefs, worldviews* etc., is based on postmodernisation, changes in the *structures* of society. Fig. 12 shows some of the identifiable changes in social structure from the modern to postmodern period.

---

2   David Wells (1995) calls it 'World Cliche Culture.' Others use the 'New Emerging World Order,' which has connotations of structuralist power mentality, but nobody yet has a name for this new civilisation.

3   Even this expression indicates the colonial and power-centred nature of the definitions of postmodernism.

Fig. 12: Postmodernisation: Structural Change from Modern to Global Culture[4]

	Structural Elements of Modernisation	Structural Elements of Late Modernity (or Postmodernisation)
Institutional Carriers	›Modern nation-state ›Industrial capitalism ›Knowledge sector (universities)	›International institutions (UN, IMF, etc.) ›The electronic superhighway ›The media
Economic	›National capitalism and communism	›Global hyper-capitalism
Production Technology	›Transition from agriculture to manufacturing	›Transition from manufacturing to information
Institutional Political Carriers and Allegiances	›Modern nation-states	›Globally connected cities (& city-states) ›Ethnic political entities
Organisational Structures	›Bureaucracies ›Hierarchies	›Networks ›Flattened levels of authority
Range of Decision-making	›Growing level of choices within a nation	›Endless expansion of choices within the global city
Modes of Relating	›In-city relationships clustered around vocation and family	›Global webs of common interest relationships electronically connected
Structural Location of Belief	›Structural relocation from centre to periphery as one social sector along with economics, politics, sociology, psychology, etc.	›Relocation from periphery to only one of multiple belief options ›Diversification of semi-formal religious communities

Fig. 12 indicates structural differences between modernisation and postmodernisation. What is not indicated is that the modern continues in parallel with the postmodern, as this is at least a generational transition.

The Globalisation Critique

Critics view this term as part of an ongoing colonialist search for a universal.[5] Such Western definition at a global level is seen as destructive to local cultures. The global culture is not just emerging from the collapse of Western cultural integration but from the interplay of six thousand cultures across the shrinking globe. As such, to define it with a Western term inferring evolution from modernism is a form of Western ar-

---

4 Developed from reflections on Van Gelder's analysis (1996).

5 Arturo Escobar, comments similarly on development as 'a top-down ethnocentric and technocratic approach that treats people and cultures as abstract concepts' to be manipulated in the name of progress, ultimately destructive of third world cultures (1999: 383).

rogance. For example, Huntington (2001) argues for nine major modern civilisations around the globe. On the other hand, he concludes that modern societies resemble each other more than traditional societies because of increased global interaction and transfer of innovations and technology and because of the transition from agricultural production to industry as the basis of modern society.

Thus, I prefer not to use "postmodern" to imply the new cosmopolis is a culture of networked cities in opposition to the old order. Rather, it is a new emerging order building on the philosophic ruins of the old. There are metanarratives, but they are morphing.[6] Yet, while bearing in mind these critiques, I *will* employ the term as a usefully descriptive category because it is popular, and opens a realm of public debate. It also facilitates analysis of the changes occurring between the coexistent urban diversity of tribal, peasant, industrial and information societies in relationships to both local and global cultural poles.

The Genesis of Postmodernism

Next, I will glance over the genesis and some characteristics of global postmodernism in some fields of knowledge, acknowledging that significant parts of Auckland society and a large portion of young adults (it is a generational change) now live within this framework. The question of how the Spirit, through the revived church, will respond and redefine these values underlies this analysis.

Postmodernism in Philosophy

Philosophers for over a century have been predicting the death of Western civilisation based on the loss of the central sources of *tradition, authority and power* based in *the church, the nation-state and the university*. The philosopher Friedrich Nietzsche (1844-1900), is considered to have begun the attack on modernity with his '*the death of God*' (the loss of the truth and power of Christianity in Western culture), leaving only '*knowledge as a will to power*' (Nietzsche, 1967), the pragmatic use of creative energies in language, values and moral systems to develop conceptions of truth, as perspectives for advancing causes or people. Because all knowledge is a matter of perspective, all interpretation is inadequate approximation, hence innately a lie, there is no truth; only *relative truths*.

This collapse of the search for universals (such as perfect beauty), devolved through the arts. I can best describe this by a presentation I used with students in the 1980's to illustrate the lostness of humanity without an integrating Christ. It summarised a work of one of Francis Schaeffer's mentors, art historian Rookmaker. He analysed the collapse of the search for absolute beauty in art (1970/1999). Symbolically, the Renaissance moved God from the centre of the artist's canvas. Now Dutch canvasses had humans at centre and God in the small picture on the wall (portraying the individual human as central authority, God as peripheral). Realism led to Cubism and Impressionism which led to abstract art. Postmodern art has no human centre. God may not be present. Spirits are. Technique and technology are present, but often warped. The

---

6 See, for example, the underlying framework in the *Global Values Study* of modernisation processes and postmodernisation (Inglehart, 1997). He rejects the extremes of philosophers like Derrida and Rorty, preferring to utilize ideas of generational shifts in thinking, rather than drastic discontinuities.

search for integration, perfect beauty and meaning for many has ceased. Experience of image remains.

The rise of *deconstructionism* as a literary theory provided the philosophical trigger for analysing these changes. Deconstructionists reject the view of structuralists that meaning is inherent in the text. It depends on the interpreter, hence there are many meanings. Jacques Derrida, in French philosophy, rejected the "metaphysics of presence" — the idea that something transcendent, eternal, is present in reality and can be described (Sherwood, 2000). Michel Foucault, reflecting on the relationship of power and knowledge (particularly in *Discipline and Punish* (1977) and the *Archaeology of Knowledge* (1972)) added that because knowledge is to name something and is an exercise of power, the great books need to be "unmasked" to show how they conceal the will to power (George, 2000). Richard Rorty adds that we cannot verify truth by correspondence between an assertion and reality through the internal coherence of the assertions themselves (1989). Thus philosophy becomes a conversation rather than discovering truth. These ideas reflect the abandonment of the search for a centre, a unity in knowledge (Grentz, 1996: 5-7).

French philosopher, Jean-François Lyotard in *The Postmodern Condition: A Report on Knowledge* characterizes "postmodernity" as "incredulity toward metanarrative" (1985: xxiv). Thus postmodernism, as a philosophy reflecting popular culture in the West lost sight first of Christendom's God in the modern era, then of modernity's humanity as authority. The loss of an external anchor for truth has resulted in there being no measure to evaluate "your truth" from "my truth." This fractionalisation results in no consensus on truth.

Yet, from dissonance, cultures seek integration[7] if they are to survive, emotionally, socially and morally. Either they stumble on in dissonance, or they die. For this reason in this study I posit postmodernism not as a rejection of metanarrative itself, but as *a transitional phase rejecting the metanarratives of an integrated modern Western worldview for the emergence of new integrations in the global/local culture.*

Conversational Space: Evangelical philosopher Francis Schaeffer developed one of the earliest popular evangelical critiques of these trends (1968a), showing that if there is no external reference point for truth, there is no lasting morality, for there is no basis (except the norms of the masses, not exactly the highest of moral bases) for judging what is moral. If there are no morals, there is only what an evangelical theologian of culture, Os Guinness (1976), writes of — the *Dust of Death,* the death of Western culture. But the end is not death and chaos as the philosophers of the largely atheistic left define, but an integrating city.

The speed of this cultural impact also recalls A.F.C. Wallace's (1956) revitalisation theory about the impact of a larger culture on a tribal people and the four possible responses that occur as they lose the integrations of their culture – gangs, new prophetic movements,

---

7   For example, the New Zealand government, in one area of social change, is currently seeking migrant policies that involve "social cohesion" which includes "belonging, participation, inclusion, recognition and legitimacy". The negative side include such things as isolation, exclusion, non-involvement, rejection and illegitimacy." (McGrath (1997)).

accommodation to the new, or anomie — only this time it is a global cultural tsunami where whole nations face these shocks and four similar possible responses.

What are the implications for revived believers in Auckland facing a culture that daily loses its commitment to truth and increasingly laughs at all authority? In what ways does the church redefine coherence and the centrality of truth for those marginalised by the oppression of incoherence in the midst of new technology? How do they portray *The Story* into a context where there is no truth, only story, with all stories of equal validity?

In this book, I am proposing a prophetic response that engages the tsunami, but creates new integrations, new metanarratives running stylistically parallel to this dominating worldview (like a surfer riding the wave), but rejecting some of its core tenets.

Physical Sciences: Death of Materialism
In the 20th century, a parallel shift occurred in the physical sciences. Chance and chaos, symbolised in the theory of relativity, or the Heisenberg uncertainty principle, replaced the absoluteness of Newtonian physics of inert matter, described in *Principia* (1687).[8] This leads Paul Davies and John Gribben in *The Matter Myth* to speak of the "Death of Materialism":

> *Newton's images of the workings of nature as an elaborate clockwork struck a deep chord. The clock epitomized order, harmony and mathematical precision, ideas that fitted well with the prevailing theology. Gone were the ancient notions of the cosmos as a living organism.... The doctrine that the physical universe consists of inert matter locked into a sort of gigantic deterministic clock has penetrated all branches of human enquiry... contributed in large part to alienating human beings from the Universe they inhabit. When extended into the domain of human affairs, such as politics or economics, machine mindedness leads to demoralization and depersonalization. People feel a sense of helplessness; they are merely 'cogs' in a machine that will lumber on regardless of their feelings or actions.... These people can take heart: materialism is dead (1991: 5-7).*

Quantum physics led to chaos theory, descriptions of nonlinear systems that become unstable and change in random yet predictable ways. The certainty of clockwork is now replaced by a world of open futures, in which even matter acquires an element of creativity. In the social sciences the reaction to behaviourism in psychology and determinism in sociology in the 1960's has also moved increasingly to open system approaches.

Yet in parallel with this loss of unity comes an all-pervasive intrusion of what postmodern critic Neil Postman (1993) calls *technopoly*, the intrusion of technology into everything from medical practice to bureaucracy to politics to religion. Ellul foresaw this decades ago (1964) in *The Technological Society*.

Conversation Space: How does the church redefine the human-matter dynamics in terms of such open-ended creativity and futurism? How can the church be faithful in defining the presence of a creative God in the nature of environmental space and network space?

---

8   This, in turn had replaced concepts of the material possessing magical or active qualities, or being infused with vitalistic forces.

Postmodernism in the Political and Economic Domain

Paralleling these shifts in the physical sciences are shifts in the broader culture occurring in the economic and political domains. As described in Fig. 12, nationally based production/consumption capitalism has become the globalised economy. Economies have moved from manufacturing to information technology. The result is a flattening of bureaucracies. This has been accelerated by rapidly expanding technology, resulting in an endless expansion of daily choices.

Concurrently, nation-state political systems have in many countries lost the allegiance of citizens who have now reverted to ethnic origins as the basis of political organisation. Tribalism and at times, balkanisation is increasing from Jerusalem to the Congo to the Maori party.[9]

Conversational Space: In the past, bishops related to prime ministers. Today in this flattened hierarchy, how does the church train its broad base to use new levels of access to directly influence national leadership?

I know urbane Christian workers and an executive who refuse or are unable to utilise email. I know of elderly folk for whom these changes are all confusion and even more confusing when brought into their safe place, the church, by enthusiastic theological college graduates bent on postmodern church growth. How does the church cater for those who opt out of the stress levels of accelerated technology into anomie?

In what ways may it affirm tribal identity, yet enhance cultural unity?

Beyond Secularism: the Structural Relocation of Belief

The church during modernisation was replaced at the centre of the city by the bank, factory and university. Post-modernity has further dispossessed it — no longer *one sector* of society as in modernity, but *one option* "for those who like that option."

Secularist philosophy (as against secularisation as process) has developed hostile to spiritual beliefs and supernatural explanations. Originally, there was that area of life that "had not yet been penetrated by religious values." Gradually however, the word came to mean, "that order of society which is neutral to the influence of religion" (Cohen, 1958: 37-38). But Newbigin argues that the state cannot be neutral in respect to other metanarratives (1986:132) so the phrase becomes one meaning hostility to religions.

Yet, this new culture is not simply secular but deeply spiritual. Moving beyond secular modernism, it involves an underlying spiritual search, yet a search largely outside traditional religious structure. *This opens a door for conversation about the good city*. Peter Lineham argues against extreme perspectives on this structural relocation of belief, indicating that church and state in New Zealand remain bound together in "unequal co-dependency" (2000a:41). The confusion for secularists is that the thesis of secularisation hasn't panned out: "It is in the West itself, not the century of secularisation, but of unprecedented religious innovation" (Turner, 1993:24). While there is a steady rise in those who have no religion or object to the question on religion in the New Zealand

---

9   Though it can be argued that this is not an increase in ethnic political identity, but a historically recurrent process for Maori, particularly at times when rights have been trampled on.

census (37% in 2001) the statistics in Chapter 4 indicate that churches in New Zealand are alive and well and with the exception of those which have bought into secular theology or are trapped in older institutional forms, they are growing. In fact, with the exception of large parts of Western Europe, the opposite to secularisation is true globally, as sociologist Peter Berger's *The Desecularization of the World* (1999) describes.[10]

Conversation Space: Ahdar has demonstrated points of conflict in New Zealand between secularists and conservative Christians (2000: 112-115), speaking of two "disestablishments" of traditional Christianity, the improbability of re-establishing a Christian state, yet the possibility that public religion may yet make a comeback, with "some unaccustomed bedfellows" in an increasingly pluralistic society (2000:76-77). The re-emergence of the search for spiritualities shows that secularism has been found wanting. While the old institutional religions are resisted, new spiritualities are being sought. The local bookshop has a shelf of books on new age religion, witchcraft, Zen Buddhism, Yoga, one or two Bibles, but nothing of substance about orthodox Christian beliefs. Our shopping centre in Glen Eden as in many Auckland suburbs, boasts a new store for witchcraft. In New Zealand this search for spirituality includes the use of Maori spirituality on public occasions with state acquiescence.[11]

Redefinition of society around "a biblical worldview" is the response of a cluster of society leaders at the Masters Institute. Ahdar gives several definitions (2000:45-54) from current discussions devolved from Harold Turner. He uses them to contrast with the "Wellington Worldview" in his model of engagement (2000:115). The idea of "worldview" jumped from missions anthropology into Evangelical Christianity through the Gospel and Cultures network,[12] and became anchored into a fight against "secular humanism as the enemy". It has been imported into New Zealand through books like *Understanding the Times*, by David A Noebel (1991) that contrast Secular Humanism, Marxist /Leninism and Biblical Christian Worldviews, or Walsh and Middleton's *The Transforming Vision: Shaping a Christian Worldview* (1984). This is a simple, though useful, way of engaging Evangelicals with the culture. I wonder if continued rethinking by Masters Institute of the anthropological dynamics of worldview may become significant. They will need to move beyond the analysis of 1980's secular humanism into postmodernism and their use of "a" Christian worldview (viz a viz the multiple worldviews in the Scriptures, influencing the multiple worldviews of cultures).

Metanarrative Loss and Redemption

Part of postmodern folklore is that the metanarratives, the great traditions, have been challenged and found wanting (Lyotard, 1985:xxiv). For example, claims of rational science as a basis for "progress" are viewed sceptically by those who have benefited by the technical progress (e.g., space research), but have been damaged by its economic oppressions (e.g., agent orange). Justice is no longer seen as a universal but only as a

---

10 See Chapter 4, A Secular Future?

11 Ahdar (2003:611-637), debates varying legal and governmental responses to indigenou Maori spirituality.

12 Partly through Kraft's ethnotheology (1979) and other evangelical missiologists. Harvey Conn's engaging *Eternal Word and Changing Worlds* trialogue between theology, anthropology and missions (1984), captures the period and issues of crossover.

rationally defensible concept within the society in which it is exercised.

Yet in the hard sciences not all agree with the philosophers. Some indicate the possibility of the creation of new metanarratives. Certainly, economic globalisation has its own narratives and the emergence of the global order involves the creation of a new language of power, extending past modernity and the developmental thinking reflected in the Club of Rome, the World Futures Society and UNESCO.

Conversation Space: I have indicated earlier an anthropological tenet that societies collapse unless they find integrations. Christians have a metanarrative. They thus need to answer how they can remain fixed on an everlasting Kingdom in service of the oppressed. And how their metanarrative can influence emergent global narratives in media, economics, governance...

Image and Substance
If we can no longer stand objectively outside and look for the grand themes, the only place to stand is on the inside. If there are no grand narratives, then there are only stories, images in juxtaposition to show that there is no point of reference. Thus design uses different fonts and left margin art irregularities and films flash multiple images without seeming connection. Baudrillard (1999) logically explains why images become disassociated from the realities they represent. Style, not meaning, becomes paramount. Since we cannot integrate meaning at depth, the surface images become the media. Body and bodily sensations receive new focus. The band takes centre stage.

Conversational Space: In this context, one response is the creation of churches that reflect postmodernism in style, without accepting postmodernism's rejection of the search for universal truth — churches of image, drama, music, changing scenes, like the Hillsborough Baptist Sunday youth services. Worship at Christian Life Centre Auckland and other central city churches involves the swingers, the shakers, the wavers, the dancers, the lights, the band and the projected image. Behind the image is the reality of Jesus who became the image of the invisible God. The correlation of the two is crucial for postmodern man and woman. On the other hand, juxtaposition of postmodern media that portrays rejection of authority, truth and substance, with a message of substance, eternal authority and truth, results in discord. Perhaps for many, it will result in a religious schizophrenia. Some retreat into the old certainties and old hymns to maintain continuity with history. Stylistically postmodern churches allow for both, usually through diverse services.

Fragmentation
With the loss of authority and metanarrative, history loses meaning and time itself fragments into a series of "presents." In politics and social structure, the loss of authority is applauded (falsely?)[13] as the expansion of democracy. In the medical field, the rejection of the formal medical profession and emergence of multiple medical traditions means a loss of the court of appeal. In deconstructionism in literature, loss of the search for universal truth has resulted in an understanding that words mean only whatever you wish them to mean, as "signs."

---

13 Barber (1996) argues that the expansion of consumer options leads to the disengagement of apathy, rather than a diffusion of power.

Fig. 13: Postmodernism: Collapsing Modernism, Emergence of Global Culture

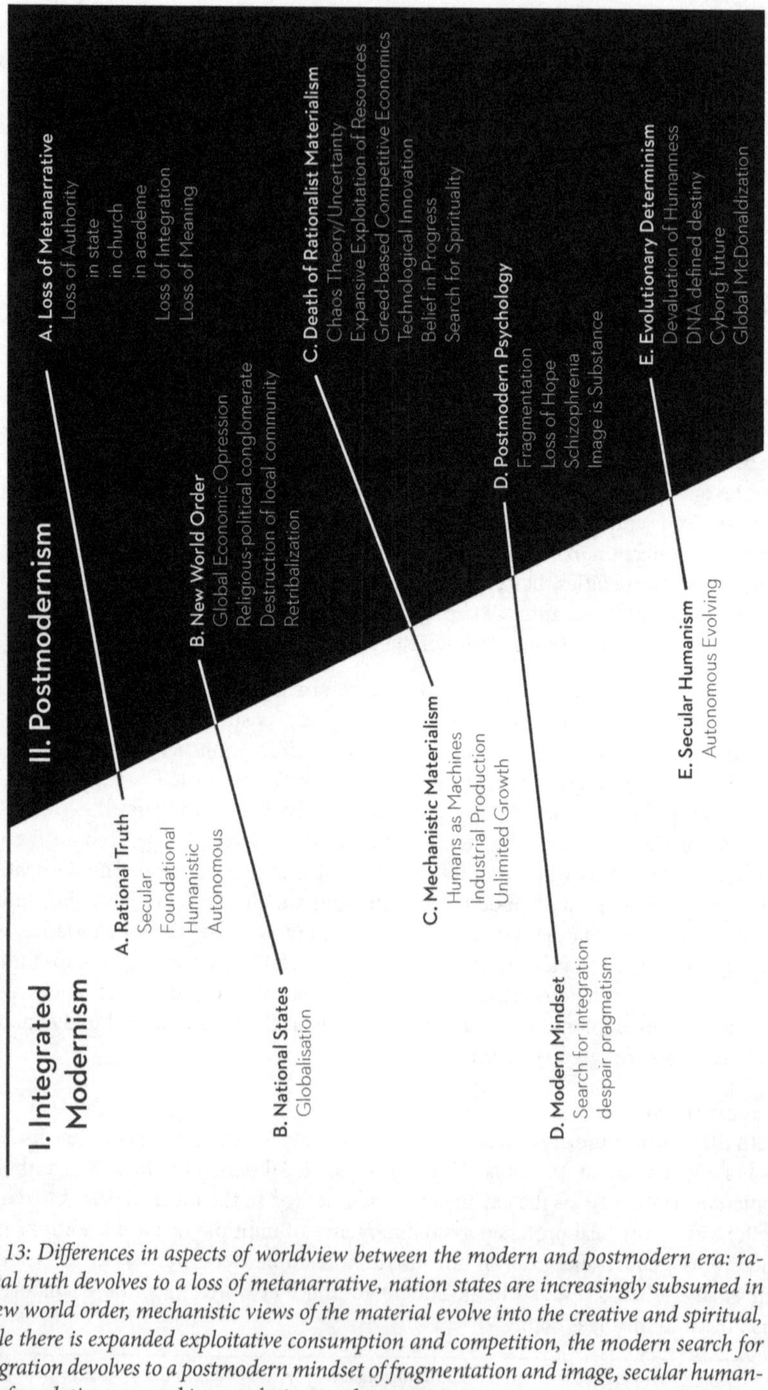

I. Integrated Modernism

A. Rational Truth
- Secular
- Foundational
- Humanistic
- Autonomous

B. National States
- Globalisation

C. Mechanistic Materialism
- Humans as Machines
- Industrial Production
- Unlimited Growth

D. Modern Mindset
- Search for integration
- despair pragmatism

E. Secular Humanism
- Autonomous Evolving

II. Postmodernism

A. Loss of Metanarrative
- Loss of Authority
  - in state
  - in church
  - in academe
- Loss of Integration
- Loss of Meaning

B. New World Order
- Global Economic Oppression
- Religious-political conglomerate
- Destruction of local community
- Retribalization

C. Death of Rationalist Materialism
- Chaos Theory/Uncertainty
- Expansive Exploitation of Resources
- Greed-based Competitive Economics
- Technological Innovation
- Belief in Progress
- Search for Spirituality

D. Postmodern Psychology
- Fragmentation
- Loss of Hope
- Schizophrenia
- Image is Substance

E. Evolutionary Determinism
- Devaluation of Humanness
- DNA defined destiny
- Cyborg future
- Global McDonaldization

Fig. 13: Differences in aspects of worldview between the modern and postmodern era: rational truth devolves to a loss of metanarrative, nation states are increasingly subsumed in a new world order, mechanistic views of the material evolve into the creative and spiritual, while there is expanded exploitative consumption and competition, the modern search for integration devolves to a postmodern mindset of fragmentation and image, secular humanistic foundations expand into evolutionary determinism.

The loss of authority and hence integrative social structure also allows opportunity for creation of darker forms of social control. Radical movements seek to hold society to ransom for good or ill — gay rights, ecology, environmentalism, justice for the oppressed… Law fragments into a collage of disjointed principles with no integrating theme.

Conversational Space: In this context, the creation of multi-generational communities of faith, where integrative belief and relational systems are transmitted across generations, provides a major source of hope for sustaining a cultural core in a way that has relational, familial, intellectual, historical and emotional integration. At the level of church and culture, is there a theology and missiology that can enable conversation between the metanarratives of the Scriptures with this fragmentation, replacing modernism in multiple sectors of society?

Psychological Schizophrenia
In the modern period, the search for self was a central theme, but outside the external authority of God it led to despair. In the postmodern period the search is abandoned, being replaced by a series of images of self that can be pulled off the shelf. This leads not to alienation but to schizophrenia and suicide. Some have highlighted Madonna as symbolizing this multiplicity of representation from Material girl, to Marilyn Monroe, to Evita, to creator of her own sexuality, to compassionate earth mother, to sensitive spiritualist (Kellner, 1995; Ward, 1997: 117-121).

Conversation Space: The embrace of the community of faith in confession and forgiveness across the damaged personalities that each one brings into it, with the catharsis of worship, confession and small group love, is a dramatic answer to a schizophrenic culture. Deeper than that is the need to generate committed communities where damaged youth, the fallout of fragmented marriage patterns, can reconnect with patterns of disciplined love and teamwork, discovering the wholeness of the fellowship of Christ. Rebuilding a culture around stable families and *whanau* (extended family) is a central platform of all the evangelical or committed Christian politicians in whatever party in New Zealand.

The Global Technological Society

Belief in Progress
The term "post"-modern rather than anti-modern implies some sense of good in modernism. Perhaps it is the belief in progress, the better life, for life is economically better this decade than last and this has been the experience for billions throughout this last century. This has rarely been true before in history.

Liberal theologians in the late 19th and early in the 20th century linked it to the moral progress of civilisation, particularly of Christendom. Auschwitz was the answer. Kosovo, two generations later, echoed the moral hollowness of European secular modernism.

What has occurred is the exponentially progressive expansion of technological innovation, with concurrent expansion of life expectancy, decrease in poverty for a significant portion of the globe, improvement in educational levels, expansion of intercultural communication through expanded travel and so on. French sociologist-theologian Ellul was one of the earliest to define *The Technological Society* (1964). Technological change has accelerated each year with a new video, PC, or new camcorder, each one better than the last.

If we can place a man on the moon and build a space station, of course we can civilize Mars! The future is perceived as unending in its technological possibilities, despite Schumacher's theme in *Small is Beautiful* (1973/1980) and other predictions about the limitation of natural resources such as *The Limits to Growth* by the Club of Rome (Meadows, Meadows, Randers, & Behrens, 1972/1977).

Conversation Space: Evangelicals with their high view of scriptural truth, also have a low view of the righteousness of humanity. They understand sin as universal and, apart from regeneration and sanctification through the Holy Spirit (i.e. conversion and discipleship), do not see religious diligence, the abolition of poverty, the expansion of education, or the creation of the welfare state as seriously decreasing that level of personal sinfulness. (That is not to say they do not see these as significant areas of social justice). Apart from the ebb and flow of righteousness through revival, they do not see societies moving towards righteousness. These views lack a serious understanding of common grace, of God-activity reflected in common humanity.

Consumer Society: Jihad vs. McWorld[14]

Within postmodernism's sense of technological progress, technology has come to define us. Barber tells us that as communist man and woman disappear and democratic man and woman disappear, what is left is consumer being, a one dimensional humanness. The world has become a global consumer culture. The only escape from this global consumer McWorld culture are the cultures of poverty. The mad rush for China and Africa is seen as an opportunity for consumption. Even the Internet is for sale now — watch it free if you watch the ads!!

The loss of citizenship is a side effect of consumerism, requiring time and energy. It is proactive, doing. The consumer by contrast is an almost passive receptor, placid, just an economic unit. When the consumer becomes the whole of our identity, even the public place has largely disappeared. The alternative according to Barber, in an echo of Schumacher, is that peoples in free communities should be the locus of self-government.

Conversational Space: These ideas closely parallel the apocalyptic thinking of most Pentecostal and evangelical believers about the future Kingdom, with their expectation of a one world socio-political-economic consumer-oriented government leading to the role of a despotic antichrist, popularised by Hal Lindsey's *The Late Great Planet Earth* (1970). This leads fundamentalists and many Pentecostals to a resistance to the UN and intrusions by the UN into New Zealand culture by such things as a bill of rights. This is in stark contrast to the optimistic view in liberal theology, the perspective of the Kingdom gradually transforming societies on earth. Such apocalyptic opposition is dulled by ever-increasing consumerism. What theological motifs will both balance out and sustain such theologies and their critiques? Is there a theological middle ground that both confronts the expanding global power structures, yet works towards gradual transformation?

---

14   Title and ideas from Benjamin Barber (1996).

Pragmatism as a Way of Life
With rejection of the spiritual for the secular and an embracing of the technological, modern personality gravitates to pragmatism, or achievement, as the measures of a man or woman. Berger, Berger and Kellner in *The Homeless Mind* (1973), identify several score characteristics of the modern mindset determined by the mechanistic, mass-production age. Humankind no longer controls the technology God has placed in its hands to manage, but rather it is defined by the technology.

Our speech is full of database terminology and talk of networking (impersonal relating across a broad spectrum of secondary relationships). Our mind chops time into manageable chunks like a mass production assembly line. Rest becomes meaningless for it does not appear to produce. The interchangeable parts of an organisation, its executives, are replaced every two to three years regardless of personality. Evaluated on performance, men and women become cogs in a machine. Postmodernism rejects this scenario in a return to new communitarianism and identity found in smaller communities, a new tribalism, or what Heelas and Woodhead in their critique of Berger's homeless mind, describe as new secondary institutions that provide transitory homes (2001).

Conversational Space: In this context, the relational Christian community is built from a biblical understanding of a spirit-infused humanness, an alternative of integration to the lostness of being — an integration of body and soul, city technology with humanity. How can the community of faith engage this technological conversation with this life-affirming humanness?

Conclusion
This analysis of movement from modernism into post-modernism defines the context in which Evangelicals and Pentecostals need to develop Transforming responses in Auckland-New Zealand. Metanarratives have been found wanting. The nature of materialism is in question. Image and media become the vehicles of cultural communication. There is a flattening of political power, and a tribalisation of politics. It is an age of fragmentation and schizophrenia. To each of these the scriptures have answers that bring integration and meaning to cultures. In the next chapter, I will expand the theme of the kingdom of God as a framework to respond to these issues.

But first, a small excursus to complete Chapter 2, an evaluation of transformational conversations as postmodern theological method. Readers may skip this, if they wish to continue with the overall flow of the main argument.

Excursus: Transformational Conversations and the Postmodern City
In this brief excursus, having looked at elements of postmodernism, I ask two questions as to how the hermeneutic of transformational conversations relates in *style* to the postmodern milieu and whether such an approach to theology is *essentially* postmodern.

Stylistic Fit with Postmodernism
First, there is a good fit between charismatic and Pentecostal oral theology as expressed in transformational conversations and the multiple stories of postmodernism, just as evan-

gelical theology is heavily entwined with modernist rationalism in style.[15]

Secondly, their experiential nature and multiple stories also relate to the search for spiritualism. Large Pentecostal churches and even charismatic St Margaret's Anglican with their media presentations, also express the overarching core of a "technique" culture, expressing image as well as search for substance (the Church Life Survey shows that substance is also welcome if imaged (Brookes, 2000)). These cultural dynamics within the movements are the context of this transformational conversations approach.

Thirdly, in the consultations and *hui* in which these transformational conversations have developed, holism is expressed by multiple stories, rather than necessarily following logical progressions towards points of universal truth. In Murphy's philosophic terms (1997:120-121) they define webs of belief not foundationalist systems. As theologian, I usually integrate the stories into a holistic summary. And leaders love this. Again, while the philosophers say "metanarrative" is rejected, I suggest that holistic processes leading to integrational truth conclusions and based on an awareness of how the disjoint elements fit together, are not unwelcome. Thus effective conversations involve both story and cosmic propositions.

Fourthly, one would expect that if charismatic Evangelicalism and Pentecostalism have migrated into postmodern styles, they would be significantly present in media, for as noted earlier in the chapter it has become the structural vehicle of postmodernism. This is the case in New Zealand music, as singers like Daniel Bedingfield rack up single after single at the top of the UK and European hit parades. Former YWAM'ers, he and his sister, Natasha, (who has done the same), are clear that their intention is to bring the Kingdom into the centre of secular music. There are others in the Kiwi music scene, less high profile, attempting the same. This is reflected in the music of the churches, the yearly Parachute weekend of thousands. Conversational theology about revival and Kingdom, becomes the theology of the balladeers.

Finally, at the core of postmodernism in philosophy is the critique of knowledge as power. Foucault's (1994: xv-xxi) assertion is that every interpretation of reality is an assertion of power. Jon Sobrino, liberation theologian, develops this in his critique of Western theology (1984:7-38). In contrast, knowledge gained by this transformational conversation approach from the bottom up has developed among the disenfranchised. This study thus illustrates a response to Sobrino's analysis of the essential demonisation of theology in its establishment nature, its use of words to control. Transformational conversations invert the power matrix.

Postmodern Evangelical Theology?

From the affirmative answer above to the question, "Can an evangelical postmodern theology *stylistically relate* to postmodern milieux?" a second question is evident, "Can we *develop an intrinsically postmodern* evangelical theological approach?"

---

15 The statements of faith of most evangelical institutions require a commitment to the infallibility of the Scriptures in various ways, statements of a foundationalism that requires significant mental gymnastics to sustain. Most seminaries are now moving to more open statements that allow for a querying of the human elements of the Scriptures (Hagner, 1998).

Charismatics and Pentecostals in this sense are postmodern phenomena, when one views postmodernism as a move from the integrative voices of Western power centres to listening to the multiple voices of the peoples. Pentecostals have rejected the language, the theology and the style of Christianity of the "official," "powerful" churches. It is a "popular religion," what Berg and Pretiz (1996), have good reason to term "grassroots Christianity" against the "survival of tradition." David Martin calls Pentecostalism "an option of the poor rather than the liberationist "option *for* the poor" (1995:27).[16]

But relating theology to the realities of the postmodern milieux does not imply full entrance into the philosophical analysis and ideas of deconstruction represented in the broad term postmodernism. We can differentiate at least two postmodern worlds:[17] urban planning, architecture, economics, politics, media

- and popular culture, where postmodernism describes real phenomena and with which transformational conversations are a good fit.

- the world of postmodern theologians and literary philosophers whose premises are speculative and, for Evangelicals, often suspect when viewed against biblical truth

Those in other disciplines have the same critique of the latter world:

> *We reject the notion that cultural construction is the only factor shaping human experience. There is an objective reality out there too and it applies to social relations as well as to natural science... when you shoot someone, that person dies...if one forgets objective engineering principles, the building may collapse... among physicists... a theory eventually triumphs or is rejected depending on how well it models and predicts that reality* (Inglehart, 1997:12,13).

This latter world, is heavily influenced by "language games" within closed academic communities, as Lyotard (1985) so aptly describes much academic theological training. These are fashioned by symbolic words, particular fashionable theological trends that owe some debt to deconstructionism[18] in literary theory, philosophy and criticism.

Theological modernism rejected the metanarratives of the Scriptures for the rationalist metanarrative as source of authority. Some postmodern theologies have attempted to continue this metanarrative to its logical conclusions — and those conclusions have proven to be an empty set of contradictions, of unending deconstructions, what Gavin Hyman in *The Predicament of Modern Theology* (2001), describes as "nihilist textualism" in which the end of foundationalism brings with it the end of theology, particu-

---

16 Pentecostalism springs up all over the world among the poor, almost spontaneously, as one would expect if it was a genuine work of the Holy Spirit, when the gospel is preached and signs and wonders occur. (Hollenweger, 1997).

17 The difficulty of using such a global description as "postmodernism" is that there are multiple ways to define postmodernity. Murphy (1997) differentiates Anglo-American postmodernity from European in philosophy. "Post-" implies not knowing exactly what...

18 A term "developed by Derrida, as an event provisionally described as reading, writing and thinking that undoes, decomposes, unsettles the established hierarchies of Western thought" (Odell-Scott, 2000:56).

larly the work of Don Cupitt (1998) in the UK and Mark Taylor (1984) in the US, both writing within the framework of Nietzsche's "death of God" and the postmodern "end of metanarrative".

I believe we need to posit another kind of postmodern theology[19] when we talk of evangelical postmodern theology. For extending liberal theology into the postmodern is not helpful for Evangelicals. For example, Kim (2000:179), in analysing the World Council of Churches gathering in Melbourne, reflects the liberal, postmodern theological literature, when she implies that to be theologically postmodern is to be "anti-" and thus will include liberationist theological stances: anti-structural, anti-establishment, anti-colonial and anti-masculine. But this is not the experience of these Pentecostal voices from the edges. These voices are postmodern in form and style, but do not confirm the categories of liberal postmodern theology. This calls into question the nature of that theology. It requires Evangelicals to posit alternative approaches relating to the "real" postmodern world.[20]

I affirm French philosopher, Jean-François Lyotard in his definition of *postmodern* as "incredulity toward metanarrative" (Lyotard, 1985:xxiv), when it is applied to some metanarratives of the modern project, but reject the underlying modernist disbelief in the metanarrative of the Scriptures (and in philosophies that subsume housing construction, milking cows and other realities that do not deconstruct!). Such affirmation, however, does not return to fundamentalism, with the metanarrative of Scripture having only one meaning that can be rationally exegeted. Postmodern understanding, that truth is multiplex not univocal, fits with Jesus', Pauline and Johannine multilevel exegetical usage of the OT, the tenor of the collation of story in the canon, Jesus' story-based didactic approach and the nature of wisdom in the Scriptures.

Thus at its heart, an evangelical postmodern hermeneutic can be partially and critically postmodern, just as evangelical theology to date has always been only partially modern. The biblical metanarrative transcends others or none. These ideas parallel, though don't exactly map another category of postmodern theology, which some term "radical orthodoxy" (John Milbank, 1999). Those in this category embrace anti-foundationalism, the narratives and the linguistic idealism of postmodernism, but attempt to recover a paradigm where theology absorbs and makes possible all other discourses (Hyman, 2001:3-4).

This is in the hope that, as postmodernism is a temporary philosophic and cultural phase between civilisations, the metanarratives that sustain and integrate our civilisation may perhaps be reformed around the eternal metanarrative. Thus, transformational conversations are neither rationalist evangelical theology nor non-integrated postmodernist.

---

19 Evangelical attempts, so far, tend to simply be critiques of elements of modern and liberal postmodern theologies (e.g. *So What Happens After Modernity? A Postmodern Agenda for Evangelical Theology* (Oden, 1995: 392-406) or Stanley Grentz, *Revisioning Evangelical Theology* (1993) or Dockery (1995). This hermeneutic of transformational conversations appears to be one of the first genuinely postmodern theologies developed.

20 Grentz indicates communitarian vs. individual, post-rational holism, spirituality-based theology as three characteristics of such theology (1995:98-101), but does not model these. This study models the first two of his categories. The analysis of how this is postmodern has come after the fact.

What has been developed here is a third way for evangelical theology — a communal transformational conversation, postmodern in that it is collaged, multivariate, story-based, yet committed to the ongoing exploration of a metanarrative.

Now, I will return to the main flow of argument, proposing the Kingdom as response to the postmodern city.

- 8 -

SPIRIT, KINGDOM AND POSTMODERN CITY

> *The Kingdom of God is the highest good. The idea of God is the highest and most comprehensive conception in philosophy; the idea of the Kingdom of God is the highest and broadest idea in sociology and ethics*
>
> (Rauschenbusch, 1916:59)

In this chapter, I propose a new evangelical understanding of the Kingdom of God as centre of a web of belief about transforming goals. This is a conversational response to themes of postmodernism in Chapter 7.

Kingdom, City, Spirit

The ultimate reign of God is integrally connected with the coming of the city of God in the final chapters of Revelations.

> *I saw the Holy City, the new Jerusalem coming down out of heaven from God, prepared as a bride, beautifully dressed for her husband* (Rev 21:2).

This bride, has been the hope of the saints, Abraham looked forward to "a city whose builder and maker is God" (Heb 11:10), a city prepared for his faithful people (11:16). "For here, we do not have an enduring city, but we are looking for the city that is to come" (13:14). The church is the bride in preparation, the city being built. The city is preceded in verse 1 with the broader context of the universal Kingdom:

> *Then I saw a new heaven and a new earth, for the first heaven and the first earth had passed away and there was no longer any sea* (Rev 21:2).

This quotation above by John, from Isaiah 65:17, is not of a creation *ex nihilo*, but a transformation. As in Genesis 1, so in this revelation of the eternal Kingdom, environmental structure precedes life-forms. But it appears to be metamorphosis, for he goes on, in verse 5, "Behold I make all things new." Paul, in Romans 8, tells us that "the whole creation groans, waiting our adoption as sons", thus this metamorphosis is integrally related to our salvation. The Kingdom involves a renewal of creation, a transformation of world and universal orders. In reference, perhaps, to the waters of primeval chaos of Genesis 1, he then states, "there was no longer any sea," and the transformation of chaos is complete.

Then is voiced a grand climax, for the crowning of the creator, his taking up his reign on earth, his Kingship, has to do with his presence with the created social creature,

And I heard a loud voice from the throne saying, "Now the dwelling of God is with humanity and he will live with them. They will be his people and God himself will be with them and be their God" (Rev 21:1-3).

"The dwelling of God, (or the tabernacle, or tent Gk: *skene*) is with humanity."[1] This is an allusion to the Hebrew *shekinah*, God's immanence both in the world and among people. It is an echo[2] of the new covenantal promise of Ezek 37:27, "My dwelling place shall be with them; and I will be their God and they shall be my people" (see Ezek 34:30; 36:28; Zech 2:11a; Lev 26:11-12). Paul links this dwelling of God among people to believers being the temple of the living God, the temple of the Spirit of God.[3] The linkage of people to city is perhaps a reflection on Ps 46:4, where the phrase "city of God" parallels "dwelling place of the most high" (Aune, 1998:1122).

Kingdom as Centre of a Web of Belief

This framework of the Kingdom of God most recently has enabled breakthroughs for Evangelicals in their involvement in transformation.[4] The theme of the city of God and framework of the Kingdom are considered here, firstly because they are both common integrative biblical themes, used by movements across history. Secondly, they are accessible, potentially popular and open up study of classic Christian theologies to Pentecostals, since they both include pneumatology. The work of the Spirit is integral to entrance, expansion and the nature of the Kingdom. The Kingdom includes the theme of the "people of God," an existing strongly held foundational theme for a "Christ against Culture" movement.

Up to this point, while the *Kingdom of God* theme is now familiar and discussed among New Zealand Pentecostal leaders, it has failed to provide broad mobilisation of the Pentecostal movement, perhaps largely because the breadth of the theme has not been extensively taught among Pentecostals. I have examined other theologies of city, justice, liberation theologies, covenants and the cosmic Christ—but these can be subsumed under the Kingdom. They also lack a popular base within these movements.

---

1 This theme has been developed from the Pentateuch through the writings and prophets.

2 In the field of intertextuality, the concept of 'allusion' and 'echo' are most useful for study of passages in Revelation. There are few direct quotations of Old Testament passages in over 473 verses in Revelations that are directly related to Old Testament passages (Moyise, 1995).

3 Moltmann examines the relationship of the Holy Spirit and *Shekinah* in detail (1991: 47-51).

4 See various discussions on the Kingdom perspective of Glasser (particularly McQuilken) and their influence on Evangelicals in Van Engen (1986).

The theme appears in Genesis,[5] though the terminology begins during the monarchy of David (Psa 45:6; 103:19; 145:11). It was the central theme in Jesus' teaching, beginning with Mark's use of it as a summary of his focus (Mark 1:15) (Beasley-Murray, 1986:71). Paul is last heard of in Rome, "preaching the Kingdom of God" (Acts 28:31). The end of the Scriptures is about the return of the King to bring his reign. It recurs uncannily in almost every generation.

This theme, in contrast to the dispensationalism of fundamentalist groups (hence breaking its interpretative power), assumes that the Scriptures are a unity.[6] While there is differentiation as to God's activity at different phases of redemption history or expressed in different narratives, this does not mean that God changes in personality, style or fundamentals. God's interventions at every phase of redemption history are consistent. The discontinuities at the incarnation, the cross and the *parousia*, are subject to the continuities of his nature.

But a further step is needed beyond existing, culturally limited,[7] evangelical theologies of the Kingdom of God, such as by Bright (1953), Ladd (1959) or sociologist Kraybill's more socially aware Anabaptist perspective (1978). We need to achieve a more comprehensive biblical understanding of the nature of the Kingdom as involving the socio-economic, spiritual and political.

Charles Van Engen (1998), reflects on missions theologian emeritus, Glasser's *The Good News of the Kingdom* (1993) (which in turn draws on Ladd (1959) and in turn Oscar Cullman's "Kingdom present and not yet" (1962)). He indicates four things the theme of the Kingdom has done or evangelical missiology:

- The Kingdom of God concept broadens missiological reflection beyond a predominantly individualised and vertical understanding of salvation to a holistic view of the interaction of the church and world.

- Glasser's Kingdom missiology breaks the impasse between evangelism and social action that has plagued Evangelicals.

- Kingdom-of-God missiology creates the possibility of new conversation among Evangelicals, representatives of the conciliar movement, Roman Catholics, Orthodox, Pentecostals and charismatic.

- Glasser's own personal pilgrimage made him deeply aware of the social and political implications of the Kingdom of God that challenges all governments, all forms of racism and all social structures that would seek to deify themselves.

Independently, Dyrness (1983/1991) working in Manila, and Bellingham in Bangladesh and India (1987), have grappled with relating the Kingdom to the social realities

---

5 Beasley-Murray, in *Jesus and the Kingdom of God*, begins the theme by examining OT theophany (1986). He points out that while the terminology Kingdom occurs only nine times and King as it refers to the Lord only forty-one times, emphasis on the ruling activity of God occurs from the time of the patriarchs (18).

6 I follow Daniel Fuller's (1992) approach beyond the popular classifications of 7 dispensational periods to lay a foundation for unity within a canonical (evangelical) view of the Scriptures. This is logical, given Evangelical's high view of revelation..

7 Middle class, economically secure, politically stable, highly educated, white American.

of poverty and oppression. The most lucid evangelical statements I have read are in Howard Snyder's *A Kingdom Manifesto* (1997). Two decades of theological conferencing by Chris Sugden and Vinay Samuel and the Transformation network produced *Mission as Transformation* (1999), with several chapters on the Kingdom. This and Glasser's teaching at Fuller have influenced the Latin American Theological Fraternity and Petersen in Latin America (1996:209-224). Brian Hathaway developed a New Zealand church-based missiology of the Kingdom (1990) reflecting these influences.

Nevertheless, with the exception of the latter, the evangelical understandings lack the comprehensiveness of social gospel conceptualisations of the Kingdom by evangelists significant in the early World Council of Churches and liberal social gospel theology, such as Rauschenbusch (1907/1968); Kagawa of Japan in *Christ and Japan*, (1934); E. Stanley Jones in India with *The Unshakeable Kingdom and the Unchanging Person* (1972); or H. Richard Niebuhr of the US (1937/1988).

Continuity and Discontinuity of the Kingdom

OT Intervention; NT Invasion

In the Old Testament, the reign of God was acknowledged and frequently he intervened in situations, applying the social, economic and political principles of his Kingdom (first part of Fig. 14). Yet the presence of God was not with humankind, his Spirit did not dwell with men and women. Thus in the times of Samson and the judges, he exercised his rule as the Spirit came upon chosen individuals for the duration of each crisis.

Then Isaiah, in the Servant Psalms, prophesies of the Servant of the Lord who would exercise his ministry through the eternal anointing of the Spirit (Isa 42:1-14; 61:1-3). This is what differentiates the New Testament from the Old — the small baby in a little manger in an insignificant town, surrounded by a host of angels, shepherds and wise men. The King has come! The Kingdom of God has invaded the Kingdom of the ruler of this world. The Kingdom is now in the midst of us! First in the Christ and then in his body, the Spirit dwells among humanity!

In the Old Testament, the King *intervened* in the life of Israel. Now he has *invaded*! His strategy? Throughout the whole world he has set up small bands of men and women (churches) at warfare with Satan, the ruler of this age. In the narratives of these guerrilla units, the principles and values of the Kingdom are demonstrated (2nd part of Fig. 14).

The Holy Spirit as First Fruits of a Future Kingdom

These principles are manifested through the power of the Spirit in transformed believers. Stronstad (1984) indicates the centrality of the anointing of the Spirit on Christ, expanded into the outpouring of the Spirit on the charismatic first church, as the integrating centre of the Kingdom in the two volume Luke-Acts story.

But the Kingdom is also still to come. Half of the parables of the Kingdom are of a present Kingdom and half of a future Kingdom.[8] Jesus came the first time, humbly,

---

8   Beasley-Murray (1986) documents these extensively. This duality (developed from Oscar Cullman (1962)) is the central thesis of Ladd's Kingdom theology that has influenced many other evangelical theologians in their progressions from fundamentalism to a holistic gospel (1959; 1974).

quietly as foretold in the four Servant Psalms of Isaiah, not as judge but as servant. He brought his Kingdom into the world. One day he will return again, to break the Kingdoms of this world and establish the rule of his Kingdom forever ((Dan 2:31-35), third part of Fig. 14).

So we enjoy a taste of its blessings here. We "have tasted of the powers of the age to come" (Heb 6:5), through the Holy Spirit . That is a power and conflict-related experience:

> But if I cast out spirits by the finger of God, then the Kingdom of God is come to you (Luke 11:20).

FIG. 14: THE KINGDOM OF GOD AS INTEGRATING BIBLICAL THEME

THE KINGDOM OF GOD IS ETERNAL, UNCHANGING

IN THE OLD TESTAMENT	IN THE NEW TESTAMENT	IN THE LAST DAYS
The King **intervenes** in the lives of: Adam, Abraham, David, Noah Moses etc.	The King **invades** history as a suffering servant	Will be the triumphal coming as the **King of kings** and as judge of all

| IN EACH INTERVENTION THE KINGDOM PRINCIPLES ARE MADE KNOWN: **SPIRITUAL, ECONOMIC, SOCIAL** THROUGH GOD'S DEALINGS WITH ISRAEL | COMMUNITIES OF THE KING MANIFEST KINGDOM **SPIRITUALITY, ECONOMICS, SOCIAL** RELATIONSHIPS | THE KINGDOM WILL RULE THE KINGDOMS OF THIS EARTH |

COVENANTS OF MERCY AND JUDGEMENT

It Is A Kingdom Present...And Not Yet!

Fig.14 indicates eternal consistencies of the Kingdom (and the covenants) and its social, spiritual and economic principles. These are contrasted with the differences in the relationship of the Kingdom of God to humanity in the Old Testament, the New Testament and after the parousia. In the Old Testament he intervenes but does not dwell. The New Covenant is of an indwelling God, choosing to suffer as servant, creating communities that model social, spiritual and economic principles. After the judgment he will rule the earth.

Sometimes, the Spirit restores our bodies through healings, though usually we have to wait for his coming when we will receive new bodies (I Cor 15:50). He gives us power over the evil one by his Spirit, but "Satan is not yet cast into the place prepared for him." At times we see clearly, as the Spirit of Truth guides us, but mostly we "see in a mirror, darkly." "On that day we will see him as he is." This imperfection means that much of what we do is incomplete, a *sign* of the fullness of the future Kingdom.[9]

Discipleship, Response to the Kingdom

Discipleship, *our human response to the Kingdom*, is a significant theme among Evangelicals, but has been disassociated from the Kingdom. It has become an extension of evangelistic motifs, popularised by the Navigators as methodologies for post-conversion sanctification, as they worked with Billy Graham in the 1950's. Its reinterpretation, if we are to understand the fullness of the Kingdom, is one key to an evangelical theology of transformation. Fig. 15, in a new way, expands discipleship from classic evangelical holiness motifs to its fuller meaning spiritually, economically and socio-politically. Foundational aspects of each of these three arenas and their relationship to the work of the Spirit are examined next.

The starting point is the common evangelical understanding of discipleship as the human "spiritual" response to acknowledge the King, to acknowledge the Lordship of Christ. Jesus left behind him the indwelling Holy Spirit in the believer, the incarnate presence of God as against his being wholly other. Indeed we cannot enter the Kingdom unless we are born again of the Spirit (John 3:1-16). Jesus did not leave us comfortless, but promised the Holy Spirit (John 14:1-7). Acts demonstrates the centrality of the work of the Holy Spirit in advancing the Kingdom.

But that hope is defined in Isaiah much more broadly than the simple indwelling of the Spirit as companion and comforter. The hope is defined as "justice for the nations," established through the anointing of the Spirit (Isa 42:1-4).[10] Jesus tells us to seek his Kingdom and his justice above all else, as a first principle of discipleship.

Disciples, Kingdom people, as a result of the indwelling Spirit, are also expansively proclamative. Because the Word was God, the communication of his being in person, we become communicating people as we enter into his being — with both word and deed being part of that communication. Jesus preached through word, deed and power, ruling over creation, for as he preached he "went about doing good and healing all who were oppressed by the devil." This he did in the "power of the Spirit"(Luke 4:14,18). Mark 3:14 tells us quite simply that the twelve were "to be with him and to be sent out to preach, with power to cast out demons."

---

9   A dialogue of international evangelical, charismatic and Pentecostal theologians was developed in three consultations in 1998, 1990 and 1994 concerning the relationship of evangelism, justice and the work of the Spirit. Key themes are summarised in Samuel and Sugden (1999).

10   For example, Waldron Scott (1980), general director of the Worldwide Evangelical Fellowship, clearly defined for Evangelicals the centrality of justice as goal based on exegeses of the Servant Psalms.

Fig. 15: Discipleship Response to a Spiritual-Economic-Socio-Political Kingdom

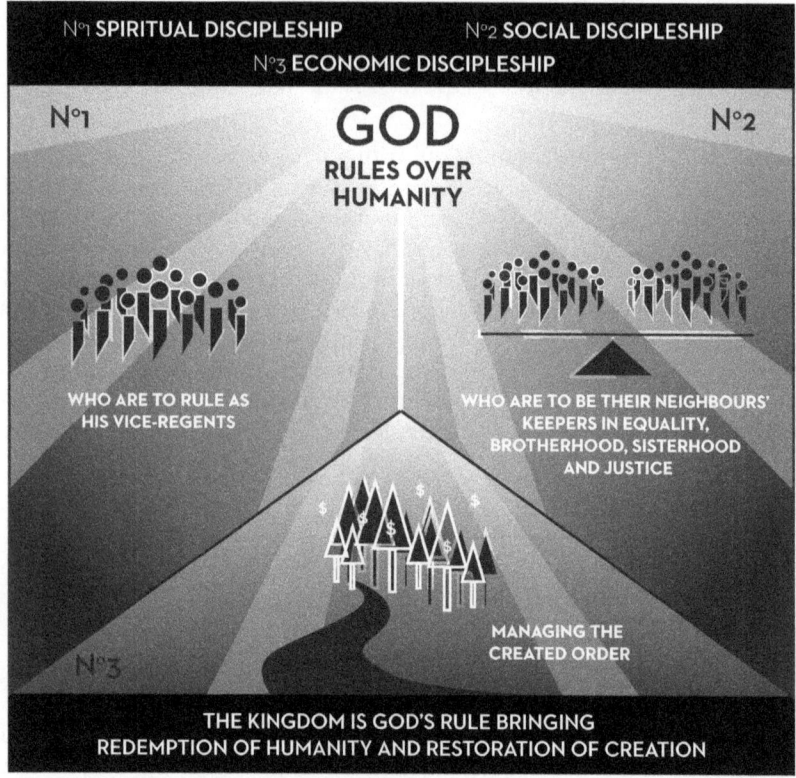

Fig. 15 indicates three sets of relationships between King, people and created order within the Genesis account. Obedient human response to the King is known as discipleship. The first two relationships, God-human, God-human-land are primarily those of authority. The human-human relationships are primarily of equality. These define the primary arenas of "spiritual" discipleship, economic discipleship and socio-political discipleship. Holistic discipleship includes all three arenas.

Along with communication of the gospel by speech is the communication of character. The fruit of the Spirit makes men and women agents of transformation by their very being. They have presence because of the presence of the Spirit. Historically, the presence and character development have been related to the exercise of spiritual disciplines in "discipleship".

- Discipleship As Methodology Or The Fruit Of The Spirit? -

> The Navigators developed from the American Evangelical centre represented by Billy Graham. Their theology builds off biblical texts to develop discipleship themes in individualistic terminology. As pietist descendants of Wesley, they have defined discipleship as the centrality of Christ, disciplines of quiet time, prayer, Bible Study, obedience and proclamation.
>
> They began as a highly influential university movement and grew rapidly in New Zealand as a significant renewal movement that has sustained the faith of thousands in fundamentalist and evangelical churches, while largely operating outside of church structure.

As one indebted to this movement for the sustaining of these disciplines over 40 years, I would affirm these as a powerful basis for sustained spirituality, nevertheless they have limitations.

Holistic Discipleship

My first step beyond the rigidity of such disciplines to more comprehensive holistic discipleship was an understanding that Jesus defines the disciplines of the Christian life not by religious rituals, but as the character qualities in his manifesto in the Sermon in the Mount (meekness, poverty of spirit, purity of heart and so on) (Grigg, 1979; 1980). Paul, the apostle, devotes the majority of his teaching not to religious methods, but to character issues.

The second step, was an understanding that these are the work of the Spirit. In the overwhelming presence of the Spirit in revival contexts, these characteristics begin to manifest. Yet they require all the above human disciplines to be sustained. However, the emphasis of the Scriptures is on these being the fruit of the Spirit, rather than the fruit of human endeavour.

Thirdly, in Luke 14:26-33, Jesus himself defines discipleship in economic (part 2 of Fig. 15) and social terms (part 3 of Fig. 15) (Scott, 1980). For discipleship, the response to the Kingdom, is not simply a spiritual relationship with God (part 1 of Fig. 15).

At a missiological level, the most powerful way I have found to move people to this understanding has been through action involving Kingdom incarnation. For Jesus' first step of discipleship, his incarnation, is a historically central socio-economic-political subversive act, not simply a spiritual act. Luke 2, in its descriptions of the incarnation, reflects the Jewish understanding of the prophets in their denunciation of social sins. The Magnificat tells us how the incarnation places the locus of economic theory at the point of uplift of the poor. The incarnation was a profoundly social act, making identification or solidarity with the poor central to social action and placing the locus of Christian mission among the poor. The incarnation was a profoundly political act, defining godly politics as politics that serve the least important of society (Grigg, 1992a; Kraybill, 1978).

It is logical that any person filled with the Holy Spirit will tend to emulate these preferences in theologies of justice, incarnation and transformation. This supernaturally happens in revivals. Jonathan Edwards, the revivalist in his post-Great Awakening

Religious Affections (Edwards, 1742/2005), asks the question, "Where does one look for true signs of revival?" His answer – "In those who seek to relieve the poor". As indicated in the diachronic survey, historically this has subverted economic, social and power structures towards good.

Incarnation among the poor confronts the powers. The preached Word results in confrontation with the powers. These two elements of incarnational and confrontational discipleship become crucial to its expansion into socio-economic political dimensions.

Jesus not only preached the presence of the Kingdom, he demonstrated that Satan's works were destroyed (Matt 12:28). When the disciples came back enthusiastic because even the demons were subject to them, he tells them "I saw Satan fall like lighting from Heaven" (Luke 10:18). Finally he "triumphed over Satan in death." Satan was rendered inoperative (I Cor 15:26; Heb 2:14). Thus spiritual warfare themes are integrally related to our understanding of the nature of the Kingdom and the clash of this Kingdom with the Kingdoms of this world, their economic, social and political issues.

> *Transformational theology is thus an expansion of discipleship, Kingdom oriented, incarnational, justice and character focused, proclamative in its central thrust and involves ongoing power confrontation with the Kingdoms of this world* (Samuel & Sugden, 1999:xvi).

Discipleship as Communal

Discipleship is also communal, not simply individualistic. A significant theological shift occurs when Evangelicals grasp that Jesus' commission was "to disciple the nations," not just individuals, but to bring the nations (*ta ethne* = peoples) under his authority.

- CHANGING THE MINDSET OF A NATION -

> Since the 1980's, Youth With a Mission (YWAM), a Pentecostal short term youth training mission, has become the biggest mission in New Zealand. It popularised Kuyper's theology, as the '7 mind moulders', looking at how to affect the mindset of a nation or city. Kuyper, a Christian theologian who became the prime minister of Holland early last century, worked extensively on the 'spheres' of Christian influence, building off Calvin's Kingdom theology (1998a; 1998b). He, in turn, built from an Augustinian framework. An underlying concept is that 'discipling the nations' involves bringing not just individuals but nations under the reign of the Kingdom. This pattern of thinking has resulted in former YWAM'ers in parliament, as business leaders and in educational reform.

The Kingdom and Postmodernism

Defining the Kingdom

Dyrness uses a simple definition of the Kingdom of God, *God's active, interventive rule over humankind and the creation*.[11] This rule has always existed and always will (indicated by the arrow in Fig. 15), defining the personal nature at the centre of the universe. While Genesis does not use the phraseology of the Kingdom of God, it lays the foundation — *"In the beginning, God..."* To speak of God's creation is to remember that God

---

11 Definition after Dyrness (1983/1991), as he seeks to relate the Kingdom to third world social issues. Intervention is a community development phrase.

created all things. He rules and reigns from before the beginning. He is King of Creation.

This is integrally connected to revival. God's Spirit was the creative breath that formed the universe. The Spirit's voice has not stopped speaking. The Spirit continues to create. The universe is thus infused with the voice and the breath and the being of a personal God. This view follows Philo and Augustine, in that God is not dependent on that universe, nor is the universe God, but matter is infused with his being, his personality, his breath.[12]

> *He does not depend on the process of nature and history for his existence, but he does have purposes that can only be realised in nature and history* (Bennett, 1941:39).

The Personality of Matter

I suggest that economic discipleship, the Christian response to fundamental postmodern questioning of rationalist materialism, beyond the transformation of Newtonian physics and the death of materialism into chaos theory or relativity, is based on an understanding of matter as infused with personality, the personality of the Spirit of God, spirit not of chaos, but of structured creativity - what the Scriptures call righteousness, wholeness, holiness. *Matter is not only, as Einstein derived, energy. Personhood is the source of the energy. Matter has an infusive personality. The universe at its heart has a personality.* Colossians 1:15-20, the grand song of the apostle about the great sovereignty of his Lord, speaks first of our Lord's creation, then of an integrational role, then of his immanence, his infusion of all in all. That song is central to our conversations with the postmodern city and the star-trek generation.

And that central personality of the universe is community, within which, the source of power and authority is the Father; the exercise of power is by the Holy Spirit. This creates a conversational space connecting with the search for creative power so central to many postmodern media productions. Relationship to the Holy Spirit as the essential creative power of the universe is central to charismatic and Pentecostal Christianity. This could place Pentecostalism at the centre of postmodern conversation. But only if it extends the conversation into the fullness of a Christian ecology and environmentalism.

The breath of God is also by nature expansive, as science has discovered in its conclusions of an infinitely expanding universe. It is the Spirit who is continually hovering over and creating cities, giving a basis for Christian involvement in all things related to construction of good cities and entrepreneurial business. These themes enable structural conversations with the post-star-trek generation that understands an expanding universe.

The Morality of the Physical World

Humanity inherits the responsibility to manage, husband, care, rule over this creation,[13] to guard over something so preciously created by God's own breath. Our relationship to creation raises a major theological question. Since the creator is moral, his creation

---

12   It is beyond the scope of these paragraphs to enter into the debate about pantheism, panentheism etc. Since such debates have not been fully reconciled historically, either theologically or philosophically, I doubt that I can do it either. Not that they are unimportant, for each perspective has logical outcomes in terms of lifestyle.

13   Darragh gives a theological analysis of the range of ways we can relate to the earth (2000:150).

must also be moral. What is the moral nature of the material? Is the world good or evil, godly or demonic?

There are opposing scriptural streams that must be held in tension. On the one hand, the Scriptures are world-affirming. God made all things good. Even in humanity's sin they remain good, though the land is cursed and work is hard. God not only created, he also loves the world and sent his Son into the world as an incarnate being in material form, affirming the importance of that material existence. These statements form the basis of conversation with society about good work, fruitful agriculture, expanding economies, etc.

On the other hand, the Scriptures are world-denying.[14] We are not "of" the world and are to separate from the world, the flesh and the devil. This fallen "world" (Gk: *Aeon* or present age) is the value system of society hostile against God. Rather than creation, the Scriptures are talking here of the derived sinful human culture of the world and demonic intrusions.

This tension is central to the metamorphosis of Evangelicalism under consideration. In seeking as part of our discipleship to "not love the world," to "not be conformed to this present age," Evangelicals in the early part of last century concluded that they should not be involved in the social, political and governmental issues of the world. Yet, St. John, tells us that "if we see our brother (or sister) in need, yet close our heart against them, how does God's love abide in us?" (1 John 3:17). According to the Old Testament concept of righteousness, right relationships with our brother are a sign of our right relationship with God. Our calling is to be "in the world but not of it."

It is as if Evangelicalism and Pentecostalism were locked into a truncated spirituality. They have focussed only on the first two steps of Matthew Fox's (1983) reiteration of paradigms of spirituality, the four paths of delight (*via positiva*), letting go (*via negativa*), creativity (*via creativa*), and compassion (i.e., celebration and peacemaking (*via transformativa*). But socio-economic discipleship in a postmodern city requires the release of creativity in the freedom and gifts of the Spirit (*via creativa*) and must move into this *via transformativa*. Socio-economic discipleship must engage the created world, enter into it after the manner of Christ, but separate from the values of the world of fallen human culture.

Beyond Inanimate Materialism
It is the empty modernist theory of inanimate materialism that is dead — not God. The new physics has blown apart the centrality of materialist doctrine. Relativity exposed the clockwork universe as shifting and warping. Chaos theory has replaced Newton's determinative machine. Chance has replaced causality. Solid matter has dissolved into apparently empty space seething with quantum activity. In its place, chaos theory has opened a future of creativity. Collaborative particles drive new forces (Davies & Gribben, 1991).

---

14 Few theological studies can match Hengel's *Property and Riches in the Early Church* (1974) for an exegesis and theology of this tension.

These changes in the underlying perception of matter mirror changes in production and the market economy. The physical materials in a silicon chip are negligible yet the information and creativity released are far more productive than the iron of steam engines that drove the industrial revolution. Human imagination and creativity has now become a major dimension of formerly mechanistic production in what is becoming known as knowledge economies.

That discovery opens up the possibility of conversation between those who know him who is creator and the wisdom of the universe[15] and the children of the Silicon Valley generation, the children of those who developed the internet, DVD and iPod.

Economic Values: Human Dignity vs. Technological Dehumanization
Again in the area of economics, one could ask, to what extent Evangelicals have enabled society to respect the dignity of the human being. Jane Kelsey, in *Reclaiming the Future: New Zealand and the Global Economy* (1999), documented the effects of overly rapid commitment to the positive benefits of free trade with concomitant loss of jobs in several sectors, including 21,000 in the textiles and clothing sector, the loss of sovereignty over many of our national assets leading to increasing foreign debt and increase in inequity and insecurity.

It is apparent, in returning to New Zealand after a decade, that governments, year by year, have increased the levels of pressure on New Zealanders to produce. This has included the increase of employment, deliberate policies to force women into the workforce in order to increase productivity (Knight & Laugeson, 2005), yearly increase of the tax take, as well as the destruction of the power of the trade unions (developed to protect the poorest workers) and collective bargaining processes and the creation of an indebted student population.

The reassertion of *human dignity* against such policies, which are based on assumptions of man the machine, woman the equal machine, is crucial for the sustaining of a just and good society. While there is no evidence of Evangelicals bringing these principles into the national legislative process, the stories in Chapter 15 each contain the application into the workplace of values of *the worth, the creativity, the dignity of each individual*. However as the stories of managers, they show an emphasis by Evangelicals on three of several major, economic themes of the Scriptures: *work, production and creativity*. These are paralleled by ministries from many churches to sectors of poor in the community, including almost every church in Auckland reaching out to migrants. These represent the search to apply two other biblical principles of *equity and redistribution*.[16]

The Biblical Critique of the Consumer Society
In a context of increasing differentials between rich and poor and expansion of indebtedness via credit card, postmodern discipleship cannot be less than economic, if it is to be true to Jesus' words. For example, following Jesus' simple statement that, "the cares of the world, the delight in riches and the desire for other things enter in and choke the Word (Mark 4:19)," classic Christian discipleship has developed another princi-

---

15 Expanded in Darragh (2000:133).
16 Brian Hathaway modelled this, both in theology and practice at Te Atatu Bible Chapel (1990).

ple in its *rejection of greed*, the accumulation of wealth and consumerism. The great transition away from this standard perhaps occurred with the failure of the puritans after Calvin, to keep regimentation on "profitable industry." As Britain led the world into the new consumer and technological age, Bishop William Temple (1881-1942) (1942:29-34) indicates that the church for 150 years failed to sustain a consistent public critique of these sins. While Christian socialism and the social gospel, spoke to the issue of *redistribution of wealth*, they did not deal with the popular value systems of ordinary Christians with a call to the principles of *co-operative economics and simplicity*, without greed, in the midst of increasingly competitive systems.

This directly contrasts with earlier Calvinism, with its understanding of the *just use of resources for the common good, frugality, diligence* and their relationship to the emergence of capitalism.[17] While we are enjoying *the expansion of wealth, the abolition of poverty and the freedom* of the middle class, we pay a price in the violation of other biblical principles of *stewardship, remaining debt-free and wealth for work* (vs. creation of paper money). One of those costs is the increasing debt burden of New Zealanders. What is a Kingdom response?

- LIBERTY TRUST: A VISION OF ESCAPING ECONOMIC BONDAGE -

> One model that breaks the power of debt in New Zealand is Liberty Trust — a cooperative venture enabling people to place their money for housing into a common pool, then making no-interest loans from that pool to others, until all in the pool have received sufficient to escape bondage to bank interest. It was born in a vision received by nurse and then discussed with Bruce MacDonald, a New Life pastor, during the renewal and has operated since 1985, setting free 220 families from the banks.

A Kingdom of Dignity: Redefining Humanness

A second response of the Kingdom to postmodernity is in the redefinition of humanness. Genesis indicates that not only does the created world a reflect a good creator, so too the creature is a reflection, a mirror of his goodness. Jesus discusses the infinite worth of a person when he queries the cost of a sparrow and the size of the hairs of our heads and tells us that our Heavenly Father cares for each of us more than these details.

Initially humanity was created in all the glory of God's image. The image is replaced by a fallen and damaged image, like the grotesque shapes of the poverty-stricken faces of the slums. Yet humanness is restored to that image by the presence of his glory upon us. This comes from the transforming Holy Spirit (II Cor 3:18). This is the end goal of discipleship.

These Kingdom presuppositions are the basis of Christian engagement in the major debates of biotechnology and psychology. Two stories illustrate this:

---

17 These are summarised in *The Protestant Work Ethic and the Rise of Capitalism* (Weber, 1980).

- DNA Determinism -

> My biochemist friend argues (while we watch our sons fight it out at soccer), that based on modern project presuppositions after B. F. Skinner and Darwin, humanity is simply a result of mechanistic process which include variations because of probabilities. If so, then there is no justification for giving people a sense of moral worth and dignity. There is no defense of innocent men and women against those who would call for a higher purpose, a rabid nationalism, a role for a super-race.

- The Source Of Psychology -

> That becomes the basis of a God-conversation with a psychologist at the other end of the field — a simple query as to whether her search for understanding of personality has led to the knowledge of the person behind the creatures.

No other philosophic or religious system beyond Christianity has such a high view of man and woman, of the dignity and worth of man and woman. They are defined not as an advanced evolutionary animal, but as created (whether that be through intelligent intervention in an evolutionary process or otherwise) by God, with a peculiar God-capacity. They are not simply extensions of levels of life, but are vice-regents of the creator. A low view of man or woman results in hierarchical oppression and slavery in each of the Hindu, Islamic or Buddhist societies with which I have dealt. While it is difficult to indicate the relationship of ethical ideas and social changes accurately, Mangalwadi has demonstrated in the Indian situation (1986; 1998; 1999) that where genuine Christianity moves, the view of the dignity of man and woman results in a democratising of social systems, in the uplift of women, in the abolition of oppression and slavery.[18]

Without such a high view of humanness, there is no option for defence of the poor. Each one must look after himself, for survival of the fittest is survival of the human race. With such a high view of humanness, the affirming of the dignity of the poor and raising them from destitution becomes a source of our future and a centre of our purpose. This becomes the basis for attempts seeking to eliminate prostitution, slavery, workplace oppression, racial, sexual and political exploitation and affirm the dignity of committed marriage, democratic ideals and so on. Jesus tells us that all will know we are disciples because of our exercise of love.

Postmodern Kingdom discipleship will involve multiple social expressions of love and affirm the fullness of the anthropological dimension.

---

18 Rauschenbush makes this theme of the *Value of Human Life*, along with the *Solidarity of the Human Family* and the importance of *Standing with the People* as the cornerstones of the *Social Principles of Jesus* (1916). The alternative view of institutional or State Christianity (viz a viz genuine or primitive Christianity) reinforcing control by an elite, and social and economic oppression, is part of Marx's critique of religion, and part of the experience of colonialisation for many.

Reviving the Corpse: Revitalisation of Postmodern Humanness

New understandings in a postmodern context, of the morality of creation, are determinative also of new understandings of the created being. Humanity has always been defined by its relationship to the creation that it is commanded to husband — "from dust we came, to dust we return" (Ecc 3:20). Discipleship can never be pursued independent of its economic dimensions.

While God is our final environment, we can only know him in the spatial and temporal forms of his creation (Dyrness, 1991(83):24).

The turning away from God by unemployed workers, dispossessed Maori tribes and affluent middle class Kiwis may all be seen as related to their alienation from their environment.[19]

Creating a new cultural value system involves repeated restatement of Kingdom values of humanity with soul, identity, meaning, accountability and an eternal future beyond being part of an evolutionary biology. In Paul Tournier's phrase (1957), there needs to be a continuing public statement of the *Meaning of Persons*.

As described in the previous chapter, fundamental to the progression from collapsing modernism into postmodernism, is the anthropological redefinition, the remaking of modern technological machine person in a clockwork universe into postmodern being. Christians now have a season in which to redefine humankind beyond modernism's machine.

Some say humanity died when its soul died, when God (Western Christendom's God?) died at the birth of the modern rationalist period. Nuttall places God's death between VE night and VJ night, between the dropping of the bomb on Hiroshima that cancelled any right to morality by authorities in the Western world of Christendom and the end of the Second World War. The soul is dead! Despair remains! Or given the speeding up of technology, schizophrenia!

Values Renewal and Redefinition of Humanness

To what extent do the fruits of the New Zealand renewal accomplish redefinition of humanness? Certainly the early phases of the renewal were phases of great release of people from bondages and times of emotional and physical healings. In the creativity of new-found spiritual gifts and prophetic words as to God's future, new identities and purposeful meaning were born. These replaced the frustrations of an often non-participative and meaningless traditional religion.

However, as indicated earlier, the significant dependence on the controls of the new experts, in the migration to Pentecostalism — those gifted with powerful sign gifts and the technique of success and the subsequent church growth institutionalisation — foreshadows a decrease in meaning. Narrow bibliolatry or fanaticism, rote liturgies of popular songs and sign-generating preachers served up in the weekly shows eventually result in disenfranchised believers without meaning.

---

19 See Snyder (1997) for an integrated theology.

The failure of Pentecostalism to develop a full-orbed biblical teaching on the nature of humanness only leads to the death of being and meaning. In the failure of the movement to expand its life into culture transformation, eventually one sees the death of culture – unless the synergy of revival from other movements continues to renew. Pentecostal rejection of intellectual pursuit needs changing into an affirmation of Spirit-directed academic discipline. If not, Pentecostalism may be expected to have little long-term conversation about meaning in an increasingly meaningless, bored, suicidal city. The alternative, a more academic approach to postmodern emergent churches, is seen by some to provide an alternative model that has intellectual validity, as well as postmodern cultural relevance (Taylor, 2004; 2005a).

On the other hand, beyond modern man and woman is another dimension, postmodern cyborg. Rats with long ears and similar genetic selective breeding experiments are now common in the University of Auckland laboratories, so my professor friend tells me. Humanoids cannot be far behind. The movie predictions in *The Six Million Dollar Man* of a partially bionic man, pale. Newspapers, talkback shows and political courts are full of wrangling over lack of ethical controls on the outcomes of new possibilities of cloning and genetic engineering. Postmodern humanity is beyond pure humanity, perhaps, at least according to Fukuyama in *Our Posthuman Future* (2002).

Frankl (1978) reflects on the uniqueness of humanity, which demands that life has meaning and purpose in an age of despair. The good news of a Kingdom of new humanity, in all its biblical comprehensiveness, provides that meaning.

The redefinition of personhood must also be related to work and rest, for in the definition of the God-human axis, we are made in the image of the Worker who rested on the Sabbath. It has importance in the regaining of the meaning of "good work," to use Schumacher's phrase (1979). Without this teaching, life in an ambitious culture ceases to have meaning — except in production and consumption of goods. With this teaching, life is filled with the creativity, the artistry, the hospitality, the grandeur of the cultures of mankind. God, the worker in the creation story, becomes the worker reflected in our story.

This element of discipleship is the work of the Spirit. Volf, disciple of Moltmann in his *Work in the Spirit* (1991:113-122), suggests a pneumatological understanding of work. In the Old Testament, the Spirit inspired craftsmen and gave David the plans for the temple. In the New Testament, this entrance of the Spirit into our beings becomes the basis of co-operation in the Spirit's ongoing creative activity in the development of the earth. This gives value to non-Christian work, providing a basis for judgement as to what work is against the Spirit. Volf believes that releasing the charisms of the Spirit gives a better basis for understanding the diversity of working roles in the postmodern city context than does the classic sense of vocation in Lutheran and historic Catholic analysis.

The Kingdom of Hope and the New World Order
Discipleship also involves us in inverse politics. The Kingdom of God is here, yet not fully realised. Until it is fully realised there will exist two different Kingdoms.

One is a Kingdom of this world, symbolised through the Scriptures and in their great climax, as Babylon, a great religious-political-economic conglomerate (Rev 17-19), that has grown out of the rebellion of humanity — its nature is that of idolatory, oppression, exploitation and unrighteousness. It is, at heart, a massive world-wide market place, eventually dominated by a single lawless authority (2 Thes 2:3-12),[20] in the midst of an increasingly lawless world.

The other is a Kingdom of the Spirit…

> For the Kingdom of God is not a matter of eating and drinking but of righteousness, peace and joy in the Holy Spirit (Rom 14:17)…yet a Kingdom that profoundly transforms economics, social relationships and political issues.

Moltmann (1998) defines theology as Kingdom-of-God theology and as Kingdom of God theology it has to be public theology. Rauschenbusch, in his simple yet masterful analysis of Jesus' understanding of the Kingdom, relates it to social structure:

> The phrase, then, embodies the social ideal of the finest religious minds of a unique people. The essential thing in it, is the projection into the future of the demand for a just social order. The prophets looked to a direct miraculous act of God to realise their vision, but they were in close touch with the facts of political life and always demanded social action on the human side (Rauschenbusch, 1916: 57).

Yet he refuses to limit the Kingdom to social structure, measuring the structures against the Kingdom not vice-versa. Along with a call to fully evangelise the world and bring the peoples into the Kingdom, he poetically called the educated of his day to full involvement in aligning existing structures with the righteousness of the Kingdom:

> A collective moral ideal is a necessity for the individual and the race. Every man must have a conscious determination to help in his own place to work out a righteous social order for and with God…We must relate (our particular job) to the supreme common task at which God and all good men are working (1916:77).

While Evangelicals are too rooted in an understanding of the nature of sin to accept either Rauschenbusch's (or Moltmann's) hope-filled progressive evolutionary view of the growth of the Kingdom and its transforming of the social structures of the earth,[21] our role should not be dissimilar to that which he states — we are to live as people of hope,[22] which involves a discipling of the structures relating them to the demands of the King. We should work with all our energy to see, "Thy kingdom come! Thy will be done on earth as in heaven!" as much as is presently possible. This should not only be

---

20 See Brazilian theologian, Carriker, for exegesis of the apocalyptic in this passage (1993: 45-55).

21 Not only Evangelicals but also the leadership of the social gospel movement rejected this. H. Richard Neibuhr came to regard Rauschenbusch's moral theology as a form of culture Protestantism' that too closely identifies the Gospel with selected cultural movements and goals. 'Rauschenbusch remained captive to the liberal impulse to equate God and God's purposes to values accepted as absolute prior to revelation, such as the common good of humanity. His Social Gospel therefore tended toward an anthropocentric and utilitarian religion that values faith in God as a means to other ends, such as economic and political reform' (Ottati, 1991:xxv).

22 As I have read the interactions of evangelical thinkers actively engaged with postmodernism, I am amazed at the constant recurrence of the theme of hope, for example Jeff Fountain's *Living as a People of Hope* (2004), as he engages similar themes to this study in the European continent.

in individual lives but in the social order of our nation and globe. This is the content of preparation for the second coming, for this gospel of the Kingdom must be preached to every people, not just as simple "Four Spiritual Laws,"[23] and a sinner's prayer, but as the gospel of the King who fills all in all and is all in all.

Rauschenbusch and the liberal social gospel may be considered as one of the final attempts to rejuvenate Western Christendom. However, postmodernism has moved into multi-religious cities and multi-ethnicity. Thus such an integrative vision as the Kingdom must grapple with its association with alternative visions inside pluralistic urbanism (Mouw & Griffioen, 1993: 110-129). I suggest that the freedom and openness of the Kingdom along with themes of reconciliation and servanthood, provide the widest metanarrative for moral dialogue and affirmation of commonalities. Humanism and rationalism fade beside the grandeur and fullness of such themes and are unable at the end of debate to define common morality, for they lack the sacrificial motivation to service that is inherent in the cross.

Paul Hiebert, one of the world's leading missionary anthropologists, with years of interfacing Hindu and Christian worldviews, once commented to me that in his studies on the options for approaching pluralism, a Christian context of tolerance and freedom created a better environment for harmony than the other major religious worldviews. Madood, a Muslim scholar, also concludes that an established religion in Anglicanism in the UK is a far better option for openness to diverse ethnicity and religion than "triumphal secularism".[24]

This appears also true when considering Hindu affirmation of plurality and its pain in caste differentials or Islamic demands for submission to Islamic law or secular frameworks within which it is difficult to deal well with morality, ethics or religious values.

In general, within such a framework of Christian tolerance, clarity of our own beliefs makes dialogue easier. I conclude that the most loving option is to call the society to be faithful to the living God, while working hard to build public space for dialogue between ethnic-religious communities within a Christian framework of freedom and tolerance.

Conclusion: Hope Beyond Postmodernity's Fractures

In this chapter, I have completed the transformational conversation concerning *goals of Transforming Revival*, glimpsing the hopes of a cultural revitalisation in response to the presence of the Spirit in the city. The holistic Kingdom provides a framework for goals that will reintegrate city culture beyond the fracturing of postmodernism. In responding to the loss of the metanarratives of modernism, it provides a powerful metanarrative around which Auckland and New Zealand can be integrated, building hope, community and coherence, diffusing power and democratising social systems. Even when the King is not acknowledged, the power of its themes are such as to significantly influence the conversation in the secular public domain concerning goals. I have related it to the economic, social, political and spiritual.

---

23   A popular small tract presentation of the gospel, developed by Campus Crusade for Christ.
24   Madood (1994:53), used in discussion of the benefit of an establishment church in Ahdar (2000: 136).

Fig. 16: Kingdom Discipleship Beyond Modernism

Kingdom Integration Beyond Modernism	Postmodern Characteristics Addressed	Values and Lifestyle of Disciples In Postmodernism
I. The personality of God infusing matter	**Failure of rationalist materialism**	
›The morality of the physical environment	›Expansive exploitation of resources	›Moral care of the environment
›Relationship to the creative power of the universe	›The search for creative power	›A healing lifestyle both of sickness and for the environment
›Biblical critique of the consumer society	›Advertised greed	›Simplicity, wealth for work, redistribution, avoidance of debt
›God as Community	›Competitive economics	›Cooperative economics
›Expansive creative structuring of the universe	›Entrepreneurial postmodern mindset ›Expansion of wealth; Technological innovation	›Affirmation of entrepreneurial care of the created order, productivity and expansion of wealth
II. Redefinition Humanness	**DNA defined evolutionary humanism**	
›The dignity and worth of humanity	›Humanness may be tampered with.	›Affirmation of the creative design of God in humanity
›The defense of the poor	›Survival of the fittest.	›Abolition of oppression and slavery, care for the damaged and less able
›The regaining of civility	›The tough Kiwi image	›Deference, respect, love in public relationships
›The meaning of personhood	›Humans as modern technological machines	›Protection of life.
›Revitalisation of postmodern humanness.	›McDonaldisation and a future of creativity	›Meaning in work as cooperation with creative Spirit. Rest in God as source of creative.

From Revival to Hope

This culminates the discussion of Part 2, in its search for end goals of Transforming Revival in the postmodern city.

Some would say that this requires more, a comprehensive program, definition of details. But the goals of any city are in constant change, so that what is needed is not a one-off strategy (that is the role of the political leadership at any given moment), but *a framework for ongoing visionary conversation.*

III. An Alternative Kingdom to the New World Order	Growth of a global religious-political-economic authority	**The Kingdom of God as a movement of people separated** from greed, sexual immorality, the passion for power, resistant to governmental intrusion, etc.
>Defense of the marginalised	>Economic oppression and exploitation	>Resistance to global domination, political & economic
>Affirmation of culture and local community	>Global domination of indigenous cultures	>Affirmation of local cultures and communities
>Creation of public space for pluralistic values	>Pluralistic dissociated communities	>Creation of public space based on moral dialogue & affirmation of God-given commonalities
IV. King and Kingdom as integrating centre	*Loss of integrated authority and truth, loss of metanarrative, image as substance*	**Coherence and centrality of truth in relationship to the King** as integrator of the universe; Coherence between image and deep meaning, hope in Kingdom
>Kingdom as both present and future	>Loss of hope under increasing oppression and lawlessness under a global world order	>Hope based on a future Kingdom >Diffusion of power, Democratising of social systems
>Kingdom as community	>Alienation / fragmentation of family	>Embrace of communities of faith

Fig. 16 relates elements of the Kingdom (Chapter 8), with elements of postmodernism (Chapter 7). The third column gives an overview of a Kingdom lifestyle (discipleship) in the cultural transition of postmodernism.

What has been achieved here has been to create the theological content to enable Pentecostals and Evangelicals to engage the anthropological, economic, and political questions about where the city is going. In Chapter 14, I will outline a strategy for engagement that requires creating conversation spaces in forums, think tanks, institutes, universities, between theologians, the technique of Christian lay experts and their non-Christian counterparts. This strategy needs to move rapidly, in order that a synergy develops across multiple sectors sufficient to catalyse a cultural revitalisation. Failure to do this in New Zealand may leave the nation in an eternal time warp of the disintegration of Postmodernity, or open the door for entrance by other oppressive metanarratives.

Fig. 16 and Fig. 17 summarize these themes, some of the modern/ postmodern characteristics they converse with from previous chapters and the necessary Kingdom lifestyle needed to engage these issues. The diagram illustrates elements of postmodernism.

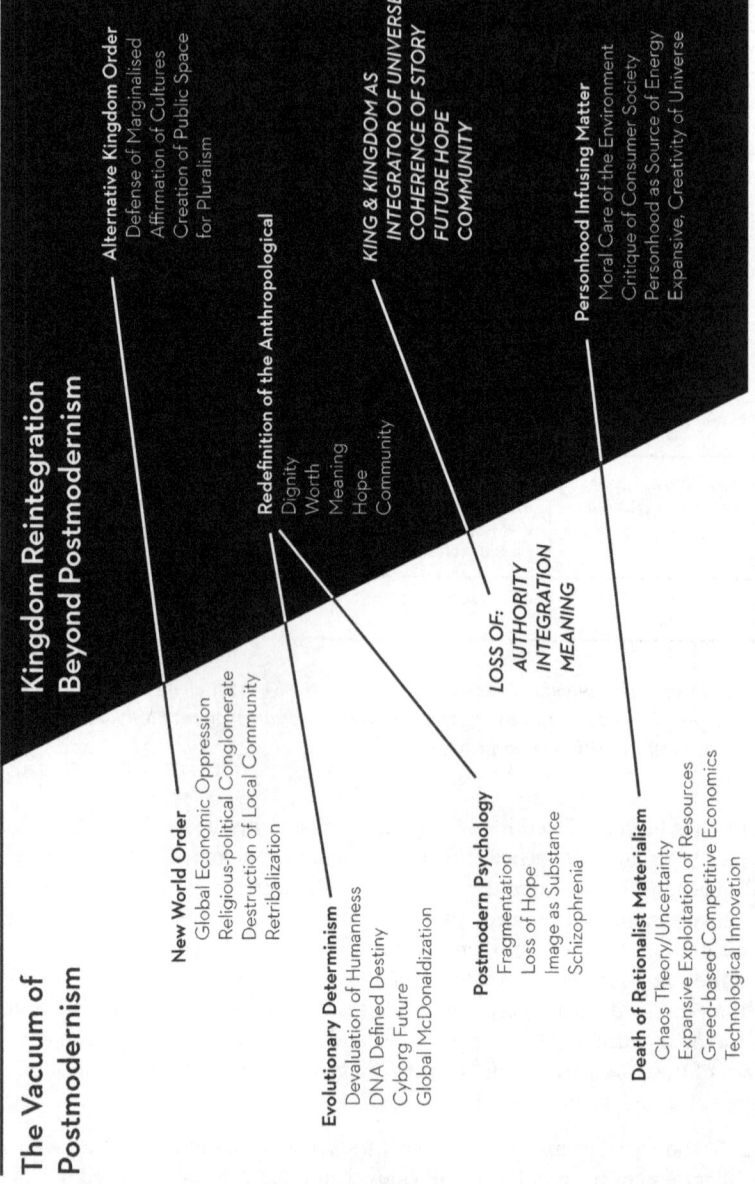

Fig. 17: Elements in the Conversation: Kingdom Integration in and Beyond Postmodernism

Fig. 17 (Following page) Shows elements of the Kingdom that create a reintegration of elements in postmodernism.

PART - THREE - PROCESSES OF CITYWIDE TRANSFORMING REVIVAL

The basis for Pentecostal social thinking and action spring from a transforming experience, an empowerment derived from an intense, transcendent sense of the divine presence

(Petersen, 1996:187).

In Part 2, conversational spaces to determine *goals of Transforming Revival* have been established. Part 3 focuses on the faith community conversation about theological and strategic *processes of Transforming Revival.*

Fig. 18: Chapters in Part 3 - Faith Community Conversation On Transforming Revival

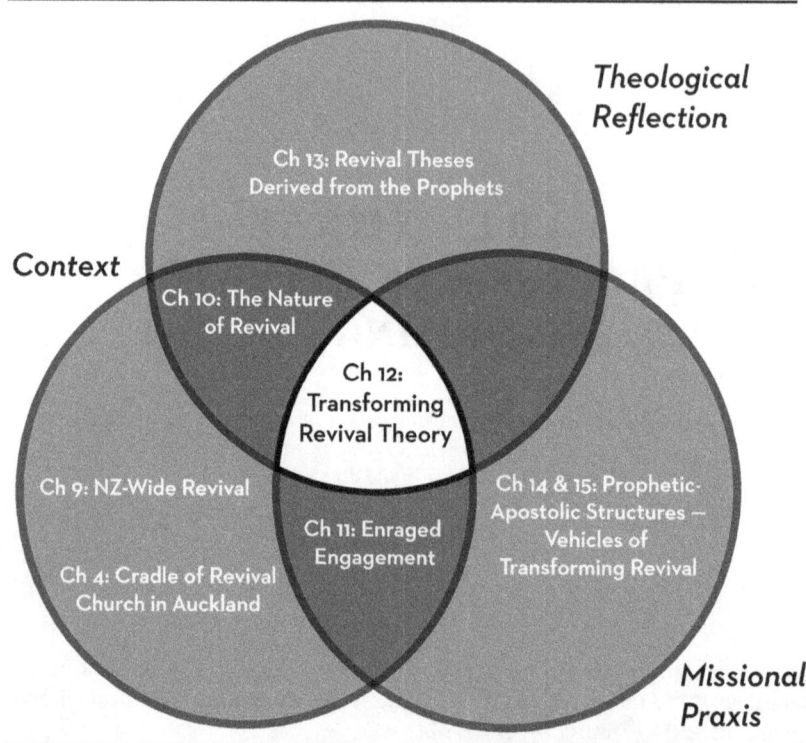

*Fig. 18: The pneumatological conversation (Step 2 of the research model), involves **Context**: Chapter 4 examined the church in Auckland as the cradle of revival. Chapters 9 and 11 examine NZ wide revival and engagement. **Theology**: Chapter 10 develops the theme of revival. **Integration**: Chapter 12 integrates these reflections into a theory of transforming revival. **Theology**: Chapter 13 expands prophetic elements of revival. **Missional Praxis**: Apostolic engagement is examined in Chapter 14 and 15.*

- 9 -

TIDES OF NATIONAL REVIVAL

"Will you not revive us again, that your people may rejoice in you"?

(Psa 85:6)

In continuing to anchor this study in the Auckland context, I will regard the wider charismatic renewal in New Zealand from 1965-1989 as a revival. In this chapter, I will test this now,[1] by examining its rise and fall against existing revival theory. Discussion follows about the capacity of the revival to progress into a subsequent phase of Transforming Revival. Based on this, I develop a theory of four phases of revival. Throughout, I identify thirteen revival principles.

My intent is to tell a simple story based on personal involvement in the revival, as the basis for reviewing missional theology rather than give a detailed history. My involvement ranges from the years 1981 to 1989, living for part of that time with Bob and Prue Wakelin, who were running Inspirational Tapes and recorded most of the major conferences in the development of the revival, and Geoff and Gayle Stevens, who exercised a prophetic role to many newly formed communities. I visited around 50 charismatic churches and communities each year I was in New Zealand, ranging from charismatic Anglican and Methodist churches to new Pentecostal ones and small fledgling communities.

---

1 Many would not call it revival. Wyn Fountain writes in Salt Shaker Letter, #47, February 2005, "In 1934 Edwin Orr came to N.Z. and he taught us to sing, "Revival is coming from North Cape to Bluff." It didn't come. Then Billy Graham came and we thought maybe this is the time. It wasn't. Along comes the charismatic renewal. We didn't call it revival, but we hoped that maybe this was going to bring just that. It didn't… Revival still evades us…Instead of revival our society has been sliding down a slippery slope of unrighteousness and social corruption. We've prayed, but prayer is not enough."

Progression into Revival

Renewal began in the early 1960's (Steel, 2003:125) as a small stream that became a river of nation-wide revival. It was preceded by a period *of brokenness and prayer*, of common believers searching for God beyond the traditions. This led to *an encounter with God* for many who are now the country's spiritual leaders. It resulted in *new patterns of worship* and the *exercise of spiritual gifts*.

George Bryant describes the sense of spiritual decline in the 1970's and 1980's:

> As the number of Christians in the mainline denominations reaches their lowest ebb ever, as the population turns in droves to atheism and agnosticism... Between 1976 and 1981 census membership of the four mainline New Zealand churches — Anglican, Roman Catholic, Presbyterian and Methodist — dropped by a massive 190,496 or 8.9%.... Mix up the philosophies of liberalism, humanism, secularism and modernism with that of materialism and you have a built in recipe for decay in Christ's church on earth (1986:3,7,9).

Into this barrenness, the testimony of new experiences of the charismatic renewal found fertile ground among lay people. The possible renewal of churches, viewed by progressive church leaders as a way to success, allowed for tacit or active assent.[2]

- THE SEARCH FOR THE SPIRIT -
H. W. Annan speaks of his experience at the early Palmerston North epicentre:

> I was immersed in the outpouring of the Holy Spirit in 1959 at Palmerston North — an experience that was to lift my vision and increase my expectation of what God wanted to do in our nation...
>
> The 60's decade was a decade of discovery... An insatiable appetite dawned upon groups of young people especially, to seek God in ways that were not taught; unstructured spontaneous prayer times, calling out to God expecting response, lying on the floor and sometimes banging on the floor with hands, weeping and praying. This hunger led to a search for answers and for books where answers may be found...
> Denominational boundaries were crossed in the search for 'enduement from on high'. The desire for evangelism surpassed the tradition of denominational loyalty. Informal gatherings in homes increased to fellowship around the quest for answers. At first the ones and two's were filled with the Holy Spirit followed by larger numbers until there was an obvious move under way. Frequently interdenominational meetings were springing up and the desire for church unity became the 'in' word.

A prophet, Arthur Wallis, travelled the land, calling for revival (Knowles, 2000:146), initiating a conference in August 1964 in Palmerston North along with Milton Smith and British revivalist Campbell McAlpine (Steel, 2003: 137). This influenced many, particularly in the Brethren movement. Orama, a renewal centre on Great Barrier Island, developed by Neville Winger, who had been reaching out to drug addicts, became a centre for teaching and encounters with the "power of God". David du Plessis (world

---

2 Davidson (1991) gives a historian's view of early progressions; Battley (1986), gives an insider's view. Knowles (2000:143-151) reflects historically as a Pentecostal on the contribution of Pentecostalism to the charismatic movement. These only cover the firsttwo decades of the revival.

leader in connecting Pentecostal, Catholic and ecumenical streams) spoke in 1964, at the first "Massey" charismatic conference. These were developed by the Anglican *Christian Advance Ministries* as yearly Summer Schools which were attended by up to 800 leaders (mainly Anglican, yet ecumenical) in Palmerston North from 1973 (Battley, 1986:49). Dennis Bennett, a leader in charismatic experience in the USA (1966); Rev Michael Harper, a respected Anglican expositor; and others, were brought in to Anglican circles, laying a solid biblical and experiential foundation for the work of the Holy Spirit and doctrine of the Baptism of the Spirit. Bob Wakelin developed Inspirational Tapes, a vehicle for distributing the teaching of many visiting charismatic teachers, such as Derek Prince. In Auckland, the ministry of Anglican evangelist Bill Subritsky and Doug Maskill resulted in thousands becoming Christians (Francis, 1993: 73-80).

- EARLY PUBLIC EXPRESSION OF REVIVAL -

> In 1969, a large march of Christians occurred along Queen St. in Auckland, with the Maori prophet-evangelist, Muri Thomson, in the forefront. It was a sign of a new generation of youth rejecting the marginalisation of classic Christianity.

All of these created *new theological paradigms* which were limited to certain issues. But those issues were significant shifts in thinking that opened up whole new fields of understanding. I can identify three aspects of significance: emphasis on the work of the Holy Spirit and her gifts; a shared theology of confessional groups and spiritual leadership based on the evidence of the power of the Spirit.

The next level of expansion was the *development of small confessional groups.* House groups and prayer groups (some would call them cells) developed. From 1971 to 1979, the *Life in the Spirit* seminars gave small group structure to the expansion of the movement. Deep relationships and spiritual ministry to personal needs occurred becoming the basis for new economic relationships, sharing of possessions and formation of communities.

As I travelled by motorbike from church to church in the 1980's, I realised that another dynamic was occurring, a *structural transformation of leadership roles* in some churches. Among Baptists, "spiritually dead" deacons' courts and elderships became transformed as elders began to be elected because of functioning spiritual giftings. House group leadership continued to provide an environment for developing leadership and the potential missionaries I was looking for.

My estimate at the time was that around four to six years after renewal began in a church, these emergent leaders found ways to outwork their spiritual fervour in new *socio-economic relationships and apostolic structures.* Hundreds volunteered for missions. 800 attended a week long Youth Missions Fest. One year, 700 signed up for *YWAM* Discipleship Training Schools. *Servants to Asia's Urban Poor,* one of the few Kiwi-born missions was birthed. All the Bible Schools were filled. The number of Bible Schools doubled to 60 (Allis, 1995).

This generated renewal of church structures within denominations and some *structural reformation of denominations* (excluding the theological training (Davidson, 1991:172)).

More than 100 committed communities formed, many from ex-Brethren fellowships in the 1970's and 1980's.[3] Milton Smith gathered leaders of these exiled communities in 1977 into a series of symposiums and conferences (Steel, 2003:141). The Anglicans and Catholics have always proved capable of enfolding new movements and the Anglicans appointed leadership to the Renewal Ministries. But despite nearly 100 Auckland clergy experiencing "the baptism of the Holy Spirit" and speaking in tongues between 1973 to 1976 under the ministry of Bill Subritszky, "the leadership of the church was not favourable" (Francis, 1993:194). Consequently the majority of parishes did not back the renewal. Presbyterians were largely trapped by their theological commitment to structural forms and existing patterns of theological training, so renewal did not result in structural reform, but contributed to the increasing polarisation between liberal and evangelical wings.[4]

Among the Baptists, renewal (affecting 25% of Baptist pastors by as early as 1975 (Brown, 1985:108)), resulted in effective local church reformation of leadership structures based on spiritual giftings and then in denominational reformation. It eventually enabled the denomination to reject the leadership of a small liberal minority and sustain a commitment to evangelical values and to growth. Increasingly pastors moved into pastoral roles through church-planting experience. The mindset of such pioneers is apostolic rather than academic. The growth of churches under such leaders forced them into prominence, with Murray Robertson recognised as having earned leadership through effectiveness in church growth, while the majority of academic trainees from the Theological College had left the pastoral ministry within a few years (though most remain active in lay, or parachurch roles).[5]

A process of *migration to institutional Pentecostalism from the charismatic movement* began. Elaine Bolitho identifies a flow of people from mainline through Baptist to Pentecostal structures (1992:114), though neither she nor I can accurately date nor measure the extent of this.[6] Fig 19 can be interpreted on this basis.

The Pentecostals' new fellowships and training schools recruited many enthusiastic leaders lacking opportunity for their gifts in other denominations with more static (rural) leadership models. Worsfold (1974:127-166) had demonstrated the necessity after the revival of the Smith Wigglesworth Crusade in the New Zealand

---

3   The Brethren (one of the major evangelistic movements of the early part of the century and major source of leaders for interdenominational evangelistic movements), consistently rejected phenomenology related to gifts of the Spirit, forcing many out of their fellowships in order to sustain this stance. These exiles carried with them the genius of this grassroots movement at establishing new fellowships, which later attached to Pentecostal (particularly New Life) or Baptist denominations.

4   From discussion with evangelical Presbyterian leaders.

5   This comment is based on personal discussion with a denominational leader as to the present roles of graduates of the Baptist College classes of the 1970's - 1980's.

6   Kevin Ward (2001: 2), documents two growing churches with 33% and 38% transfer from mainline churches. It would be unwise to generalize from his figures, beyond saying that in general the transfer is significant. Knowles discusses some of the factors and particularly a sectarian, "come out" of the "old wineskins" mentality of the New Life churches, towards mainline charismatics (2000:104-5).

context of the 1920's, of creating cell and authority structures to harvest the fruits of renewal. After a period of freedom, the renewal of that period became formed Elim and AOG denominations.[7]

Negative critiques of Pentecostalism grow from the pain of mainline pastors from whom sheep have departed. These represent a great weakening of mainline churches, a great loss of leadership. Faced with old doctrines and structures that had been found wanting, yet a new-found spirituality among their people and new patterns of small group leadership, the nature of pastoral leadership had to change rapidly to survive.

I suggest that the end of the renewal was 1989 (not that the Spirit stopped working in isolated outbreaks of revival, but that the nation-wide movement halted). When the renewal became denominationalised (Davidson and Battey identify 1989 (1991:171)[8]), then it stumbled. Rather than being a "church across the churches" (*ecclesia inter ecclesiae*) it once again became pastorally controlled. We are too close to that date to state this categorically. Fig 20 indicates the same.

FIG. 19: BAPTIST NATIONAL ANNUAL BAPTISMS AND MEMBERSHIP

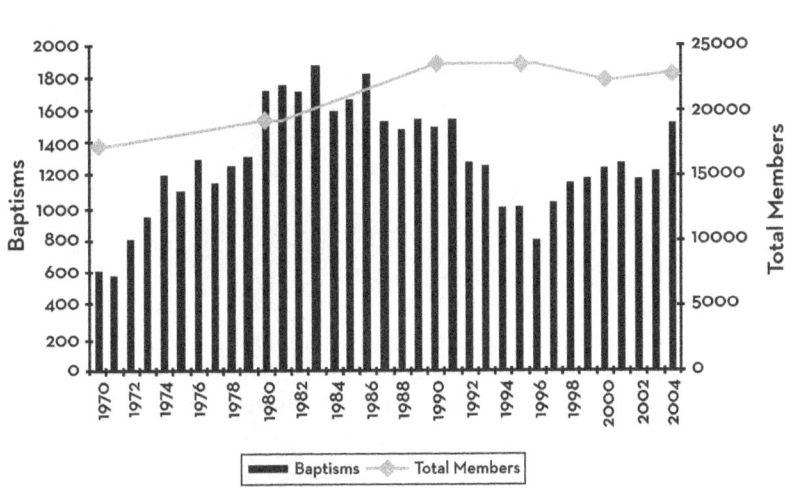

---

7   At a global level, Wagner (1998:29), Schaller (1995:17, 53), and Neighbour (1988), all with decades of global ministry in renewal of denominational churches, have concluded that the establishing of new structures ('new wineskins' (1991)), is critical if growth of the church is to occur.

8   Wyn Fountain, a leader in the development of *Life in the Spirit Seminars* in personal conversation, indicated this as one turning point away from growth of the movement. On the other hand, Peter Robertson, with a roving prophetic ministry, has indicated in conversation, an extended season of growth through to 1996 derived from the intrusion of elements of the Toronto blessing (an outbreak of revival in Toronto descended from the Vineyard movement) into the New Zealand scene.

Fig. 19 [9] shows the increase of baptisms in Baptist churches during the revival (1970-1991), decreasing from 1992 to 1996 (because of the loss of revival or migration to Pentecostalism?). The subsequent increase indicates post-revival consolidation, more effective theological training and new structural developments post-revival (or does it show a reversion from Pentecostalism?). The fruit of revival peaked in membership, again with a (7 year?) time lag. Membership has become less significant for a generation that does not commit easily to institutions, but does reflect baptismal and attendance growth with a 5-8 year time lag.

The phases identified in this story have included the following elements, which I have identified at four phases of expansion:

Phase 1: Personal Renewal
1. **Human Precondition**:
searching, prayer, brokenness and repentance.
2. **Divine Presence**:
outpouring of the Spirit in power and cleansing.
3. **Personal Renewal**
4. **New Theological Paradigms**

Phase 2: Small Group Renewal
5. **Small Confessional Groups**
6. **New Socio-Economic Relationships**

Phase 3: Structural Renewal
7. **Structural Renewal** of church leadership roles
8. **Structural Reformation** of denominations
9. **Migration** to institutional Pentecostalism from the revival movement

Phase 4: Cultural Engagement
10. **Initial Engagement** in social issues

Principles in the Rise of the New Zealand Revival

To analyse the rise and decline of this revival, I will correlate some of the principles in the schemata above with global principles of revival that I have developed over the years (based on the literature and recent research, but drawing largely on Pierson and Snyder). The next chapter integrates these into a more comprehensive theory.

Human Preconditions: Prayer, Confession, Brokenness

All the theological literature and much of the historical analysis of revivals points to a sense of desperation, as seen earlier in Annan's comments. Wallis has adequately justified this from Scriptures (1956: 99-137). I also identified above the expansion of confessional groups in this revival. There is a linkage between the outpouring of the Spirit, and theology and practice of public confession (Hessian, c1960).

Confessional groups sprang up everywhere. Prayer groups, house groups and cell groups were integral in this New Zealand charismatic renewal and they normally broke denominational barriers. This parallels a diversity of small group structures that

---

9   Source, NZ Baptist annual statistics, Lynne Taylor and Lindsay Jones.

Fig. 20: Expanding Phases in the New Zealand Revival

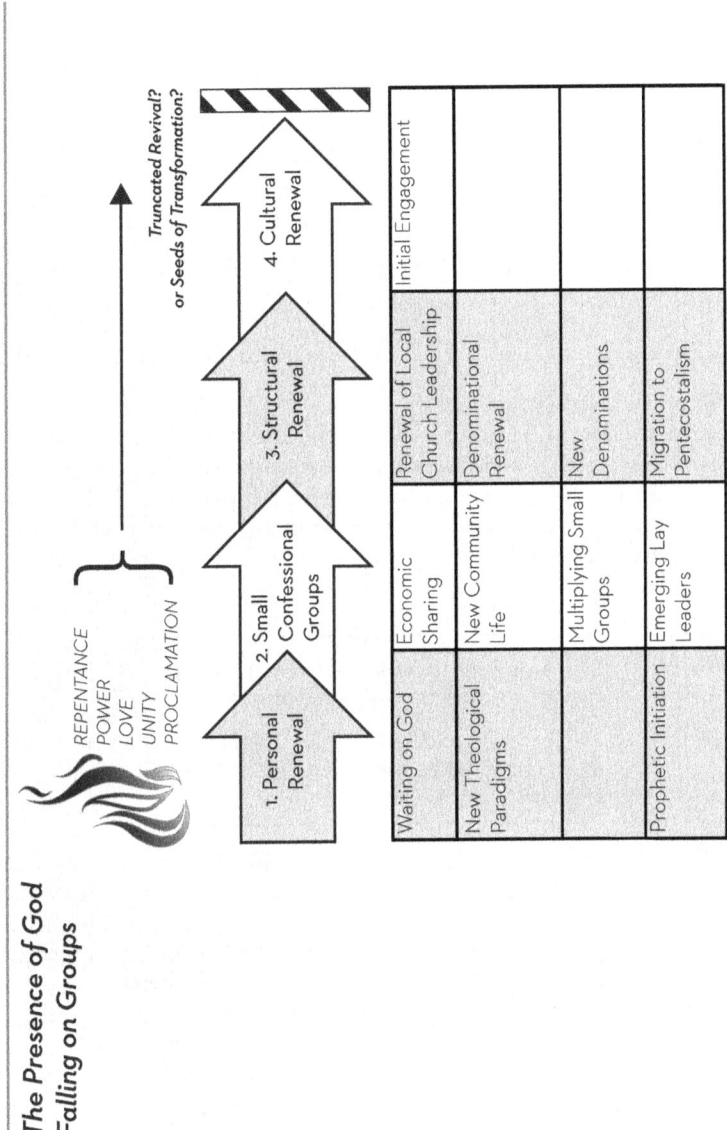

Fig. 20 shows four expanding phases and some principles that occur at each phase, demonstrated in the New Zealand revival. It also shows the truncation of the revival.

have been identified in different revivals, for example Wesley's bands as discipleship groups (see Snyder, 1989/1997: 222-230), team ministries in the Indonesian and Timor revivals (Koch, 1970), small groups in Presbyterian revival in Ghana (Dadzaa, 1993), or cell group structures sustaining revival in other nations (Neighbour, 1995: 20-37). The biblical basis is found in the "eating house to house" dynamics in Acts 2 and 4. To summarize:

Principle 1 –	Human Precondition: Revivals are preceded by a sense of spiritual desperation, repentance and prayer.
Principle 2 –	Confession: A commonly shared folk theology of confession and brokenness is foundational to revival.
Principle 3 –	Small Groups: Revival multiplies through confessional small group structures (Tanner, c1995:220).[10]

Leadership Renewal: Lay Training

The creation of a layer of cell group leaders in churches received impetus from within the renewal. Beyond cell group leadership, some leadership training infrastructures for lay leaders developed, largely among Pentecostals rather than the mainline denominations, apart from the Anglican-led *Life in the Spirit* seminars, then tightly franchised *Alpha* programs.[11] These congregational leadership training processes illustrate two missiological principles:

Principle 4 –	Lay Leadership: Revival is sustained in contexts where new training structures for lay leadership can be developed.
Principle 5 –	Lay Leadership and Small Groups: The small group is the initial context for the release of lay leadership (Snyder, 1989/1997:230, 252-258).

Beyond the early revival phases, and at a higher level, the changes to the Education Act of 1989 and the creation of the New Zealand Qualifications Authority (NZQA) allowed pathways for accelerated development of training schools that had been birthed during these years, such as Faith Bible College in Tauranga, or New Covenant International Bible College in Auckland. After two decades where the only recognized New Zealand-based theological qualifications for Evangelicals had been bachelors degrees from the Bible College of New Zealand or Carey Baptist College, or degrees at either St Johns, or University of Otago (where liberal theology was the norm), suddenly there was a possibility of recognised academic courses and eventually masters degrees. A theological sector within NZQA was developed with significant involvement from within the Pentecostal sector and from the Bible College of New Zealand.

---

10 This is one of the hallmarks of the ongoing East African revival, identified by Hessian in a major contribution to revival theory.

11 The Alpha Programs are a series of small group evenings utilising an apologetic video series that leads people through the gospel and encounter with the Holy Spirit.

The majority of new Bible Schools created during the renewal were Pentecostal. Bruce Patrick (home director for the Baptists) and Marjory Gibson, however, created a churchplanters' training school (which was after a few years reintegrated with the Baptist College in order to "consolidate resources"). Though improving quality of existing institutions, Presbyterians and Anglicans created no significant new training structures.

These leadership structures have implications for transformation. *New Covenant Bible College*, one of the leading Pentecostal Bible Colleges for some years, recently developed several courses on issues related to social change and others related to cross-cultural bridge-building. *Upper Hutt Christian Fellowship*, a significant centre of post-charismatic Pentecostalism has developed an NZQA recognised course from Dennis Peacock's material on social analysis. *The Bible College of New Zealand* has also broadened its theological training to cover many aspects of social issues. One of their courses deals with Workplace Theology. This is the fruit of reflection for years by Alistair McKenzie (http://www.faithatwork.org.nz/) in Christchurch. Martien Kelderman in Auckland took similar processes into local churches. Derek Christiansen has been developing similar themes at *Carey Baptist College*.

Theological Renewal Releases Energy
Each of the four phases requires new clusters of ideas in their development. Kuhn's concept of "paradigm shifts" has become popular terminology, indicating ideas that open up whole new fields of knowledge. Snyder comments, "Church history shows that conceptual renewal has often been at the heart of revival movements" (1989/1997:289).

Burns discusses the return to simplicity of doctrine, particularly the doctrine of the cross as central in all revivals, cutting through overlays (1909/1960:45). This is dramatically confirmed by study of the sustained East African Revival (Hessian, c1960). Pierson adds the theme of authority in spiritual conflict (1985:3). These appear to be critical factors in the personal renewal phase.

In Phase 2, as mentioned, theologies of gifts of the Spirit, lay leadership and small groups (part of a global emphasis in the 1970's), accomplished this return to the simplicity of the cross in the New Zealand charismatic renewal. These small groups affirmed the cross, as people confessed sin to each other and prayed for each other's healing.

- SMALL GROUP HEALING -

> I recall a period when a pneumatic drill operator and his wife were praying with me in a group. They did not know me, but week by week, the Lord would reveal issues in my spirit to the pneumatic drill operator, an unlettered man with a big heart. "What is that dagger in your back?" was the first query and I knew all the pain of a recent betrayal and felt the healing love of God enter into that void. Over eight weeks, step by step, each "word from God" brought healing to deeper levels of spirit or body, till a decade old sickness was completely healed, my spirit was alive with his presence and I could walk back into the pain of missionary advance.

New paradigms of leadership and institutional models were needed in phase 3. This was difficult within the mainline churches, with theological rationales for older traditions of leadership. New lay leaders became frustrated and after a few years would often give up. Consequently, I identify a third wave of theological change sustaining the revival for a few years as charismatic renewal began to wane. In the migration of renewed believers from renewed churches to institutional Pentecostalism, processes of learning new Pentecostal leadership styles and church growth theologies released new energies. This confirms the previously mentioned turning towards simplicity — in this case a turning towards simplicity of church structure, leadership and theology.

This study proposes that a theological breakthrough is now needed to sustain momentum into phase 4 and the full purposes of revival, that of a social vision of the city of God and Kingdom of God[12] being fully manifest in the human city. It must be simple, hence the focus on these two themes. It must involve the cross, in this case a progression from private to public repentance.[13] In summary:

> Principle 6 –   *Theological Renewal: Revival requires theological change at each phase that releases new energy* (Lovelace, 1979: 381-383; Pierson, 1998: 3a; Snyder, 1989/1997: 289).

Pierson adds a strategic element to this principle of conceptual renewal:

> Principle 7 –   *Information Flow: Central co-ordination of information flow is critical in sustaining revival movements* (1998:3a).[14]

This is evidenced in the way pastoral leadership of churches in renewal was well networked through yearly Charismatic Renewal Conferences at Massey, preparing them to bless the lay movements infiltrating their churches.

- SMALL GROUP MULTIPLICATION -

> Expansion came notably with the *Life in the Spirit* seminars that drove the flow of ideas and dynamic networking. This is being repeated now with *Alpha* courses, following a similar but evangelistic model of small groups, having involved 50,000 people by the year 2000.[15]

---

12 Similar proposals have been surfacing across the globe among Evangelicals since the mid 1990's, for example Peterson's proposal of the Kingdom as foundational for a "Social Doctrine for Pentecostals in Latin America" (1996: 209-222).

13 Yet even in proposing this, I wonder if the costliness of the way of the cross is sufficiently strong to generate another wave of revival.

14 A corollary of this, is the challenge underlying this study, of developing a transformation network. Unless it can integrate a central cadre with funded base structure, from whom information on new transformational theology flows, it will not develop a movement dynamic.

15 Figure from Fr. Ray Muller, NZ director of Alpha.

Such information flow[16] implies resources for a co-ordinating office, conferencing and publications, leading to pragmatic factors in a theory of sustainable revival.

Movement Dynamics: Revival from the Edges and Institutionalism

Anthropologist A.F.C. Wallace, in a highly recognised study, *Revitalization Movements: Some Theoretical Considerations for Their Comparative Study* (1956) speaks of five stages in revitalisation of culture from steady state to a period of individual stress and then cultural distortion, followed by a period of revitalisation and a new steady state. Pierson's historical missiology identifies the epicentre of such change:

> Principle 8 –   *Diffused Sources: Renewal does not emanate from ecclesiastical centres but from the pioneering edges* (Pierson, 1998:3a).

Again, this was evident in the centrality of the *Life in the Spirit* seminars, the visiting prophets, the Massey conferences, the welcoming of ministry by Pentecostal leaders, the small groups. These things did not come from Bishops' conferences.[17]

The movement also displayed all five dynamics described by Gerlach and Hine's study on movements (1970:xvii):

> Principle 9 –   *Cellular Structure: A revival movement will have five structural characteristics: face-to-face recruiting, personal commitment, multi-cellular small-group structures, an ideology which codifies values and goals, opposition by existing power structures.*

These were evident in the wave of charismatic renewal of the 1970's, but my observation is that they are no longer significantly apparent in charismatic movements in mainline churches. A case can be made for their consistent presence in Pentecostal church structure. The opposition indicated in the last point was intense in the early days of the movement, but became a dull rumble as the movement gained in popularity. In contrast, Pentecostals still find themselves in conflict with older ecclesiastical power centres.

While revival starts on the edges, sustaining it requires institutional support. The sustaining of the charismatic renewal is largely attributed to institutional support within the Christian Advance Ministries in the Anglican communion and particularly in the early years to support from Pentecostal leadership in New Zealand (Knowles, 2000:172). Baptists, for some time, sought this route, appointing some charismatic home mission directors and regional superintendents. However, in the end, the non-directive denominational decision-making processes resulted in collective non-affirmation. Charismatic renewal does not even feature in the executive secretary's ten-year denominational report in 2000 (Brown, 2000). Home mission leaders are now consultants reviewing

---

16 Montgomery develops theoretical constructs that can be applied to information flow and mission, in his analysis of Diffusion Theory and Missions (1999:29-44).

17 Principle 8 can be derived by extension of Principles 61-68 of Fink and Stark on Professional Ecclesiastics (Stark & Finke, 2000: 283).

structural health of churches. On the other hand, some of these are men come from the renewal and these new consultant processes include issues of renewal in the Spirit.

> Principle 10 –   Institutional Support: Expansion and consummation of revival requires structural and theological support by denominational leadership.

Entropy: Decline and Failure to Develop Transforming Revival

The above contrast of the New Zealand charismatic renewal with revival theses may have been sufficient to indicate the validity of presuming the New Zealand revival as a genuine work of the Holy Spirit. I will now identify factors that eventually betrayed the heart of the renewal, moving it into an entropic state. These may also have killed the possibility of it becoming a Transforming Revival. The factors do not however, negate the early phases of growth of the renewal as a work of the Spirit.

The Periodicity of Revival

Revival literature struggles with issues of timing and extent (I will deal with this more thoroughly in the next chapter).

> Principle 11 –   Periodicity: Revivals have a built in time limit and periodicity.

Burns (1909/1960), defining the laws of revival, identifies periodicity as a factor: "Every revival has a time limit... The constant factor, is that whatever the size of the wave, it has its limits marked out for it." Thus, on the one hand, the decline of a nation-wide, interdenominational renewal was to be expected. On the other hand, causes of decline can be examined. Violation of any one of a number of revival principles can cause the death of a revival. Orr, interprets the death of the Welsh revival as largely resulting from its genius, the lack of organisation by its leadership (Joyner, 1993:17). The Maori revival of last century was largely halted by the taking of Maori land and Maori Wars (Tippett, 1971:64-68). Historians, with their skills, may evaluate these violations more accurately for this New Zealand revival, but among them, I suggest the following:

Loss of the Prayer Movements

Beginning with the united prayer of Acts 2 and Acts 4, revival literature confirms the pre-existence of prayer movements. It would be difficult to cite any book on revival that did not begin with this presupposition. While revivals are the sovereign acts of the grace of God, they also appear to be in response to the pleas of his children. Tanner identifies both a sense of crisis and the intercessory stage, as prerequisites (c1995:215-6). Both have been demonstrated above for the early charismatic movement of the 1960's and 1970's. With the cessation of the Massey conferences and loss of information flows by 1989, the prayer movements dissipated, despite the ongoing communications from Brian Caughley and *Intercessors for New Zealand*. This violated a universal principle which I will summarize as:

Principle 12 –   Hungry Prayer: Revivals begin and expand in prayer movements representing a hunger for God.

- COLLECTIVE PRAYER — PREDICTOR OF SOCIAL ACTIVISM -

By 1996, attempts to encourage city-wide prayer meetings in Auckland, met with insignificant responses. After the collapse around 1989, of the revival dynamic and then the prayer movements generated in the renewal, there was no apparent sense of need for prayer across the city and little linkage between existing prayer groups.

After several attempts, by the end of 2000, John Fulford, a denominational leader of the Church of Christ, was able to link an infrastructure of prayer leaders and city-wide prayer events. It included all night prayer meetings, 24 hour prayer vigils involving multiple churches, prayer summits,[18] and a March for Jesus as an act of public prayer, but lacked any wave of enthusiasm.

Discussions with Colin Shaw, a prayer summit leader from Australia, after he had travelled the country in 2004, confirmed there was little *hunger* for prayer.

Structural Issues: Loss of Small Confessional Groups
I have already identified the confessional group dynamic as essential to maintaining revival. My observation (not easily verified) is that the emphasis in the renewal moved from the confessional, healing, small group to the frontal, anointed pastor. More directive Pentecostal leadership styles replaced the grassroots, charismatic Spirit-led movement. Pentecostal pastoral enthusiasm for the rightness of their beliefs and sense of being anointed by God, plus the more directional leadership styles imported from US sources by many of these groups, added to general ignorance of what had been happening culturally in terms of diffusion of leadership under the Spirit in the indigenous renewal. Confession is not highly valued by performance-focussed pastors.

By the late 1990's, a general decline of small groups was apparent,[19] certainly in the mainline churches — perhaps due to these cultural styles of leadership, perhaps due to increasing economic stress on couples, most likely due to the loss of information flow and training from a central revival cadre. This was despite some nation-wide attempts to develop cell-group structures under strong pastors, some linked to the global cell-group movement of Ralph Neighbour, Nev Chamberlain and Ben Wong.[20] In contrast, the larger charismatic and Pentecostal churches still maintain significant cell group

---

18 Prayer summits developed in revival contexts in the Seattle region in the US. Groups of pastors or leaders go away for some days with no agenda but to wait on God. Confession of sin and healing of disunity occurs.

19 A statement that needs examination of numbers of groups during these years in various denominations and churches. Baptists have been keeping records in the last few years which could be analysed.

20 Ralph Neighbour developed materials (1988; 1995: http://www.ccmnglobal.com/) on cell-group based church development in the hierarchical and responsive Southern US. In non-hierarchical and somewhat unresponsive Kiwi contexts, his methodology has not been so fruitful.

structures that provide pastoral care for about 30%[21] of their membership and contexts for leadership development. While these are encouraged to focus on evangelism after the model of Ralph Neighbour, my observation is that the generally unresponsive context of Pakeha culture, renders them more pastoral in style.[22]

Leadership Issues: Loss of the Cell Group Leadership
Many lay leaders who emerged in renewed mainline churches found, after periods in church leadership teams, that the theologically-trained pastors (viz-a-viz pastors trained in group and movement dynamics) often could not lead them. This appears to be largely because of the 400 year old process of formally appointing or electing pastors based on a tradition of academic training (in largely liberal European theologies). The style of leadership, understanding of pastoral roles and thinking, contrasted with how lay people were now emerging into leadership through demonstrated spiritual gifting and its fruit as they led cell groups. The need for cell-group level training processes for Kiwi contexts was acute.

This reflects the nature of Kiwi society. Whereas Americans think of franchising both business and spirituality, Kiwis both lack the resources and the population base to do this well, so tend to depend on marketable religious products from the US or, as with the Alpha course, from the UK. US approaches did not fit culturally, such as Ralph Neighbour's cell group model, so were generally unsustainable. The Alpha course had a better cultural fit, plus a marketing niche within Anglicanism.

Many lay leaders moved to Pentecostal churches, whose pastoral emergence processes depend on fruitfulness not academic ability. This was perhaps wise, as Jesus states that new wine needs new wine skins (Snyder, 1996b). This often provided a learning context for several more years before new difficulties appeared, often related to serving under spiritually gifted pastors but usually with minimal theological and professional pastoral training. These elements plus directive leadership styles would often cause a second round of disillusionment.

There are perhaps several thousand such lay leaders now living outside the church in Auckland, either hurt, disappointed, or seeking to follow the Lord through independent small house group models (Jamieson, 2000). My observation is that they generally failed to sustain spirituality through the blessings and trials of marriage, pressures of work demands or failure, though some have been sustained for many years. Even interlinked small groups do not allow for the full operation of the fivefold leadership gifts of Ephesians 4. Structured movements are required.[23]

---

21 Figure derived from questioning of leaders as I travel. Generally it is around 30%. One church indicated 85% in cells, but checking this out showed less than 50%. The CLS survey results of 1997 showed 33% Baptist, 36% Brethren down to 14% Methodist in small prayer/study groups (Brookes & Curnow, 1998: A-6). My observation is that higher figures appear to be related to more evangelical doctrinal stance of congregations.

22 This may be one factor explaining Kevin Ward's figure of only 3.9% conversions from non-churched contexts at one of the "models" of New Zealand church growth, Spreydon Baptist, which has utilised small groups extensively over the years.

23 These are reflections based on my analyses of committed communities of the early Irish monks and the preaching friars, when I was first forming apostolic orders among the poor (Grigg, 1986).

- Cell Groups At The Edges Of Revival -

> I encountered one example of a successful group however, as I was waiting for my son's moment of fame at the school cross-country. We discussed my friend's 20 year pilgrimage from involvement in a large charismatic church, to his enjoyment for some years of meeting every Friday with a small group of several couples. "We minister in seminars to churches so we don't lack connection to the wider body of Christ. But, we are able live out real Christianity in the small group without all the politics of church thrown in. This is real. We deal with heart issues."

At higher leadership levels, the expansion of Bible schools moved to a consolidation phase, reducing them from a peak of sixty-two to eventually forty-two providers as of 1999, while numbers of theological students continued to climb dramatically from 2,644 heads in 1988 to 5,230 in 1999 (Knox, 2004:76-77). This reflects both the desire for personal growth and educational expansion in general, including foreign student growth, but also expanding pastoral and leadership training, largely outside of the denominational training schools.

Theological Issues: Decrease of Spirituality
The lack of major breakthroughs into consistent patterns of small group leadership training in New Zealand charismatic churches results in failure to pastor individuals in lifestyles of holiness. This has natural corollaries — loss of committed spirituality among charismatics, deadness in worship, and drifting off of the sheep.

It is also helpful to note the fundamentalist critique that charismatic theology of spiritual experiences initiates a never-ending search for the ultimate spiritual experience, which never occurs. The conflict between the monthly ups and downs of life — success and failure, sickness and health, poverty and affluence — and often a positive theology that is close to absolute in its belief that God brings prosperity, health, magnificent displays of the supernatural and success to all who follow him, eventually creates too great a dissonance for people.

Jamieson (2000), indicates this includes disillusionment with church structures and power relationships and dissatisfaction with the inadequacy of personal faith to influence society. (Jamieson's study however, based on interviews, does not significantly address the wider social phenomenon of dislocation in the city and its impact on dislocation from the church). Urban social change causes the morphing and breakdown of socially supportive Christian contexts over extended periods. My perception is that lack of such long-term social contexts makes the above dissonance untenable, leading to loss of faith, or as Knowles (2004:56) summarizes, "inability to move to higher levels of spirituality" that require questioning and academic reflection. Positively, such dissatisfaction means that many people are ready for a call into a spirituality that involves deeper theological reflection and social action.

The classical evangelical commitment to separation from the world of drunkenness, gambling, immorality and vices has become blurred, as in many churches wealthier

---

A seminal book is Charles Mellis, Committed Communities (1976).

people came in for whom social drinking, dancing, and the ease of materialism were normal parts of life. In this materialist context, the sacrificial lifestyles of the missionary-oriented Evangelicals of last century has to some extent dissipated.[24]

This loss of spirituality and separateness anticipates loss of motivation for social change, since the emergence of change agents is accelerated in families from revival contexts where the search for perfection is emphasised (McClelland, 1962:165-178). This loss of clarity as to what disciples are to separate from, violates a significant principle developed by Pierson:

> Principle 13 – Revival as dis-enculturation is crucial for the ongoing work of the Holy Spirit (1998:3).

Holiness involves separation from at least the values of the world. According to the apostle Paul, consumption, wrongful sensuality and spirituality are incompatible bedfellows (Col 3:5). Christ is against culture — when the cultural traits are sinful, he resists. The early revival demarcation between spirituality and sensuality has been blurred in attempts to relate to the postmodern world. This is a significant factor in the death of renewal. This issue is very apparent to migrant leaders:

- MIGRANT EVALUATIONS OF NZ EVANGELICAL SPIRITUALITY -

> They come as missionaries bringing renewal of inner holiness and prayer: evangelical Indian friends, from a tradition of regulated prayer morning and evening; evangelical Korean Presbyterians, known for their early morning prayer meeting patterns; my Brazilian wife from an evangelical context of intense activism and devotion. They conclude that the New Zealand Evangelical and Pentecostal church is too weak spiritually to influence this nation for God. Their message is one of repentance for laxity and the necessity of revival and holiness.

Cultural Incompatibility: Dependency on American Models

New Zealanders still depend for theological validity on outside sources — Catholics for decades on the Irish, Anglicans on the English and more recently Pentecostals on the US. This allows both the possibility of openness to significant teaching on social involvement from groups like Regent College in Vancouver, or Tony Campolo of Eastern College, or reversions by Pentecostal leadership to American Pentecostal or right-wing, fundamentalist, American political agendas. In the postmodern city, some aspects are a good fit for the sector which is Americanised, particularly the managerial and business leadership sector.

- "SUCCESSFUL" POSTMODERN GLOBALIZED CHURCH -

> Walking into the new building of the rapidly grown Christian Life Centre of Auckland is like walking into a medium sized Assemblies of God church in the US, with a complete high profile media/worship show in full gear. The reproduction came via Australia. Because the church ministers to the needs of 5000 in many creative ways and

---

24 Quebedeaux analyses this for the US in *The Worldly Evangelicals* (1978), Bruce does the same from a UK Perspective (2001:90).

> affirms cultural diversity in its style, it believes it has created a new and more effective indigenous Christian culture. The values and culture derive from elsewhere, but success in numbers and finances indicate that a culturally modified version from elsewhere is meeting peoples' needs within the globalized sector of the postmodern diversity of Auckland.

On the other hand, the heavy dependence for teaching in most Pentecostal denominations, on "anointed" (= "well marketed"?) American models, has also included a remarkable intrusion of American hierarchical concepts of spiritual authority[25] as against the egalitarianism of Kiwi culture and of the early renewal.

Too Rapid Institutionalism, Poor Institutionalisation

Over the years, I have utilised a principle that administrative structures must follow not lead the development of ministry. I am suggesting here that institutionalisation into Pentecostalism occurred too quickly with this renewal. On the other hand, the evangelical denominations in general failed to denominationally institutionalise cell groups and leadership training, leaving them with renewed people and renewed worship, but not transformed church structures with accessible pathways to leadership.

Beginning with Weber's "Routinisation of Charisma" (Weber, 1947a), there are numerous models of institutionalisation that could be used to analyse this. Among them, O'Dea (1961) identifies five dilemmas in the institutionalisation of religion:[26] (1) the dilemma of mixed *motivation*, where the single minded goal is replaced by self interest (1961:304); (2) the symbolic dilemma, focused on the transmission of the charismatic through rituals vs. the development of inauthentic rituals; (3) the dilemma of administrative order in institution building versus the freedom of the Spirit; (4) delimitation, the balance between the need for concrete definitions versus the substitution of law for charisma; (5) the dilemma of inappropriate controls and accommodation to the larger society.

My above comments show that I perceive both the need for positive progressions into structural integrations of the revival and some serious negative elements in the speed and manner of such progressions bringing much of the NZ Revival under Pentecostal controls. Using O'Dea's categories:

(1) the rapidity of institutionalisation into Pentecostalism in New Zealand very quickly diverted the revival from its motivation on release of the Spirit, to become driven by *motivation* to successful institutionalisation, (i.e. successful church growth in new congregations) perhaps largely because of the economic necessities of aspiring pastors for a sufficient membership base to sustain their own salary and the costs of institutional growth towards such a goal, perhaps because church growth was the clear goal of these

---

25 In struggling to analyse NZ and Australian conflicts with American concepts of authority in missions these can be considered to have been strongly influenced by US roots in hierarchical authority models with significant migration from hierarchical Germanic culture, its militarization, the emergence of Management by Objectives in business vs. the New Zealand experience of migration of poor British seeking to found a haven from the oppressive British enclosures and aristocracy, with strong anti-authoritarian values.

26 Utilized by Poloma (1997) in analysing the "Toronto Blessing", a revival in Toronto in the 1990's.

denominations more than renewal (Pentecostals saw little merit in renewing mainline churches). The Pentecostal structuralist model of church growth replaced the model of freedom in the charismatic renewal. This has resulted positively in consolidation of the fruit of the renewal, but negatively it also has created a culture of power and control in many groups.[27] This is both a financial and a theological issue. Theologies of "the anointing" resting on leadership, of the need for "spiritual covering"[28], meaning submission to directive leadership, meshed with abuse or poor use of "words of wisdom and knowledge" (direct revelations from the Lord into people's lives).

(2) This has often been accompanied by inauthentic rituals in worship "to sustain the work of the Spirit", when that Spirit has often departed. In the name of revival, revival has often been muted by fixed structural forms (patterns of worship such as leading singing into a period where all pray together in tongues, (or in Korean Pentecostal churches, great shouting in prayer), modes of prophetic voice, styles of leadership, sloganised theologies developed in foreign contexts (even though Pentecostal pastors swear they are indigenous), and high resistance to the Spirit's creativity in generating new patterns of reflective theology that are not part of the imported Pentecostal traditions.

(3) O'dea uses the phrase administrative controls. Again there are positive and negative aspects to this process. I perceive this in the centralisation of the fruit of revival under pastoral controls. My observation[29] is that in the transition to Pentecostalism, the sheep have often been well pastored. Yet there are glaring pastoral enigmas. Particularly destructive have been imported American theologies that prevent people from challenging senior pastors over their actions and morals.[30]

(4) Overly legalistic definitions These have not been sustainable in postmodern Kiwi contexts, so are less of an issue. Perhaps the lack of stricness may have hastened subsequent re-enculturation with worldly values.

(5) Accommodation to materialism by many larger churches has often tended to exceed necessary levels and has quenched the work of the Spirit. The imported American "prosperity gospel" and "health and wealth" theologies that indicate a church is successful if growing and large, all contribute to the structural model. I will develop this in the next section.

These issues would not necessarily perceived negatively by those migrating from the mainline churches. People like a secure place, they like ritual and performances and there is often little discernment about the marketing rhetoric of Pentecostalism that requires pastors to affirm their actions as "being from God" for survival in their market niche. However, the issues are perceived strongly by those migrating out of these churches.

---

27 Kevin Ward indicates the dissonance that this causes for baby boomers and for children of postmodernism, results in a drifting off of believers (2001: 6).

28 I began to hear this term in the mid 1970's. Knowles links it to the teachings of David Ellis of the Ashburton New Life (2000: 236).

29 It was heartening eight years after penning this, to have Knowles confirm these thoughts, with an analysis of similar issues (2004: 53-55).

30 One could include multiple cameos from discussions on this point, but it is ethically inappropriate.

These are very broad comments, for Pentecostalism has tremendous internal variations, even among leaders of any one of its denominations, and such generalisations do not take into account the greater indigeneity of New Life and Apostolic streams, where many of these issues have been faced and a balance of progressions sought. While such comments reflect a cursory participant-observer consideration of these dilemmas, as a small aspect in a wider thesis, they are nevertheless from one who has at times sympathetically lived within and advocated Pentecostal structural frameworks among the poor (Grigg, 1992/2004: Chap 15, 16). A sociologist needs to research this across several Pentecostal denominations, with those who have migrated.[31] Diary notes on a visit to one church show some issues:

- LIMITATIONS OF SPIRITUAL AUTHORITY AND CONTROL -

> It was an independent Pentecostal church of 350, built up over 11 years, with wonderful worship. To accomplish this growth, the pastor and his wife had exercised strong authority. This was given and supported by the people, initially because of the pastor and his wife's loving relationships with a core team and their sense of divine calling to the leadership of the church.
>
> Over the longer term, this was backed up by their experience and their gifts as teachers, administrators and preachers and the sense by many, of the peoples' needs being met. This leadership developed a style of speaking directly 'from the Lord' into peoples problems, building the churches around their personal sense of vision and need for a successful church (with assent from their eldership), ways of testing people's loyalties and directive organisational styles. In this situation, a good leadership team had developed, which balanced out most extremes in the leadership style.

This strongly directive leadership style may be preferable to another dynamic. In general, Pakeha Kiwis are averse to authority as reflected in comments against structure that I have heard in many smaller house churches and fellowships. I would suggest that the historic scoffing against authority of the lower class British migrants in New Zealand transmuted into a peculiar trait of rejection of authority in New Zealand culture. When this rejection is affirmed as spiritual, it can cement the group as a new (and in their eyes, more spiritual?) alternative, but never fully confront this underlying value system.

In all of the above, the balance and speed of institutionalisation become critical.

Failure to Move to Socio-Economic Revival
The NZ revival showed fruit in new economics, as have other revivals. Economic communities developed, many becoming landed communities; concern for the poor that enabled initiation of Servants to Asia's Urban Poor; and several new work schemes for poor people.[32] New social dynamics developed as new fellowships formed.

---

31 The appropriate level of these tensions might need to be examined within each phase of A.F.C. Wallace's revitalisation movements theory (2003), see pp. 191, (a model from Europe may be found in Need & Evans, 2004).

32 The Apostolics, particularly, were able to set up numerous work schemes with government funding, thus enhancing their entrance to poorer sectors of society.

Prophetically, some leaders called the church to live simply, live for the poor, do justice and seek racial reconciliation. The book of Acts is clear about these economic dimensions of the revived lifestyle (Acts 2: 44-45; 4: 32-34). Pierson has identified them in several evangelical revival movements in history (Waldensians, Lollards, Hutterites, Moravians (1998:vi)). Many heard these as a call from God and obeyed. Others and in general most Christians, became trapped by survival or consumer materialism. The result predicted in the Scriptures is that the hunger for God and commitment to community declined. This affects the work of the Spirit.

For many who transferred to Pentecostalism, a further step away from these issues occurred with the importation (at times via Australia) of the American "prosperity gospel". This has become particularly true for the mega-churches descended from American AOG models as they drew in many from mainline and other Pentecostal churches in the 1990's. Christian Life Centre in Auckland perceives their teaching on materialistic success as a positive "release from a spirit of poverty" – choosing to oppose the teaching from within the renewal to "live simply that others may simply live." High pastoral salaries and luxurious living are cited as evidence of successful Christianity.[33] Brian Tamaki, bishop of the Destiny Churches, interviewed on Radio Rhema, stated that this kind of lifestyle set a model for his flock.[34]

Central in the Acts 2 passage on Pentecost is the multiracial mix of the peoples. President of YWAM and New Zealand leader in reconciliation, John Dawson, developed comprehensive theologies about the relationship of revival and reconciliation between peoples (1996). Several prophets called the church elders in local areas to go and sit with the Maori elders, listen to their wounds and seek reconciliation (Clover, 1996; Grigg, 2001b). The renewed church, in general, did not obey. Returning to several churches where this message was received, I found there had been no significant action. (I personally wonder if God could have released a wave of revival among Maori. This would have created a synergistic impact on the Pakeha community. It did not happen). This contrasts with the obedience of many liberal leaders in mainline churches who sought such just reconciliation between the peoples.

Thus, I am suggesting that the grass roots work of the Holy Spirit in a renewal of humility, simplicity, reconciliation, unity and purity became focused on front-led revivalists with symbols of spiritual power affirmed by materialism. History tells us that sensuality[35], accumulation of wealth and seeking power are often not far away from such power-symbols.

In summary, renewal did not move to its socio-economic outworking.

---

33 Knowles identifies these same issues (2004: 57).
34 9 a.m. interview with Bob McCoskrie, Tuesday 17th, May 2005.
35 It is inappropriate to document discipline of pastors falling into immorality in these movements, some of which (e.g. New Life) have put significant pastoral accountability structures in place. There is no evidence that this arena of sin is greater or less than of other denominations.

Revival, Launching Pad for Transformation?

In conclusion, a movement ascribed to the Holy Spirit has been authenticated in this chapter as a genuine revival when examined against principles in the theological and historical literature of revival. But it stumbled, as many revivals do, for revivals are multivariate and these multiple variables need to function in synergy. The information flow and leadership from the revival core was redirected; intercessory movements and hunger for revival declined. Pastors began to redirect the revival from its role in creating new freedoms for spiritual gifts to local (pastorally controlled) institutional church growth. Despite some prophets, the revival leadership in the main, had not moved theologically beyond spiritual experience to define issues of reconciliation, economic repentance and social sins.

My theological interpretation of this, is that people began to falter in obedience to what the Spirit was saying across the country. Spirituality began to die and as that happens people turn to pursuing the good life with its affluence and to the cult. The religious show began to take over on Sunday mornings from the confessional group on weekdays, affirming these changes with an imported churchy "signs, success, health and wealth" gospel that directly contradicted what revival leaders believed the Spirit had been saying to the churches.

Yet the revived individuals and the missional structures they have generated (remnant missional clusters of the revival, along with the institutionalised post-revival structures of congregational-based Pentecostalism), are now potential sources of new cultural energy. This study proposes that redirection of revival to transformational ends remains a possibility.

However, the loss of renewal dynamics and transition of many activist Christians from classic churches with their deeper level of theological and historical reflection on the faith, presages a possible lack of momentum for sustaining cultural change and predict a likely reversion to Pentecostal fundamentalism, unless new theological paradigms are disseminated…

I wish to move from this story to a comprehensive model of revival, as a basis for then developing such a paradigm in a theology of Transforming Revival.

- 10 -

THE NATURE OF REVIVAL

The Holy Ghost seemed to come upon the congregation like a mighty rushing wind... In my prayer, the power of God came down and gave a great shock — such an abiding shock I never knew before... The place was rent with the power and presence of God.

John Whitefield[1]

A common web of belief about *revival*, that has been largely consistent over 300 years, framed the pneumatological conversation of the last chapter. However, over the last two decades these beliefs have been engaging new mega-urban issues and mutating into a new global web of belief. In this chapter, I extend the literature survey of Chapter 3 and the participant-observation of Chapter 9 into the writings of the students of revival (historians, theologians and social scientists). Common themes from *Lukan* accounts, germane to such analyses, introduce this to show a foundational web in one gospel author that underlies the present web. I then, step by step, expand the initial definition from the literature. I next examine elements of *revival movements*. "Revival Principles" are then summarized into a theory.

Areas where these common definitions are inadequate are then examined and a new (third) web of belief concerning Transforming Revival is discussed. Then, seeking to understand possible transitions from an evangelical web of belief to the proposed Transforming Revival web of belief, I examine revival as central to Evangelicalism, as evidenced in the shift in power to entrepreneurs. I take a brief but necessary excursus on the nature of glossolalia and examine the wider theme of spiritual gifts as foundational for extending revival into transformation.

---

[1] From an old message, source noted as from Whitefield's journal. A summary of such phenomenological revival features in the Wesley's and Whitefield's ministries is given in *The Nature of Revival* (Weakley, 1987)

Literature on Revival

While the phenomena of revivals and revival movements derives from the Scriptures, the evangelical use[2] of "revival of religion" came to prominence with Whitefield in his spawning of the Great Awakening in England. The interpretations of revival in the writings of Jonathon Edwards, in the early decades of the American colonies, were popularised by the early-mid 19th century Finney's *Laws of Revival* (Burns, 1909/1993; Finney, 1836/1987; Weakley, 1987). They emphasised the necessity of conversion, the depravity of humanity, repentance from sin and unity among believers. Leonard Ravenhill promulgated these ideas popularly last century (1979; 1986) (including a visit to New Zealand). These began a genre of primarily *theological* interpretations of revival, based on sets of principles.[3]

Edwin Orr, worldwide revivalist and author of over 50 books on revival became the definitive author on the topic from a *historical* then a global point of view. (e.g. 1955; 1972; 1975a; 1975b; 1975c). However, his very rigid categories, formed by 1955, progress no further. He viewed revival and evangelism as closely intertwined and defined the cause of revival as the preaching of the Word of God, resulting in conviction, confession, repentance from sin and restitution. These result in public witness. Outcomes of revival are seen in multiple good works by individuals (for example, 1972: 232). Emeritus missions historian at Fuller, Pierson (1998), in his unpublished analysis of revival movements within church history, has expanded Orr's theses into several historical theses which influence my discussion.

Church Growth guru, McGavran, did the seminal thinking on the relationship of revival and church growth (1970:186-203). Alan Tippett (1971; 1973; 1987), brought anthropology into the study of revival, particularly developing McGavran's ideas of "web movements," and "people movements." These are germane to my discussion on spatial expansion of urban revival movements. East African revivalist, Roy Hessian, in *The Calvary Road* (c1960), developed a paradigm of "brokenness" as source of sustainable revival.

At a more academic theological level, reformed theologian, Lovelace, in *Dynamics of the Spiritual Life* (1979) developed ideas on sustainable revival based on a Reformed analysis. I do not use this significantly, as I find it lacks roots in the typical experiences of revival, hence tends to confuse, with imposed rather than grounded theological paradigms. In contrast, Free Methodist revival theologian, Snyder, in *Signs of the Spirit* (1989/1997) and *Radical Renewal: The Problem of Wineskins Today* (1996b), integrated ideas from the above underlying works into a systemic *historical, sociological and theological* theory of revival. Snyder developed a model of five dimensions of renewal: personal; corporate; conceptual; structural and missiological, affirming that renewal "may begin in any one or more of these five ways," though he later refers to "concentric ripples in a pond" (293).

---

2 Revival is an uncommon theme in liberal literature. Interestingly, Moltmann in his representation of World Council of Churches; thinking in *The Spirit of Life* (1991), says nothing about revival, none of the authors above being mentioned, perhaps showing the great divide between the institutional ecumenical churches of traditional Christendom in Europe and the accelerating global Evangelical and Pentecostal movements..

3 e.g. (Autrey, 1968; Kaiser Jr., 1986).

I build from these, particularly Snyder, but seek to extend revival into the arena of cultural engagement and revival. I reflect on several major theories from diverse disciplines on the relationship of revival movements and culture. In developing a theory for *revival movements*, I utilise the influential *anthropological* model of revitalisation by A.F.C. Wallace (2003), in his attempt to define rapid cultural change within total cultural systems, built largely from studies of tribal cultural movements.

The above authors are foundational for the new experimentalists in the field, who seek to interpret contemporary revival issues. While many of these are trained academic missiologists, they write popularly. Spiritual warfare is a major popular theme, recurring throughout the Catholic saints and Protestant history. Ed Murphy in his *Handbook of Spiritual Warfare* (1996), gives a definitive six hundred page Pentecostal view of these issues.[4] Aldrich builds on experiences of catalysing prayer for revival and develops the idea of "prayer summits" as source of revival (1992), a model that has been utilised in New Zealand. Haggard (1995) expands on city-wide unity as a basis for revival – a theological thesis that as leaders in the AD2000 movement we have experimented with for 15 years and that significant leaders have come to question as a demonstrable missiological statement (though this is not as yet published material).

Peter Wagner writes in areas of church growth. He has built beyond my early works on city leadership teams of apostles and prophets as expressed in the AD2000 leadership (Grigg, 1997d:57-62) and also developed the idea of mega-church leaders as city apostles (1993; 1998; 1999), an idea accepted by many globally, but seen as seriously flawed by other Evangelicals (again, unpublished). Silvoso's (1994) ideas of city-wide revival strategies and spiritual warfare encapsulate some years of group dialogues of city leaders. Frangipane complements these in the area of a biblical theology of revival and the city (1991). The international president of YWAM, John Dawson (1989; 1996), develops a foundational idea of revival derived from reconciliation of peoples through "identificational repentance", using experiences between Maori and Pakeha in New Zealand.[5] These are all part of a field of current academic and popular debate. This study is within this genre, as part of a network seeking to understand revival in postmodern cities.

Significant in studies of revival in New Zealand is Brian Hathaway's *Beyond Renewal: The Kingdom of God* (1990) which reflects our early experiences of relating the Kingdom to renewal and develops a missiology for the local congregation. Wyn Fountain, in a self published document, *The Restoration of Hope for the Transformation of Our Nation* (1996), introduced themes into New Zealand, influencing (or influenced by?) his son, Jeff Fountain (2004), a YWAM leader who has been coordinating Hope for Europe and part of the AD2000 network which was central to these global discussions. Other published works on this field in New Zealand are largely historical. Worsfold (1974), did significant research on the development of the Apostolic church, including information about the Smith Wigglesworth revival of 1922-23 in Wellington. Missionary anthropol-

---

4 The Evangelical Missiological Society has published several critiques of these themes popularised by Wagner (McConnell, 1997). They tend to critique his hermeneutical style and popularist approach, which does not necessarily negate the themes themselves, but the nuances of derivation and hence current global extremes in application.

5 Critiques in Orme (2004: 147-163).

ogist Alan Tippett, does a riveting analysis of the conversion and discipling movement of the Maori people in the mid 19th century (1971:40-75). Evans and McKenzie supplement this (1999:2-30). Edwin Orr's experiences in New Zealand (1936), are also more autobiographical, coming before his period of global revival analysis. Brett Knowles' *The History of a New Zealand Pentecostal Movement* (2000) correlates early years of the New Zealand revival with the New Life churches.

How do these theological explanations relate to the analysis of revival movements in sociology? Missiology can utilise scripture as a foundation, and describe the person of the Holy Spirit as the source of revival. In contrast, sociology has to do with social configurations, and the social origins of religion, exemplified by Durkheim (1915/1965) at the beginning of last century as he identified religion as primarily performing the vital social functions of social integration and solidarity that derive from a system of shared beliefs. It can only describe the phenomenology of movement growth, and interpret human or institutional elements within that. "Revival" is not utilised by sociologists in the theological sense defined in this study, as a revival generated by the person of the Holy Spirit, but more generally as a revitalisation (Wallace, 2003) of religious institutions and/or belief systems not dissimilar in use to revival of a cultural system, political ideas, or philosophy.

In contrast with its use in examining tribal religious movements in anthropology, its use occurs occasionally in sociological discussions[6] on the expansion of Christianity, for example, in recent Eastern Europe and Russia (Greeley, 2004) or on revival of Islam (Voll, 1968). Greeley examines the contextual factors in Russia, both the persistence of 1000 year old religion, and a vacuum of belief in the demise of communism, a great vacuum causing a demand for spirituality and religion.

The recent relevant debates (in some ways cross-Atlantic debates (Crockett & O'Leary, 2004:1-11)), in sociology of religion have rather been between proponents of secularisation theory, its critics, and Stark's more recent application of economic theory to sociology of religion (Stark & Bainbridge, 1985; Finke & Stark, 2000). He tries to explain the religious pluralism in the US, proposing that demand for religion is somewhat constant, caused by the need to explain human existence. He develops ninety-nine propositions that cover many areas of church growth. Unfortunately he did not include in these the arena of revival. It would be of interest in another study to review the theological principles of revival movements in this study from a sociological perspective and add to his wider theory.

Underlying Biblical Web of Belief

The following simple definition of core revival elements, will be expanded step by step to encompass the commonly held web of belief:

Principle 14 –	*Divine Outpouring: Revival is the outpouring of the Holy Spirit on groups.*

---

6   None of the major missiological writers mentioned in this chapter feature in the recent major writings of sociology of religion.

The biblical basis for such a theology of revival focuses on Pentecost:

> When the day of Pentecost came, they were all together in one place. Suddenly a sound like a blowing of a violent wind came from heaven and filled the whole house where they were sitting. They saw what seemed to be tongues of fire that separated and came to rest on each of them. All of them were filled with the Holy Spirit and began to speak in other tongues as the Holy Spirit enabled them (Acts 2: 1-4).

Luke describes a unique communal event, the beginning of the creation of the church, yet without its breaking with the temple or synagogue.[7] Acts 4:31-34 recounts another experience of the Holy Spirit sovereignly falling on a group, with a different phenomenology but similar socio-economic, evangelistic and spiritual results. At each expansion of the church across ethnic divides the group phenomena is repeated — as Peter and John are sent to the half-caste Samaritans they lay hands on them and they receive the Spirit (Acts 8:15-17) and when Peter preaches to the Gentile Cornelius' house, "the Holy Spirit came on all who heard the message" (Acts 10:44; 11:15). Joel 2:28,29 is used to interpret this, indicates that the coming of the Spirit would be on all God's people, not just prophet, priest and king. Thus this falling has to do with the empowering of the laity.

Secondly, I utilise Joel's word "outpouring" to indicate the divine sovereignty and the overwhelming nature of the Holy Spirit on *groups*. They were *all* filled in a baptism of the Spirit (an immersion, Acts 1:4,5), a coming upon them (1:8; 2:3), an overwhelming. Moltmann extrapolates, "The Spirit always descends on the whole congregation and cannot be claimed by anyone as his or her possession. This has been so since the first Pentecostal congregation we hear about in Acts 2" (1998: 57).

Yet thirdly, the divine action relates to collective spiritual hunger. Each group mentioned in Acts, experiences unity and seeks God – "they all joined together constantly in prayer" (1:14). Jesus told them to wait for the promise, which they did in prayer, in the Scriptures and in unity. This leads to a theme I recall as a child, reading from late 19th century books sent to me by my grandmother, of "tarrying," waiting on him together, as the human prerequisite for revival (cf. Edwards, 1990:72ff).

> Did Luke intend his readers to infer that the first coming of the Spirit was made possible, on the human side, through the willingness of the disciples to pray and meditate on the Scriptures and through their refusal to allow any discord or withdrawal from fellowship to erect a barrier to that coming? This possibility cannot be lightly dismissed (Hull, 1967:48).

Luke's description is informed by some Old Testament theophanies.

> It is interesting to note the parallels to various Old Testament theophanies where God comes down and there is fire on the mountain and Moses or someone is given a word to speak for the Lord (Ezek 19:18; 2 Sam 22:16; Ezek 13:13). In those events as well, we are talking about the experiences of a group of God's people when together (Witherington, 1998:132).

These OT theophanies include presence, empowerment, signs and wonders. These NT passages discussed so far speak of the action of the Holy Spirit upon (or baptizing) a group, with concomitant, though varying, signs and wonders, particularly speaking in other languages.

---

7   With its birthing as an *ecclesia* in a synagogue (Ladd, 1974:342), was the church inherently designed to always be a renewal movement, always an *ecclesia in ecclesia*?

These experiences are spoken of, in what Moltmann calls "movement metaphors," of rushing wind and flaming fire (1991:278). The action of the Holy Spirit is external, starting from heaven. Using other metaphors, it is a coming upon like a dove, a pouring out (2:17f; 10:45), a baptism (1:5, 11:16), resulting in an internal indwelling, a filling of the Spirit.

Every occurrence in Acts also resulted in bold proclamation.

In summary, we may extend my simple definition to a basic Lukan definition:

> Principle 15 – Lukan basis for revival: Revival involves communal waiting, unity and prayer for his presence, divine outpouring on groups, empowerment, bold proclamation, signs and wonders.

I wish to expand on these characteristics from the literature.

Principles of Revival

The Initiating Manifestation of Divine Presence

The central element of revival I have identified in principle 14 is the initiating manifestation of God. Typical of revival experiences, is David Brainerd's record of the birth of revival among American Indians in 1745:

> The power of God seemed to descend upon the assembly 'like a rushing mighty wind' and with an astonishing energy bore down all before it. I stood amazed at the influence that seized the audience almost universally and could compare it to nothing more aptly than the irresistible force of a mighty torrent... Almost all persons of all ages were bowed down with concern together and scarce one was able to withstand the shock of this surprising operation.[8]

This central element is captured in popular British revivalist, Selwyn Hughes' definition, "A high voltage burst of spiritual energy and supernatural power" resulting in:

- An intense, palpable and extraordinary sense of God's presence.
- A deep desire to be rid of all sin.
- A powerful impact on the wider community (Hughes, 2003:21).

Holiness, Repentance, Confession and Conversion

Hughes' second point illustrates one of the evidences that these dynamics are from God — the evidence of holiness. She is the *Holy* Spirit, as against other spirits, whose names indicate the nature of their being, or the human spirit, which can generate its own phenomenology. There is deep soul-level awareness of sin and truth occurring in the presence of the Holy bringing repentance by both Christians and in conversion of non-Christians.

> Suddenly the power of the Spirit comes upon them and they are brought into a new and more profound awareness of the truths that they had previously held intellectually and per-

---

[8] Quoted in *In the Day of They Power* (Wallis, 2005).

haps at a deeper level too. They are humbled and they are convicted of sin, they are terrified at themselves… So the two main characteristics of revival are first, this extraordinary enlivening of members of the church and second, the conversion of masses of people who have been outside in indifference and sin (Jones, 1959).

Revival's integral connection to sin and its opposite, holiness are both causal and resultant relationships. Causal: outpourings occur in response to conviction and repentance of sin caused by preaching. Resultant: the presence of God falling results in conviction of sin.

> *Principle 16 –*   *Holiness: The sudden, transcendent sense of the presence of the Holy Spirit causes personal spiritual change, holiness and striving after holiness.*

But repentance is not limited to believers. Conversion of many is normative, just as it was in the book of Acts, with the conversion of 3000, then 5000. Orr's definitions of revival are the most used and consistently include four phenomena:

- revival includes some repetition of the phenomena of the Acts of the Apostles
- groups collectively experiencing the divine presence with resultant empowering
- a revitalizing of nominal Christians
- and conversions of outsiders as a result of the divine encounter (various writings by Orr).

> *Principle 17 –*   *Conversion: The overwhelming presence of God causes conversion of non-believers.*

Manifestations of Power
Beginning with the noise of Pentecost (the sound of a rushing wind) and the brilliance of 120 fires settling on each one, followed by the speaking in other tongues, the phenomenology of revival is a major field of social research and theologizing. If the Spirit of God (or any spirit) comes in power, one would expect diverse phenomena. The Scriptures outline the nature of these, but descriptively, not exhaustively.

As a participant-observer, I find manifestations differ from culture to culture – often a deep silence, broken by outbreaks of sobbing, weeping repentance. In other cultures, sudden outbreaks of cultural dance forms occur as people are set free from sin to rejoice. People fall, shake, quake (source of the name of the denomination), speak in other languages, prophesy, demons manifest, etc. The most beautiful event I have been involved in was watching a paralysed ballerina, set free into the most beautiful dance of worship. Overwhelming divine encounters, power seen in healing and deliverance, love, resultant worship – all are repeated elements. It is difficult to write of it in the midst of experiencing it. This study is a poor reflection on transforming experiences and "empowerment derived from an intense, transcendent sense of divine presence"

(Petersen, 1996:187). This aspect also differentiates spiritual revival from common understandings of organisational revival, or cultural revival included in Wallace's revitalisation theories – I am talking of revival ascribed to the Holy Spirit.

> Principle 18 –   *Manifestations of Power: The presence of the Spirit is observable through diverse manifestations of power.*
>
> *Corollary: Manifestations of power may be tested against scripture as to their validity as manifestations of the Holy Spirit.*

Socio-Economic Fruit

This study relates the impact of revival to social transformation. A starting point is the evidence in the revival scenes in the Acts 2 community and again in Acts 4:32-34. They are stories of a new social community and new redistributive economics matching the new spirituality. This new socio-economics was surely based on the disciples' training by Jesus and their modelling the nature of the new Kingdom, an eternal jubilee of redistribution of wealth and equality across social classes (Grigg, 1981; 1985/2004; Snyder, 1997:67-76).

The literature documents such results repeatedly. The following is a typical story:

> *Before the (Welsh) revival there had been an almost plague of drunkenness and gambling. During the revival, taverns were either closed or turned into meeting halls. Instead of wasting their earnings on drinking and gambling, workers started taking their wages home to their families. Because of the conviction of the Holy Spirit, restitution became a fruit of repentance and outstanding debts were being paid by thousands of young converts. These two factors alone resulted in a substantial economic impact on the whole community...business founded on honourable trades and products prospered. Those that traded on vice went out of business. Possibly never before in history has an entire society been so profoundly transformed by a spiritual revival in such a short time* (Joyner, 1993:76,77).

> Principle 19 –   *Socio-economic change: Revival immediately results in positive changes in social and economic relationships.*

Character Transformation

Luke, in his accounts, emphasises love and unity leading up to and following Pentecost. Others have the same emphasis on love. Pierson (1998:IV), perhaps reflecting sociologist Berger (1954:480), summarises one evidence as, "Revival decreases distances between individuals, male and female, rich and poor, church and church." Gordon Wakefield (1976:76), describing the effects on Wesley, calls it "the burning charity." Moltmann (1991:280), speaking of the images of the Spirit says, "the raging tempest and raging fire are also images of the *eternal love* which creates life and energises it from within."

The fruits of the Spirit in Galatians 5:22, 23 represent key characteristics of the future Kingdom. One would expect that love, joy, peace, patience, kindness are heightened with the inbreaking of the Spirit in revival.

- THE PRESENCE OF GOD, HEALING AND SPIRITUAL ENCOUNTER -

> Some years ago, over a period of six months I interviewed more than 50 people 'slain in the Spirit', after they had fallen onto the floor in a type of slumber in revival meetings under the overwhelming 'presence of God'. Each identified a deep sense of the love of God as the Spirit healed inner traumas, speaking of her purposes and revealed aspects of his person. Unlike hypnosis or demonic possession, they were able, if they wished, to allow or halt the activity of the Holy Spirit. Most preferred to bathe in the Spirit's presence. I have spoken to some years later. These experiences marked a turning point in their personal lives, marriages and ministries.

> Principle 20 –   Love: A psychological sense[9] of the love of God marks those who walk in revival (Hessian, c1960:22-28). It transforms social relationships.

My proposal is that this principle becomes a basis for considering a theory of Transforming Revival. One could take the fruit of the Spirit, the first fruits of the inbreaking future Kingdom and muse on their effect on any city. What happens when love, joy and peace sweep over a sector of a city? What is the impact on violence and dissension in homes? What happens when patience, kindness and goodness become the norm in the civic square? How do faithfulness, gentleness and self-control affect families and media presentations?

George Thomas, professor of sociology at Arizona State University, in his *Revivalism and Cultural Change*, analyses such dynamics in the second awakening in the US:

> Revivalism as it evolved in the North and West led to moral crusades that had the goal of morally defining citizenship and the nation: the Kingdom of God would be established by the moral actions of citizens…Antislavery and temperance grew directly out of revivalism (1989:63).

The Expansion of Revival Movements

Beyond these principles of revival, expansion of the concept of "groups" in the definition requires both theological and sociological development of a "revival movement" theory. Among the diverse definitions available, Snyder defines "a renewal movement" as,

> *a sociologically and theologically definable religious resurgence which arises and remains within, or in continuity with, historic Christianity and which has a significant (potential*

---

9   When examining these and other phenomena, I had the privilege of an African classmate who had a doctorate in psychology and was studying theology. Over hamburgers, he would discuss with us the phenomenology we were observing and describe how he could cause the same phenomena through psychological means and had observed them being prouced through the control of people through other spirits. Thus the phenomena themselves do not verify the nature of the Spirit of God being behind them. They do verify the presence of overwhelming spiritual powers upon people. Other biblical tests for fruit in character, healing, affirmation of Christ as Lord are needed - in the case of the phenomenology of 'being slain in the Spirit', the long-term deep level healing and love and the ministering of that love to others.

> ly measurable) impact on the larger church in terms of number of adherents, intensity of belief and commitment and/or the creation or revitalization of institutional expressions of the church (1989/1997:34).

This is a very church-focused definition. Orr uses the term "evangelical awakenings".[10] Lovelace comments that "revival," "renewal" and "awakening," "usually are used synonymously for broad-scale movements of the Holy Spirit's work in renewing spiritual vitality in the church and in fostering its expansion in mission and evangelism" (1979: 21).

The repetition of revival dynamics is foundational to the rapid expansion of Evangelicalism and Pentecostalism, both of which can be perceived as *the fruit of series of revival movements occurring across multiple cultures, with overlapping timeframes*. There is an expanding literature on revival themes that grows from interpreting these movements.[11]

Two popular missiological terms are helpful. *People groups* is a sociological concept used in missiology by Donald McGavran (1970:223ff), the founder of church growth theory and marketed by Ralph Winters globally.[12] Flow of ideas (or the transmission of the power of the Spirit) within such groups is rapid, through webs of relational ties until it meets a racial, ethnic, class or other barrier (a *web movement*).[13] There is usually a multiplier effect that is often graphed to show an exponential spread of the gospel as revival dynamics expand – until they hit barriers of war, famine, other catastrophe, or heresy that curtail expansion.

The idea of web movements can be utilised to understand revival movements within the Scriptures. We can consider the structure of Acts as built around several web movements – the multiplication within the Jerusalem Jewish community up until Acts 8:1, at which time, "there arose a great persecution in Jerusalem and they were all scattered everywhere." Then a transition across a barrier as the Holy Spirit is poured out on Gentile communities: through Philip to the Ethiopian eunuch, then Peter and John, bringing the power of the Holy Spirit to the Samaritans, then from Peter to Cornelius the Roman, where again the Holy Spirit fell. From Acts 13 on, it is the story of another web movement throughout the Roman Empire, pioneered (though not exclusively) by the apostle Paul in the trade language and at the trade centres.

---

10 Language has now moved on and a cursory look at the web shows the word "awakening" now commonly used for those awakening into spiritist experiences. For this reason, I have not used it.

11 Analyses of the revivals in Europe and the US have reoccurred regularly (for some sources see the extensive summaries at www.revival-library.org/. These are now being supplemented by theses on revival across many nations (e.g. *Spiritual Awakening: A Theological and Historical Study of Four Waves in the Korean Church* (Han, 1991); or *Lessons from the Revival in Argentina* (Richardson, 1998); or *Spontaneous Combustion: Grass-Roots Christianity, Latin American Style* (Berg & Pretiz, 1996)).

12 A People Group is "a significantly large grouping of individuals who perceive themselves to have a common affinity for one another because of their shared language, religion, ethnicity, residence, occupation, class or caste, situation, etc., or combinations of these." For evangelistic purposes, it is "the largest group within which the gospel can spread as a church planting movement without encountering barriers of understanding or acceptance" (Winter & Koch, 1999: 514).

13 See Tippett, (1971:40-59, 198-220) for example, and his figures on the expansion of Christianity among Maori in the 19th century.

Limited Time Frames and Periodicity of Revival

Movement dynamics have to do with time and space. Revival theories tend to consider four temporal questions — the speed of initiation; the timing of revivals; their limited time frames and the periodicity of revival. There are some areas of agreement but generally these are matters of historical, sociological and theological speculation.

Suddenly: Acts 2 begins with a "Suddenly". Revival involves sudden intervention (for descriptions from the scriptures see Wallis, 1956:61-63). It is as if a mighty wind passes by and all are left touched by it, as it moves rapidly to another region.

> *What happened in the time of Hezekiah was 'done so quickly' and the same was true 700 year later, when on the day of Pentecost, "Suddenly a sound like the blowing of a violent wind came from heaven and filled the whole house..."(Acts 2:2). No matter how long people have been praying for it or expecting it, when it comes it is always full of surprise* (Edwards, 1990:29).

Periodicity: I have also struggled theologically (as have the revivalists) with the reasons why, in the Scriptures, there is periodicity. Biblically, there is an outbreak of the empowering of the Spirit and the miraculous around Moses. Then occasional outbreaks throughout the Judges, followed by a gap until Solomon's temple, then to Elijah and Elisha, on to Ezra and the rebuilding of Jerusalem, then another recognised gap until the coming of Christ and the apostolic age.

If the question is phrased, "Why should God only choose certain times to anoint his people?" one should search for patterns of affirmation of new epochs, new ages of his working with his people, as Moses created the nation, Solomon dedicated a temple, Jesus brought a Kingdom and the apostles a church age. On the other hand, how do we explain Elijah, Elisha and Samson, who did not initiate new epochs? The tenor of the book of Judges and the periodic rise of the prophets indicates a process of generational outbreaks of phenomenology around prophetic figures. Perhaps both elements need to be integrated into any theory of revival.

Jonathon Edwards defines failure of revival in theological terms as "periods of spiritual decline occur in history because the gravity of indwelling sin keeps pulling believers first into formal religion and then into apostasy" (Lovelace 1979:40). This affirms the scribal commentary on the stories of Judges and the Kings in the Old Testament, where outbreaks of divine presence and the miraculous are related to obedience and his absence related to disobedience. If revival is integrally connected with public repentance (either cause or response to the presence of God on groups), then it is reasonable to presume the decline of revival relates to the resurfacing of sin in the public square and consequent loss of the presence of God.

Is there a possibility of sustainability? Hessian (c1960), documents the sustained East African revival patterns, based on continual confession of sin between believers.

Lovelace (1979:32, 62-80) contrasts two theological models of revival. The first is an oscillating model of decline and renewal, gross apostasy and call to national repentance. He links it to generational history, prefering a second model of continuous revival based on Acts.[14] I find this difficult, as the Lukan account is too limited in time frame to make a strong case. The scattering of Acts 8:1 occurred probably within 3-4 years of the falling of the Spirit at Pentecost and the subsequent accounts in Acts focus on the Pauline web more than the scattered early Jerusalem church.

Looking at such movements from a more human perspective, mathematical chaos theory proves useful. It demonstrates periodicity of patterns for varying combinations of multiple variables (e.g., from the multiple variables that go into weather forecasting, certain repeating patterns such as cyclones can be predicted in general). Revival movements certainly are complex combinations of multiple variables, crystallising in common configurations at certain periods.

Toynbee, in his study of the wider phenomena of civilisations comes to a similar conclusion, of two modes or rhythms, periodic movements within progressive major development of civilisations (1972:159). Thus, Like Toynbee and in accord with a biblical concept of time (not linear Western, not cyclic Eastern, but directional and seasonal), I am integrating both of Lovelace's models.

Principle 21 –	*Periodicity and Continuity: 'Revival movements' are an expanding series of interrelated outpourings of the Spirit, within the ongoing expansion of Christianity.*
Principle 22 –	*Multivariate Periodicity: At a human level, revival will be sustained for a period when a cluster of critical variables continue to operate in synergy.*
Principle 23 –	*Quiescent Revival: A 'sustainable but seasonal model' of revival involves a phase of healthy quiet growth beyond the period of sudden visitation of the Spirit.*

This latter phase produces revival outgrowths, structures that engage in cultural transformation between the period when all the critical variables are working together and the next period of integration of these variables.

According to "The Revival Website" which extensively documents six ages of worldwide revivals (revival-library.org, 25 Feb 2004), these seasons appear to be nearly generational. McLoughlin, as a scholarly historian (1978:v), documents four spiritual-cultural awakenings in the US (1730-1760, 1800-1830, 1890-1920, 1960-1990). Some generations miss revival completely, as is seen in the gaps in these.

The lack of a new season of visitation, if the critical variables do not reconstitute themselves after the phase of quiet structuring, may produce an alternative life-destroying institutional growth phase coupled with spiritual decline then apostasy. I would suggest this has happened within New Zealand Methodism and parts of New Zealand Presbyterianism. The consensus of the writers appears to be that these periods of decline parallel

---

14 Norman Grubb (1997), had earlier popularised this phrase in *Continuous Revival*, an analysis of the ongoing East African Revival.

the loss of morality in the broader culture, as Evangelicals believe has happened in New Zealand between the decades between the 1960's to 1990's, with the accelerating decay of these mainline denominations over 40 or more years, and before the NZ revival could generate enough maturity and fruit to reverse these processes .

Spatial Expansion of Revival Movements

This seasonal but sustainable model also marries perspectives on spatial expansion of revival.

Revival of existing churches: Throughout history the intensity and focus of revival as divine visitation on groups of existing believers has consistently occurred for limited seasons only. In this context, the human structuring that enables ongoing progression of the work of the Spirit may or may not develop, for it often is not part of the structures of what is being revived. For example, the Welsh revival movement conserved little fruit as it contained such an aversion to ongoing structure.[15]

Revival through new discipling webs: Jesus' departing words in the Markan addendum (Mark 16:17,18) indicates outbreaks of signs and wonders during evangelistic phases. This correlates with the global anecdotal evidence. Such revival movements may be defined missiologically as web-movements of divine manifestations resulting from small group conversions. Thousands of such movements occur around the world involving direct intervention of the Holy Spirit in divine encounters, signs and wonders as evangelistic and discipling work progresses.[16] The multiplication of these is often sustained for decades. Beginning with Tippett's anthropological exploration (1971) of the phenomenology in McGavran's people movement thesis (1970:333-353), there is a literature of over four thousand church growth studies related to such movements over the last 30 years, many documenting such signs and wonders. Such studies usefully explain some of the Pentecostal denominational growth dynamics in New Zealand, as ideas from this school have often determined New Zealand church leader's goals.

- INITIATING A "PEOPLE MOVEMENT" REVIVAL -

> While living in the slums of Manila, I was involved in the discipling of two families from among the Ibanag people. The father of one of these families, a professor of anthropology, returned to his people, was asked by the priest to preach, began to heal the sick and cast out demons. Within 6 months, 1500 people had stopped dealing with the spirits and begun to follow Christ. We asked one mission to translate the Scriptures into their language. The Navigators and Reach developed small group discipling processes for these people. Today tens of thousands are following Christ among those 350,000 people. These have begun to reach some of the neighbouring people groups with different languages.

---

15 *The Plan Was Not to Plan* (1988: 791).

16 David Barrett (1988: 791) documents 42.1% of Protestants in Latin America in indigenous churches in 1985. Berg and Pretiz indicate grass-roots indigenous churches at 25% to 53% of Evangelicals in selected Latin cities (1996:51).

The common thread of the falling of the Spirit on groups with signs and wonders is part of both dynamics. Because of the intentional structure of evangelistic mission and subsequent catechetic or discipling processes, the second kind of discipling movement often has a longer sustaining structure. The divine and human elements operate in a synergy.

Revivals and the Core Values of Evangelicalism

The deeper I have researched, the more evident it has become that revival is foundational to Evangelicalism. I have already noted the high view of Scripture, the crucicentric nature of Evangelicalism and its evangelistic centre. The *sequitur* is that revivals (centred on the preaching of the cross) produce Evangelicals. The corollary is that Evangelicalism does not exist apart from revivals. For each outpouring of the Spirit in Acts results in bold evangelistic activity. The second corollary is that since Evangelicalism is essentially revivalistic, attempts to restrict outbreaks of revival phenomena will fail, as seen with the exodus of thousands of those touched by the Spirit from fundamentalist Brethren fellowships in the early phases of the New Zealand revival.

Revivals: Power Shift to Lay Entrepreneurs

Two other significant themes among Evangelicals directly emerge from revival sources: power shifts to lay entrepreneurs and the spiritual unity of believers.[17] I will review the first of these.

I have already indicated that Pentecost was a giving of the Holy Spirit to common people. Literature of the 1980's indicated that lay leadership develops when there are small group structures (as seen in the last chapter). Snyder's extensive comparison of the pietists, Moravians and Methodists forms the basis of his theories on revival:

> All three movements were in effect ecclesiolae in ecclesia... Pietism had its collegia pietatis; the Moravians organised distinct communities; and the Methodists were organized into smaller, more tightly knit groups called "bands." Spener advocated greater emphasis on the 'spiritual priesthood' as a means of reform and Zinzendorf and Wesley had rather elaborate theories of ministry or church, as we shall see, which allowed for the use of various kinds of "lay" ministers (Snyder 1989:33).

Evangelicalism and Pentecostalism are populist movements, with leadership emergence patterns for the common person who can appeal to the masses, recruit followers and build them into participative communities of faith. Such movements build an *espirit de corps* in opposition to that from which they have come (Gerlach & Hein, 1970:370-77). - a privileged, well funded, theologically-trained clerical class. Hatch demonstrates how in America the process of democratisation of the church was as much a conquest of class as it was a conquest of theology. What this has meant,

> is that at the psychological centre of much evangelical faith are two ideas that are also at the heart of the practice of democracy: (1) the audience is sovereign and (2) ideas find legitimacy and value only within the marketplace (Hatch, 1989:46).

---

17 I have developed some aspects of unity in *Transforming Cities* (Grigg, 1997d). I have excluded a section on this essential element of revival from this study, as it is not germane to the thesis.

The Latin (Berg & Pretiz, 1996) and New Zealand experiences are not apparently different. Baptists in New Zealand recently reaffirmed their position against ordaining clergy. The Brethren generally refuse to ordain a pastor, each assembly being led by an eldership (though this is changing). Pentecostal leadership development has little to do with academics and much to do with proven leadership. These are peoples' churches.

> Principle 24 – Empowered Common People: Revivals empower ordinary individuals as lay leaders (Snyder, 1989/1997:279). They are an enfranchisement of the laity, a defrocking of ecclesiastical controls on the knowledge of God, a radical power shift from institution to movement.

Pentecostal Spirituality: The Inbreaking of the Holy Spirit

Having examined the relationship of revival to Evangelicalism, there are additional elements of revivalism in Pentecostalism that need consideration. While initially rejecting its evangelical mother, Pentecostal history builds on and embraces the charismatic Evangelical core. A theology of "spiritual gifts as evidence of the Holy Spirit" jumped the fence between these movements in the late 1960's, globally and in New Zealand (Knowles, 2000: 101-105). But the mark of Pentecostalism has been its emphasis on *glossolalia*, rendering it necessary, for completeness, to take a brief excursus.

Glossolalia

The hallmark of Pentecostalism is the doctrine that the "baptism of the Spirit" is evidenced by one spiritual gift — speaking in tongues (based on the three events of Acts 2:4; 10:46; 19:6 and the debates of 1 Corinthians 12 and 14 as to the exercise of the gift). Many evangelicals reject the necessary evidence of *glossolalia* and the concept of the baptism of the Spirit as a second experience following conversion (e.g. Ladd, 1974: 345), though a second experience fits well with Anglican and Catholic perspectives of infant baptism and subsequent confirmation.

Spiritual, psychological or historical analysis of *glossolalia* are not central to this study but require comment.. There is a significant literature on *glossolalia* from within and without the Pentecostal movements. There is plenty of evidence for its historical appearance throughout history as an aspect of Christian phenomenology.[18] Newt Maloney has a comprehensive summary of last century's psychological assessment of *glossolalia* (1985). Morton Kelsey (1999; 1977; 1991), explores many aspects of Christian and charismatic phenomenology from a Jungian perspective. Suffice to state that socially it is an initiation into some of these movements; biblically, it is a gift that is seen as of worth (1 Cor 12, 14); practically, for some of its recipients, it is seen as significant in prayer, worship and deliverance.[19]

Yet, recognising that readers may have rejected the validity of such experiences because of their strangeness, it seems appropriate to indicate the biblical and histori-

---

18 Stanley Burgess, for example, has a three volume analysis of the Holy Spirit in Eastern, Western and early church traditions (1997a; 1997b; 1997c.)

19 At a personal level, when involved in deliverance of individuals from demons, this is an essential gift. It facilitates clarity of communication and identification of the particular demons, usually essential before deliverance can occur. For others, the gift is more utilised in worship.

cal Christian commonness of *glossolalia* and related phenomena. Such phenomena include deliverance, shaking, quaking (source of the denominational name), falling down under the power of the Spirit (being "slain in the Spirit" in Pentecostal terms), words of knowledge (direct revelation of another's situation or of sin) and so on.

Without formal analysis in phenomenology of religion, the logic is simply, "If the presence of God fell on you in power, what physical effects would you expect to see? How would your body react? If the power of the Spirit fell on groups, what phenomena would you expect?"

The answer can be derived in four ways, (a) from the written Word of God,[20] (b) from documented historical occurrences, (c) from contrasts with parallel power encounters with the occult and (d) from examination of present-day experiences. There are consistent answers to all four and among the phenomena, speaking in tongues is a part of the repeated evidence.

Aberrations in usage, as with any common phenomena. are documented (e.g. in the Corinthian church). Despite the sometimes peripheral and sometimes central place of such phenomena in revivals, they are well circumscribed in the structural norms of most Pentecostal denominations. Such aberrations would be a poor basis for rejection of the phenomena.

However, speaking in tongues is only one of the spiritual gifts that the apostle Paul exhorts believers to seek, a minor gifting. It is from a theology of the higher gifts that I wish to derive a theology of Transforming Revival. Since this theme of gifts is central to revival theology from at least the time of Irving in the 1830's, a charismatic theology of social change will only be popularly received if anchored in a theology of spiritual gifting.

Integrated Theory: Phases of Revival

In this chapter I have analysed the popular web of belief about *the nature of revival* starting with its roots in the Lukan accounts and identifying 24 principles. Revival, as understood by revivalists, includes a *time of tarrying*, then *divine outpouring of the Holy Spirit* on groups, with *signs or wonders*, causative or resulting from *conviction of sin* among believers and unbelievers alike, *public repentance*, deep *love, character change, bold declaration* of the reality of his presence and a *multiplication of power* to other groups through those touched.

The expansion of the Spirit's outpouring on groups results in *revival movements*. I have extended missiological theories of revival by examining three questions: the relationship of revival and time, differentiating people group and web movement theories and contrasting urban movement synergies with rural web movements. This leads to a *sustainable but seasonal model* of revival based on a multivariate synergy.

---

20 For a scholarly biblical analysis of debates on the nature of this gift see Keener (2001:171-186).

Fig. 21: Common Web of Belief about Phases of Revival Movements

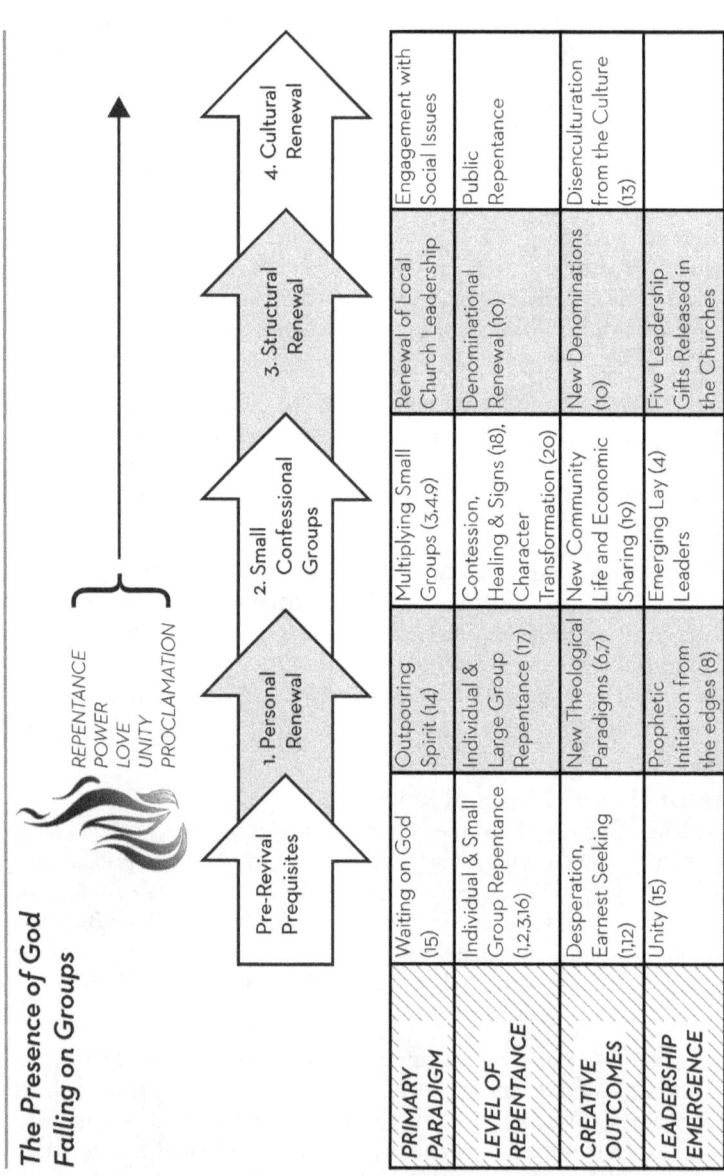

Fig. 21: Revival Movements are generated by the empowering presence of God on groups releasing processes of power, love, unity and proclamation resulting in four expanding phases (Revival principles in brackets).

In Fig. 21 I integrate the recent web of belief among evangelical and Pentecostal thinkers about revival movement progressions[21] as the presence of God affects four phases: first, personal revival; secondly, small confessional groups; thirdly, structural renewal of churches and denominations. Fourthly, I propose that consummated or Transforming Revival achieves deeper engagement with the culture. The culture may or may not respond and be revitalized (as a fifth dynamic?). Movement dynamics may be truncated at any step.

FIG. 22: PROCESSES COMMON TO ALL LEVELS OF REVIVAL MOVEMENTS

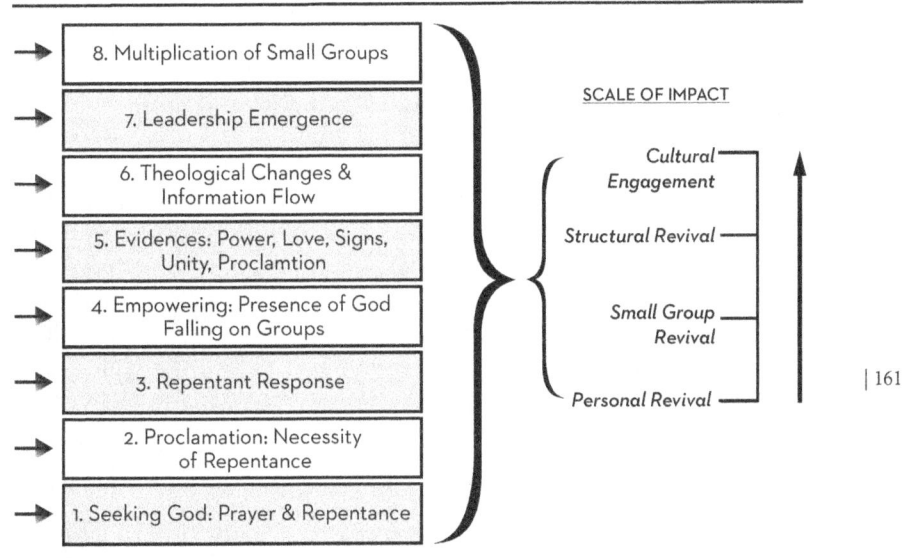

Fig. 22: Common Processes: At each phase, the same processes of seeking God in prayer and repentance, his intervention and anointing and resultant love and power are evident. Information flow and theological transformation are required at each phase, though different information and different theological issues. New styles of leadership need to develop at each phase and each phase necessitates a process of small groups, though these differ in type as the revival expands

The processes at each level though similar, are of differing scale, thus with different dynamics. Conceptual renewal is included in the process of the work of the Spirit in Fig. 22 (rather than as one level in Fig. 21),[22] along with the dynamics of repentance, release of love, unity, signs and power in proclamation, information flow, leadership emergence and multiplication of small groups for each phase. For example, conceptual

---

21 The complexity of the processes implies diversity. Snyder appears to indicate that there is not necessarily a progression but that revival may impact different arenas at different times (1996b: 293).

22 Snyder includes it as one of his five dimensions of renewal (1989/1997: 288-289), but it appears to me that the principle of theological change occurs at each level.

change required for cultural engagement is much more complex than for personal revival, with very different information flows.

I have shown aspects of transitions from an evangelical web of belief to a new Transforming Revival web of belief. In the next chapter, I examine pressures that have accelerated engagement in transformation of New Zealand.

- 11 -

Revival & Enraged Engagement

> *In KiwiKulture we aim to fill life with meaning by getting everyone a good education, building a sound economy and providing full employment. This will liberate us to be a nation of devout hedonists in which we live our lives for our own leisures and pleasures.*
>
> Paul Windsor on Kiwikulture (1994)

Moving from revival in New Zealand and a theory of revival dynamics, this chapter progresses to the fourth phase of cultural engagement in the New Zealand revival. This, the first action-reflection research cycle (p 18), employed to ground the theory of Transforming Revival, will reflect on the build up to engagement. Chapter 14 will reflect on engagement in multiple city sectors by the Vision for Auckland city leadership.

Beginning with identification of progressions in these movements and analysis of rage as catalyst to action, this chapter asks of the period prior to the research in 1970-1996, "What pushed New Zealand Pentecostals and charismatics into social engagement?"

Revival, Theology and Social Engagement

The entrance stories in the first chapter, plus the historical experiences of revival in Chapter 10 give biblical and historical reasons for expecting engagement to result from revival. But it does not always happen. In one of his last public lectures, Edwin Orr discussed with us his conclusion, over the years, that revival "may or may not" lead to significant socio-economic-political change (1955:95-113, 125). His response confused me, because despite his years of research there was a lack of conciseness as to cause and effect, almost a classic (for Evangelicals of those days) unwillingness to examine the social implications of the gospel. It seemed to me, reading book after book about revivals, that the social outworkings depend on the leadership given and theology taught, either before or during their progress.

This conclusion was reinforced by a two-year period in the American charismatic Vineyard movement of John Wimber. He carried one of my books about the poor with him for a few months and was much influenced by a friend, Jackie Pullinger, who works among the poor in Hong Kong - both of us teaching that the fruit of renewal was to preach the gospel to the poor. He sought to focus his movement towards the poor. It was too difficult to turn the movement, when the underlying principles had not been built in from its foundations. I concluded that theological factors preceding (or during) revivals are crucial to their outcomes. Thus a theology of *Transforming Revival* becomes essential.

Manifestations of the Passion, Zeal and Anger of the Holy Spirit

The natural progression from revival to engagement also does not explain the passion and the speed of such processes among NZ charismatics.

Wallace (1956) describes some precipitating mechanisms that switch religious movements from upholding the social order towards social change. Mechanisms may include class reaction to oppression, frustration of interest, loss of social control. They may result from social disorganisation and anomie or some form of deprivation.[1] Sociologist of religion, Gerlach (1974:671-676), rejected the view that early American Pentecostalism (and we can apply his analysis to many renewal structures) was primarily an expression of frustration and resignation, but was a movement that created ingenious mechanisms for extending its influence by diffused leadership, flexible resilient structures and semi-autonomous cells.

> Such ideology encourages individual and group persistence, risk taking, sacrifice for the cause, identifies an unjust opposition, strong enough to challenge but eventually overcome and bridge-burning acts that set the participant apart from the established order and often from past associations (681).

So which of these have been factors in the transition? My observation is that the precipitating factors have been a quiet anger at perceived governmental leadership into national cultural and moral disintegration and failure to listen to the voice of the people! This is akin to Wallace's "class reaction to oppression; frustration of interest." But the anger has found fertile ground in these renewed people with a sense of destiny.[2]

Theology of Rage

Anger, or more poetically, *rage*, is an interesting phenomenon in the building of movements. Here, I examine it theologically, as a response of the grief of the Spirit. There is an interesting interplay between grief and anger in the Godhead, expressed in the prophets. Jewish activist Alinsky (1969), as the founder of community organisation theory, James Cone (1972; 1975) and others, of African-American liberation theology, along with Frantz Fanon (1986) and other leftist activists of various hues, have defined such grief-anger as the essential propellant for movements of change.

---

1   The social science literature on social dislocation, cognitive dissonance, status discontent theories as possible causes of the emergence of the "New Christian Right" in the UK are discussed in Hunt (2002).

2   Gerlach's rejection of frustration in the formation of these movements is correct. The frustration in this case causes their conversion from sectarian non-involvement to proactive social activism.

The evangelical mindset in New Zealand included a perceived disempowerment, shock at the rapid breakdown of social structure, a quiet rage at their sense of the loss of legitimacy and morality of the established church, then anger at the "benign" governments of New Zealand.

However, this loss of respect for governing authorities "appointed by God," violates a serious Pentecostal theme, one reflecting the intrusive American value on submission to directive authority, a theme of largely unquestioning respect/obedience to authority within the church and in government. Governments must be benign, for they are God-appointed and Governments themselves say they are benign! The centuries of non-conformist English roots have been largely forgotten.[3]

Theological Evaluation of Progressions to Rage Activism

The Ten Commandments (nine of them generally understood as universals) are a reasonable starting place for theological evaluation of these social phenomena. I will present an evangelical perspective of social disintegration in New Zealand over the past decades, as Evangelical Christians evaluated changes in the culture (particularly family breakdown and loss of morality in political leadership), against the Ten Commandments. Rather than a balanced evaluation of the culture, this is a judgement made against a high ideal.

If these movements indeed involve people of the Spirit, the apparent judgemental nature of Evangelicals is unsurprising. Indeed, it would be evidence of the work of the Spirit. Jesus indicates primary roles of the Spirit in convicting of sin and judgement (John 16:8-10).

Generational Change in a Modernist Nation

To develop a baseline, we can return to the 1950's. New Zealand had come of age economically and began to see itself as a base of international heroes – Sir Edmund Hillary; or 'the boot', Don Clark, in rugby. It began to distance itself from its colonial master in terms of identity and economically. With sufficient economic security people began to experiment and choose preferred careers. It was a good time, when people felt good about their own progress and about their good nation. This was also the heyday of full churches, which rode on this season of new cultural identity and integration.

The seeds of collapse were inherent in the cultural integration and economic success. This was most apparent to Evangelicals in progressive family breakdown. Along with the technology of the condom in 1964, rock and roll created, perhaps for the first time, a new youth culture. The songs of the Beatles, the Rolling Stones and others about free love created a cultural rejection of abstinence and authority. Thus a confluence of economics, technological abrogation of temperance in morality and popular cultural rejection of social controls, began the unravelling of the secure family – for which New Zealanders had aspired for 100 years. By the 1970's, along with the drunken immorality of the Saturday night party, came the cohabitation of students in mixed flats, then the increasing incidence of *de facto* marital relationships, finally resulting

---

3   This would not be true among most Baptist churches which value independence and individuality highly - perhaps reflecting those non-conformist roots.

in a generation of broken families with single mothers raising the children. At least in sexual *mores*, the morality of the church was no longer acknowledged.

Evans tracks these progressions through specific issues as they moved into the deletion of Christian principles as the basis for law (1992). The removal of fault as a divorce criterion in 1980, replaced Christian principles with more secular grounds for divorce. There was increasing recognition of *de facto* marriage (in contrast to laws against "living in sin"). In 1986, in relationship to the Family Proceedings Act (7a), marriage was defined to include "a relationship in which the parties are or have been living as husband and wife although not legally married to each other."

Judged against the seventh and tenth commandment, "You shall not commit adultery," and "You shall not covet your neighbour's wife," Evangelicals perceived a loss of values. Given this logical basis, we would expect a grieving of the Spirit.

Imposition of Moral Vision

By the late 1980's, the demanding drive for economic and social security of early New Zealand pioneers and nation-builders had generally been met across the nation. New visions beyond economic security and stable families were needed as people now had time to be and do what they desired. My analysis is that the nation faltered as it moved into this phase of "freedom to be". While it defined its economic goals, it failed to define its ideals in terms of moral vision that reflected the Kingdom of God. The good life became the life of ease, as Paul Windsor aptly states, "The children of the good life are emerging as hedonists whose primary pursuit is leisure and pleasure" (1994). In this vacuum, with the appointment of Helen Clark as prime minister, began what is commonly called a period of social engineering, the imposition of other moral visions, leftist agendas built on solid economic gains by the capitalist economy, and including strong feminist/lesbian/homosexual agendas (Paterson, 2005). This "moral vision" was at odds with evangelical beliefs.

Turning Point Events

As those types of Christianity linked to the state declined in influence, Evangelicals and Pentecostals were emerging as a potential force numerically to fill the gap. However, up until the 1980's, Evangelicals had retrenched into non-involvement in public issues. The shocks of some events in the 1980's and beyond reversed that trend. At issue in this study, is the extent and future of that reversal. Ahdar's (2000: 9-23) significant analysis, parallels, from a legal perspective, the theological analysis of this chapter. He describes three phases of disestablishment of religion to the point of marginalisation in the 1960's. He calls the response, 'awakening from slumber'.

Ryan (1986), in another significant study, indicates the increasing consternation in the 1980's of conservative Christians at the process of secularisation, the lost role of the churches as major social legitimizers and the "moral crisis." But this does not explain why, in New Zealand, many Evangelicals changed from what H. Richard Niebuhr (1951/1956) describes as a Christ-against-culture insulation to active involvement in Christ-transformer-of-culture activism over two decades.

Several confrontatational events, "stands for righteousness," in New Zealand seem significant in building a momentum for changes in theological stance: Patricia Bartlett's 41,000 signature petition against pornography, nudity and homosexuality sparked by the show *Oh Calcutta!* in 1970 (rejected); the Jesus Marches of 1972 (Shaw, 1972); and a petition of 835,000 signatures in opposition to the Homosexual Law Reform of 1985 (rejected). The cycle has repeated again with the Destiny Marches against further Homosexual Law Reform (pilloried) in 2005. John Evans (1992), links the early events to an early phase of emergence of socially active conservative churches as they sought to deal with the issues of a sexually permissive society.[4] These actions were seen by Evangelicals not primarily as political responses but as public statements of repentance, attempts to avert the judgement of a grief-stricken God.

Alternatives to Individualism and Consumerism
To the children of the revival, the first commandment, "to have no other gods before me," and the tenth commandment "to not covet" became abrogated in a culture of advertising, with affluence as the purpose of life. Logic again would lead us to expect the grief of the Holy Spirit. This grief was outworked by many new evangelical children of the revival seeking to opt out of society. Numbers sought to build alternative communities, live lives of simplicity and struggled with creating alternative economic structures.[5]

In the 1970's, as charismatic renewal swept the country, many families formed communities to demonstrate alternative models of ownership and use of possessions. Some of these later became churches. Perhaps this reflected Kiwi culture; New Zealand has, according to Sargisson and Sargent (2004: cover), more intentional communities per capita than any country. For many, such as the Paengaroa community, with which Milton Smith became associated and out of which Comvita Healthfoods developed as a multinational, it was an extension of their conversion from a hippy lifestyle.[6] But by the 1990's, most Christian communities had collapsed, particularly those built around possession of land.[7]

On the other hand, not many sought alternative economic approaches – there was little integrated economic theology to draw from, as Catholic and WCC theologies had been rejected – we were just producing the early papers on simplicity, redistribution, co-operative economics (Grigg, 1981; 1984/2004:87-95; 1985; 1985/2004; McInnes, 1980 and communications from Tear Fund).

Yet looking toward the 1990's, despite the imported American Pentecostal *prosperity gospel* taught in the larger descendent churches of the AOG,[8] which affirmed success

---

4   This view perhaps reflects his selection of interviewees among Calvinist-fundamentalist leaders in the Christian Heritage Political Party.
5   Brian Hathaway captures the core of the teaching that a number of leaders shared (1990:127-155).
6   As an example of such communal dynamics, see extensive discussion of its rise and implosion in Milton Smith's biography (Steel, 2003).
7   Sargisson states that more New Zealand and more religious communities survive than in other countries (Sargisson & Sargent, 2004: xv). This was not the case with these early charismatic communities.
8   See David Martin's rhetoric on the same conflict of economic values among Pentecostals in

measured in financial terms, these early simplicity themes have resurfaced (Benge, 2003; Hathaway, 1990; Hofmans-Sheard, 2003). Thus internal unity on the use of wealth within Evangelicalism is not assured, though the prosperity gospel has become a dominant theme.[9] After thirty years and initial motivation to experiment with economic alternatives, the commandment to not covet has ceased to be a major source of rage. The dulling of holy anger by consumerism was predicted by Jesus 2000 years ago in Matt 6:24.

Abortion

Typical of the evangelical perceptions of the decline in morality through these decades was concern about the increase in abortions.[10] Since the 1960's, the increase in extramarital relationships and children born out of wedlock had escalated. This increased pressure to legalise abortion, not merely from medical necessity, but essentially on demand.

The Evangelical and Catholic Christian response was dramatic, incensed and sustained until the early 1990's. There have been multiple attempts to publicise and highlight "the murder of the unborn child." Despite the level of protest, the government first pushed through acts legislating for abortion effectively on demand, following the 1977 Royal Commission on Contraception, Sterilisation and Abortion. Evangelicals contend that the law has consistently violated the sixth commandment, "You shall not murder."

The Sensual Environment

Evangelicals are also a significant presence in family counselling sectors of society, an indicator of the importance placed on family. "Traditional family values," generally defines the family as a two parent intergenerational family that remains fundamental to civil society.[11]

To many Evangelicals, the loss of marriage as the foundational institution in society appears more like a rout than a gradual decline. 20% of the population are formally in extramarital relationships, or divorced or separated (Statistics New Zealand, 2002:148-9). 41% of births are outside of marriage (Doyle, 2001).[12] But yearly, the figures increase. Figures released by Statistics New Zealand in November 2004, show that of women in their early 20s the proportion cohabiting rose from 19 percent in 1981 to 71 percent by 2001. In the same period the number of married women in this age group fell from 58,000 to 10,000.

Latin America (Martin, 2002: 88).

9   In discussions with Evangelical leaders in business in Auckland, I realised the extent of this. Since there is little economic teaching in these churches and less on redistribution, my observations are that their agendas have come to be set by the Business Round Table. The prosperity gospel is compatible with these views.

10 6000 in 1936, 8789 in 1987, 16,103 in 2000, of which 15,800 were authorised on the grounds of 'serious danger to the mental health of the woman or girl' (Statistics New Zealand, 2002: 190).

11 At least on this issue, Maxim Institute represent the Evangelical voice (New Zealand Association of Christian Schools, 2005b).

12 Doyle (2001) analyses this trend across the industrialised nations, where New Zealand stands as one of the higher ranked nations.

A courageous journalist, Ian Wishart, described an avowed agenda of Helen Clark, as Labour prime minister, to advance the goals of the gay and lesbian community (2003: 32-41).[13] Evangelicals and Pentecostals take as normative the apostle Paul's identification of homosexual activity as the last step in his description of the moral breakdown in Romans 1:18-32. Decriminalisation of homosexual activity and the active promulgation of homosexual lifestyles felt to my evangelical friends like national rape. Mick Duncan describes the Destiny March in response to the 2005 steps in this progression as a "public display of outrage" (2005:13,14).

- Polarising National Leadership -

> I witnessed a spontaneous burst of applause by a group of Christian leaders from across the denominational and political spectrum, when a brother declared that he planned to stand against her in the next elections. The emotion and unity in that outburst were caused by deep anger and frustration at Helen Clark's previous day's "engineering" of the legalisation of prostitution. Particularly as a good number of Christians across the nation are involved in rescuing people from abuse within prostitution and homosexual lifestyles. Many are also involved in caring for AIDS victims.

This stance on purity has been sustained in an environment where increasingly overarching themes on television include both permissive sensuality outside of marriage and overt homosexual acts. The appointment of practicing homosexuals to the leadership of TVNZ and pressure directly by the prime minister, Helen Clark, to screen homosexual shows in earlier time slots (Wishart, 2003: 39), is seen as highly intrusive governmental aggression against godly child-raising. The censorship laws from the 1980's had no intention of excluding anything except the worst kinds of immorality or violence and certainly were not directed towards positively affirming committed marital relationships. Few use them, recognizing that they will not bring about any censorship appropriate for children. The government censor is clear that sexual scenes between consenting adults are acceptable within his frame of reference.[14]

- Failed Censorship Laws -

> A letter to TV3 after they showed public nudity to my 12 year old son at 7 p.m. on Campbell Live on May 4, 2005, went through their complaints review process. My complaint was rejected as "this was not unacceptable to a significant number of viewers." They consider it would "not have caused distress or offence". "naked breasts …are not of themselves obscene, indecent, or upsetting to children". They needed to uphold "freedom of speech."

Alternative Media, Alternative Education
The anger has produced alternative evangelical radio stations and ShineTV as a channel within SkyTV. The increasing intrusion of television into the living room and computer into the bedroom raised the spectre of a generation of children not

---

13 The steps in an agenda outlined in documents in feminist meetings in the 1970's have been followed in detail (Paterson, 2005).

14 Late night TV interview 9th Sept 2003, TV1.

raised by parents with Christian values but by values beamed by a largely uncensored media into homes. Christians of all hues, who were serious in their commitment to purity, understood that the extension of the commandment against adultery by Jesus, to not even look lustfully on a woman, had become an impossibility in most homes, including Christian ones.

The affirmation of premarital sex in public school sex education and refusal to modify this stance to include abstinence, led to the search for alternative Christian schools — even at great financial cost to evangelical parents.[15] Middleton Grange School, the first of a new breed of Christian schools was started by a group of concerned Evangelicals and people with a Reformed tradition in Christchurch in 1964. In 1976, Rob Wheeler, a leader of the New Life stream of Pentecostal churches had observed Accelerated Christian Education schools in USA and saw the opportunity to re-establish Christian schooling in NZ and protect their children from rampant humanism in state schools. In the late 1970's about 20 schools using ACE were set up by local churches around NZ. There are nearly 90 schools in NZ with an Evangelical or Pentecostal distinctive, with over 12,000 students. Added to this, about 4000 children are being home schooled for Christian reasons (New Zealand Association of Christian Schools, 2005a).

The 1990s also saw the establishment of Christian teacher education establishments. Two began in 1993, namely MASTERS Institute which is now based in Mt Roskill in Auckland and Bethlehem Institute in Tauranga.

Thus, Evangelical/Pentecostal reactions have created attempts to both engage society in anger and to withdraw into new alternative structures. Perceptions of the violated ten commandments — loss of respect for parents, murder of children, free adultery, a culture of covetousness — underlie an evangelical perception of disintegrating core moral values. If the revival was a genuine work of the Spirit, I would have expected the grief of the Spirit to manifest itself in increased public judgement and angry rage by Evangelicals.

Opiate to the Rage
Looking at other social developments, new cultural integrations were developing that (in Marxist terminology), acted as an opiate to the anger, blunting the drive towards activism and encouraging many Pentecostal churches, particularly those with strong numbers of business people, to affirm the status quo. Sustained economic growth in the 1990's and increased consumerism; greater freedom for women who desired to be in the workforce; increased opportunity for entrepreneurial development; expansion of international trade; the development of multiculturalism; greater ecological awareness; the opening of the tertiary education system to greater experimentation; the Waitangi Tribunal and reconciliation processes between Pakeha and Maori – these could all be seen as good and godly progressions towards a more just society.

Even if Evangelicals sometimes lacked the theological frameworks to understand God and productive economics, expansion of creativity, or redressing of injustices,

---

15 Knowles describes the initial impetus for these with the introduction of the ACE system from the States among the indigenous (New Life) churches (2000).

they were buoyed by these apparent advances in society to remain in society and its economic structures.

Reaction + Vacuum + Cultural Dependency = Confrontation

These tensions generated reactions at some turning points, fermenting the rise of the New Christian Right. There was a determination to move from symbolic public repentance and enter the realm of public policy, once it became apparent that elected public officials would not respond on moral issues to the voices of those who cared about Christian morality.[16] But there was no heritage to draw from concerning social transformation and little social analysis. Rejection of the National Council of Churches for its perceived denial of the full authority of the Scriptures meant traditional theological views on involvement in public affairs were unacceptable.

The barriers caused by disestablishment of traditional Christian religion were not well analysed. One was privatisation of religion (confining it to the private realm).

> *The privatisation of religion is now being experienced with full vigour. A cultural Christian establishment had shielded Christians from the full effects of privatisation. In this sense the thorough privatisation of relig9ion was never achieved for the* de jure *disestablishment was offset by a continued* de facto *establishment of a cultural Christianity. This cultural hegemony has now gone, leaving many Conservative Christians feeling bewildered and vulnerable. Their religion really is privatized now, in law and in fact* (Ahdar, 2000:112).

It took some years for a number of evangelical leaders to conclude that Christian agendas in the public domain were best phrased in secular language to attain public validity – this is a language of rationality, not of subjectivism, emotion or anything that could be labelled religious, superstitious or sectarian. This became a significant principle behind development of the United Futures party,[17] along with an understanding that politics involves the art of compromise. However failure in their coalition arrangements to confront Labour lesbian/gay agendas effectively, largely lost them the confidence of the Evangelicals.

One failed attempt at analysis was the use of "secular humanism" to define the enemy. in the 1980's.[18] It was not the label secular Kiwis used of themselves, so Christians found themselves shadow boxing.

Given this analysis of the final death-throes of privileged Christendom, there were, insuperable barriers to anything beyond ineffectual and conflictual prophetic engagement. Ahdar, when discussing the prevailing "Wellington Worldview", the philosophy underlying the New Zealand legal system, "the taken for granted way of perceiving reality", speaks of several characteristics: [1] neutrality concerning the conception of the good society, [2] privatisation of religion, [3] rationality (vs. religion which in-

---

16 Ruth Smithies with Catholic Peace and Justice Commission and Peter Lineham expressed the same perception (Lineham, 2004:149)..

17 Personal discussions with Bernie Ogilvie, United Futures MP.

18 For example, the Coalition of Concerned Citizens, in 1987, published articles on humanism in the Media, in the Classroom, as a Global Plan, etc., distributing 105,000 copies through Challenge Weekly (17 Apr., 1987).

volves subjectivism, emotion and superstition) and [4] a doctrine of progress (some improvement in moral and political understanding and behaviour) (2000:75-85). Using a confrontational approach did not produce a breakthrough in any of these four characteristics. It was a difficult task and Evangelicals came up like boxers, battered and reeling, unable to grasp what had happened to them. Wrong cultural analysis and inadequate strategy as to the level at which change should be attempted lead to frustration.

Lineham adds to Ahdar's themes changes in governmental style from one based on principle to one driven by expert consultant advice (2004:147-151), while identifying modifications to this approach with MMP[19] and changes of government. This demonstrates the necessity of Evangelicals to coordinate consultations of experts in major sectors of society, training them in critical theological frameworks (Chapter 8) and seeking to define middle axioms so that they can then work out specific expert responses as issues surface. This necessitates think tanks, forums, institutes and eventually universities. These steps were neither strategised nor executed, as the focus of energy was on creating political parties.

Global Sources of Evangelical Social Theology

Social and political involvement in New Zealand, however, has to be evaluated in terms of both internal and external stimuli. Interestingly the same progressions into active political involvement have been occurring among Latin American Pentecostals during the same period (Petersen, 1996:115).[20] Is this a natural progression or is it being accelerated by global connections between national leaderships from these countries through the seminary systems and global networks like Lausanne?

Mainstream Evangelicalism had been slowly expanding social theology aided by other sources than revival. Theologically, the 1974 Lausanne Covenant, filtered down to leading New Zealand Evangelicals. Another source was the global Tertiary Students' Christian Fellowship (TSCF), the major evangelical student movement up until the 1980's. It was enthused with Francis Schaeffer's theological critiques of Western culture (1968a; 1968b; 1981: including his Christian response to secular humanism) and this heritage has continued on into many people's lives and roles in social leadership. My perception is that no movement dynamic eventually has come from it, perhaps because of historical decisions as to the non-hierarchical nature of leadership in TSCF.

I evaluate it as having produced "sleepers", now successful in their professions and in significant social roles, with a background of thinking about social issues, but waiting to be activated by an apostolic and networking dynamic. These are salt and light people who were left without national leadership structures and synergistic relationships by TSCF, which in other countries, such as India, developed graduate networks of significance.

---

19 MMP = Mixed Member Proportional (MMP) voting system introduced to New Zealand in 1996, where New Zealanders vote once for a candidate and once for a party in the same national elections.

20 See also the extensive reflections on an ambiguity of responses across Latin America in Martin (2002: 88-98).

- John Skeates: Manager Of Corporate Culture Change -

> Typical is John Skeates, formerly marketing manager of a New Zealand multinational pharmaceutical corporation who in student years had studied Francis Schaeffer. He found increasing disparity between the Sunday morning worship and focus on building the local church and his desire to bring freedom into oppressive working relationships. This led to experimentation with his own consulting company to bring principles of the Kingdom into envisioning and team building processes of companies. Eventually he moved back into management believing he could better accomplish his purpose from within a corporate role. The avenues to express this were not found in the local churches. The synergistic relationships with like-minded CEO's has been difficult to find.

I also suggest that lack of synergistic structures is partially caused by the minimal New Zealand evangelical connections to global evangelical centres of transformational theology in the Lausanne Movement, the Gospel and Cultures Network and urban transformation movements. While some leaders bridged to these movements, they were not significant in terms of setting the directions of activism. A sign of this was the return of Dr Harold Turner[21] to New Zealand, a companion of Lesslie Newbigin in the global *Gospel and Cultures Network*. He was hailed with great acclaim. A cluster of leaders around him developed the *DeepSight Trust: A New Zealand Initiative for Religion and Cultures* (2005). The return of Bruce and Kathleen Nichols from forty years in India, as leaders of the *World Evangelical Theological Commission*, was less acclaimed but has led to significant expansion of Vision Network task forces in theology, science and faith and the environment.

Connections to the fundamentalist and Pentecostal heartland of the Southern USA opened the door for an influx of right-wing fundamentalist approaches to combat something labelled "secular humanism".[22] "It served as a convenient shorthand label for the enemy and as a seemingly compelling socio-philosophical explanation of why permissiveness was increasing" (Ahdar, 2000: 61). The Coalition of Concerned Citizens and from its demise, the significantly fundamentalist and Dutch Reformed Christian Heritage Party and then the Christian Coalition all expressed the groping of a soul, subject to the whims of each right-wing guru imported by some enthusiastic Pentecostal or fundamentalist.

These approaches may have expressed the Southern US heartland but not the New Zealand soul. The American Religious Right is known for state enforcement of personal morality, its conservative tenor of thought, its nationalistic fervour and its free market capitalism (Ansley, 1988; Neuhaus, 1984). The common people of New Zealand rejected these *en mass*.

> *This was the lasting dilemma for many conservative Christians. The situation was perceived to be serious. The solution was clear and uncompromising: the state enactment of biblical principles. However the only way this could be achieved was by winning political office and that now does not seem likely. The electorate seems to have rejected*

---

21 Some autobiographical reflections in *The Laughter of Providence* (Turner, 2001).
22 Ahdar gives some of the roots of its development in New Zealand (2000: 58-61).

the cure; it perhaps has even rejected the diagnosis (Evans, 1992:320).

My observation is that this kind of response will keep recurring as fundamentalism consistently reappears. The latest expression (in 2004) has been the expansion of the fundamentalist Pentecostal Destiny Church into catalysing a political party with its own polarising public marches.

These movements also manifest characteristics of absolutist and entrepre-neurial business nature of fundamentalist and Pentecostal Christianity:

- They want change *now*.
- Social analysis is not part of their heritage, so largely uncritical importation of US models is acceptable.
- Theological astuteness is not recognised as significant among leaders of these movements, so little political theological reflection occurs. Since Tom Marshall, no theologically literate yet pneumatologically anointed national figure has arisen.
- An absolutism in theology. Unity with other Christians was not a priority, so Calvinists such as lead the Christian Heritage Party made absolutist claims to represent the Christian views of New Zealand ignoring other Christian perspectives.
- Power is an important theme for Pentecostal leadership, so placing Christians in points of governmental power seemed the logical objective.
- The dispersed authority and financial structures of these movements meant that short bursts of activity around issues could be sustained, but rarely long-term resourcing.

Faced with a nation without apparent moral leadership and without, in their opinion, effective voices from the traditional churches, charismatics and Pentecostals began to flip-flop between expressing social outrage and retreating into hopes of sudden revival. However, many leaders began to search for a more effective integrative theology and strategy that would enable effective action. Politically, apart from a dozen committed Christians scattered through Labour, New Zealand First and the National Party,[23] the influence of Kingdom theology enabled several to become members of government through the United Futures Party in 2001, with a clearer understanding of the complexity of political processes based on the Kingdom of God.

But Kingdom theology, while known in name, was not widely understood. Training of experts in the implications of theology and particularly the Kingdom of God for their fields was minimal. And given the centrality of the work of the Spirit to these movements, such a theology would need to be derived from pneumatology, but that thinking had not been done. Revival slowed. Lack of effective cultural analysis and a theological core were major factors in it failing to engage the issues of the day.

To fill this gap, the next chapter develops a theory of Transforming Revival, based on the release of spiritual gifts in revival.

---

23 One or two from each party attended a Vision Network election thinktank, March, 2005 and identified other committed Christians across all the parties except the Greens.

- 12 -

CITYWIDE TRANSFORMING REVIVAL

> *I have understood that the most fruitful approach to developing the theological foundations for a social ethic for Hispanic Pentecostalism rests in the development of a social spirituality. This spirituality must emerge and thus cohere with Hispanic Pentecostal experience — particularly as it relates to the ministry of the Spirit*
>
> Eldon Villafañe (1993b:193).

This chapter expands revival and revival movement theories of the previous chapters into a theory of *Citywide Transforming Revival* as part of a proposal to fill the theological vacuum identified in the previous chapter.

Interpreting Loss of the Presence

Is such a theory necessary? I have already alluded to the loss of the national revival dynamic, how it failed to some extent through redirection from biblical ends of releasing the laity to bring the Kingdom into society, into a pastorally-controlled institutional focus on the intermediate goal of church growth, accelerated in the migration to Pentecostalism.

Part of the difficulty for charismatic leaders in New Zealand was to interpret the loss of presence and power. The decline of the New Zealand-wide revival appears to have been largely due to too rapid institutionalisation, lack of sustained theological development, failure to develop leadership training and breakdown of information flow from core leadership as it became denominationalised. However, it is difficult for leaders to tell the people that revival has died because of leadership failures.

Failure to teach the relationship of repentance, changes in economic and social lifestyles, reconciliation and social justice are factors and such issues are more understandable. However, to a large extent, apology for the failure of leadership in these issues has been largely absent in evangelical churches. The issues remained outside the theological framework of most.

In the vacuum of explanation for the loss of the presence, many people touched by the revival migrated to Pentecostal churches. However, interpretataions of why God had lifted his hand, were also not part of Pentecostal teaching. Instead, (along with the real ongoing presence of God on some touched by the revival), imported specialist revivalists, or those gifted in sign gifts and more fervent attempts to recall the former presence of God, became normative.

- Nz Prophet Of Revival -

> I worshipped, listening to one of New Zealand's godly prophets. When he speaks, in a down to earth Kiwi honesty, there is evidence of the presence of God on him, as he shakes. When he prays for people they fall down under the power of God. These signs affirm to Assemblies of God people his words about upcoming revival. Such words repeat a hundred years of institutionalised oral tradition within the Assemblies of God.

I do not wish to imply that God is not at work or that spiritual growth is not occurring through such prophets. But that is neither revival, nor Transforming Revival. It is expansion of institutional themes through those with prophetic giftings. Another strange phenomenon, is the dependence on American "prophets." I listened to the advertising about a new "prophetic" magazine on Radio Rhema.[1] The magazine includes "articles by various prophetic leaders" (it then mentioned three American authors, recognised as godly prophets in their contexts, but unconnected with New Zealand).

Better explanation is needed! It is not honest to keep prophesying, "Revival is coming! Revival is coming!" without defining the nature of obedience once revival has come.

I now offer an alternative framework, by developing a theory of Transforming Revival, beginning with several principles already developed in the analysis of revival. The foundational principle I have identified as the coming of the Spirit in power:

> Transforming Revival 1 – *Communal Presence: The cause of Transforming Revival in the city is the overwhelming presence of God among the people of God.*

At the same time, revival has to be defined in terms of the relationship of the Holy Spirit and the public square. This I have expressed in the second principle:

---

1   15 Feb, 2005.

> Transforming Revival 2 – *Consummation and Cultural Revitalisation: Revivals progress to consummation in a phase of transformation that involves cultural engagement, with the possibilities of cultural revitalisation if there is a response of public repentance.*

Two other principles of theological progressions have been identified:

> Transforming Revival 3 – *New Theologies: Revival movements are often initiated by a small shift in theological thinking that releases energy for change* (Lovelace, 1979:381-383; Pierson, 1985:3a).

> Transforming Revival 4 – *Necessity of Integrative Theology: Revivals result in long-term social transformation if they have disseminated theologies that support such an activity* (Orr 1955:95-113, 125)).

Fig. 23 portrays the processes proposed and some of the principles discussed in this chapter. The theme of the last chapter can be added to the principles already observed:

> Transforming Revival 5 – *Public Grief-Anger: One of the evidences of a movement being Spirit-filled is grief-anger, when biblical ethics are violated in the public arena.*

An interesting paradox of Christian character and the nature of the Spirit is the juxtaposition of this grief and anger with deep love. The revival principle of the release of love in Chapter 10, gives rise to the next proposals concerning love and consensus-seeking, when it is extended from the level of individual revival to social levels.

> Transforming Revival 6 – *Increased Love: Transforming Revival within extensive sectors of a city increases love and unity in the public square.*

This has a corollary:

> Transforming Revival 7 – *Consensus Seeking: Transforming Revival unfolds a divine sensitivity to others, greatly enhancing an environment for truth and consensus seeking.*

How did I reach these conclusions? In my first years grappling with injustice in the slums of Manila, I taught an analysis on Isaiah 58 that showed progressions towards a righteous society, and progressions away from righteousness in Isaiah 59. One foundational element in a good society derived from these passages is the capacity for truth-seeking public dialogue on issues. This enables consensus seeking. Ungodliness entwined with "lying tongues," causes divisiveness and eventually both oppression and a response of violence in Isaiah 59. The release of love and unity should create men and women with greater capacity and perception towards seeking consensus and truth. James tells us that people of the Spirit move away from dogmatism and absolutism to an openness to reason (3:16, 17).

- Dick Hubbard: Social Entrepreneur -

> Dick Hubbard, businessman, has for some years sought to develop businesses based on social responsibility. Evaluating the behaviour of the previous mayor as unnecessarily abrasive, in 2004 he stood for the mayoralty and won, in order to bring a graciousness into the civic forum. The decision to do so was made with his wife, in the context of seeking God.[2]

Urban Plurality and Citywide Revival

The second corollary has to do with breaking down existing barriers:

> Transforming Revival 8 – *Reconciliation: Revivals move peoples towards reconciliation, both racial and ecumenical.*

Cultural and economic barriers exist between cultural groups within any mega-city. In a larger city such as Auckland, several migrant groups are large enough to coexist with others but function largely within their own circles. The revival has generated men and women of the Spirit in Auckland who are actively working to integrate new communities and dialogue with leadership of entrenched cultural groups. Teaching theologies of reconciliation accelerates such processes and surely must be the work of the Holy Spirit.

- Called to Reconcile -

> "I run reconciliation classes for Maori and Pakeha," she said at the end of a seminar on a Vision for Auckland. "That is wonderful! Who helped you to get into this?" "Just the Lord! I'm charismatic and the Lord began to speak to me about this in pictures, so I just began, then I studied it at university. Now as a lecturer, I give seminars up and down the country."

This leads to my focus on a postmodern mega-city. In a mega-city, in contrast with the mono-cultural rural town, we need to evaluate the idea of synergies.[3] With the emergence of mega-cities, there are new limitations but also new possibilities of city-wide revival. Transforming Revival involves not only the expansion of one revival movement, but also the impact of synergistic movements on whole cities or cultures.

Historic revival has often been within tribal or people groups such as the Naga people in India, the Maori of the 19th century, the Walamo tribes of Ethiopia (1937-43) or the Welsh Revival of 1904, or uniform cultural contexts where rapid people-movement dynamics have exploded, such as in Korea. In each case, it institutes a phase of new cultural

---

2   Summary of a presentation by the mayor's wife, Jan, 2005 at a Vision for Auckland breakfast.
3   Synergy is defined here as 'the combined effect of organisms co-operating together, that exceeds the sum of the individual efforts'.

interpretations after cultural disintegration or damage.

In contrast, experience with city leadership teams gives little evidence of complex, pluralistic cities entering into sustainable Transforming Revival from a single dramatic event as portrayed in the transformation videos of George Otis, Jr (1999).[4] On the other hand progressions in some cities — the Brazilian cities, Manila, Mumbai, Chennai, Nairobi and elsewhere, indicate the possibilities of *synergistic* change.

In terms of revival synergy in Auckland the gospel has moved rapidly among migrant mainland Chinese (but less among Taiwanese). Another style of Christianity appears among Koreans and totally independent webs occur among Fijian Indians and wealthy, highly educated Tamil and Malayalam migrants from South India. The size of each ethnic or linguistic population limits each movement. Although barriers between them hinder the rapid flow of the work of the Holy Spirit in a citywide movement, I have observed a number of events now where the Holy Spirit is released upon groups of leaders which include people from these diverse cultural backgrounds. There is a releasing of love and a desire to work together.

> Transforming Revival 9 – *Synergy: Citywide revival movements occur when a synergy develops between web movements in a number of ethnic, racial or social sectors, so that each contributes to the others at crucial points.*

The theological and praxis themes being reworked in this study are part of the ongoing global search for such dynamics. Knowles (2004:50-51) discusses *factors of reinforcement*, referring to social factors in society that reinforce certain elements of Pentecostal belief. I suggest the term can be applied to reinforcement between similar revival movements within the geographic space of a mega-city.

Revival: Necessary Or Sufficient Condition for Transformation?

Popular NZ Pentecostalism holds that revival and subsequent filling of churches automatically results in social transformation. This view raises the questions, "Is spiritual revival a precursor to social change movements towards righteousness? To what extent? Under what conditions?"

Latourette (1953/1975: 1019) and Lovelace (1979:354-400) demonstrate a positive relationship between revival, lasting personal moral change and change in public morality. There is also generally not a major *social vision* driving revival, except the desire for righteousness in the nation and its leadership and for repentance for its sins. But this has moderating factors. It needed the hard social analysis of Wilberforce and the Clapham

---

4   Transformations videos from George Otis Jr. (1999), have taken themes we developed in the AD2000 cities network in 1991 (Grigg, 1997d: 78-83) that were subsequently utilised by the US city leaders' network linking revival to transformation. Otis' derives his understanding of transformation from Ray Bakke. But he appears to confirm Pentecostal beliefs that simply by prayer, cities can be changed, ignoring the hard work of intense academic study and community organising needed to confront philosophies and the society-building that is required along with God's interventions and answers. This may be unintentional.

sect to follow through and achieve the social change that Wesley began.

FIG. 23: PROPOSED WEB OF BELIEF: PHASES OF TRANSFORMING REVIVAL

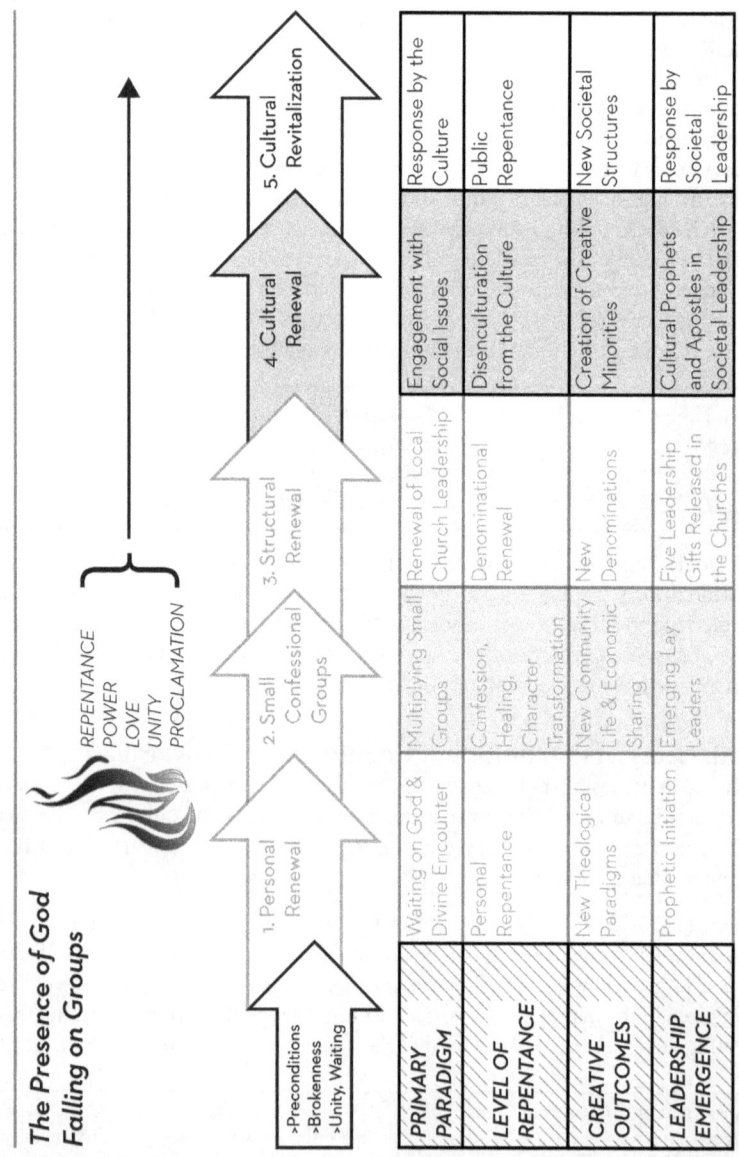

Fig. 23 portrays the five phases of Transforming Revival and some of the elements that occur at each phase (table) and across all phases (repentance, power, love, unity, proclamation.

I suggest however, that revival is not a necessity for social change. The necessary basis is God's activity revealed in common grace on good men and women, resulting in social change towards the highest good. In other words, God's character revealed in the commonality of human goodness is often manifest in good secular people seeking social change. They may or may not be Christians or godly. Thus:

> Transforming Revival 10 – *Significance: Revival is a positive factor in social change towards righteousness.*

> Transforming Revival 11 – *Necessary Condition? Revival is not a necessary condition for transformation but accelerates it and is essential for its completion.*

The logic is as follows:

- The work of the Spirit, life-giver of humanity, is essential for social change towards righteousness.
    - The Spirit is always active in the common affairs of humankind.
    - The Spirit is always active in the church to some extent.
        Thus revival is not a necessary condition for the Spirit's work in church or community
- However, the work of the Spirit is mightily released in church and community during revival.
    - During and as a fruit of revivals, the Spirit's increased activity and freedom to operate accelerates processes of social change towards righteousness.

Also:

> Transforming Revival 12 – *Sufficient: There is not always a 'sufficient' relationship to say that revivals release 'significant' positive social transformation.*

This leads to the question, "To what extent do revivals accelerate social change?" I suggest that a major factor in this involves transformation theologies inherent in the revival web of belief. For these social visions are determined by multivariate sources. There are multiple visions, "calls to activism" within revivals. There are also social visions within the church prior to or subsequent to revivals, influencing the speed of social change.

Release of Entrepreneurial Mindset as Source of Transformation

This leads to another set of questions. Among Pentecostals, does the rejection of the "oppression" of traditional theological frameworks (or "theological corruption") of traditional church structures involve rejection of oppression per se within the broader society? The global analysis gives no consensus on this issue (Berg & Pretiz, 1996: 162;

Martin, 2002: 88-98). Sepulveda, seeking to answer this question in Chile, notes:

> *Social scientists' opinion of Pentecostalism is shown among others in the following expressions: opium, domination via religion, religious proclamation of social conformism, "refuge of the masses"* (1989:81).

Whether this reflects reality or the presuppositions of social scientists is an open question. However, alignment of Latin Pentecostalism with US Anglo evangelical missionary non-involvement in social issues would indicate its truth. Personal discussions with Brazilian and other Latin national evangelical leaders, analysing the extent of social involvement, have identified non-involvement as a major problem. This is a "live and let live" religion.

On the other hand, that is not irrelevant. Voluntary organisations build up "social capital" (Ammerman, 1997: 367-8; Greerley, 1990:154-5) through networks between state and individual. In that sense it is a political act simply to create a layer of institutions which could be integrated into an emerging civil society. Likewise, it is a political act to establish free space and to create models of self-government and participation with a flat hierarchy of management (Martin, 1995:29). Emilio Willems (1967), studied Pentecostals in Chile and Brazil and found that their faith helped them overcome anomie (a sense of loss and disorientation). Other anthropologists mention upward mobility through the mutual support system of the Pentecostal faith community, the acquisition of skills through lay participation in church activities, the preference that honesty gives in job hunting and a greater number of self-employed people (Berg & Pretiz, 1996:163-167).

I observe that at least Auckland Pentecostals include a higher number of contractors and entrepreneurial business people, compared with the number of managers and employees I see in the Baptist and Presbyterian churches.

Such a release of leadership resembles the concept of entrepreneurship. It is a crucial component of Transforming Revival missiology. McClelland (1962), building off Max Weber's understandings of the relationships of religion and economic growth (1963c; 1980), analysed the psychological roots of entrepreneurs. He demonstrated that fifty years after religious (Christian or Muslim) revival , there is economic peak, as children born in the revival turn their diligence, sense of divine purpose, destiny and perfectionism (holiness), not necessarily to religion alone, but to business. As a result, they rise to be the economic leaders of society. There is another development study I read thirty years ago, concerning the psychological roots of entrepreneurs (Hagen, 1971). A suppressed minority in a society, when given freedom will produce highly driven and gifted leaders into upper levels of that society. Would this be true of Evangelicals, with their sense of suppression of morality by Labour's social engineering?

Thus, the fullness of revival may well result in entrepreneurial structures; the biblical terminology is perhaps prophetic and apostolic structures modelling or calling out in the public square for repentance. These then require responses of repentance by the leaders of city structures for the culture to move into cultural revitalisation.

To accelerate the synergy between these, I suggest three missional elements need to be catalysed by city leadership teams:

- Missional Theology: Revival teachers must be informed by full-orbed transformational theological themes of the city of God and Kingdom.
- Missional Structures: Synergistic city-wide structures must be developed to facilitate interaction between apostolic and prophetic nuclei for social change.
- Missional Synergy: Transformational movements need to occur simultaneously or progressively in different sectors of the church, of the ethnicities, classes and structures of the city, with relational communication between them.

Thus, the following are tentatively proposed:

> Transforming Revival 13 – *Empowerment: The empowerment processes of revival produce entrepreneurs. The biblical terminology for the primary giftings in such people is prophetic and apostleship.*

> Transforming Revival 14 – *Secular Location of the Apostolate: Entrepreneurs re leased in revival create not only new churches, but new Christian organisations influencing the secular and new structures in secular careers.*

Transformation of Nooks and Crannies

The previous chapters indicate the natural periodic re-emergence of existential charismatic styles of Christianity, with their strange contrast to academic Christian formulations. It is a contrast in style, in content, and in nature of vision. Stylistically, the social impacts of revival movements do not stem from a social vision, finely manicured in sacred halls of learning and gazing into the future. They rather stem from divine encounters, divine empowerment and response to the present.

"Jesus' ethics is neither a call to repentance in light of an immanent Kingdom nor a blueprint for bringing about the perfect society on earth" (Dempster, 1999:62). Instead, as Richard Neibuhr develops (1963), Jesus' ethic is a "response ethic." Indeed revivals seem to be like salt or light in their penetration style. They are a series of dancing stories, responding to contexts. The Holy Spirit is the master of the dance. She utilises multiple theological paradigms in the creation of their synergies.

> Transforming Revival 15 – *Incremental: Transforming Revivals are incremental, wending their way or darting their way into the nooks and crannies of society, without necessarily conforming to a global master theology.*

On the other hand, there is a tension between freedom of the Spirit and her operation in spiritual leadership, part of which is to envision, and to understand the signs of the times.

> Transforming Revival 16 – *Human Integration: Wise citywide leadership integrates theology and strategy, to maximise synergy between grassroots expressions and facilitate progressions in revival to social transformation.*

Putting It All Together

In this chapter and the last, and in Fig. 23, I have built from the twenty-four principles of revival/revival movements by developing sixteen Transforming Revival principles.[5] This has been framed by reviewing the eight processes of revival and expanding their application from the initiating *communal presence* (Principle 1) of the Spirit to *cultural engagement* and *consummation in cultural revitalisation* (2) in columns 4 and 5 of Fig 23.

These include the *sensitivity* and *reconciliation* (8) that the Spirit invokes in communities of believers that results in *grief and anger in the public square* (5) along with *loving and consensus-seeking behaviours* (6,7). Such revival *empowers and releases entrepreneurs* into secular arenas of society. Consummation depends on *information flow* of *new theological paradigms* (3) and teaching of an *underlying theology of social change* (4). It relates to the *release of prophetic and apostolic leaders* and *empowerment* (13) of common people full of the Spirit who *incrementally transform the nooks and crannies* (15) of society. These are not to be located primarily in the cultic centres (congregations) but in *creation of godly social structures* (14).

The new paradigm of Transforming Revival rejects the notion that revival automatically results in city-wide transformation simply through prayer, as (inadvertently?) portrayed by recent marketing from the US. Instead, I have identified that revivals are *not always sufficient* (12) to release *significant* positive social transformation(10) nor *necessary* (11), since the Spirit also works through common grace. I have expanded revival principles into a theory of *incremental* (15), *seasonal, synergistic* (9), *city-wide Transforming Revival*.

Leadership is necessary to integrate such progressions of theology, structure and synergies (16). Among the primary gifts initiated and released in revival are those of the prophet. An expanded Pentecostal understanding of the prophetic is now proposed as a further step in developing a theology of the process of Transforming Revival.

---

5   These forty principles could have been added to sociologists of religion, Stark and Finkes 99 propositions, (2000: 277-286) as there is a large gap in their theory related to revival. However, it is difficult to mesh the diverse disciplines, as the sociological definition of revival begins from quite different presuppostions. Despite their impassioned plea for a faith-based approach to sociology of religion (pp 11-21), I could not overcome the issue of having premised this study on the personhood of the Holy Spirit, a theological premise, and of revival emanating from this person, not simply from sociological forces..

- 13 -

PROPHETIC SOURCES OF TRANSFORMATION IN URBAN CULTURES

The work of culture and the creation of enduring institutions are the realisation of visions and dreams of relatively small creative elites who by inspiration project a future worthy of imitation (mimesis). The immediate consequence of their actions may appear to be failure....

(Tonsor, 1998:99)

The Spirit of Creative Minorities

There are prophetic elements in each of the five phases of Transforming Revival in the previous chapters. How do the Scriptures inform the nature of the prophetic in initiating revival movements (phase 1), in cultural engagement (phase 4) and in generating the response of cultural revitalisation (phase 5)?

Arnold Toynbee, argues in his monumental *Study of History* (1972:127ff) for the determinative role of creative minorities in the development of civilisations. I examine this by reflecting on characteristics of the prophetic in the anthropology of religion and in theology, so as to expand limited Pentecostal understandings. I then supplement this by identifying significant prophetic roles in the Old Testament prophets and Jesus. This results in definition of eight prophetic roles, measurable as a revival enters into cultural engagement.

In examining *the first phase of initiation of movements*, A.F.C. Wallace identifies the prophetic as the beginning of revitalisation movements (including revivals). "With a few exceptions, every religious revitalisation movement with which I am acquainted has been originally conceived in one or several hallucinatory visions by a single individual. A supernatural being appears to the prophet-to-be ..." (2003:17). The dreamer preaches his revelations: he becomes a prophet, makes converts. Wallace, building on Max Weber's understanding of charisma (1947b), indicates that because of the moral ascendancy and uncanny authority of the charismatic leader, his/her followers organise into a movement. "Followers defer to the charismatic leader, not because of his status in existing authority structure, but because of his fascinating personal "power" often ascribed to supernatural sources and validated in successful performance."

Wallace studied primarily tribal contexts. This book deal with city leadership in a multi-sectored, multi-ethnic city, involving "tribal leadership" of the religious movements in the revival, as well as the emergence of Christian leaders in social leadership roles.[1]

The released creativity of the Holy Spirit in the *second and third phase*, beyond the initiation of revival, involves releasing prophetic giftings to new prophets in the midst of revival. The emphasis on this particular gift is reasonable as the Scriptures elevate the desire for the gift of prophesying[2] above all others (1 Cor 14: 1, 2).

The training of the *nebiim*, the school of prophets of Elijah, included a linking of the ecstasy of worship and power gifts, to an expectation of speaking the direct oracle, the Word from God. Similarly, the charismatic movement and Pentecostalism expanded for millions today into the exercise of types of prophetic ministry accompanied by similar manifestations.

There is a parallel between Old Testament prophetic activity and that of the New Testament prophets. This contrasts with most Pentecostal understandings of New Testament prophetic roles as primarily within the church, while Old Testament roles were towards society - therefore the church has no responsibility for the prophetic to society – a spurious argument from silence, as in the first decades of the church there were few in positions to speak prophetically to nations.

Gentile (2002: 143-157) in an extensive chapter "Comparing Prophecy in both Testaments" writes,

> *The term prophet is used by both ancient Hebrews and the early Church and the Christians did not seem to struggle with a difference in meaning. They saw continuity between the Hebrew prophets and the New Testament prophets…Some important variations did exist in the use of prophecy between the two Testaments [He analyses six]…but the essence of prophecy has not changed.*

I add to this continuum the parallels with sociological and anthropological studies. Overholt, for example interfaces anthropological studies with Biblical studies of the

---

[1] Leadership of religious movements is difficult to interpret with organisational leadership paradigms. When considered as clans that make up tribes, the model matches more readily the dynamics of roles, authority and leadership emergence.

[2] While strong Calvinistic teaching emphasises the intellectual and didactic nature of the preacher as prophet in 1 Cor 14:1-3, the context of Paul's discussion relates to ecstatic abuse and charismatic manifestations - not dissimilar to the context of sociological (Weber, 1963a) and anthropological definitions of the prophet.

prophetic (1996); or at the foundations of sociology, Weber reflects on the nature of the exemplary and ethical prophets (Morris, 1987; Weber, 1963b), not just as a spiritual gift in Christian circles but as one that can be manifested in the context of other religions. Thus, the occurrence of the prophetic appears to be consistent across time and cultures. This gift may be utilised by the Holy Spirit or by other spirits, or be an expression of the human spirit of an individual. The testing of the Spirits and of prophecy required by Scripture are useful in determining the difference. Kurt Koch, psychiatrist and theologian summarizes differentiation from a psychoanalytic perspective (1972/1994:268); Gentile analyses the theological basis for differentiation (2002: 330-351).

Phase 4 of cultural engagement involves the expanding network of creative change agents and prophetic institutions at city leadership levels. In my earlier studies of city leaderships globally, there are generally many prophetic persons recognised in a megacity at culture changing leadership levels. Not scores; and not just individuals.

The unity and communality of these is a crucial issue. The relationship of these prophets to the apostles who would implement and structure their movements is also crucial. I have dealt with the nature of prayer and networking elements of this in *Transforming Cities* on "Building City Leadership Teams" (Grigg, 1997d:53-66). Such leadership teams, with their networked institutions, may become a creative prophetic minority within a culture.

Whitefield, the prophet of the First Great Awakening, along with Charles Wesley, its poet and its apostolic organiser John Wesley, demonstrate such unity, developed in revival experiences.

> At New Years 1739, George Whitefield, my brother Charles, three others and I, with about sixty of our brethren, were present at a love feast in Fetter Lane. About three in the morning, as we were continuing in prayer, the power of God came upon us so mightily that many cried out in holy joy, while others were knocked to the ground. As soon as we were recovered a little from the awe and amazement at the presence of God, we broke out in one voice, "We praise Thee, O God; we acknowledge Thee to be Lord." (Weakley, 1987:75).

Phase 5 involves a cultural response of repentance, a rapid cultural change of direction, an acceptance of the alternative public consciousness created by the prophets – a cultural revitalisation.

> *The invention of a culture by a creative minority is rarely the work of a dominant minority employing the mechanisms of power* (Tonsor, 1998: 92).

Redefining the Nature of Prophecy

To accomplish the fourth and fifth phases in the multi-sectoral milieux of 21st century cities requires redefinition for Pentecostals and charismatics, an expansion of their popular understandings of the prophecy from a cultic, church-centred view to the comprehensiveness of national and city-level prophecy. Pentecostal professor at Fuller, Robeck indicates alternative definitions:

- A predictive word of future events. (This, he indicates, has ancient precedents but is an insufficient basis for understanding the gift).
- An oracle, spontaneously inspired by the Holy Spirit and spoken in a specific situation.
- A form of expositional preaching from the biblical text.
- A public pronouncement of a moral or ethical nature that confronts society.

Pentecostal and charismatic Christians tend to emphasize the nature of prophecy as spontaneous, though many allow for the prophetic gifts to function in 'anointed' preaching and in some 'inspired' social commentary (Robeck, 1988:728).

Among Pentecostals, some prophets rove among the churches and have *words of knowledge* for people. These are direct revelations of the needs and directions of people's lives. The validity of one who calls himself a prophet is confirmed by the clarity and accuracy of these perceptions. The following story illustrates their significance.

- Two Prophets From The South -

> Twenty students and staff in an Auckland Bible School sit quietly praying, occasionally led in some rousing choruses, arms uplifted. In between, two prophets 'from the South Island', call out one or two, lay hands on them and pray, identifying elements of God's call on their lives, defining areas of sin, inviting the Spirit to bring healing. There is the sense of the presence of God at many points. Knowing many of the students personally, I am silent witness to the veracity of many things said by these two farmers who knew nothing of these students before.

But the theological path into new patterns of social transformation is found in the expansion of the nature of the prophetic role in charismatic and Pentecostal thought to include all four of Robeck's categories. Theological integrity requires it. This involves an expansion from simple emphasis on the spontaneous oracle, to an understanding of the full declamatory force of the prophets as social conscience, as oracles at the public level. It also meshes the spontaneity of the oracle with wisdom and understanding of contemporary issues.

Dispensationalism and reductionism in fundamentalist groups and the narrowness of Pentecostal definitions of the prophetic role generally preclude addressing social issues for both groups and exclude a lifetime of intellectual study or the kind of social analysis such as Moses and Isaiah were skilled in. Such study tends to be relegated to "less spiritual" patterns of Christianity (i.e. non-Sirit-lead mainline churches).

Yet biblically, the prophetic word of judgement and hope is much more complex than simple words of knowledge. The prophetic imagination interprets social analysis in the light of the underlying spiritual dynamics, but without social analysis there is little accurate perception of the issues. In a complex society, that involves *both* intuitive understanding and complex social analysis.

On the other hand, one must not err in overemphasising social analysis not rooted in divine revelation. Some it is true, like Isaiah or Ezekiel, had highly formulated academic and literary social analyses. Others such as Joel or Jonah, appear to have heard directly from God in divine inspiration related only cursorily to any intellectual analysis. Ultimately, the core of the prophetic word has the Pentecostal emphasis on direct oracle, commonly understood to involve the "word of wisdom" and the "word of knowledge" of I Corinthians 12:8 and 14:6.

In this vein, Walter Brueggeman argues from the Scriptures for freedom from stereotypes of prophets as foretellers or social protesters to a wider cultural leadership role:

> *The prophet is primarily addressing the underlying vision of the nation. He is energising that 'dominant consciousness within the culture and energising persons and communities with the promise of another time and situation towards which the community can move* (1978:15).

Prophetic Sources of Revival in Urban Cultures

I will review roles of several OT prophets to illustrate the prophetic role in the fourth and fifth phases of Transforming Revival. This is a conversation between a modern prophetic emphasis and the OT prophets. based on the principle of continuity of prophetic styles across the OT, NT and the present. My categories have been formed by years of reflection on the classics of Heschel (2001), Brueggeman (1978), Harold Knight (1947) and Rauschenbusch (1907/1991), in their in-depth studies of the prophetic, supplemented by Weber's sociological studies (1963a) and anthropological studies of the prophetic in tribal movements. What is new is connecting these themes to revival in the city.

If we turn to the Transforming Revival of the nation of Israel under Moses, we find the model of a prophet giving a *recurrent call for repentance by oppressive leadership*, a pattern repeated throughout the Scriptures. Moses' prophetic thunder against Pharaoh, can be understood in terms of *revelation and repentant response* of one people against the unrepentant response of Pharaoh.

The *appearance of a new social reality* through his words is unprecedented and unrepeated. The corollary is that without prophecy, new social realities do not emerge and old social realities decline in evil and corruption. In the process of a nation morally decaying, the failure of the prophetic voice in the public square is as much at fault as ungodly leadership.[3]

The results of a time of prophetic encounter required the *remaking of a moral value system*, expressed in the Ten Commandments. Later this study will return to the *progression of prophetic to apostolic*, but it is significant to note Moses modelling this combination, as over forty years, he builds a people of God from an oppressed people, *transforming the mindset of poverty and dependency*.

Jeremiah also highlights crucial prophetic roles in an urban and globalized context of non-responsiveness not dissimilar to New Zealand, where prophetic cultural engagement has met with a cold shoulder from the nation's leaders. Jeremiah 8:4-9:26

---

3   I define moral decay in this study as the opposite of transformation towards the principles of the Kingdom of God - mismanagement of creation, destructive patterns of social relationships, loss of values of truth, love, patience, kindness in the public square etc.

is a collection of prophetic sayings concerning national evil, against the city-state of Jerusalem-Judah, in a time of momentous social change.[4]

The "revival" under Josiah had collapsed. The prophet *highlights the non-responsiveness* of this people, using rhetorical questions, "Why then have these people turned away? Why does Jerusalem always turn away" (8:4,5). Then in verse 7, Jeremiah examines their fickleness by using an analogy from nature, "Even the stork in the sky knows her appointed seasons and the dove, the swift and the thrush observe the time of their migration. But my people do not know the requirements of the Lord."

Here is an indication of the first step in the prophetic role in bringing revival, the cry against the blindness of the people to their own sin and identification of it as a time of repentance.

Then Jeremiah moves to an oracle of *judgement on the people* as a whole (10-12), with a *question about shame*: "Are they ashamed of their loathsome conduct? No, they have no shame at all; they do not even know how to blush" (12). Heschel (1965:112-114), speaks of such "loss of embarrassment" as a decisive step towards "loss of humanness."

Jeremiah goes on to speak of the lack of shalom, peace and of future judgment. Why is there no healing? "Is there no balm in Gilead?" he asks. Gilead was the valley of healing, the place of spices and medicinal herbs. Only later (30:17), we find a promise to the chastised, humbled and repentant ones of a healed future, "'But I will restore you to health and heal your wounds,' declares the Lord." This is part of the prophet's wider role, *to envision a future of hope* for the exiles, both within Babylon (29:4-7) and beyond, "for I know the plans I have for you, says the Lord, to give you a future and a hope" (29:11).

In the first twenty-four chapters of his book, Ezekiel looks from exile at his nation and city of Jerusalem. This is a conversation with the people of his city *predicting its fall, specifying the sources of its judgements*. He speaks of the sins of leadership: "Her officials within her are like wolves tearing their prey…" (Ezek 22:27). Then he defines a new kind of leader, the intercessor, "I looked for one among them who would build up the wall and stand before me in the gap on behalf of the land so I would not have to destroy it but I found none…"(Ezek 22:30). Ezekiel's cry is for an intercessor who engages in a "conversation," "petition," "pleading" for the people, before the Lord.[5]

This concept of an intercessor is more than the Pentecostal definition of one who simply prays with intensity. The location of such a person is one who "stands in place," "stands between," and as such prays with knowledge and wisdom. In Ezekiel 13:5, he defines the qualities of a true prophet as one who goes up to the gaps in the wall and repairs them, so that it will stand firm in the day of battle. This may be correlated to the concept in 3:17-21 and 33:7-9 of the *prophets being like watchmen* on the walls, sounding the trumpet of alarm (Jer 6:17), the progress of a battle (I Sam 14:16) or

---

[4] Though Craigie (1991) places it in the latter part of Josiah's reign because of the sense of failure of reform and Kidner (1985) puts it in the early period of his prophesying because of similarities with chapters 2-6..

[5] See Vines analysis of "intercessions" (uperentulcanv) (1996: 330).

the approach of messengers (II Sam 18:24-27). There is documented evidence globally supporting the thesis that the creation of intercessory movements in the city is the source of motivation, mobilisation, new vision for rebuilding.[6] But ten years of such documentation have also left some city leaders who have worked with this thesis skeptical that the common idea of intercessors, dissociated from the hard work of engagement in the public forum, is significant for social change.

The prophets declared *God's concern for justice within society*. The historical books also show the outworking of such a theme. Nehemiah, the builder of a city, models this understanding of the completed prophetic. He begins where Ezekiel has left us — as a weeping intercessor serving a meal to a King. Then the tears of intercession are converted into audacious action with a plan that a worthy King would respond to. His rebuilding Jerusalem is used as a model of urban rebuilding through community organisation.[7] It includes divine encounter, envisaging, resourcing, mobilising of the people, dealing with opposition, developing teamwork, strategy and sustaining discipline. *Activists may experience the divine call in the midst of an intercessory lifestyle*.

The role of the apostle, evangelist, prophet, pastor-teacher is to prepare workers for such public service (Eph 4:11, 12). I suggest that the training of functional prophets occurs in the training of Nehemiahs, men and women who intercede between God and the people as they serve the nation in public affairs, neither neglecting the intercessory closet, nor the public debate.

Jesus' Model of Defining Core Values

In seeking to understand the prophetic element in *processes* of Transforming Revival, what is the focus of Jesus, the ultimate prophet? His emphasis was neither dismantling society, nor building its physical structure but inaugurating a new value system and a new web of relationships. His prophetic critique was direct, forceful, cutting to the values of the culture. His was *a creation of alternative spiritual, personal and social values* of the Sermon on the Mount, then an *apostolic process of building those prophetic values into the character* of the disciples and their communal relationships. The model of Jesus requires us to examine the value changes that might mark Transforming Revival in Auckland and how to embody these into structures that become the vehicle of the ongoing prophetic voice.

Personal values are part of the daily transformational conversation for many revived believers as they are forced into prophetic definition of values by confrontations with the culture of the office or government-imposed values in the school system.

- Values Education -

> As my children learned to read in class J1 with officially approved government readers, I noticed that none of the readers contained any values teaching (with the exception of tolerance of cultural pluralism). I took William Bennett's *Book of Virtues* to the

---

6   See Grigg, (1997b) for sources. It has been a major theme in John Dawson's and Wagner's works. Silvoso builds his city-reaching strategy around it (1994).

7   Alinsky (1969), an atheistic Jew, used it as the basis of theories of community organising.

> principal and asked if there was any statement in the school's policy about teaching values. There was not.
>
> Should there be? I suggested that I was coming from a Christian perspective, but that William Bennett, in the *Book of Virtues* (1993), had developed a compendium of stories for moulding children's values around universally acceptable themes such as self-discipline, compassion, responsibility, friendship, work, courage, perseverance, honesty, loyalty, faith, love and so on, that could be used across cultures and religions. The school then introduced an alternative to *Bible in Schools* developed along Bennett's lines, but led by a Hindu Brahmin!

The use of values brings problems. Ball (1996), demonstrates how pervasive use of the word "values" in its derivation from the social sciences has subsumed issues of moral principle, religious conviction and ethical precept into a single category. This legitimises a fact/ value distinction where values say nothing of the thing judged but become merely an expression of the speaker's attitudes — and hence meaningless.

Secondly, the possibilities of establishing a consensus on values in a postmodern city are limited. Brazilian Catholic urban theologian, Libanio, in "The Structure of Values" demonstrates the disintegrating effects of postmodern urbanism on a values system:

> Modern urbanism presents a horizon of pluralistic values, conflicting, subjective, individualistic, fragmented. Pluralistic, because they have developed in diverse cultural and religious traditions. Conflicting, because they reflect fundamentally different postures about life, humanity and the Transcendental. Individualistically subjective, because people may oscillate in their own acceptance of universals, without sensing an obligation to follow all norms. Fragmented, because their values don't necessarily come from a unified tradition and may be incompatible
>
> (Libanio, 2001: 178, tr. from Portuguese, mine).

Yet there is evidence for teaching on values change to be a fruitful field of social change in education, business and medicine.[8] It anchors transformational theology into the locus of specialist social issues and of professionals who are Christians. Given the genesis of Pentecostalism as a values-based movement (Sheppard, 1988:796; Martin, 1995:27), redefinition of some cultural values is a significant possibility.

On the other hand, Pentecostals and to a lesser extent charismatic Evangelicals, are activists. Two recent studies have sought to develop a Pentecostal social ethic in Latin America, based on ethics as pneumatological (Petersen, 1996:186-226; Villafañe, 1993b: 193-221). They focus on both the pneumatological and the Kingdom of God. My observation is that the ethics taught among Pentecostals tend to develop in action more than being related to a theology of being. Thus, an arbitrary choice has been made to include values in the broader activist theme of the Kingdom of God of Chapter 8.

---

8   See *Accent on Values Emerging in Universities, Workplace* (Lynch, 2000). Gavin Ellis identifies some values issues in *Towards Shared Values* (2000).

Conclusion

I have examined the prophetic at each phase of Transforming Revival, expanding the nature of the prophetic from Pentecostal definitions and considering revival as a process for developing a creative minority (phase 3 & 4). At times, with divine intervention or because of repentant response, the whole culture may move into a cultural revitalisation and the prophetic becomes the basis of an apostolic building phase (phase 5). These become the basis of eight measurable characteristics of prophetic initiation at phase 4. A cursory glance at the New Zealand revival, using these criteria, indicates them present, apart from failure of the culture to move from lack of shame to a repentant response.

Apostolic engagement in sectors of society where creative minorities and prophetic roles are developing will be examined in the next chapter.

- 14 -

APOSTOLIC STRUCTURES AS TRANSFORMING VOICES

Mission structures are a kind of 'theology on four wheels', enfleshed demonstrations of a theoretical orientation to the world... they are windows that allow one to peer closely at the underpinnings of a given theology of mission.

(Skreslet, 1999:2)

In Chapter 13, I examined prophetic processes that initiate each of the proposed revival stages one to four. In this chapter, I explore the spiritual gift of apostle in *apostolic engagement* with social leadership. This develops from the earlier question, as to what has forced the dramatic reversal from non-engagement to aggressive activism in social issues. I examine elements of the apostolic that begin in revival and that transition revival into cultural renewal. The process of calling people to aspire to leadership roles in society is prophetic. The apostolic deploys and develops such prophets and creative minorities, sustains momentum and creates movement dynamics for change.

I expand the concept of the apostolic,[1] based on reflections on Scripture and history and in terms of missional action. A simple 7-step apostolic / prophetic movement model for analysing structural developments of *engagement* in multiple social sectors is proposed. Some proposals are made for further expansion and evaluation beyond

---

1   Although I have taught Weber's routinisation of charisma over the years (Weber, 1947a), as a useful understanding of the prophetic, the multiple bases of authority in leadership, and progressions to institutionalisation, it has seemed that he does not clearly differentiate the transitions from prophetic to apostolic roles well On the other hand, it seems that in business literature, the frequent differentiation of roles have parallels to the five leadership giftings of Ephesians 4:11,12. This chapter could easily be expanded into both of these fields – sociology of religion or management studies. Space precludes either.

engagement. This is an insider's evaluation based on stories from leaders within each sector of society. Some are included.

Recent evangelical literature on this topic (see *Literature on Transforming New Zealand Social Vision*), has largely been concerned with public policy and governmental relationships to the churches. For many years, I have wondered "Why such a focus on power?" Perhaps it reflects a New Zealand cultural understanding that governments are all-empowering. I posit an alternative underlying presupposition that policy change at such a level cannot be done by enthusiasts overnight. That seems reasonable.

A second assumption is that the primary locus of social change is not at governmental level but at the level of the experts in social sectors.[2] If there is an ongoing process of theological reflection and action by cadres of leaders in each sector, which results in the values and collective thinking being transferred from generation to generation of leaders, these experts are likely to engage and significantly influence both the cultures within that sector and through that, policy-making bodies. Such assumptions lead me to the idea of think tanks, forums, institutes and eventually universities.

Redefining the Nature of the Apostolic

The *apostolic* in missions, for Evangelicals and Pentecostals, is related to the role of multiplication of local congregations, based on a reading of the scriptures that formation of new faith communities follows Paul's practice of creating new congregations imaging Jewish synagogue styles. In contrast, I suggest that:

Transforming Revival 17–	*Transforming Revival involves an understanding of the apostolic role as the creation of entrepreneurial structures which speak of the nature of God's activity in secular arenas.*

This significantly extends existing global revival theory. While coordinator of the AD2000 Cities Network, I developed the phraseology of apostolic and prophetic city leadership teams in the global conversation on city transformation in 1991, beginning from experiences in Kolkata (Grigg, 1997d:54-66). Peter Wagner subsequently publicised the concept of city leadership teams of apostles and prophets for transformation globally (1998; 1999), though some organisational dynamics he has used to execute this, have drawn heavy (though largely unpublished) criticism of the connotations of power inherent in the idea.

---

2   This assumption has been strengthened by Eisenstadt's analysis of Weber, "In general, it seems that such transforming tendencies of religious and ideological systems and movements tend to be greater, the more they are borne and promoted by relatively cohesive elites with a strong sense of self-identity, and especially by secondary elites which, while somewhat distant from the central ruling one, yet maintain positive solidary orientations to the center and are not entirely alienated from the pre-existing elites and from the broader groups of society" (Weber, 1968: xlvii). I first came across this in Tippett's story of the conversion webs in Southern Polynesia, where conversion of a significant number of heads of tribes was a prerequisite for the King to eat the sacred turtle and (since no calamity happened), declare Tonga a Christian nation (Tippett, 1971).

In contrast to such writings focussed on pastoral leaders developing into apostolic roles, I expand the concept of apostolicity into leadership in secular social sectors. Thus I seek to move the conversation from an integrational level of city leadership to the diffusion of the apostolic into social leadership. Australian Assemblies of God pastor, James Thwaites, in *The Church Beyond the Congregation,* gives an alternative Pentecostal "creation" theological framework for such a discussion (1997; 1999).

Biblical Understanding of Apostolic Entrepreneurs

Some simple definition is needed. Of the functional roles released in revival the pre-eminent one is that of the apostle. The Greek *apostolos* ("one sent forth"), emphasizes elements of commission — carrying the full authority and responsibility of the sender for a definite mission, used for emissaries sent from the Emperor with full imperial authority (Harrison, 1984).

Jesus highlights the divine order with a saying attributed to God himself, but found nowhere in the Old Testament, "God in his wisdom said, 'I will send them prophets and apostles...'" (Luke 11:49). Jesus himself is the supreme apostle (Heb 3:1), often speaking of being sent from the Father and sending the twelve as the Father had sent him. This "sentness with authority", has always been interpreted primarily as referring to the designated twelve apostles, imparted with authority to preach, teach, heal and deliver. However, historically there has also been an understanding of the expansion of these gifts in the apostolate.

Working from within the "pneumatological apostolic mindset" of expanding new church movements, charismatic and Pentecostal understanding grows from a view of an ever-changing gift of the Spirit in action. This contrasts deeply with views based on apostolic succession and the defence of authority of office in state churches. It regards the apostle as a continuing functional role within the church. For the Scriptures speak of other apostles than the twelve (Paul (Gal 1:1); Paul and Barnabas (Acts 14:4,14); Paul, Timothy and Silas (I Thes 2:6); probably Andronicus and a (probably female) apostle, Junias (Rom 16:7); James, Jesus' brother (Gal 1:19), along with the other apostles of I Cor 15:5-8. In II Cor 8:23, two unnamed brethren are named "apostles to the churches." In Phil 2:5, Epaphroditus is referred to as "your apostle." The word is also used in a general sense as "messenger" in John 13:16 (Vine et al., 1996:31).

Apostolic Multiplication of Congregations

The preceding chapters on revival have led me to seek to define a new ecclesiology. I have suggested that post-revival emphases on church growth as goal, with its institutionalisation of cultic religion, (i.e., its focus of local church, pastor, collection plate, ritualistic worship (even speaking in tongues) in Sunday morning worship), has been a limited conservation goal within a broad movement of the Spirit. The alternative principle:

> Transforming Revival 18 – *Releasing the Apostolic: A primary goal of revival is to set people free into new apostolic directions outside the cloisters.*

This affirms missiologist Bosch's major thesis that true ecclesiology is primarily missional, not cultic (1991: chapter 1).

The tenor of the book of Ephesians is of the global Church as the agent of transformation. In it, the apostle examines the purposes of history and sees that through the Church, the many-sided wisdom of God is manifested to the powers (Eph 3:10). But the barrier for Evangelicals has been the definition of the local church. If this is re-examined then an understanding of the apostolic, prophetic and evangelistic giftings and their utilisation within secular arenas suddenly becomes obvious.

For Evangelicals there has been a history of theology since the reformation, elevating the local, geographically defined congregational structures known as "the local church." These theologies grew among Anabaptists as the normative, indeed, absolutist model, identified with "the New Testament church." They were modelled after the congregational structures of the monasteries, the set apart ones, the religious. With the destruction of the monasteries, anyone could now be one of the "religious" while joining as a lay person into these local congregations. This became "*the* church." Elders were elders in this local congregation. When towns became filled with Methodist, Baptist and Presbyterian churches, each felt they should have elders (or the equivalent, depending on their nomenclature).

However, it is not the "local church" to whom Paul writes in his letters, but the church or the faithful in the city of.... The elders, overseers and deacons are those of Philippi (Phil 1:2) or in every town in Crete (Titus 1:6).... He wrote to city-wide churches with a variety of structures.

Church growth theory has worsened this problem by defining the apostolic as the multiplication of these "local churches". This unfortunately locks the New Zealand Evangelical church, which is heavily influenced by these theories, into a theological time warp. The evidence in the Scriptures indicates the pioneering of many different Kingdom structures depending on the city and the culture. There is evidence of many small groups, house churches and larger congregational structures in these biblical cities. However, the leaders of these groups are connected across the city. These city churches are diverse structurally and in terms of leadership.

Other Apostolic Structures
Missiological theory identifies seven Church structures that historically continue to recur.[3] To understand social penetration, we need to look carefully at these missional structures in the city.

Today, in mega-cities, clusters and communities of intensely committed men and women, choosing lifestyles of devotion and involvement with the needy, multiply. Focussed around small training centres, they are often committed to Jesus' ideals of simplicity and sacrifice.

---

3   1. Local congregations, 2. denominations, 3. training centres, 4. service organisations, 5. missions societies, 6. renewal movements, 7. global inter-church networks (Glasser, 1993). This historical reality is in direct conflict with the commonly held Pentecostal view that if the church was fully functional, parachurch organisations would disappear, for all must be under the authority of the apostles and pastors in local churches (Holding, 2005).

Non-Church Apostolic Movement

> One such group in Auckland is Wai Ora, working with at-risk teenagers. They follow a pattern of evangelism and discipleship based on open homes and extended family living. Typical are Ian and Debby who have spent ten years having teenage kids in trouble with the police living in their home, running weekly clubs for the kids in trouble at the local schools and quietly bringing the Kingdom to some of the most dysfunctional families. Their support structure has been in meeting with other leaders committed to similar programs.

These are not local churches[4] but they are Church. This raises the question as to whether the strong identification of the apostolic gifting with (local) churchplanting in the literature is correct. These groups often have an apostolic leadership style.

In most cases it is not the holding structure of the local worshipping parish, the paramission structures but the missional structures, which bring growth and dynamic change in the local church.

Apostolic And Pastoral City Leadership Styles

> This was very evident in Christchurch, where I met first with a group of six men with apostolic and prophetic giftings and facilitated them in mapping out various major directions of the church in the city. In the afternoon, I met with pastoral leaders and asked the same questions. At the end of the afternoon with them there was no apparent direction. Until I showed them the morning's work! The response was an immediate affirmation.

Similarly, the database behind this study identified over 700 Protestant mission structures within the Auckland church, half Protestant, half Catholic. Alpha courses drive evangelism in many churches; Dynamite Bay programs resource many effective children's outreaches; Youth for Christ and Parachute Extreme see perhaps more effective penetration of youth culture than the work of all the church youth groups which feed off the dynamic they generate; Christian schools provide a base for sustenance of Protestant and Catholic congregations and so on.

This on the ground evidence again raises the question of whether releasing apostolic giftings into mission in the secular arenas, semi-autonomous from the local worshipping congregations is a more significant structural step into the future than the present focus of the theology of the apostolic as local congregational development (i.e. church growth).[5]

---

4   Classical sociology from Troelsch on has used only a church-sect dichotmomy. It appears to me that the area of church-mission structural differentiation is required with an additional analysis of mission structures. This would add dramatically to Stark's 99 propositions on the sociology of religion (2000:277-286), drawing on Winters seminal works on missional orders as a polar type (1974) and Mellis' concept of missional community (1976).

5   Tillapagh (1985) some 25 years ago, was widely accepted when he broached the same thesis within mainline church growth theory. His model was the expansion of the local church into secular ministries. He built from a limited theology of spiritual giftings not the function of the apostolic/prophetic gifts.

> Transforming Revival 19 – *The development of apostolic structures in secular society is a primary means of expanding revival into transformation.*

On the positive side, many urban anthropologists have identified the significant relational ties of modern urbanites as being in the local geographic community rather than the working environment, the networked and associational relationships. Response to this has been the foundational theory behind the Catholic worker-priests in France and workers movements and Industrial Mission movement within liberal Protestant circles of the 1960's.[6]

Against this, the failure of the Catholic worker-priest movement parallels the lack of expected fruit of the Industrial Missions. Evangelicals have presupposed this to be because of the lack of an evangelistic component to the theologies of these movements.[7] This is perhaps true, but I wonder if the analysis is wholly valid or if there is another social reality at work. Based on urban theory, the workplace is a secondary relational context.

Similarly, it has become obvious that attempts to develop businesspersons' ministries have grown healthily then faltered several times in the city, largely because their wives and children are based in the local community. Missional structures must be apostolic and evangelistic to be sustainable, but sustainability requires fulfilling familial functions — this is better done in the local community congregation. Participants in industrial or business mission live with this tension.

The following shows how use of small transformational groups is not without its difficulties:

- SMALL GROUP STRUGGLES -

> Wyn Fountain writes, "I have been trying for years to establish a group of businessmen who would meet together and relate together for the purpose of encouraging an apostolic team to lead the way in penetrating society… this has never come to pass. I have challenged the group of ten men that I meet together with each week and the response has been that they are still working through their own theological and philosophical bases, let alone their personal relationships with their wives, families and staff and other stake holders. They are making progress and some are nearly ready to put time and energy into other people's lives, businesses and so on. In the meantime they are all working hard to keep their own businesses afloat and they find that meeting once a week is all they can manage. Men with initiative and drive are already involved in various activities that place heavy demands on their time, energy and money…"

Other ongoing experiments in apostolic non-church mission have been occurring among Evangelicals in the city:

---

6   For background on the development of industrial missions model in New Zealand see Horrill (1995) and Buckle (1978).

7   For example, core Asian documents contain the following rhetoric against evangelism, in describing industrial mission: "IT IS NOT: preaching at the factory gate… A proselytising or propaganda agency with an ulterior motive behind all its concern… A recruiting centre for the church's membership" (Daniel, 1970).

- Navigators: Non-Church Church -

> The Navigators for years have met in small groups in homes or in the business sector of the city for Bible studies. They are mission. They choose not to worship or celebrate the sacraments, so as not to offend the 'local church'. They encourage people to be involved in their local church, but the primary relationships remain within the discipling groups.

The third option for social engagement (viz-a-viz local congregational growth and apostolic structures in social sectors), is that of large inner-city churches with apostolic ministries into social sectors. This is being experimented with around the world. Generally, the centripetal pull into large church growth appears counterproductive to this vision. To grow a large church rapidly requires concentration on that goal alone.[8] Centrifugal activity is usually seen as counterproductive to it, so takes a back seat to those ministries that can be controlled and produce numbers in the worship service.[9]

- Developing The Apostolic From Within The Mega-Church -

> Ken Youngson is involved in one of these experiments. He is Community Outreach pastor at CLCA in Mt Eden. The church has grown over 13 years to about 5000 members through dynamic leadership, both through healthy evangelism and in drawing in good disenfranchised Christian leaders from other churches in the city. Ken's role involved the pioneering of street ministries to prostitutes on K. Rd., the development of a counselling centre on the church property, sports ministries and a yearly conference targeting business people and social transformation. Ken was released from the church to develop Quantum Sports Ministry.

Transformational Conversation: Apostolic and Prophetic Engagement

Having reviewed the nature of the apostolic in the scriptures, then from missions theory and local practice considered its implications as a primarily ex-cloister gifting, this chapter next examines aspects of "engagement" of the prophetic and apostolic with Auckland as a means of anchoring this theology.

"Engagement"[10] involves connecting the conversations. While the outlines of the transformational conversation have been drafted, engagement questions whether the conversationalists are speaking to each other or past each other (or simply into thin air). Are the prophets and apostles developing voices and structural expressions of those voices, that relate to the structures and issues of society?

---

8   Wagner has recently popularised the idea of the apostolic (1998). He ignores the suffering pioneer missionary and ascribes the role to apostolic development of mega-church structures. While his work is descriptive of an aspect of emerging reality, this present thesis counters this cultic-focused model of the apostolic. I base this on the view that the cultic and non-crucicentric power, wealth and prosperity centres of mega-church growth are counter to the primary processes of revival. Paul modelled his apostleship through suffering, humility and a lifestyle of financial sacrifice (II Cor 6:4-10).

9   Principles 61-68 on Professional Ecclesiastics justify this statement (Stark & Finke,2000: 283).

10 The study evolved into a focus on 'engagement' as indicator. As of 1998, that was as far as much of evangelicalism had progressed. Secondary studies are needed to examine 'impact'. By 2005, that was becoming a viable option, but beyond the scope of this study.

Methodology: Identifying Structural Change and Values Change

"Transforming a city" is a phrase with two monolithic categories, "transformation" and "city". Yoder's (1996) major critique of Neibuhr's Christ and culture thesis, is of his monolithic categories of "Christ" and of "culture." This leads me to the premise that while it is difficult to define and engage an entire city or social sector as good or evil, godly or demonised,[11] it may be possible to see and engage parts of it as categorised by qualities of good or evil, godly or demonised.

I propose that strategic transformation of a city requires analysis at three levels of city structures, soul and spirit in a number of social sectors, identifying nodes and linkages within these and the nature of change needed in each.

The nodes of a structure are here defined as people in loci of decision-making or execution. The linkages are inanimate policies, procedures, patterns of implementation, communications processes and so on. Take, for example, the nodes and linkages of the educational structure of a nation. Policy (linkage 1) is formulated by the governing parliamentary chamber (node 1), under the leadership of a secretary of education (node 2), then quantified into operating procedures (linkage 2), by bureaucrats (node 3) and implemented (linkage 3), by principals (node 4) and educators (node 5). Both nodes and linkages can be good or evil, godly or demonised — or neutral.

The relationships of God, humankind and creation together make up what is called "the social order." The matrix of the social order differs from culture to culture. Penetrating the nodes and linkages of that matrix is essential in bringing each social order under the authority of the King, discipling that nation.

Movement Engagement Analysis

What are the mechanics of engaging each of these nodes and linkages in the postmodern era? Experiences bringing together global consultations leads me to emphasise the synergy derived from moving from consultations to networks (Garvin, 1998) to alliances, think tanks and partnerships (Grigg, 1997d: 67-70), all based on prayer movements.

VisionNZ developed as a national network linking the religious leadership around the evangelistic mandate. It began with a national church growth research process reported in 1987 (Fernandez & Hall, 1987) and has built through several conferences into a networking movement with diffused authority. By 1996, it had expanded evangelistic concepts to integrate aspects of transformational theology, broadening evangelistic networks to include the context of social transformation, in essence providing a national movement that connects theologians, churchmen and those at the coal-face of evangelism. *Vision for Auckland* sought to anchor this at the city level.

Networks at any level require staffing and ongoing funding sources to be sustainable. This has been minimal but progressive with *VisionNZ*, through the transition of Graeme Lee from politician to national leader, then the restructuring as *Vision Network* with the appointment of Glynn Carpenter as national director. The retrenchment in

---

11 Tippett (1987) and Koch (1972/1994) among others, have taxonomies for demonisation, both anthropological and theological. Here it is used loosely for any intrusion of demonic activity into a social structure.

2004 of the Christian Council of Aoteoroa – New Zealand, positioned it as a national voice for the wider Protestant church, with welcome involvement of Catholic representatives.[12]

Fig. 24, "Generating Kingdom Movements in Society," below, shows a progression proposed in 1995 (Grigg, 1997a), for the growth of a transformational movement structure based on various strategic elements developed in this study. It is integral to the structure of Vision Network and is based on the expansion of the prophetic into the apostolic. I proposed seven *elements of engagement* (Phase 4 of the Transforming Revival dynamic), that require networking to develop an impact in each social sector:

Fig. 24: Transforming Revival: Generating Kingdom Movements in Society

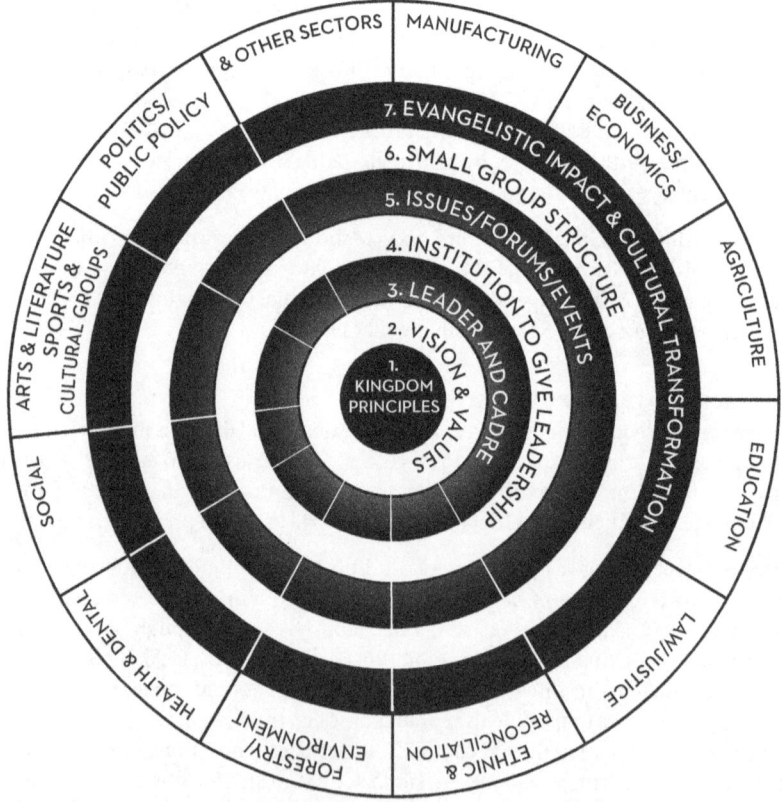

Fig.24: A missiological framework for engagement: seven steps in multiple social sectors towards a movement that engages the culture.

---

12 Its council involves significant leaders from all the major denominations, and there are current discussions (2005) with representatives of the former CCANZ (Council of Churches of Aotearoa – New Zealand), as to its potential role as a national voice.

1. **Theology:** Central to integration of such a model is a clear theological vision.[13] A common theology around revival and the Kingdom is proposed, offering a theological rationale, for a national strategic framework of social engagement.

2. **Vision and Values:** What should each sector of a city or nation look like if acknowledging the Kingdom — education, politics, business, trade unions, manufacturing, the arts, city planning and so on? What values are important in this?

3. **A Leader and Cadre** of totally committed leaders: Movements are developed by face-to-face recruitment into cell-like groups with costly mission goals.

4. **Infrastructure:** What structures are needed to effect change? It may simply be an office and a fax machine. It may be a training institution. There has to be enough operational capacity to develop an information flow of vision, values and theology and enable coalescence of leadership of the multiplying small groups.

5. **Engagement with the Public Arena:**[14] What symbols are needed in the political arena, the architecture, the media, the publishing in the city, to communicate these values for each sector? How are forums, publications and events to be utilised to highlight issues?

For example, in the above example, I resolved the educational structure of a city into nodes and linkages. Which of these levels have personnel and issues that can be impacted by the principles of the Kingdom? What is the appropriate cultural strategy for each node and linkage in each sector?

6. **A Small Group Dynamic:** Movements are based on small committed groups which deal with the ethical issues that Christians and non-Christians face (an inclusive transformational goal) and point to Christ as solution to these issues (an inclusive evangelistic goal). They require some basic structure and appropriate informational materials related to the sector of society they are penetrating.

7. **The Goals:** The objective is the full declaration of the Word of God into each sector of the culture, resulting in individual salvation (entrance to the Kingdom) and social and cultural transformation (reflecting the values of the Kingdom). I suggest this can be measured by the creation of new covenantal structures in each sector of society, just as Kagawa's Kingdom-building work in Japan was measured by the creation of trade unions, credit co-operatives, and the reconstruction of Tokyo without slums (Davey, 2000).

---

13 *The Ecumenical Conference on Life and Work* that preceded the *World Council of Churches* before the second World War, intended to formulate some united action, but could not for lack of clear theological vision concerning the relationship of church and society - an important lesson (Duff, 1956:28-31).

14 Theologies for creation of public space (freedom of the individual, separation of church and state), were at the core of reformation and post-reformation emergence of Evangelical movements. See de Castro (2000) and Maggay (1994).

Conversational Engagement

Fig. 24 provides a basis for analysing conversational engagement. The following Fig. 25 suggests how more quantitative research about levels of engagement could be developed and as an example, indicates my view of existing dynamics in Auckland.[15] The following stories are also representative.

Based on my involvement with city leaders around the world, in most cities business networks are the first to develop significant processes. If we consider engagement by the business community in Auckland, the prophetic figure of Wyn Fountain looms large.

FIG. 25: ESTIMATING TRANSFORMATIONAL ENGAGEMENT OF EVANGELICALS IN AUCKLAND

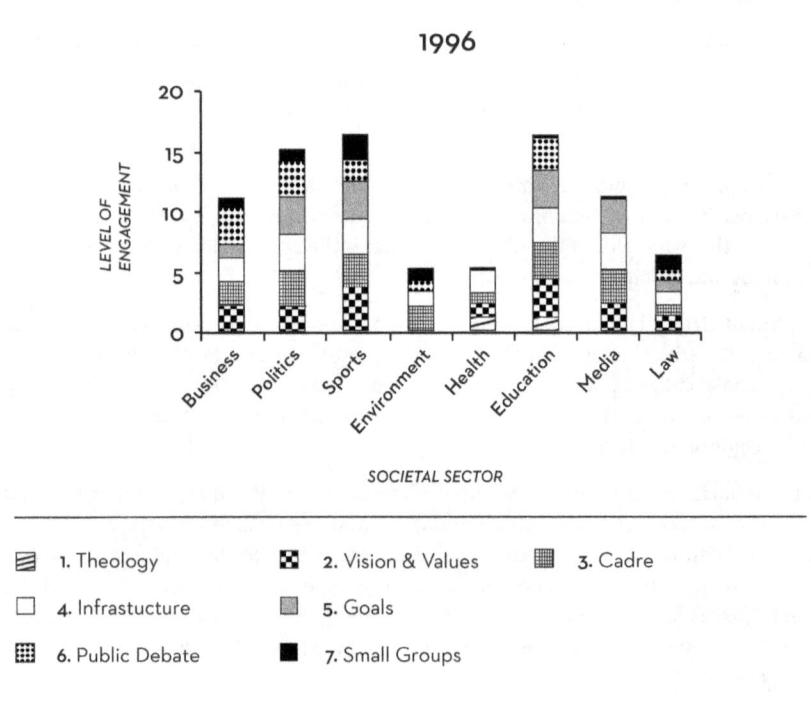

---

15 Full analysis would involve another phase in the helical cycle of research, moving from the case study, participant-observer roles to a fuller sociological analysis. This was beyond the parameters of a primarily theological study. It could also be useful to compare these with graphs of the Catholic and liberal church engagement in each sector over the same time.

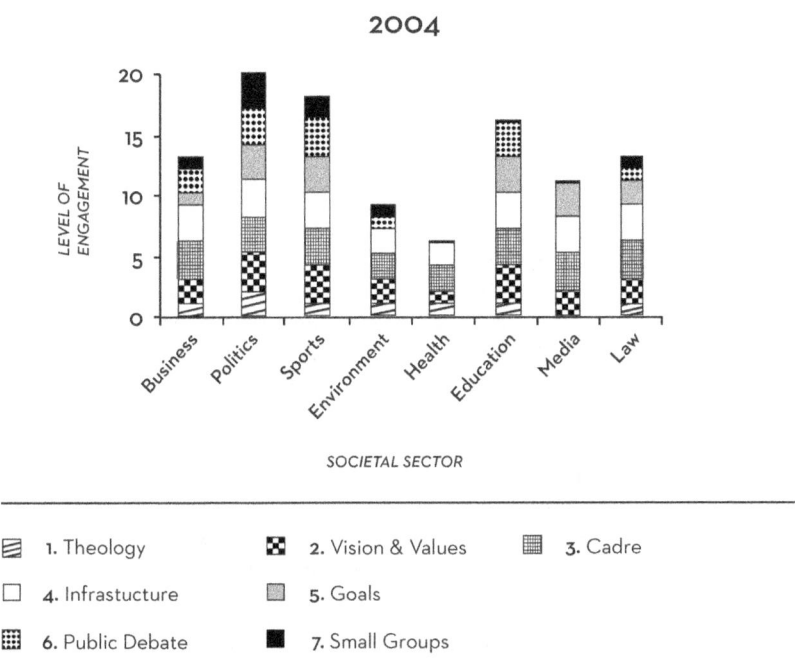

Fig. 25: An approach to comparing levels of engagement in various social sectors by evaluating the seven steps of engagement in Fig. 24 by a four point scale for each step. 0 for no evidence of that factor to 3 for significant evidence. Values given are my estimate for each sector in Auckland in 1996 and 2005.

- WYN FOUNTAIN AND THE BUSINESS ROUNDTABLE -

Wyn, an 80-year-old businessman, was a leader in the renewal movement. Over the years, he has published, in pragmatic Kiwi businessman style, booklets and articles on areas of theology for business (Step 1 in Fig. 24).

He co-ordinated business forums with Christians, creating a vision for transforming business (Step 2). Out of this a network of committed businessmen has developed (3, 4). Collective strategy and goals have been difficult to develop (5). Wyn set up forums (6) to stimulate debate on issues of ethics and morality in the conduct of business and civil society in general. World-known speakers such as Michael Novak and Paul Johnson were made available to these forums by the Business Roundtable These were not set up as specifically Christian functions, but both speakers came from Catholic roots. They emphasised that successful capitalism must be controlled by the exercise of conscience, informed by a point of reference outside the humanist emphasis. These

> forums ceased when the Business for Social Responsibility was formed in Auckland, as an organisation seeking to apply these principles into practice. More recently, Wyn established small *Omega* groups of business people (7).

Martien Kelderman, was appointed to Bible College to train business people in Kingdom theology. This has resulted in many church seminars on the workplace. The next chapter will also indicate the roles of other business people in these progressions.

In the political realm, right-wing fundamentalist attempts at Christian parties described earlier largely failed. The Christian Democrats, in joining a sitting member to become the Futures Party, developed a different model of inclusiveness that in the 2002 resulted in the election of several Catholic and Protestant charismatics, with wide support from the Evangelical community. But they failed to effectively confront Prime Minister, Helen Clark's aggressive secularism and feminist/gay agendas (Wishart, 2003) and together with the Labour government's unwillingness to listen to the moral concerns of its people (Carnichan, 2004), eventually splitting from the coalition and losing what evangelical support there had been. The earlier failures nevertheless have produced several politically active Evangelicals and a number of politically-savvy Evangelical leaders — some in other parties. However, little clear theological reflection has developed on thenature of Christian involvement in politics.[16]

The increasing Christian presence in sports and sports media is largely due to the expansion of Pacific Islanders in this sector, who tend to come from Christian and increasingly evangelical backgrounds, as second generation migrants move to English speaking and often Pentecostal churches.

In contrast to these sectors, the health sector has a large number of committed Evangelicals (several have estimated that 25-30% of the medical schools are committed Christians). Many are in influential roles. For example, Christian involvement has been significantly effective in the rehabilitation processes of Mason Clinic for psychologically disturbed prisoners. Key leaders training medical students are Evangelicals. However there is no overall process for developing specific Christian strategies for this sector. The evangelical Christian Medical Fellowship has been nationally networked and met quarterly for over 15 years to listen to speakers. The TSCF model has meant leadership is not apostolically defined but based around the idea of fellowship. It has resulted in a few public forums but appears to lack strategic objectives for changing the medical environment.

Given the extent of environmental teaching in the Scriptures, the lack of significant impact on environmental discussions and policy appears to be a major gap. A network was formed in the early 1990's by then university chaplain, Ray Galvin, but has

---

16 There have been numerous articles, but no development of a comprehensive evangelical theology in New Zealand. (From overseas, see Grant, 1987b; Mouw, 1976; Neuhaus, 1984; Newbigin, 1981; Niebuhr, 1932; Whitehead, 1994; Wogaman, 1988). On the other hand, Ahdar and Stenhouse (from a legal perspective (Ahdar, 2000; 2003; Ahdar & Stenhouse, 2000)), Jonathon Boston (from a public policy perspective), and Lineham (from a historical perspective (2000a; 2004)) have all written on the relationship of Church and State, from evangelical theological frameworks.

not been sustained with any significant voice.

- ENVIRONMENTAL NETWORK -

> In February, 2005, a cluster of leaders, motivated by Bruce Nicholls with his years of networking in India, came together to listen to Christian experts in environmental areas and to formulate an initial strategy for developing an environmental theology. Out of this group, Arocha, a global group initiated an NZ chapter.

Such leadership is linked to regular intakes of environmental studies students from the US at Kodesh community.

Education Act changes in 1989 and the development of New Zealand Qualifications Authority as an accrediting body with the Christian Theological and Ministries Training Sector has enabled Pentecostal Bible schools to enter into consistent educational upgrading. It has also brought Pentecostal schools into significant dialogue with traditional theological training which includes serious attention to justice and social change.

Some leaders have also been working towards visions of Christian Universities as possible long-term institutional bases for a national leadership infrastructure, particularly Bethlehem College in Tauranga (Bethlehem College, 2004).

- BEV NORSWORTHY: CHRISTIAN TEACHERS TRAINING COLLEGE OF AOTEAROA -

> Bev Norsworthy and others have single-mindedly focused on bringing the Kingdom into the educational sector, through the Christian Teachers Training College of Aotearoa. These teachers continue to network across the sector. This has become a centre for training students in Christian worldview thinking, now called Masters Institute, led by Patrick Baker (Masters Institute, 2004).

- BRUCE LOGAN: PROPHET OF EDUCATIONAL VALUES -

> Bruce Logan wrote a bimonthly magazine, *Cutting Edge*, dealing with public policy particularly in education and Christian values, engaging in frequent public debate. It reads like an Oxford magazine, but it is consistently engaging issues. This became the catalyst for the development of Maxim Institute. Maxim has broadened this engagement in public debate from educational to social and political issues. It is regarded by many, including leading Evangelicals, as confrontational and rightwing (e.g. Lineham, 2004:165), but affirmed for its commitment to engagement.

Values education in schools has brought these issues into the public arena. More than a score of evangelical Christian schools have sprung up in a desire to create a morally-based educational environment. Others prefer to influence the values of existing secular education.

- JOHN HEENAN: VALUES EDUCATION -

> Cornerstone Values is a program developed by John Heenan (c2002) that has focussed on this idea. It has developed the eight values in "The Abolition of Man" by C. S. Lewis into a values curriculum for schools. It does not mention Christ but produces a standard of right and wrong for students. Forty schools have accepted it for use.

Conversation between Evangelicals and Pentecostals and the media is also relatively insignificant. American evangelists and Brian Tamaki of Destiny Church pay their way onto certain TV channels. NZ evangelical or Pentecostal-developed TV programs do not feature more than once a week. March for Jesus, gatherings of thousands held each year, featured a mere two minute slot on the news in contrast with the Hero Parade, a parade affirming gay and lesbian lifestyles, which collects both news and review time.

- RESPONSES TO ANTI-CHRISTIAN MEDIA BIAS -

> In response to the Church Life Survey, the New Zealand Herald published a scathing headline about decline of churches. This was followed by TVNZ's portrayal of classic Christian beliefs as a thing of the past.
>
> This burdened several evangelical leaders as they met to discuss issues. 'How do you address the issue of closed doors for Christians at the Herald, at TVNZ and elsewhere?' An immediate response was to find a person to collect clippings to document the bias within the Herald.
>
> 'The doors are not closed, though there may be bias. We simply need to come up with positive media objectives. We need a task force which will define the objectives, similar to the way the Marxists and homosexuals identify key places in society into which to get their people. We need people who the media can contact with issues, that the media like, public spokespeople.'

No serious action was taken.[17] This may be contrasted with many positive activities involving Evangelicals and charismatics in media events from Ian Grant's frequent youth and family TV programs, to Rob Harley's TVNZ documentaries of New Zealand Christians and other heroes pioneering against odds to serve the poor and bring justice.

- TREVOR YAXLEY: MEDIA DREAM -

> Typical of the stories encountered during this study is that of Trevor Yaxley, a converted businessman, who during the renewal, developed a national evangelistic movement and then Lifeway Bible School. In 1991 they 'heard from God' about Family Television Network. By 1996, he had developed television production studios and training, then a free to air station. ShineTV is a family friendly channel launched on SKY TV, 2001.

This is complemented by the development among Pentecostals of a postmodern music culture, spearheaded by the large inner city churches. This has resulted in curiosity among

---

17 Harold Turner discusses the issues of church and media at length (Turner, 1996).

the media as to why a number of top performers are Evangelical Christians: Brooke Fraser, Stereogram, Daniel and Natasha Bedingfield, Dave Dobbins of the Ladds…

- POSTMODERN MUSIC CULTURE: PARACHUTE FESTIVAL EXTREME -

> *Parachute Festival* claims to be the third biggest Christian music festival in the world. Over 18,000 young people attended the 12th yearly festival at Matamata in Feb, 2000, 25,000 were expected in 2005. The festival affirms all forms of youth music from 40 different bands on five separate stages in an attempt to inspire young people to follow Jesus.
>
> Delirious are loud and ragey enough to cut it with the youth culture of today and yet lead singer Martin Smith, is a man who's so passionate about worship that he easily combines the two. Add in the waterslides, weird haircuts, a massive tent town, comprehensive seminar programme on youth issues and a village full of food and the momentum keeps building year by year (Francis, 2000).

One of the most advanced sectors is that of family counselling. The Christian Counsellors Association has a significant standing with the Psychological Association of New Zealand.[18] Part of this has to do with marriage and family development.

- MARRIAGE AND FAMILY RETREATS -

> 'Get Away for a Weekend to Remember' says the advertisement for Family Life NZ, identifying a weekend of seminars and husband-wife discussion on roles, conflict, forgiveness, anger, intimacy. On the opposite page *Marriage Ministries International* advertises a course, "Good marriage, bad marriages, stale marriages. Any couple can benefit from God's plan for marriage!"
>
> Meanwhile, the popular *Parenting With Confidence* seminars that have touched scores of thousands of people in New Zealand, led by the popular TV host of youth programs, Ian Grant, is featured in another corner. On the back page is a *School of Biblical Counselling* and an advertisement for a conference for ministering to homosexuals entitled 'Pursuing Sexual and Relational Wholeness' (2000).

The rapid expansion of abortion and the loss of public support to fight it indicates that such ventures, while noble and assisting many, are not at a sufficient national level to reverse what Evangelicals view as declining moral trends. An alliance of Evangelicals and Catholics on these issues has seemed powerless against the much smaller abortion lobby.

- PETITIONS AGAINST EXPANDED ABORTION LEGALISATION -

> In Feb. 2000 with a petition of 30,084 signatures requested Parliament to give statutory recognition to the unborn child as a human being with an inalienable right to life.
>
> A survey by A. C. Nielson showed that support for such legal protection had decreased from 40% to 34%, while opposition had increased from 35% to 53% over ten years. The pro-life analysis of this included comment that with an increase of abortions to 15,000 per year, 'tens of thousands of New Zealanders who have experienced abortion in their

---

18 Comment from John Sturt, pioneer of the Christian counselling sector.

> family or amongst their circle of friends have been coerced by this culture of death into supporting abortion' (Orr, 1999)

Frequently, the Vision for Auckland leaders commented that the family is the essential building block of a healthy society. One necessary area of healing is the restoration of many men who have lost their role as heads of homes, or become trapped by the effects of their sexual freedom within the culture.

- PROMISEKEEPERS: ALTERNATIVE COMMUNITIES OF PURITY -

> The growth of Promisekeepers, a movement of men making commitments to fidelity in marriage with gatherings yearly of several thousand, has resulted in small covenantal groups of men in many churches and provided a public symbolism around the sanctity of marriage. While its roots are in Midwest US Evangelicalism (Abraham, 1997; Claussen, 2000), leadership in New Zealand has been built around Paul Subritsky, son of an evangelist at the centre of the charismatic renewal in the 1970's and 1980's.

Evaluation of Engagement

Reading these structural transformational visions born in seasons of charismatic renewal, is like watching a child taking its first steps, or a teenager oscillating between identity and confusion. It is both glorious in the evident actions of faith, in the panorama of boldness and sad in the inadequacy of underlying theological frameworks, structural wisdom and effectiveness.

It confirms (1) that renewal releases energy for social change. It also confirms (2) that underlying theological development and (3) expansion of structural networks is needed. This leaves me recognising (4) that these are neither available nor developing rapidly enough for renewal to become Transforming Revival. Thus cultural revitalisation will not be generated, unless... apostolic and prophetic leadership takes these embryonic building blocks and fosters them into an effective synergistic movement for change.

This study has examined the missiological ramifications of revival theology in Auckland as far as engagement. Next, as an example of the process of engagement, I examine creation of theology in the business sector.

- 15 -

Transforming Business Culture

This chapter summarizes stories from the business sector in more depth in order to demonstrate the necessity and process for formulating a theology of the Kingdom transforming business.

Patrick Lynch (2000), executive director of the Catholic Education Office, identified growing trends in ethical business and values-based business education. During this study I became acquainted with numerous evangelical business people with a passion to influence business culture. Can evangelical business leaders influence the directions of such discussions? Based on the seven steps described in the previous chapter is there enough theological integration and reflection to enable the passion for change to move to productive action?

The stories of fifteen Evangelical/Pentecostal business people were gathered and eleven edited and published. Several of them are part of the top echelon of business leadership in the city, others were in significant management roles, some ran small businesses. These stories were analyzed for biblical themes. While too small a sample for comprehensive analysis, I was amazed at the extent to which they illustrated how theologies are developing in this sector and the comprehensive spread of those theologies across the Scriptures. The following is a summary analysis of the business stories. The complete stories may be read in *Creating an Auckland Business Theology* (Grigg, 2000a).

Eleven Business Stories

Clearly evangelical business people have patterns of deep spirituality and well-developed value systems. Unbeknown to themselves, they also are creators of theology. That is evident when one businessman (some names withheld for personal reasons) hears a message on tithing, applies it in his company and finds the sudden response of God's blessing. Or, when a second struggles with an ethical response to being undercut by former employees. Both find themselves entering into and being embraced by the unusual character of God in the midst of the chaotic realities of life. That is theology – reflection on the knowing of God.

The stories included a dramatic range of themes from Genesis to Revelation. They begin in Genesis 1, with the God of creativity, foundational to Peter Haythornthwaite's values and the success of his advertising company, *Peter Haythornthwaite Design (PHD)*. His desire is to see people "go beyond, to break down the barriers, to do something new and fresh, beyond the preconceived idea." Craig Weston's business management consulting company extends the creativity theme into an Inspired Solutions Group, expanding on the role of the Holy Spirit, the breath of life behind creation.

Peter further develops the theme in Genesis 3 of men and women made in the image of God, in his approach to "treating clients as a treasure" and his desire to inspire people "who may feel like failures, that they can become the person they're destined to be." Bruce Nicholson, Manufacturing Manager of Kalamazoo, follows the same theme upholding the dignity of women in the workplace by removing pornography and creating a pleasant work environment. The fatherhood of God is inherent in the strong sense of caring and providing, evident in most stories of the managers.

Lucy Clancie of the Sanitarium Company, expands on the Genesis concept of God who structures, as they have structured into a business their theology of health, based on the Mosaic law. The ten commandments of Exodus for Dick Hubbard of Businesses for Social Responsibility and the fruit of the Spirit in Galatians 5:22,23 for John Sax, Chief Executive of Southpark Corporation, give foundations for personal and business ethics.

Wyn Fountain, retired clothing manufacturer, illuminated the sovereignty of God over fallen humankind as he reflected in a Psalmist-like manner on the ups and downs of life and of good and evil men around him in the early years. That theme echoes in several of these stories. The prophets are not absent, beginning with the modelling of the prophetic in Wyn Fountain's life and David Hope-Cross's (company director of Bayer and Agfa) desire to see a prophetic voice to the economic powers.

Related to the New Testament, ecclesiology is inherent in most of these stories, from Wyn's rejection of the institutional church as largely irrelevant, to other's total commitment to support a church which has supported them. A new pattern of theology that sees the church as networks in the community rather than the gathered congregation on Sunday morning in a building in essence redefines the church as mission in the workplace. Ken Eagle, Managing Director, Cambridge Consulting Services, like many of us from Navigator or YWAM backgrounds, has been operating with Jesus' model of the mission team as being church for some years while sustaining commitments to a traditional church.

Dick Hubbard emphasizes responsibility, hard work and discipline as outworkings of Christian values. He talks of pressing through in the tough times. This relates to Ken Eagle's reflections on a life of faith and faithfulness, based on Jesus' promises to answer prayer in John 14 and 16. Faith in a long-term vision and an awareness of God's timing are significant for another entrepreneur. This reflects Solomon's wisdom in Ecclesiastes 3: "There is a time for everything under the sun."

Fig. 26: Conversational Sources of Auckland Business Theology

BUSINESS CONVERSATION THEMES	BIBLICAL CONVERSATION THEMES	SOURCES OF THEOLOGY FOR BUSINESS LEADERS	THEIR BIBLICAL SOURCES
CREATIVITY	>Releasing full potential, human dignity	Charismatic renewal	Gen 1
PRODUCTIVITY	>God made it fruitful >Hard work >God of blessing >Tithing releases blessing	Pentecostal pastor	Gen 1; John 15:7, 16
PEOPLE-CENTRED MANAGEMENT	>Loving relationships >Management in different social spheres >Harmonious work environment >Pastoral care >Redemptive leadership, forgiveness	Washington Prayer Breakfast Industrial Mission	1 Cor 13; 1John 4:7-21 1 John 1:9-10
ETHICS IN BUSINESS	>Integrity, financial honesty >God of faithfulness >Ten Commandments >Fruit of the Spirit	Seventh Day Adventist doctrine	Exodus 20:2-17 Gal 5:22,23
STRUGGLE AGAINST BUSINESS UPS AND DOWNS	>Spiritual warfare >Sovereignty of God >Life of faith	Popular Pentecostal theology	Eph 6:10-20
HANDLING POWER PLAYS	>Sovereignty of God >Trust in God's purposes	Navigator discipling	Psalms
POSITIVE MENTAL ATTITUDE	>Problems as opportunities for faith and prayer >Spirituality heightening the intellectual integration of logic, intuition, emotions	Indian Christian reflection	1 Cor 1:20-25
CAREER COMMITMENT	>Business as a vocation	Book: The Other Hundred Hours[1]	
MENTORING EXCELLENCE	>Discipleship >Holiness, search for perfection	The Navigators, Revival Theology	II Tim 2:2-6
RESPONSIBLE ECONOMIC POLICY AND STRUCTURES	>Prophetic voice to the economic powers	World Council of Churches Theology, Pentecostal spiritual warfare themes	Eph 6:10-20

Fig.26: A summary of themes, sources of theologies and motivating Scriptures of eleven Auckland businesspeople.

Affirmation of business as a vocation, a theme of Timothy and Titus, is needed. This sense of calling is strong in every story. It expresses an inner spirituality. Ajayan Abraham, Indian student, reflecting on this, includes in his definition of spirituality, "The spiritual person always embodies critical intellectual capabilities such as heightened awareness that sees problems as challenges or that blends logic and intuition." That spirituality is expressed in love, forgiveness, ability to perceive the next steps, faith, investment in others, redemptive leadership and so on. The development of a business spirituality for Kiwis in business requires some further discussion.

Integrity marks Rodney Dawson's (Managing Director, Leaders with a Vision Int'l) search and, is a common theme in all these stories. It is based on the nature of the God of faithfulness, regular confession of sin and the search for a holy life. Practically, Peter Haythornthwaite relates it to the paying of accounts promptly.

John Sax has a Johannine-like emphasis on the centrality of love and relationships. Indeed, most identified a pleasant, just and interactive environment as an essential Christian management value. Peter extends this to a sphere management philosophy without hierarchy. The biblical foundations for either of these poles of management style require important levels of debate. David Hope-Cross has thought extensively of pastoral care for staff.

Expansion of a Theology of the Apostolic into Business Culture

Earlier, I commented on the release of the apostolic and prophetic as significant in moving from revival dynamics to Transforming Revival. Elements of this were evident in the stories of these businessman. The concept, described in the previous chapter, of an apostle as one called and sent directly by God, includes lay persons with a sense of vocation. One aspect of an apostolic gift is one who pioneers new God-infused structures and is gifted in organisational leadership. The definition of an apostle as one with a sense of both creation of new structure and "sentness," can include an entrepreneur, a business leader, a trade union leader or community organizer who possess a sense of godly vocation. (This illustrates the primary thesis of Volf in his *Pneumatological Theology of Work* (1991: 69-154), a derivative of Moltmann's (1993) creation-oriented pneumatology).

By defining the apostle as one who speaks a message, one can include a business leader who interprets business values in the light of God's Word, one who creates business culture in a manner that reflects the creator. By defining the apostle as one who evangelizes and sees much fruit conserved into groups, one can also include a business leader who reaches out to his people and creates evangelistic momentum and discipleship cells among those he or she touches.

Redefinging the apostle as anointed by God and affirmed by signs and wonders, one would anticipate both the blessing of God and the unusual activity of the Spirit on these men and women in their business dealings. (This aspect was not specifically explored in the study, but was indicated in several of their comments.)

The underlying Evangelical and Pentecostal commitment to evangelism was evident. This is usually significant in apostolic roles. Ken models this par excellence. Sanitarium model it as structural witness and in the environment of prayer and caring within the organisation. Craig Weston ended up with an evangelistic Alpha course as a result of discussion of vision and values within his organisation. Rodney Dawson prays at the beginning of seminars and people are shocked, confront their backsliding, turn to Christ or are strangely moved.

Given these understandings of the apostolic, it became evident from these stories, that there are a number of such apostolic leaders in the business world and other professions around Auckland.

Integration of the Theological Conversation

This above brief integration shows business people developing action theologies, from the whole gamut of the Scriptures. Multiple life stories are connected to multiple biblical narratives and teachings. What is not evident is an integrating theological plot that meshes the sub-themes. My observation is that the paucity of theological input on business themes meant that each had latched on to themes that had touched an issue – the diversity of sources is indication of this paucity.

Lack of integration of their theologies with others led most to identify the need for consultation and resultant publications to generate a full-orbed theology in order to do what David Hope-Cross cried out for:

> *The churches have lost the prophetic voice in society and they have lost the right to speak the Word of God into society. The world is ruled by economic powers, so it is important that Christian business people speak out for God and try to have an impact on society.*

From Fractured Stories to Kingdom Theologies

As an illustration of the use of the Kingdom in practice at a grassroots level, I will now consider the Kingdom as a theme to serve the business leaders in their conversation about transforming Auckland's business culture. Fig. 27 shows the key themes of their grassroots conversations and biblical source. The final column indicates ways these could be integrated within a Kingdom framework.

Fig. 27: Auckland Business Theology and the Kingdom of God

BUSINESS CONVERSATION THEMES	THE BUSINESS PEOPLE'S BIBLICAL CONVERSATION THEMES	THEIR BIBLICAL SOURCES	PARALLEL KINGDOM THEMES
CREATIVITY	>Releasing full potential, human dignity	Gen 1	Kingdom and humanness Kingdom and mustard seed and yeast (Matt 13:31-34)
PRODUCTIVITY	>God made it fruitful >Hard work >God of blessing >Tithing releases blessing	Gen 1; John 15:7, 16	Kingdom economic principles (Matt 18:23-35; 20:1-16; 21:28-31; 21:33-44) Parable of the sower of the seed of the Kingdom (Matt 13:1-23)
PEOPLE-CENTRED MANAGEMENT	>Loving relationships >Management in different social spheres >Harmonious work environment >Pastoral care >Redemptive leadership, forgiveness	1 Cor 13; 1John 4:7-21 1 John 1:9-10	Kingdom social principles Love as great commandment (Matt 22:32-40) Kingdom theology of work
ETHICS IN BUSINESS	>Integrity, financial honesty >God of faithfulness >Ten Commandments >Fruit of the Spirit	Exodus 20:2-17 Gal 5:22,23	The King as supreme sustainer Kingdom & faithfulness (Matt 25:1-13; 25:14-30) Kingdom and social order (Matt 22:2-14)
STRUGGLE AGAINST BUSINESS UPS AND DOWNS	>Spiritual warfare >Sovereignty of God >Life of faith	Eph 6:10-20	Kingdoms in conflict (Matt 16:19) Kingdom and mustard seed and yeast (Matt 13:31-34)
HANDLING POWER PLAYS	>Sovereignty of God >Trust in God's purposes	Psalms	Kingdom leadership (Matt 18:1-4; 20:1-16, 21; 23:1-14)
POSITIVE MENTAL ATTITUDE	>Problems as opportunities for faith and prayer >Spirituality heightening the intellectual integration of logic, intuition, emotions	1 Cor 1:20-25	Kingdom and mustard seed and yeast (Matt 13:31-34) The Spirit and the Kingdom
CAREER COMMITMENT	>Business as a vocation		Kingdom and hiring workers (Matt 20: 1-16)
MENTORING EXCELLENCE	>Discipleship >Holiness, search for perfection	II Tim 2:2-6	Discipleship as response to King
RESPONSIBLE ECONOMIC POLICY AND STRUCTURES	>Prophetic voice to the economic powers	Eph 6:10-20	Kingdom economics Kingdom conflict

Fig. 27 shows a correlation between the ad hoc *business theologies of Fig. 26, their sources and the theme of the Kingdom. This shows both the spread of theologies involved and demonstrates the Kingdom as an integrating interpretive framework.*

FINISHING A CONVERSATION—
EXTENDING THE DREAMING

Beneath the Surface

Never-ending transformational conversations allow for multiple permutations. So as we get up from our coffee, allow me to wrap up, so that for our next coffee we may start at a new place.

You have engaged in a conversation envisioning the Spirit of God as he hovers and creates, intervenes and renews the people of a city. A conversation to get inside revival theory, beyond the "God will come and all will change!", to a clarity as to processes, dynamics, phases and principles from initial encounters with the Holy Spirit to cultural revitalisation — what I have termed *Transforming Revival* where the Spirit revitalises all aspects of the city culture with her presence. Imagine the implications of this conversation a few decades hence.

For example, extending the data in the early chapter on the church in Auckland:

- we will have seen the rapid increase of experiences with the Spirit of God among new Polynesian churches.
- the expansion of a new wave of Maori revival on the urban maraes.
- the explosion of deep prayerful, meditative, activist spirituality from Chinese, Korean, and Indian congregations.
- such that even Pakeha have become increasingly responsive to the touch of the comforting Spirit in the midst of What Os Guineess calls the death of their culture.
- Sadly, many liberal or traditional (largely Pakeha) churches will have died, but their facilities will have been taken over by these vibrant groups.

This is already happening:

- NEW SOUNDS OF REVIVAL -

> On Saturday morning, I woke to a roaring sound like surf breaking. The phone rang. "You'd better get down here. The Spirit of God has come."
>
> The sound I was hearing was a roar of praise, worship and weeping emanating from the ministry base a few blocks away. Young athletes and performers travelling with the "Impact World Tour" had assembled for three days of commissioning and orientation. Their goal, after two years of preparation, was to hit over fifty cities and towns across New Zealand in waves of evangelism, followed by stadium events.
>
> Loren Cunningham, Winkie Pratney and I entered the courtyard to find young people overwhelmed by the presence of God. I stood next to people who seemed far away in another dimension. It has not stopped. The downtown Auckland evening meetings for leaders were packed to capacity and in the small remote first city of the tour, Gisbourne, the three nights drew 11,000 people, one third of the population.
>
> Email from John Dawson, President, Youth With A Mission
>
> In a few weeks public evangelism had reached over 200,000 people across the nation, of whom 20,000 had indicated a desire to turn from sin and become Christians. The leaders of the process had been obedient to the prophets in the earlier revival to begin with Maori. Indeed, it was so multicultural as to be owned by the Maori and Polynesians.

Decades from now among these groups these early phases of revival, the descending presence, will keep jumping boundaries between groups creating a synergy between these ethnic movements into their second and third.

If the expansion of theology into the fullness of the Kingdom of God continues to expand among these movements (and that is a big if...) these entrepreneurial children of migrants will bring a sense of godly hope after the disintegration of postmodern culture. As these migrant cultures take greater and greater place centre stage in the nation, and in education, Christian values will increasingly surface in the restructuring of post-postmodernism. A restructuing around the integrative themes of the Spirit and the Kingdom of God will move into Phase 4.

Imagine postmodernism has disappeared (if it ever did exist), as the nation has reintegrated around this Kingdom theme, thus redefining the nature of humanness, the dignity of each individual, the protection of the unborn, the defence of the poor, swearing and pride in abusive language will become unpopular. Our understanding of our relationship to the created order will be determined by the mandate to care for it, such that it is replenished and sustained, cooperative economic systems will increasingly be replacing greed-driven capitalism, simplicity will be a popular mantra, and foreign ownership of resources and means of production step by step be decreased. The King himself will increasingly be central in peoples thinking, while hospitality to and inclusion of the marginalised and the religious minorities will be affirmed, though not uncritically be allowed to dominate national values.

The early leadership by evangelical children of revival and the emergent engagements illustrated in this book will have broken through the governmental barriers into two Christian Universities; refined political reflection institutes will be engaging all parties; extensive rethinking of economic systems based on Biblical principles of production, creativity, cooperative economics, limitations on greed, etc. will be subjects at regular economic forum; in Education, values will be significantly evident in curricula; in Forestry, ownership will have been devolved to NZ cooperative processes, and protection of native forests replaced the rape of the native forests in order to plant ecologically destructive pine trees; in Law, Christian ethics groups will have been proposing quiet reforms...

Perhaps... for as we are conversing, hope grows. The phone rings with a call from a leader as to how to cluster others to examine national transformation later in the year, how to create enough unity within Evangelicalism for agreement about issues around the treaty of Waitangi... A brother enters to discuss the development of the ethnic leaders hui...

On the other hand...crime, divorce, abortion, suicide rates show no sign of decline; abusive language and lack of civility mark the schoolyard; drunken orgys occur every Saturday night all over the city, banks continue to fleece the unsuspecting...

Perhaps! There has been revival as documented here. Evangelicals have become enraged and the beginnings of an engaged and creative minority for social change have appeared, but there has been little theological reflection or clarity of goals and we are far from seeing major paradigm shifts of culture. Transforming Revival is not yet evident.

Scattered through the study are evidences of issues, which together will preclude these sizeable movements from using their critical mass for significant social transformation. The work of the Holy Spirit will be slowed by reversions to reductionist views of revival, anti-intellectualism and absolutism. A general dislocation of these movements from the mainline denominations will likely continue, hence lack of access to traditional theologies on social issues, along with a loss of holiness, and institutionalism of the renewal and traditions that preclude expansion of theologies of social change.

So, in the midst of advance and retreat, we wait for this time of seeing the full fruit of the revival, of seeing the city squares filled with the hovering, creating Spirit of fire, love, unity, comfort and counsel. Meanwhile let us work with all our energy to expand her penetration into every nook and cranny of the city.

To Finish the Conversation

This study has examined a dynamic with many signs of being a work of the Spirit of God, a revival in a modern/postmodern city, resulting in the fruit of leaders who desire transformation of city culture. While this revival has caused church growth and some social engagement, its embryonic prophetic and apostolic social theology and structures have not yet resulted in the critical mass to significantly impact the city.

Yet as it progresses we expect Citywide Transforming Revival to engage the postmodern city resulting in the revitalisation of postmodern humanness, community and identity, moral relationship to the material environment and an alternative Kingdom order to the New World Order.

On the other hand, it is not evident that there is sufficient momentum for these hopes to be fulfilled. Yet, one hopes! The lack of response by secular leaders in New Zealand may mean that transforming engagement, in the end is not matched with cultural revitalisation. Yet the strange twists of divine intervention in Moses and Nehemiah support the logic of this study with an unknown factor, a sovereign God acting on behalf of praying people. One measures the human, studies the realities and hopes. Yet one expects, beyond reasonable hope.

These theologies and processes indicate ways forward not only in Auckland, but globally, in the development of the work of a sovereign Holy Spirit in postmodern city transformation.

I hope you enjoyed your coffee. May God grant what we ask!

- CONVERSATIONAL SOURCES -

Abraham, Ken. (1997). Who Are the Promise Keepers? New York: Doubleday.

Ahdar, Rex. (2000). World's Colliding: Conservative Christians and the Law. Gower House, Croft Road, Aldershot, Hants GU11 3HR, England: Dartmouth Publishing and Burlington, VT: Ashgate.

---. (2003). Indigenous Spiritual Concerns and the Secular State: Some Developments in New Zealand. Oxford Journal of Legal Studies, 23 (4), 611-637.

Ahdar, Rex & Stenhouse, John (Eds.). (2000). God and Government. Dunedin: University of Otago Press.

Aldrich, Joe. (1992). Prayer Summits. Portland, OR: Multnomah Press.

Alinsky, Saul. (1969). Reveille for Radicals. New York: Vintage Books.

Allis, David. (1995). Training Centres' Directory. Auckland: Urban Leadership Foundation.

Alton, David. (1991). Faith in Britain. London: Hodder and Stoughton.

Ammerman, Nancy. (1987). Bible Believers: Fundamentalists in the Modern World. Brunswick and London: Rutgers University Press.

---. (1997). Congregation and Community. Brunswick and London: Rutgers University Press.

Ansley, B. (1988, 26 Oct.). The Growing Might of the Moral Right. New Zealand Listener, pp. 16-18.

Aune, Dave E. (Ed.). (1998). Revelation 17-22. Nashville: Thomas Nelson.

Autrey, C. E. (1968). Renewals before Pentecost. Tennessee: Broadman Press.

Bakke, Ray. (1987). The Urban Christian. Downers Grove, IL: IVP Press.

---. (1997). A Theology As Big As the City. Downers Grove, IL: IVP Press.

Ball, Terence. (1996). The Mushy World of Moral Relativism: "What's Wrong With Values?" Oxford Review, (May 1996).

Barber, Benjamin & Schultz, Andrea. (1996). Jihad vs. McWorld: How the Planet is Both Falling Apart and Coming Together. New York: Random House.

Barrett, David, Kurian, George & Johnson, Todd. (2001). World Christian Encyclopedia (2nd ed.). Oxford: Oxford university Press.

Battley, Don. (1986). Charismatic Renewal: A View from the Inside. Ecumenical Review, (Jan 1986).

Batty, Michael & Longley, Paul. (1994). Fractal Cities. San Diego: Academic Press.

Baudrillard, Jean. (1999). The Revenge of the Crystal: Selected Writings on the Object and its Destiny. Leichhardt: Pluto Press.

Bauman, Zygmunt. (2000). Liquid Modernity. Cambridge: Polity Publishers.

Bausch, William J. (1984). Storytelling, Imagination and Faith. Mystic, Conn: Twenty-Third.

Beasley-Murray, G.R. (1986). Jesus and the Kingdom of God. Grand Rapids: Eerdmans.

Bebbington, D.W. (1989). Evangelicalism in Modern Britain: A History From 1730's to the1980's. London: Unwin Hyman.

Bellah, Robert. (1976). The Broken Covenant. New York: Seabury.

Bellingham, G.R. (1987). A Biblical Approach to Social Transformation. Unpublished D. Min Thesis, Eastern Baptist Seminary, Philadelphia.

Benge, Diane. (2003). Abundance and Waste. Reality, 56, 7.

Bennett, J. C. (1941). Christian Realism. New York: Charles Scribner's Sons.

Bennett, William (Ed.). (1993). The Book of Virtues: A Treasury of Great Moral Stories. New York: Simon and Schuster.

Berg, Mike & Pretiz, Paul. (1996). Spontaneous Combustion: Grass Roots Christianity, Latin American Style. Pasadena: William Carey Library.

Berger, Peter. (1954). The Sociological Study of Sectarianism. Social Research,, 21 (4, Winter 1954), 467-485.

--- (Ed.). (1999). The Desecularization of the World: Resurgent Religion and World Politics. Grand Rapids, MI: Eerdmans.

Berger, Peter L., Berger, Brigitte & Kellner, Hansfried. (1973). The Homeless Mind: Modernization and Consciousness. New York: Random House.

Bethlehem College. (2004). The First Five Years of Bethlehem College. Retrieved Dec 30,2004, from http://www.beth.school.nz/history/beginnings.htm.

Bevans, Stephen B., S.V.D. (1996). Models of Contextual Theology. Maryknoll: Orbis.

Bishop, Wendy. (1999). Ethnographic Writing Research. Portsmouth, NH: Boynton/Cook Publishers.

Bolitho, Elaine. (1992). In This World - Baptist and Methodist Churches in New Zealand 1948-1988. Unpublished PhD Thesis in World Religions, Victoria University of Wellington, Wellington.

Booth, William. (1890). In Darkest England and the Way Out. London: Salvation Army.

Bosch, David. (1991). Transforming Mission: Paradigm Shifts in Theology of Mission. Maryknoll, NY: Orbis.

Brierley, Peter (Ed.). (1991). Prospects for the Nineties: Trends and Tables from the English Church Census. London: MARC Europe.

Bright, John. (1953). The Kingdom of God :The Biblical Concept and its Meaning for the Church. Nashville: Abingdon Press.

Brookes, Norman. (2000). Impact! Communicating the Faith. P.O. Box 28-843, Remuera, Auckland: Church

Life Survey.

Brookes, Norman & Curnow, Steve. (1998). Lifting the Lid on the New Zealand Church. In Norman Brookes & Steve Curnow (Eds.), Shaping a Future. Adelaide: Open Book Publishers; Wellington, NZ: Church Life Survey.

Brown, Colin. (1985). The Charismatic Movement. In Brian Colless & Peter Donovan (Eds.), Religion in New Zealand Society. Palmerston North: Dunmore Press.

Brown, Ian. (2000, Nov). Executive Secretary's Report. New Zealand Baptist.

Bruce, Steve. (2001). Peter Berger and Study of Religions. In Linda Woodhead (Ed.), Peter Berger and the Study of Religion (pp. 87-111). London and New York: Routledge.

---. (2004). The Social Organization of Diffuse Beliefs and the Future of Cultic Religion. In Alasdair Crockett & Richard O'Leary (Eds.), Patterns and Processes of Religious Change in Modern Industrial Societies (pp. 231-255). Lewiston, New York and Lampeter, Ceredigon, Wales: Edwin Mellen Press.

Brueggeman, Walter. (1977). The Land. Philadelphia: Fortress Press.

---. (1978). The Prophetic Imagination. Philadelphia: Fortress.

---. (1982). Genesis. Atlanta, GA: John Knox Press.

---. (1997). Theology of the Old Testament: Testimony, Dispute, Advocacy. Minneapolis: Fortress Press.

Bryant, George. (1981). New Zealand 2001. Auckland: Cassells.

Buckle, E.G. (1978). Paroikia: the House Alongside: An Account of Developments in Ministry in Some of Auckland's New Urban Areas. Auckland: Diocese of Auckland.

Burgess, Stanley M. (1997a). The Holy Spirit: Medieval, Roman Catholic and Reformation Traditions. Peabody, Massachusets: Hendrikson Publishers, P.O. Box 3473, Peabody, Massachusets 01961-3473.

---. (1997b). The Holy Spirit: Ancient Traditions. Peabody, MA: Hendrikson Publishers.

---. (1997c). The Holy Spirit: Eastern Christian Traditions. Peabody, Massachusetts: Hendrikson Publishers.

Burns, James. (1909/1993). The Laws of Revival. Wheaton, IL: Billy Graham Evangelistic Association.

Busch, Eberhard. (1976). Karl Barth: His Life from Letters and Autobiographical Texts. Philadelphia: Fortress Press.

Carnichan, Hamish. (2004). Vox Populi: Can Binding Referenda Rein in Bad Government. Investigate, February 2004, 44-51.

Carriker, C. Timothy. (1993). Missiological Hermeneutic and Pauline Apocalyptic Eschatology. In Charles van Engen, Dean S. Gilliland & Paul Pierson (Eds.), The Good News of the Kingdom (pp. 45-55). Maryknoll: Orbis.

Castro, Emilio. (1993). Themes in Theology of Mission Arising Out of Canberra. In Charles van Engen, Dean S. Gilliland & Paul Pierson (Eds.), The Good News of the Kingdom (pp. 127-136). Maryknoll: Orbis.

Childs, Brevards. (1960). Myth and Reality in the Old Testament. London: SCM.

---. (1970). Biblical Theology in Crisis. Philadelphia: Westminster.

---. (1979). Introduction to the Old Testament as Scripture. Philadelphia: Westminster.

Christian, Jayakumar. (1999). God of the Empty-Handed. Monrovia, CA: MARC.

Church of England of New Zealand. (1974). Commission on the Charismatic Movement Report. Paper presented at the General Synod of the Church of the Province of New Zealand, Christchurch.

Claussen, Dane S. (Ed.). (2000). The Promise Keepers: Essays on Masculinity and Christianity. Jefferson, NC and London: McFarland and Company, Inc.

Clover, Gary. (1996). A Gospel Imperative for New Zealand Christians: Honour the Treaty of Waitangi as a Sacred Covenant of Equity and Partnership Between "Tangata Whenua" and "Tangata Treaty". Unpublished paper, VisionNZ Reconciliation Network, Auckland.

Cohen, Arthur. (1958). Religion and the Free Society. 60 East 42nd Street, New York 17, NY: The Fund for the Republic.

Colson, Charles. (1987). Kingdoms in Conflict. Grand Rapids: Zondervan.

---. (1989). Against the Night: Living in the New Dark Ages. Ann Arbor, MI: Word Publishing.

Cone, James H. (1972). Black Spirituals: A Theological Interpretation. Theology Today, 29 (No. 1, April 1972).

---. (1975). God of the Oppressed. New York: Seabury Press.

Conn, Harvey. (1992). Genesis as Urban Prologue. In Roger Greenway (Ed.), Discipling the City. Grand Rapids, MI: Baker Book House.

---. (1993). A Contextual Theology of Mission for the City. In Charles van Engen, Dean S. Gilliland & Paul Pierson (Eds.), The Good News of the Kingdom (pp. 96-104). Maryknoll: Orbis.

Fig Harvey, ed. Urban Mission. P.O. Box 27009, Philadelphia, PA19118: Westminster Seminary.

Cox, Harvey. (1965). The Secular City, Secularization and Urbanization in Theological Perspective. New York: MacMillan.

---. (1984). Religion in the Secular City. New York: Simon and Schuster.

---. (1995). Fire from Heaven: The Rise of Pentecostal Spirituality and the Reshaping of Religion in the Twenty-First Century. Reading, MA: Addison-Wesley.

Craigie, Peter C., Page H. Kelley & Joel F. Drinkard, Jr. (1991). Jeremiah 1-25 (Vol. 26). Dallas: Word.

Cullman, Oscar. (1962). Christ and Time. London: SCM.

Cupitt, Don. (1998). Post-Christianity. In Paul Heelas (Ed.), Religion, Modernity and Postmodernity (pp. 218-232). Oxford: Blackwell.

Dadzaa, Guggisberg Aku. (1993). Mobilization of the Church for Effective Evangelism through Small Groups. Unpublished DMin, Westminster Seminary, Philadelphia.

Daniel, Harry F.J. (1970). Urban Industrial Mission in Asia. International Review of Mission, LIX (234), 189-197.

Darragh, Neil. (1995). Doing Theology Ourselves: A Guide to Research and Action. Auckland, New Zealand: Accent Publications (a Division of Snedden and Cervin Pub. Ltd).

---. (2000). At Home in the Earth. Auckland: Accent.

---. (2004). The Future of Christian Thought in the South. In John Stenhouse, Brett Knowles & Antony Wood (Eds.), The Future of Christianity: Historical, Sociological, Political and Theological Perspectives from New Zealand. Adelaide: ATF Press.

Davey, Cyril. (2000). Saint in the Slums: Kagawa of Japan. Jersey City: Parkwest Publications.

Davidson, Allan. (1991). Christianity in Aoteoroa: A History of Church and Society in New Zealand. Wellington: Education for Ministry.

Davies, Paul & Gribben, John. (1991). The Matter Myth: Towards 21st Century Science. London: Viking and Penguin.

Dawson, John. (1989). Taking Our Cities for God. Lake Mary, FL: Creation House.

---. (1996). Healing America's Wounds. Ventura: Regal Books.

de Castro, Cloves Pinto. (2000). Por Uma Fé Cidadã: A Dimensaõ Pública da Igreja. Saõ Paulo: Edições Loyola.

de Soto, Hernando. (1989). The Other Path (June Abbott, Trans.). New York: Harper & Row.

Dear, Michael J. (2000). The Postmodern Urban Condition. Oxford: Blackwell Publishers.

Deepsight Trust. (2005). The Deepsight Trust. Retrieved May 23, 2005, from http://www.deepsight.org/deepsight/index.htm.

Dempster, Murray. (1999). A Theology of the Kingdom - A Pentecostal Contribution. In Vinay Samuel & Chris Sugden (Eds.), Mission as Transformation (pp. 45-75). Oxford: Regnum Books International.

Dewalt, Kathleen, Dewalt, Billie & Wayland, Coral B. (1998). Participant Observation. In H. Russell Bernard (Ed.), Handbook of Methods in Cultural Anthropology. Walnut Creek, CA: AltaMira Press and London: Sage Publications.

Dickie, Hugh. (1997). The Kids-Count '96 Survey. In Bruce Patrick (Ed.), New Vision New Zealand II. Auckland: VisionNZ.

Dockery, David S. (Ed.). (1995). The Challenge of Postmodernity: An Evangelical Engagement. Grand Rapids, MI: Baker Book House.

Donovan, Peter. (2000). Civic Responsibilities of the Church to People of Other Faiths. In Rex Ahdar & John Stenhouse (Eds.), God and Government: The New Zealand Experience (pp. 77-91). Dunedin: University of Otago Press.

Dorfman, Robert. (1970). The Functions of the City. In Anthony H. Pascal (Ed.), Thinking About Cities: New Perspectives on Urban Problems. Santa Monica: The Rand Corporation.

Dorrien, Gary. (1995). Soul in Society. Minneapolis, MN: Augsberg Fortress.

---. (2001). Berger: theology and sociology. In Linda Woodhead (Ed.), Peter Berger and the Study of Religion (pp. 26-39). London and New York: Routledge.

Dow, Malcolm. (2005). An Evangelical Response to Postmodernity. Retrieved 11 Nov, 2005, from http://www.bethtephillah.com/articles/postmodernthesis.html.

Doyle, Rodger. (2001). Going Solo: Unwed Motherhood in Industrial Nations Rises. Scientific American (January 2001), 24.

Duff, Edward. (1956). The Social Thought of the World Council of Churches. London: Longmans.

Duncan, Michael. (2005, April 2005). Destiny March: Public Display of Outrage. Baptist, 121, 13-14.

Durkheim, Emile. (1915/1965). The Elementary Forms of the Religious Life. New York: George Allen and Unwin Ltd and the Free Press.

Dyrness, William. (1983/1991). Let the Earth Rejoice! A Biblical Theology of Holistic Mission. Pasadena: Fuller Seminary Press.

Dyson, R.W. (Ed.). (1998). Augustine: The

City of God Against the Pagans. Cambridge: Cambridge Press.
Edwards, Brian. (1990). A People Saturated with God. Avon: Evangelical Press.
Edwards, Jonathon. (1742/2005). Religious Affections. Retrieved Oct 12, 2005, from http://graciouscall.org/books/edwards/religious/ra3_8.shtml#RTFToC33.
Ellis, Gavin. (2000, Dec 2-3, 2000). Towards Shared Values. Weekend Herald, p. A23.
Elliston, Edgar J. (1997). Missiology: A Multidisciplinary Research Based Discipline. In Introduction to Missiological Research (pp. 207-220). Pasadena: Unpublished manuscript.
Ellul, Jacques. (1964). The Technological Society. NY: Random House, Vintage Books.
---. (1997). The Meaning of the City. Greenwood, SC: Attic Press.
Escobar, Arturo. (1999). The Invention of Development. Current History (November 1999), 382-386.
Evans, John Adsett. (1992). Church-State Relations in New Zealand: 1940-1990. Unpublished D. Phil. Thesis, Otago University, Dunedin.
Evans, Robert & McKenzie, Roy. (1999). Evangelical Revivals in New Zealand. Wellington: Colcom Press, Epworth Bookshop.
Fackre, Gabriel. (1983). Narrative Theology: An Overview. Interpretation, 37 (No. 4 (October)), 340-353.
Fanon, Frantz. (1967). (1986). The Wretched of the Earth. New York: Grove.
Fernandez, Wolfgang & Hall, Bob. (1987). Initial Findings of a Research Analysis on the People and Church of New Zealand. Wellington: Dawn Strategy Committee.
Festinger, Leon. (1959). A Theory of Cognitive Dissonance. London: Tavistock.
Finke, R. & Stark, R. (2000). Acts of Faith. Berkeley: University of California Press.
Finlay, Graeme. (2004). God's Books: Genetics and Genesis. Auckland: TELOS, P.O. Box 56167, Dominion Road, Auckland 10303, New Zealand.
Finney, Charles. (1836/1987). Principles of Revival. Minneapolis: Bethany.
Foucault, Michel. (1972). The Archaeology of Knowledge (A.M. Sheridan Smith, Trans.). New York: Pantheon.
---. (1977). Discipline and Punish: the Birth of the Prison (Alan Sheridan, Trans.). New York: Pantheon.
Foucault, Michel & James D. Faubion ed. (1994). Power. New York: The New Press.
Fountain, Jeff. (2004). Living as a People of Hope. Rotterdam, the Netherlands: Initialmedia, Hope for Europe.
Fountain, Wyn. (1996). The Restoration of Hope for the Transformation of Our Nation. 2 California Place, Kohimarama, Auckland.
---. (c1980). The Other Hundred Hours. Auckland: Wyn Fountain.
Fox, Matthew. (1983). Original Blessing. Santa Fe, NM: Bear and Company.
Francis, Vic. (1993). On the Cutting Edge: The Bill Subritsky Story. Auckland: Dove Ministries and Sovereign World Ltd, Po Box 777, Tonbridge, Kent TN11 9XT.
Frangipane, Francis. (1991). The House of the Lord. Lake Mary, FL: Creation House.
Frankl, Viktor. (1978). The Unheard Cry for Meaning: Psychotherapy and Humanism. New York: Simon and Schuster.
Fukuyama, Francis. (2002). Our Posthuman Future: Consequences of the Biotechnology Revolution. New York: Picador.

Fuller, Daniel P. (1992). The Unity of the Bible. Grand Rapids: Zondervan.

Gale, Stephen & Moore, Eric G. (1975). The Manipulated City. Chicago: Maarufa Press.

Garriott, Craig W. (1966). Leadership Development in the Multiethnic Church. Urban Mission, 13 (No 4, June 1996), 24-37.

Garvin, Mal. (1998). The Divine Art of Networking. Gordon St, Poatina, Tasmania: Whitestone, Fusion Australia.

Gentile, Ernest B. (2002). Your Sons and Daughters Shall Prophesy: Prophetic Gifts in Ministry Today. Grand Rapids: Chosen Books.

George, Mark K. (2000). Foucault. In A.K.M. Adam (Ed.), Handbook of Postmodern Biblical Interpretation (pp. 91-98). St Louis: Chalice Press.

Gerlach, Luther P. (1974). Pentecostalism: Revolution or Counter Revolution. In Iwing I. Zaretsky & Mark P. Leone (Eds.), Religious Movements in Contemporary America. Princeton, NJ: Princeton University Press.

Gerlach, Luther P. & Hein, V.H. (1970). People, Power, Change: Movements of Social Transformation. NY: Bobbs-Merrill Co.

Giddens, Anthony. (1990). The Consequences of Modernity. Stanford, CA: Stanford University Press.

Gill, Robin. (1999). Churchgoing and Christian Ethics. Cambridge: Cambridge University Press.

---. (2003). The Empty Church Revisited. Aldershot, Hants, GU11 3HR, England: Ashgate Publishing Company.

Gilling, Brian. (1989). Mass Evangelism in Mid-Twentieth Century New Zealand. In Douglas Pratt (Ed.), Rescue the Perishing (Vol. 1, pp. 43-53). Auckland: College Communications.

Glasser, Arthur. (1993). The Good News of the Kingdom. Maryknoll: Orbis.

Gleick, James. (1987). Chaos: Making a New Science. New York: Penguin.

Gmelch, George & Zenner, Walter P. (Eds.). (1996). Urban Life: Readings in Urban Anthropology, 3rd edn. Prospects Heights, IL: Waveland Press Inc.

Grant, George. (1987a). Bringing in the Sheaves: Transforming Poverty into Productivity. Fort Worth, TX: Dominion Press.

---. (1987b). The Changing of the Guard: Biblical Principals for Political Action. Fort Worth, Texas: Dominion Press.

Greeley, Andrew. (2004). A Religious Revival in Europe. In Alasdair Crockett & Richard O'Leary (Eds.), Patterns and Processes of Religious Change in Modern Industrial Societies (pp. 165 - 189). Lewiston, New York and Lampeter, Ceredigon, Wales: Edwin Mellen Press.

Greenway, Roger & Monsma, Timothy. (1989a). Cities: Mission New Frontiers. Grand Rapids, MI: Baker.

---. (1989b). The Intersecting Veins of the City. In Cities: Missions New Frontiers. Grand Rapids, MI: Baker.

Greenway, Roger S. (1978). Apostles to the City. Grand Rapids: Baker Book House.

---. (1979). Discipling the City: Theological Reflections on Urban Mission. Grand Rapids: Baker.

Greerley, Andrew. (1990). The Catholic Myth: The Behaviour and Beliefs of American Catholics. New York: Charles Scribner's Sons.

---. (2004). A Religious Revival in Europe? In Alasdair Crockett & Richard O'Leary (Eds.), Patterns and Processes of Religious Change in Modern Industrial Societies (pp. 165-189). Lewiston, New York and Lampeter, Ceredigon, Wales:

Edwin Mellen Press.

Grentz, Stanley. (1995). Star Trek and the Next Generation. In David S. Dockery (Ed.), The Challenge of Postmodernism: An Evangelical Engagement. Grand Rapids, MI: Baker.

---. (1996). A Primer on Postmodernism. Grand Rapids: Eerdmans.

---. (1993). Revisioning Evangelical Theology. Downers Grove, IL: Intervarsity Press.

Griffith, Brian. (1982). Morality and the Market Place: Christian Alternatives to Capitalism and Socialism. London: Hodder & Stoughton.

---. (1984). The Creation of Wealth. London: Hodder & Stoughton.

---. (1985). Monetarism and Morality: A Response to the Bishops. London: Centre for Policy Studies.

Grigg, Viv. (1979, October 1979). Discipleship. Reach Communiqué, 1.

---. (1980, First Quarter, 1980). The Disciple and Self. Reach Communiqué, 2.

---. (1981, 3rd quarter, 1981). The Disciple and Possessions. Reach Communiqué, 11.

---. (1984/2004). Companion to the Poor. Monrovia, CA: Authentic Media (revised and updated), originally Abatross: Sydney (1984), revised MARC: Monrovia (1990)).

---. (1985). The Lifestyle and Values of Servants. Auckland: Urban Leadership Foundation.

---. (1985/2004). Biblical Reflections on Land and Land Rights. Auckland: Urban Leadership Foundation.

---. (1986). SERVANTS: A Protestant Missionary Order With Vows of Simplicity and Non-Destitute Poverty. Auckland: Urban Leadership Foundation.

---. (1992/2004). Cry of the Urban Poor. London: Authentic Press.

---. (1992a). Church of the Poor. In Roger Greenway (Ed.), Discipling the City: A Comprehensive Approach to Urban Mission (pp. 159-170). Grand Rapids, Michigan: Baker.

---. (1996). AD2000 Cities Database, Global Ministry Mapping System CD, from http://www.gmi.org/research/database.htm#Countries,%20Provinces,%20 Cities.

---. (1997a). Transforming the Soul of Kiwi Cities. In Bruce Patrick (Ed.), New Vision New Zealand (Vol. II, pp. 106-126). Auckland: VisionNZ.

---. (1997b). Transforming the Soul of the Nation. In Bruce Patrick (Ed.), Vision New Zealand Congress (1997). Auckland: Vision New Zealand.

---. (1997c, Nov 15, 2001). 72 Goals for Auckland. Retrieved Mar 10, 2009, http://urbanleaders.org/home/index.php?option=com_content&view=article&id=12&Itemid=69.

---. (1997d). Transforming Cities: An Urban Leadership Guide. Auckland: Urban Leadership Foundation, P.O. Box 20-524, Glen Eden, Auckland.

---. (1999a, 1999, Mar 5-7th). Vision for Auckland Hui. Paper presented at the Vision for Auckland Hui, Te Ngira Marae, Papakura.

---. (2000a). Creating an Auckland Business Theology. P.O. Box 20-524, Auckland: Urban Leadership Foundation.

---. (2000b, Nov 2000). Urban Theology as Transformational Conversation: Hermeneutics for the Post-Modern Cities. Retrieved Dec 8, 2001, from http://pcbc.webjournals.org/articles/1/11/2000/3177.htm.

---. (2000d, Nov 15, 2001). The Vision for Auckland Transformation Network. Retrieved Mar 15, 2009, http://www.urbanleaders.org/home/index.php?option=com_content&view=artic

le&id=66&Itemid=67
---. (2001a, Nov 15, 2001). Processes in Transforming Auckland. Retrieved Feb 15, 2009, http://www.urbanleaders.org/home/index.php?option=com_content&view=article&id=64&Itemid=64.
---. (2001b, Nov 15, 2001). Healing Cultural Fractures. Retrieved Feb 10, 2009 http://www.urbanleaders.org/home/index.php?option=com_content&view=article&id=67&Itemid=70
---. (2005a). Envisioning a Cultural Revitalization. Paper presented at the Christian Leaders Congress, Waikanae.
---. (2005b, 14 October, 2005). Revival Growth in Auckland: Dispelling the Myth of a Dying Church. Retrieved 10 Mar, 2009 http://www.urbanleaders.org/home/index.php?option=com_content&view=article&id=65&Itemid=66.
Grimstead, Jay. (2005). Coalition on Revival. http://www.angelfire.com/ca4/cor/ , accessed May 21, 2005.
--- (Ed.). (1990). The Christian World View Documents. Sunnyvale, CA: The Coalition on Revival.
Grubb, Norman. (1997). Continuous Revival. Fort Washington, PA: Christian Literature Crusade.
Guinness, Os. (1976). The Dust of Death. Madison: IVCF.
Gulick, John. (1989). The Humanity of Cities: An Introduction to Urban Societies. Westport, Connecticut: Bergin and Garvey.
Hagen, Everett E. (1971). Personality and Entrepreneurship: How Economic Growth Begins: A Theory of Social Change. In Jason L. Finkle & Richard W. Gable (Eds.), Political Development and Social Change. New York: Wiley & Sons.
Haggard, Ted. (1995). Primary Purpose. Lake Mary, FL: Creation House.
Hagner, Donald. (1998). The New Testament and Criticism: Looking at the Twenty-first Century. Theology, News and Notes, 7-10.
Hall, Douglas. (c1985). Systems Thinking and the Urban Church. In Christianity in Boston (pp. A-1 - A-12). Boston: Emmanuel Gospel Centre.
Hamilton, Victor P. (1990). The Book of Genesis: Chapters 1-17. Grand Rapids: Eerdmans.
Han, P. (1991). Spiritual Awakening: A Theological and Historical Study of Four Waves in the Korean Church. Fuller Theological Seminary, Pasadena, CA.
Harrison, E.F. (1984). Apostle, Apostleship. In Walter Ellwell (Ed.), Evangelical Dictionary of Theology (pp. 70-72). Grand Rapids: Baker Book House.
Hatch, Nathan. (1989). The Democratization of American Christianity. New Haven: Yale University Press.
Hathaway, Brian. (1990). Beyond Renewal: The Kingdom of God. Milton Keynes, England: Word Books.
Heelas, Paul & Woodhead, Linda. (2001). Homeless minds today? In Paul Heelas & Linda Woodhead (Eds.), Peter Berger and the Study of Religion. London and New York: Routledge.
Heenan, John. (c2002). Teaching Character Through Cornerstone Values. PO 348, Alexandra, New Zealand: NZ Foundation for Character Education.
Hengel, Martin. (1974). Property and Riches in the Early Church. Philadelphia: Fortress Press.
Heschel, Abraham. (1965). Who is Man? Stanford: Stanford University Press.
---. (2001). The Prophets. New York: HarperCollins.
Hessian, Roy. (c1960). The Calvary Road. London: Christian Literature Crusade.
Hiebert, Paul. (1982). The Flaw of the Ex-

cluded Middle. Missiology, 10 (1 (Jan 1982)), 35-47.

Hiebert, Paul & Hertig, Young. (1993). Asian Immigrants in American Cities. Urban Mission, 10, 15-24.

Hiebert, Paul & Meneses, Eloise Hiebert. (1995). Incarnational Ministry: Planting Churches in Band, Tribal, Peasant and Urban Societies. Grand Rapids, MI: Baker.

Hitchcock, James. (1996). The Guilty Secret of Liberal Christianity. New Oxford Review (Oct 1996).

Hofmans-Sheard. (2003). Addicted to Consumption. Reality, 56, 22-26.

Holding, Rob (Writer) (2005). Interview with Brian Tamaki: Radio Rhema.

Holland, Dick. (1996). Wakey, Wakey or Don't: Christian Church Trends in New Zealand. Auckland: St Stephen's Church, Ponsonby.

Hollenweger, Walter J. (1997). Pentecostalism: Origins and Developments Worldwide. Peabody, MA: Hendrickson Publishers.

Horrill, Seton. (1995). Forging a Workplace Mission. Orewa: Inter-Church Trade and Industry Mission.

Hughes, Selwyn. (2003). Why Revival Waits. Waverley Abbey House, Waverley Lane, Farnham, Surrey GU9 8EP, UK: CWR.

Hull, J. E. (1967). The Holy Spirit in the Acts of the Apostles. London: Lutterworth Press.

Hunt, Stephen J. (2002). Religion in Western Society. New York: Palgrave.

Huntington, Samuel P. (1993). The Clash of Civilizations. Foreign Affairs, 72 (3), 22-40.

---. (2001). The Many Faces of the Future: Why we'll never have a universal civilization. In Robert M. Jackson (Ed.), Global Issues 00/01. Sluice Dock, Guilford, Connecticut 06437: Dushkin/McGraw Hill.

Hyman, Gavin. (2001). The Predicament of Postmodern Theology. London: Westminster John Knox Press.

Inglehart, Ronald. (1997). Modernization and Postmodernization: Cultural, Economic and Political Change in 43 Societies. New Jersey: Princeton University Press.

Iremonger, F.A. (1948). William Temple, Archbishop of Canterbury: His Life and Letters. Oxford: Oxford Press.

Jackson, Hugh. (1987). Churches and People in Australia and New Zealand, 1860-1930. Wellington: Allen and Unwin/Port Nicholson Press.

Jacobs, Jane. (1984). Cities and the Wealth of Nations. The Atlantic Monthly (Mar/Apr 1984).

Jamieson, Alan. (2000). A Churchless Faith: Faith Outside the Evangelical Pentecostal/Charismatic Church of New Zealand. Wellington: Philip Garside Publishing.

Johnstone, Patrick & Mandryk, Jason. (2001). Operation World. London: OM Publishers.

Jones, E. Stanley. (1972). The Unshakeable Kingdom and the Unchanging Person. New York: Abingdon.

Jones, Martin Lloyd. (1959). Revival: An Historical and Theological Survey. Paper presented at the Puritan and Reformed Studies Conference.

Joyner, Rick. (1993). The World Aflame: The Welsh Revival and its Lessons for Our Time. Charlotte, NC: Morningstar.

Kagawa, Toyohiko. (1934). Christ and Japan (William Axling, Trans.). London: SCM.

Kaiser Jr., Walter C. (1986). Quest for Renewal. Chicago: Moody Press.

Keener, Craig S. (2001). Gift and Giver: The

Holy Spirit for Today. Grand Rapids, MI: Baker.

Kellner, Douglas. (1995). Media Culture: Cultural Studies, Identity and Politics Between Modern and Postmodern. New York and London: Routledge.

Kelsey, Jane. (1999). Reclaiming the Future: New Zealand and the Global Economy. Wellington: Bridget Williams Books.

Kelsey, Morton. (1977). The Christian and the Supernatural. London: Search Press.

---. (1991). God, Dreams and Revelation. Minneapolis: Augsberg Fortress Publications.

---. (1995). Healing and Christianity: A Classic Study. Minneapolis: Augsberg Fortress.

Kidner, Derek. (1967). Genesis. London: Tyndale Press.

---. (1985). The Wisdom of Proverbs, Job & Ecclesiastes. Downers Grove, IL: IVP.

Kim, Kirsteen. (2000). Post-Modern Mission: A Paradigm Shift in David Bosch's Theology of Mission? International Review of Missions, LXXXIX, No 353 (April 2000), 172-179.

Knight, Harold. (1947). The Hebrew Prophetic Consciousness. London: Lutterworth Press.

Knight, Kim & Laugeson, Ruth. (2005, Feb 13, 2005). All in a day's work. Sunday Star Time, p. C3.

Knowles, Brett. (2000). The History of a New Zealand Pentecostal Movement : The New Life Churches of New Zealand from 1946 to 1979. Lewiston, NY: Edwin Mellen Press.

---. (2004). Is the Future of Western Christianity a Pentecostal One? A Conversation with Harvey Cox. In John Stenhouse, Brett Knowles & Antony Wood (Eds.), The Future of Christianity (pp. 39-59). Adelaide: ATF.

Knox, Bruce. (2004). Christian Allegiance is Declining, Yet... In John Stenhouse, Brett Knowles & Antony Wood (Eds.), The Future of Christianity. Adelaide: ATF.

Knox, R.A. (1962). Enthusiasm. Oxford: Clarendon Press.

Koch, Kurt. (1970). The Revival in Indonesia. 7501 Burghausen Blvd, Western Germany: Evangelization Publishers.

---. (1972/1994). Christian Counselling and Occultism (fr German, Trans.). Grand Rapids: Kregel.

Kraft, Charles. (1979). Christianity in Culture: A Study in Dynamic Biblical Theologizing in Cross-Cultural Perspective. Maryknoll: Orbis Books.

Kraybill, Donald B. (1978). The Upside Down Kingdom. Scottsdale, PA: Herald Press.

Kuhn, Thomas. (1962/1970). The Structure of Scientific Revolutions. Chicago: University of Chicago Press.

Kuyper, Abraham. (1998a). A Centennial Reader. Grand Rapids: Eerdmans.

---. (1998b). Creating a Christian Worldview: Abraham Kuyper's Lectures on Calvinism. Grand Rapids: Eerdmans.

Ladd, George Eldon. (1959). The Gospel of the Kingdom. Grand Rapids: Eerdmans.

---. (1974). A Theology of the New Testament. Grand Rapids, MI: Eerdmans.

Latourette, Kenneth Scott. (1953/1975). History of Christianity, 2 vols. New York: Harper and Row.

Lausanne Committee for World Evangelization. (1974). Let the Earth Rejoice! Paper presented at the Lausanne Congress on World Evangelization, Lausanne, Switzerland.

Lewis, Oscar. (1966). "The Culture of Poverty." Scientific American, 215 (4), 3-9.

Libanio, Joao Batista. (2001). As Lógicas da Cidade: O Impacto Sobre a Fé e Sob o Impacto da Fé. São Paulo: Edições Loyola.

Lindsay, Hal. (1970). The Late Great Planet Earth. Grand Rapids: Zondervan.

Lineham, Peter. (2000a). Government Support of the Churches in the Modern Era. In Rex Ahdar & John Stenhouse (Eds.), God and Government: The New Zealand Experience (pp. 41-58). Dunedin: University of Otago Press.

---. (2000b). Three Types of Church. In Ree Bodde & Hugh Dempster (Eds.), Thinking Outside the Square: Church in Middle Earth (pp. 199-224). Auckland: St Columba's Press & Journeyings.

---. (2004). Social Policy and the Churches in the 1990's and Beyond. In John Stenhouse, Brett Knowles & Antony Wood (Eds.), The Future of Christianity. Adelaide: Australian Theological Forum.

Linthicum, Robert. (1991a). City of God, City of Satan: A Biblical Theology of the Urban Church. Grand Rapids, MI: Zondervan.

---. (1991b). Empowering the Poor. Monrovia, California: MARC.

Littell, Franklin H. (1962). From State Church to Pluralism. Doubleday: Anchor Book.

Lovelace, Richard. (1979). Dynamics of the Spiritual Life: An Evangelical Theology of Renewal. Downers Grove, IL: InterVarsity Press.

Lupton, Robert. (1993). Return Flight: Community Development Through Reneighboring Our Cities: FCS Urban Ministries Inc, 750 Glenwood Ave, SE, P.O. Box 17628, Atlanta, GA 30316, USA.

Lynch, Frank. (c1979). Lowland Filipino Values. Manila: Ateneo de Manila.

Lynch, Pat. (2000, May 5, 2000). Accent on values emerging in universities, workplace. NZ Herald, p. A11.

Lyotard, Jean-Francois. (1985). The Postmodern Condition: A Report on Knowledge (Brian Massumi, Trans.). Minneapolis: University of Minnesota Press.

MacIntyre, Alasdair. (1988). Whose Justice? Which Rationality? Notre Dame, IN: University of Notre Dame Press.

Madood, Tariq. (1994). Establishment, Multiculturalism and British Citizenship. Political Quarterly, 65, 53-73.

Maggay, Melba Padilla. (1994). Transforming Society. Oxford: Regnum.

Maloney, H. Newton & Lovekin, A. Adams. (1985). Glossolalia: Behavioural Science Perspectives on Speaking in Tongues. New York: Oxford University Press.

Mangalwadi, Vishal. (1986). Truth and Social Reform. New Delhi: TRACI.

---. (1998). India: The Grand Experiment. Farnham, Surrey, England: Pippa Ran Books.

---. (1999). The Legacy of William Carey. Wheaton, IL: Crossway Books.

Marquardt, Manfred. (1992). John Wesley's Social Ethics: Praxis and Principles (John E Steely & Stephen Gunter, Trans.). Nashville: Abingdon Press.

Marsden, George. (1997). The Outrageous Idea of Christian Scholarship. Oxford: Oxford University Press.

Martin, David. (1990). Tongues of Fire: The Explosion of Protestantism in Latin America. Cambridge, MA: Basil Blackwell.

---. (1995). Wesley's World Revolution. National Review (December 31, 1995), 26-30.

---. (2002). Pentecostalism: The World Their

Parish. Oxford: Blackwell.

Martin, Margaret Reid (Ed.). (1983). Finding the Way: New Zealand Christians Look Forward: Joint Board of Christian Education.

Masters Institute. (2004). History and Beliefs of Masters Institute. Retrieved 30 Dec, 2004, from http://www.masters.ac.nz/welcome/history.html.

McClelland, David C. (1962). Business Drive and National Achievement. Harvard Business Review, XL (No. 4), 165-178.

McConnell, C. Douglas (Ed.). (1997). The Holy Spirit and Mission Dynamics (Vol. 5). Pasadena: William Carey Library.

McGavran, Donald. (1970). Understanding Church Growth. Grand Rapids: Eerdmans.

McInnes, John. (1980). The New Pilgrims: Living as Christians in the Technological Society. Sydney: Albatross and Lion UK ; Ronald N. Haynes USA 1981.

McLoughlin, William G. (1978). Revivals, Awakenings and Reform: An Essay on Religious and Social Change in America, 1607-1977. Chicago and London: University of Chicago Press.

Meadows, Donella H., Meadows, Dennis L., Randers, Jorgen & Behrens, William W. (1972/1977). The Limits to Growth (2nd ed.): New American Library.

Mellis, Charles. (1976). Committed Communities. Pasadena: William Carey Library Pub.

Milbank, John, Catherine Pickstock, and Graham Ward (Ed.). (1999). Radical Orthodoxy: A New Theology. London: Routledge.

Miller, Gordon. (2003). A Beginner's Guide to the NZ Church. Retrieved June 3, 2005.

Moltmann, Jürgen. (1991). The Spirit of Life: A Universal Affirmation (Margaret Kohl, Trans.). London: SCM Press Ltd.

---. (1993). God in Creation: A New Theology of Creation and the Spirit of God. Philadelphia: Fortress.

---. (1997). The Holy Spirit and the Source of Life (Margaret Kohl, Trans.). London: SCM.

---. (1998). The Source of Life: The Holy Spirit and the Theology of Life. Minneapolis: Fortress Press.

Montgomery, Robert. (1999). Introduction to the Sociology of Missions. Westport, Connecticut; London: Praeger.

Morris, Brian. (1987). Anthropological Studies of Religion. Cambridge: Cambridge University Press.

Mouw, R. J. (1973). Political Evangelism. Grand Rapids: Eerdmans.

---. (1976). Politics and the Biblical Drama. Grand Rapids: Eerdmans.

Mouw, R. J. & Griffioen, Sandra. (1993). Pluralisms and Horizons. Grand Rapids: Eerdmans.

Moyise, Steve. (1995). The Old Testament in the Book of Revelation. Sheffield: Sheffield Academic Press.

Mumford, Lewis. (1969). The City in History, Its Origins, Its Transformations, and Its Prospects. New York: Harcourt, Brace & World.

Murphy, Ed. (1996). The Handbook of Spiritual Warfare. Nashville: Thomas Nelson.

Murphy, Nancey. (1997). Anglo-American Postmodernity. Boulder, CO: Westview Press.

Need, Ariana & Evans, Geoffrey. (2004).

Religious Mobility in Post-Communist Eastern Europe. In Alistair Crockett & Richard O'Leary (Eds.), Patterns and Processes of Religious Change in Modern Industrial Societies (Vol. 68, pp. 191-206). Lewiston; Queenston; Lampeter: The Edwin Mellen Press.

Neighbour, Ralph Jr. (1988). The Shepherd's Guidebook. P.O. Box 19888, Houston, Texas 77224: Touch Outreach Ministries Inc.

---. (1995). Where Do We Go From Here? A Guidebook to the Cell Church. Singapore: Touch Publications, Touch Resources #06-00, 66/68 East Coast Road, Singapore 1542.

Neuhaus, R.J. (1984). The Naked Public Square: Religion and Democracy in America. Grand Rapids: Eerdmans.

New Covenant International Bible College. (2001). Kaupapa i te Whanau: Our Children - Tomorrow's Families. Paper presented at the Kaupapa i te Whanau: Our Children - Tomorrow's Families, Auckland.

New Zealand Association of Christian Schools. (2005a). A Brief Summary of the History of Christian Schooling in New Zealand. Retrieved 15 May, 2005, from http://www.christianschools.org.nz/history.htm.

---. (2005b). Maxim Institute. Retrieved May 23, 2005, from http://www.christianschools.org.nz/maxim.htm.

Newbigin, Lesslie. (1981). Politics and the Covenant. Theology, LXXXIV (Sept 1981 no 701).

---. (1986). Foolishness to the Greeks: The Gospel and Western Culture. Grand Rapids: Eerdmans.

---. (1989). The Gospel in a Pluralist Society. Grand Rapids: Eerdmans.

Nichol, Christopher & Vietch, James. (1981). Christians in Public Planning. Wellington: Tertiary Christian Studies Program.

Niebuhr, H. Richard. (1937/1988). The Kingdom of God in America: Wesleyan University Press.

---. (1951/1956). Christ and Culture. New York: Harper & Row.

---. (1963). The Responsible Self. New York, NY: Harper and Row.

Niebuhr, Reinhold. (1932). Moral Man and Immoral Society: A Study in Ethics and Politics. New York: Charles Scribner's Sons.

Nietzsche, Friedrich. (1967). The Will to Power (Walter Kaufman & R.J. Hollingdale, Trans.). New York: Random House.

Noebel, David A. (1991). Understanding the Times. Manitou Springs, CO: Summit Press.

Norris, Pippa & Inglehart, Ronald. (2004). Sacred and Secular: Religion and Politics Worldwide. Cambridge: Cambridge University Press.

North, Gary. (1986). Honest Money: Biblical Principles of Money and Banking. Fort Worth, Texas: Dominion Press.

Noth, Martin. (1957/1981). The Deuteronomic History (from German, Trans.). Sheffield: Journal for the Study of the Old Testament Press.

O'Dea, Thomas. (1961). Five Dilemmas in the Institutionalization of Religion. Journal for the Scientific Study of Religion (1), 30-41.

Odell-Scott, David W. (2000). Deconstruction. In A.K.M. Adam (Ed.), Handbook of Postmodern Biblical Interpretation. St Louis, MO: Chalice Press.

Oden, Thomas. (1995). So What Happens after Modernity? A Postmodern

Agenda for Evangelical Theology. In David S. Dockery (Ed.), The Challenge of Postmodernism (pp. 392-406). Grand rapids, MI: Baker Books.

Orme, John H. (2004). Identificational Repentance and Strategic Spiritual Warfare: A Hermeneutical Case Study. In C Douglas McConnell (Ed.), The Holy Spirit and Mission Dynamics. Pasadena: William Carey Library.

Orr, J. Edwin. (1936). All Your Need: 10,000 Miles of Miracle Through Australia and New Zealand. London: Marshall, Morgan and Scott.

---. (1955). The Second Evangelical Awakening. London: Marshall, Morgan and Scott.

---. (1972). Campus Aflame: A History of Evangelical Awakenings in Collegiate Communities. Ventura: Regal.

---. (1973). The Flaming Tongue. Chicago: Moody Press.

---. (1975a). Evangelical Awakenings in Southern Asia. Minneapolis: Bethany Fellowship.

---. (1975b). Evangelical Awakenings in Africa. Minneapolis: Bethany Fellowship.

---. (1975c). Evangelical Awakenings in Eastern Asia. Minneapolis: Bethany Fellowship.

Orr, Ken. (1999, December 1999). Views on abortion more polarised. Humanity, 23, 9.

Ortiz, Manuel. (1993). Insights into the Second Generation Hispanic. Urban Mission, 10 (No. 4, June 1993).

Osborne, Grant R. (1991). The Hermeneutical Spiral: A Comprehensive Introduction to Biblical Interpretation. Downers Grove, IL: IVP Press.

Otis Jr., George. (1999). Transformations [Video]. Seattle: Sentinel Group.

Ottati, Douglas F. (1991). Foreword. In Walter Rauschenbusch (Ed.), Christianity and the Social Crisis (pp. xi-xxxviii). Louisville, KY: Westminster/John Knox Press.

Overholt, Thomas W. (1996). Cultural Anthropology and the Old Testament. Minneapolis: Fortress.

Packer, J.I. (1976). Fundamentalism and the Word of God. Downers Grove, IL: IVP.

Palen, J. John. (1996). The Urban World (5th ed.). Guilford, CT: McGraw Hill.

Pannenberg, Wolfhart. (1995). Anthropology in Theological Perspective. Philadelphia: Westminster.

Paterson, Sandra. (2005, May 14,2005). Feminist agenda reaches fruition. Weekend Herald, p. 23.

Patrick, Bruce (Ed.). (1993). The Vision New Zealand Congress. 427 Queen St, Auckland: VisionNZ.

--- (1993). New Vision New Zealand. Auckland: VisionNZ.

--- (1997a). New Vision New Zealand II. Auckland: VisionNZ.

--- (1997b). The Vision New Zealand Congress 1997. Auckland: VisionNZ.

Peacocke, Dennis. (1989). Winning the Battle for the Minds of Men. Santa Rosa, CA: Alive and Free.

Pentecost, Edward C. (c1979). Reaching the Unreached. Unpublished PhD in Missiology, Fuller Theological Seminary, Pasadena.

Perdue, Leo G. (1994). The Collapse of History: Restructuring Old Testament Theology. Minneapolis: Fortress Press.

Petersen, Douglas. (1996). Not by Might Nor by Power: A Pentecostal Theology of Social Concern in Latin America. Oxford: Regnum Books.

Pierson, Paul. (1985). Historical Development of the Christian Movement Course Notes. Pasadena: Fuller Theological Seminary, School of World Missions.

---. (1998). History of Theology of Evangelical Awakenings Course Notes. Pasadena: Fuller Theological Seminary, School of World Missions.

Poloma, Margaret M. (1997). The "Toronto Blessing": Charisma, Institutionalization, and Revival. Journal for the Scientific Study of Religion, 36 (2), 257-271.

Postman, Neil. (1993). Technopoly: The Surrender to Popular Culture. New York: Vintage Books.

Preston, Ronald. (1981). William Temple as Social Theologian. Theology, LXXXIV (701), 334-341.

Quebedeaux, Richard. (1978). The Worldly Evangelicals. New York: Harper & Row.

Quine, W.V.O. & Ullian, J.S. (1978). The Web of Belief (2nd ed.). New York: Random House.

Ramos, Arivaldo. (1995). Veja Sua Cidade Com Outos Olhos: Ação da Igreja na Cidade. São Paulo: Editora Sepal.

Randerson, Richard. (1987). Christian Ethics and the New Zealand Economy. Wellington: Department of Christian Education, Diocese of Wellington.

---. (1992). Hearts and Minds: A Place for People in a Market Economy. Wellington: Social Responsibility Commission of the Anglican Church.

Rauschenbusch, Walter. (1907/1968). The Righteousness of the Kingdom. Nashville: Abingdon.

---. (1907/1991). Christianity and the Social Crisis. Louisville, KY: Westminster/John Knox Press.

---. (1916). The Social Principles of Jesus. London: YMCA Association Press.

---. (1917). A Theology for The Social Gospel. New York: MacMillan.

Ravenhill, Leonard. (1979). Why Revival Tarries. Minneapolis: Bethany House.

---. (1986). Revival Gods Way. Minneapolis: Bethany House.

Reid, Gavin. (1972). The Elaborate Funeral - man, doom and God. London: Hodder & Stoughton.

Richardson, Amie. (2004, 18 July 2004). Fashionable flock worships in style. Sunday Star Times.

Richardson, Michael Donald. (1998). Lessons from the Revival in Argentina. Unpublished D. Min., Fuller Theological Seminary, Pasadena.

Riddell, Michael. (1998). Threshold of the Future: Reforming the Church in the Post-Christian West. London: SPCK.

Robeck, Jr., C. M. (1988). Gift of Prophecy. In Stanley M. Burgess & Gary B McGee (Eds.), Dictionary of Pentecostal and Charismatic Movements (pp. 728-740). Grand Rapids, MI: Zondervan.

Roman Catholic and Anglican Bishops of New Zealand (Ed.). (1990). Te Ara Tika - The Way Ahead. Wellington: Anglican and Catholic Communications.

Rookmaker, H.R. (1970/1999). Modern Art and the Death of a Culture. Wheaton, IL: Crossway Books.

Roper, Brian. (2005). Prosperity for all? : economic, social and political change in New Zealand since 1935. Southbank, Vic.: Thomson Learning.

Rorty, Richard. (1989). Contingency,

Irony and Solidarity. Cambridge: Cambridge University Press.

Ryan, A. (1986). 'For God, Country and Family': Populist Moralism and the New Zealand Moral Right. New Zealand Sociology, 1 (2), 104-112.

Samuel, Vinay & Sugden, Chris (Eds.). (1999). Mission as Transformation: A Theology of the Whole Gospel. Oxford: Regnum Books.

Santos, Milton. (1979). The Shared Space (from Portuguese edition (1975) by Chris Gerry, Trans.). London and New York: Methuen.

Sargisson, Lucy & Sargent, Lyman Tower. (2004). Living in Utopia: New Zealand's Intentional Communities. Aldershot, England: Ashgate Publishing.

Schaeffer, Francis. (1968a). Escape from Reason. Downers Grove, IL: IVP.

---. (1968b). The God Who is There. Downers Grove, IL: InterVarsity Press.

---. (1981). A Christian Manifesto. Westchester, IL: Crossway Books.

Schaller, Lyle. (1995). The New Reformation. Nashville: Abingdon Press.

Schumacher, E.F. (1973/1980). Small is Beautiful. London: Abacus.

---. (1979). Good Work. New York: Harper and Row.

Scott, Waldron. (1980). Bring Forth Justice: A Contemporary Perspective on Mission. Grand Rapids: Eerdmans.

Sepulveda, Juan. (1989). Pentecostalism and Popular Religiosity. International Review of Missions, 78, Jan 1989 (80-88).

Shaw, Trevor (Ed.). (1972). The Jesus Marches 1972. Auckland: Challenge Weekly.

Shenk, Wilbert R. (1995). Write the Vision. Harrisburg, PA: Trinity Press International.

Sherwood, Yvonne. (2000). Derrida. In A.K.M. Adam (Ed.), Handbook of Postmodern Biblical Interpretation (pp. 69-76). St Louis, Missouri: Chalice Press.

Shipp, Glover. (1992). On the Urban Scene, We Must Know the Territory. Journal of Applied Missiology, 03 (1).

Shwartz, Christian A. (1996). Natural Church Development. D-25924 Emmelsbull, Germany: C & P Publishing.

Signpost Communications. (1992). Probing Further. Wellington: Signpost Communications.

Silvoso, Ed. (1994). That None Should Perish. Ventura: Regal Books.

Smidt, Corwin E., Kellstedt, Lyman A., Green, John C. & Guth, James L. (1999). The Spirit-Filled Moves in Contemporary America: A Survey Perspective. In Edith L. Blumhofer, Russell P. Spittler & Grant A. Wacker (Eds.), Pentecostal Currents in American Protestantism (pp. 111-130): University of Illinois.

Smith, David W. (1998). Transforming the World. Exeter, UK: Paternoster.

Smithies, Ruth & Wilson, Helen (Eds.). (1993). Making Choices - Social Justice for Our Times. Wellington: Epworth Bookroom.

Snyder, Howard. (1989/1997). Signs of the Spirit. Eugene, OR: Wipf and Stock Publishers.

---. (1991). Models of The Kingdom. Nashville: Abingdon Press.

---. (1996a). Liberating the Church. Eugene, OR: Wipf and Stock Publishers.

---. (1996b). Radical Renewal: The Problem of Wineskins Today. Singapore:

Touch Publications.

---. (1996c). The Radical Wesley and Patterns for Church Renewal. Eugene, OR: Wipf and Stock Publishers.

---. (1997). A Kingdom Manifesto. Eugene, OR: Wipf and Stock Publishers (1985 edn. by IVP).

---. (1999). Models of the Kingdom: Sorting out the Practical Meaning of God's Reign. In Vinay Samuel & Chris Sugden (Eds.), Mission as Transformation (pp. 118-133). Oxford: Regnum.

Sobrino, Jon. (1984). The True Church and the Poor. Maryknoll: Orbis.

Soja, Edward. (1989/1997). Postmodern Geographies: The Reassertion of Space in Critical Social Theory. London: Verso Books.

Stark, Rodney & Bainbridge, William Sims. (1985). The Future of Religion. Berkeley: University of California.

Stark, Rodney & Finke, Roger. (2000). Acts of Faith: Explaining the Human Side of Religion. Berkeley, Los Angeles and London: University of California Press.

Stark, Rodney & Glock, Charles Y. (1968). American Piety: the Nature of Religious Commitment. Berkeley: University of California Press.

Statistics New Zealand. (2002). New Zealand Official Yearbook 2002. Wellington: David Bateman.

---. (2005). Table 16: Religious Affiliation (Total Responses)(1)(2)(3) and Sex "for the Census Usually Resident Population Count, 1991, 1996 and 2001". Retrieved 19 October, 2005, from http://www.stats.govt.nz/census/cultural-diversity-tables.htm.

Steel, Natalie. (2003). Milton Smith: A Man After God's Heart. Auckland: Castle Publishing.

Stenger, Mary Ann & Stone, Ronald H. (2002). Dialogues of Paul Tillich. Macon, GA: Mercer University Press.

Stenhouse, John & Knowles, Brett (Eds.). (2004). The Future of Christianity : Historical, Sociological, Political and Theological Perspectives from New Zealand. Adelaide [S.Aust.]: ATF Press.

Stibbe, Mark W.G. (1994). A British Appraisal. Journal of Pentecostal Theology (4), 5-16.

Stronstad, Roger. (1984). The Charismatic Theology of St. Luke. Peabody, MA: Hendrickson Publishers.

Swanson, Eric. (2003). Ten Paradigm Shifts Towards Transformation. Retrieved Oct 6, 2003, from http://www.urban-ministries.org/Articles/paradigm.htm.

Tanner, John David. (c1995). Insights into the Nature, Course and Demise of Spiritual Awakenings. Unpublished paper, School of World Missions, Fuller Theological Seminary, Pasadena.

Taylor, Mark. (1984). Erring: A Postmodern A/Theology. Chicago: University of Chicago Press.

Taylor, Steve. (2004). A New Way of Being Church. University of Otago, Dunedin.

---. (2005a). Emergentys/Out of Bounds Church : Learning to Create a Community of Faith in a Culture of Change (EMERGENTYS). Grand Rapids, MI: Zondervan.

---. (2005b, July 28, 2005). postgraduate emerging church research. Retrieved 25 October, 2005, from http://www.emergentkiwi.org.nz/archives/postgraduate_emerging_church_research.php.

Temple, William. (1942). Christianity and the Social Order. New York: Penguin.

Thomas, George M. (1989). Revivalism and Cultural Change: Christianity, Nation Building and the Market in Nineteenth Century United States. Chicago: Chicago University Press.

Thurow, Lester. (1996). The Future of Capitalism: How Today's Forces will Shape Tomorrow's World. 9 Atchison St., St Leonards, NSW 2065, Australia: Allen and Unwin.

Thwaites, James. (1997). The Cry of the Apostolic. In Renegotiating the Church Contract: The Death and Life of the 21st Century Church. London: Paternoster Publishing.

---. (1999). The Church Beyond the Congregation. Carlisle, Cumbria, UK: Paternoster Press.

Tillapagh, Frank. (1985). Unleashing the Church: Getting People Out of the Fortress and into the Ministry. Ventura, CA: Regal Books.

The Times. (1922, May 31). Faith Healing: Extraordinary Scenes at Town Hall: the Deaf Made to Hear. The Times.

Tippett, Alan. (1971). People Movements in Southern Polynesia. Chicago: Moody Bible Institute.

---. (1973). Missiology, a New Discipline. In Alvin Martin (Ed.), The Means of World Evangelization. Pasadena: William Carey Library.

---. (1987). Introduction to Missiology. Pasadena: William Carey Library.

Tonna, Benjamin. (1982). A Gospel for the Cities A Socio-Theology of Urban Ministry. Maryknoll: Orbis.

Tonsor, Stephen. (1998). What to Do While Awaiting the Apocalypse: The Role of Creative Minorities in a Time of Cultural Crisis. Grand Rapids: Eerdmans.

Tournier, Paul. (1957). The Meaning of Persons. London: SCM.

Toynbee, Arnold. (1972). A Study of History (First Abridged One volume Edition ed.). Oxford: Oxford University Press.

Troeltsch, Ernst. (1911/1960). The Social Teaching of the Christian Churches (Olive Wyon, Trans.). New York: Harper and Row.

Turner, Harold. (1993). The Gospel's Mission to Culture. Latimer, 112, 23-35.

---. (1996, December 1966). Religion in the N.Z. Herald. New Slant, 1-7.

---. (2001). The Laughter of Providence. Auckland: Deepsight Trust.

Van Engen, Charles. (1996). Mission on the Way: Issues in Mission Theology. Grand Rapids, MI: Baker Book House.

---. (1998). The Gospel Story: Mission of, in, and on the Way. Fuller Theological Seminary

Theology, News and Notes, June1988.

Van Gelder, Craig. (1996). The Great New Fact of Our Day: America As a Mission Field. In George R. Hunsberger & Craig Van Gelder (Eds.), Church Between Gospel and Culture (Vol. 57-68, pp. 57-68). Grand Rapids: Eerdmans.

Van Seters, John. (1983). In Search of History: Historiography in the Ancient World and the Origins of Biblical History. New Haven: Yale University Press.

---. (1999). The Pentateuch: A Social Science Commentary. Sheffield: Sheffield Academic Press.

Vanhoozer, Kevin J. (1995). Mapping Evangelical Theology in a Postmodern World. Trinity Journal, 16.

Vause, Doug. (1997). Powers in the City. Carey Baptist College, ACTE, University of Auckland, Auckland.

Villafañe, Eldin. (1993a). Evangelizing Immigrants in Transition. Urban Mission, 10 (No. 4, June 1993).

---. (1993b). The Liberating Spirit: Toward an Hispanic American Pentecostal Social Ethic. Grand Rapids: Eerdmans.

Vine, W.E., Unger, Merrill F. & Jr., William White (Eds.). (1996). Complete Expository Dictionary of Old and New Testament Words. Nashville, TN: Thomas Nelson.

Volf, Miroslav. (1991). Work in the Spirit: Toward a Theology of Work. London: Oxford Press.

Voll, John O. (1968). Islam: Continuity and Change in the Modern World. Boulder, Colorado: Westview Press; Harlow: Longman.

Von Rad, Gerhard. (1962). Old Testament Theology 1: The Theology of Israel's Historical Traditions (Vol. 1).

Wagner, C. Peter. (1993). Breaking Strongholds in Your City. Ventura: Regal.

---. (1998). The New Apostolic Churches. Ventura: Gospel Light.

---. (1999). Churchquake: How the New Apostolic Reformation is Shaking Up the Church as We Know It. Ventura: Gospel Light.

Wakefield, Gordon. (1976). Fire of Love: The Spirituality of Wesley. London: Darton, Longman and Todd.

Wallace, A.F.C. (1956). Revitalization Movements: Some Theoretical Considerations for Their Comparative Study. American Anthropologist (58), 264-281.

---. (2003). Revitalization Movements. In Robert S Grumet (Ed.), Revitalizations and Mazeways (pp. 9-29). Lincoln and London: University of Nebraska Press.

Wallis, Arthur. (1956). In the Day of Thy Power. London: Christian Literature Crusade.

---. (2005). In the Day of They Power. Retrieved May 23, 2005, from http://www.revival-library.org/index.html?http://www.revival-library.org/catalogues/cat_home.htm.

Walsh & Middleton. (1984). The Transforming Vision: Shaping a Christian Worldview. Downers Grove: Intervarsity Press.

Ward, Glen. (1997). Teach Yourself Postmodernism. London: Hodder & Stoughton.

Ward, Kevin. (2000). Religion in a Post-aquarian Age. Retrieved 4 May 2005, 2005, from http://www.missionstudies.org/anzams/2000/post-aquarian.htm.

---. (2001). Christendom, Clericalism, Church and Context: Finding Categories of Connexion in a Culture Without a Christian Memory. Dunedin: Presbyterian School of Ministry.

---. (2002). Rugby and the Church: Worlds in Conflict. Reality.

---. (2004). Is New Zealand's Future Churchless? Retrieved May 5, 2005, from http://www.schoolofministry.ac.nz/kevinward/.

---. (2004a). Changing Patterns of Church in Christchurch from 1960 to 1990, from http://www.schoolofministry.ac.nz/kevinward/.

Weakley, Clare George, Jr. (Ed.). (1987). The Nature of Revival. Minneapolis: Bethany.

Weber, Max. (1921/1958). The City. New York, NY: The Free Press.

---. (1947a). The Pure Types of Legitimate Authority (A. R. Henderson and Talcott Parsons, Trans.). In Theory of Social and Economic Organization. London: MacMillan Company.
---. (1947b). The Theory of Social and Economic Organization (A.M. Henderson & Talcott Parsons, Trans.). New York: Free Press.
---. (1963a). The Prophet (Ephraim Fischoff, Trans.). In The Sociology of Religion. London: Beacon Press.
---. (1963b). The Sociology of Religion (Ephraim Fischoff, Trans.). London: Beacon Press.
---. (1968). Introduction. In S. N. Eisenstadt (Ed.), On Charisma and Institution Building. Chicago: University of Chicago Press.
---. (1980). The Protestant Work Ethic and the Spirit of Capitalism (Talcott Parsons, Trans.). London: Unwin.
Webster, Alan. (2001). Spiral of Values: the Flow from Survival Values to Global Consciousness. P.O. Box 566, Hawera, New Zealand: Alpha Publications.
Webster, Alan & Perry, Paul. (1989). The Religious Factor in New Zealand Society: A Report of the New Zealand Study of Values. P.O. Box 9046, Terrace End, Palmerston North: Alpha Publications.
---. (1992). What Difference Does it Make? Values and Faith in a Shifting Culture. Palmerston North: Alpha.
Wellhausen, Julius. (1885). Prolegomena to the History of Ancient Israel (J.S. Black & A. Menzies, Trans.). Edinburgh: A. & C. Black.
Wells, David F. (1995). God in the Wasteland: The Reality of Truth in a World of Fading Dreams. Grand Rapids, MI: Eerdmans.
Westermann, Claus. (1974). Creation (S.J. John Scullion, Trans.). London: SPCK.
---. (1980). The Promises of the Fathers. Philadelphia: Fortress Press.
White, Lynne. (1967). The Historical Roots of Our Ecological Crisis. Science (155), 1203-1207.
Whitehead, John. (1994). Christians Involved in the Political Process. Chicago: Moody Press.
Wilberforce, William. (1797). A Practical View of the Prevailing Religious System of Professed Christians in the Higher and Middle Classes in this Country Contrasted with Real Christianity. London: Available at Porteous Library, London University Library.
Willems, Emilio. (1967). Followers of the New Faith: Culture Change and the Rise of Protestantism in Brazil and Chile. Nashville: Vanderbilt University Press.
Wilson, Bryan. (1976). Contemporary Transformations of Religion. Oxford: Clarendon Press.
---. (2004). Preface. In Alasdair Crockett & Richard O'Leary (Eds.), Patterns and Processes of Religious Change in Modern Industrial Societies. Lewiston, New York and Lampeter, Ceredigon, Wales: Edwin Mellen Press.
Wimber, John. (1985). Power Evangelism. San Francisco: Harper and Row.
Windsor, Paul. (1994). KiwiKulture: Towards a Definition. In John Crawshaw & Wayne Kirkland (Eds.), New Zealand Made. Wellington: Signposts Communications Trust.
Winter, Ralph D. & Koch, Bruce. (1999). Finishing the Task: The Unreached

Peoples Challenge. In Ralph D. Winter & Steven C. Hawthorne (Eds.), Perspectives on the World Christian Movement (Third ed., pp. 509-524). Pasadena: William Carey Library.

Winters, Ralph. (1974). The Two Structures of God's Redemptive Mission. Missiology, II, No. 1, Jan. 1974.

Wirth, Louis. (1996). Urbanism As a Way of Life. In George Gmelch & Walter P. Zenner (Eds.), Urban Life: Readings in Urban Anthropology (3rd ed., pp. pp13-34). Prospect Heights, IL: Waveland Press.

Wishart, Ian. (2003, November 2003). The Siege of Helengrad: Angel of Light or Muldoonista. Investigate, 32-41.

Witherington, Ben, III,. (1998). The Acts of the Apostles: A Socio-Rhetorical Commentary. Grand Rapids: Eerdmans and Paternoster Press: Carlisle.

Withy, Alan. (1993). Who's Growing, Who's Not. In New Vision New Zealand (pp. 120-145). Auckland: Vision New Zealand.

Wogaman, J. P. (1988). A Christian Perspective on Politics. Philadelphia: Fortress Press and London: SCM Press.

World Evangelical Fellowship. (1983). Transformation: The Church in Response to Human Need. Paper presented at the Church in Response to Human Need, Wheaton.

Worsfold, J.E. (1974). A History of the Charismatic Movement in New Zealand. Yorkshire: Julian Literature Trust.

Yoder, John Howard. (1996). How H. Richard Niebuhr Reasoned: A Critique of Christ and Culture. In Glen H. Stassen, D.M. Yeager & John Howard Yoder (Eds.), Authentic Transformation: A New Vision of Christ and Culture. Nashville: Abingdon Press.

- INDEX -

A

abortion, 168, 209–10, 219, 235
action, 9, 13–14, 20–21, 23–24, 29–30, 32, 35, 57, 59, 107, 140, 148–49, 163, 191–92, 194–96, 210–11; action-reflection, 14, 24, 29, 163, 195, 224; ethics from action, 192; God of, 20–21, 23; group, 9, 14; missional, 29, 194; public, 57; social, 35, 102, 107, 116, 137; stories, 24, 29–30; of the Holy Spirit, 148–49; transforming, 32, 59
Acts, 8, 25, 102, 105, 130, 134, 142, 148–51, 153–55, 157–58, 196, 230, 242
Adsett, John, 226
Ahdar, Rex, 11, 40, 70, 90, 117, 166, 171, 173, 206, 221, 225, 232
Allen, Les, 29
Allis, David, 53, 125, 221
Alton, David, 221
anger, 14, 164–65, 169–70, 177, 184, 209
Anglican, 12, 17, 38, 40, 42, 46–47, 53, 74, 96, 117, 123–26, 130–31, 133, 136, 138, 236
apostles, 31, 107, 109, 150, 154, 187, 191, 194, 196–97, 200, 214, 227, 229–30, 242; city leadership teams of, 146, 195
apostolic, 10, 53, 56, 126, 141, 172, 183, 189, 194–200, 202, 210, 214–15, 219, 239
Apostolic church, 47, 146
apostolic structures, 125, 194, 197, 199–200
Assembly of God, 42, 53, 127, 142, 167
attendance, 9, 18, 33, 42, 44–48, 50–53, 125, 128, 174, 209
Auckland, 9–11, 14–15, 39, 41–44, 46–55, 57–58, 60, 69–72, 74–76, 78–80, 125, 135–36, 178–79, 200–201, 204–6, 228–29; churches, 41, 44, 51, 198; population, 45–46

B

Babylon, 61, 67, 116, 190
Bakke, Ray, 64, 179, 221
Baptist, 35, 41–42, 46–47, 51–53, 91, 126–28, 130–31, 136, 165, 182, 197, 222–23, 225, 240
Barber, Benjamin, 91, 94, 221
Barrett, David, 12, 42, 156, 222

Barth, Karl, 17, 39, 223
Bartlett, Patricia, 167
Bateman, David, 238
Bedingfield, Daniel, 96; Natasha, 209
Bellah, Robert, 58, 222
Bellingham, Rob, ii, 102, 222
Bennett, Dennis, 125
Bennett, John, 34, 109, 192, 222
Bennett, William, 192
Berger, Peter, 27, 49, 95, 151, 222–23, 225, 229
Bible College: Faith, 130; New Covenant, 74, 130–31; of New Zealand, 10, 130–31, 206
Blackwell, Basil, 224, 232–33
Bolitho, Elaine, 126, 222
Bosch, David, 13, 34, 38, 60, 197, 222, 231
Boston, Jonathon, 206
Brookes, Norman, 47, 51, 96, 222–23
Bruce, Steve, 49, 56, 138, 173, 223, 231, 235, 241
Brueggeman, Walter, 65, 189, 223
Bryant, George, 39, 124, 223
Burgess, Stanley, 32, 158, 223, 236
business, 15, 70, 74, 78, 108–9, 136, 138–39, 151, 168, 170, 174, 182, 199–200, 203–6, 210–16, 233; leaders, 15, 108, 214–15
Business Roundtable, 205

C

Campolo, Tony, 138
capitalism, 35–36, 84, 89, 112, 173, 205, 218, 228, 239, 241
Carey, William, 232
Catholic, 14, 23, 32, 37, 39–42, 44–46, 48, 50–52, 55, 57, 74, 124–25, 167–68, 198–99, 204–6, 236; Church, 50–51
Caughley, Brian, 17, 134, 165
CCC (Central City Church), 53, 91
cell groups, 128, 135–37
census figures, 48
chaos theory, 23–24, 88, 109–10
charismatic renewal, 7, 9, 41–42, 52–53, 123–24, 132–33, 140, 210, 222
Christ, 10, 12–14, 16–18, 28–30, 36–38, 46–48, 60–62, 92–94, 102–4, 106–8, 134–38, 156, 200–204, 214–16, 242; atoning work of, 11–12; cosmic, 28, 101
Christianity, expansion of, 147, 153, 155
Christians, committed, 55, 174, 206
Christiansen, Derek, 131
Christian values, 170, 207, 212, 218
church: attendance, 18, 42, 44–48, 50, 52–53; ethnic, 44, 47–48, 51, 55; leaders, 14, 47, 53, 74, 91, 169, 186; mainline, 42, 51–52, 126–27, 132–33, 135, 140, 142; structures, 56, 107, 125, 132, 137, 197
church growth, 13, 56, 126, 139–40, 145–47, 175, 196, 198, 219
church history, 13, 18, 31, 131, 145, 225
Church Life Survey, 46–47, 50–51, 96, 208, 223
city, 8–9, 15–16, 21–25, 29–30, 59–61, 63–76, 78–80, 100–101, 117–19, 176–79, 189–91, 197–201, 203, 217–19, 224–30, 239–40; cubic, 64; culture, 217, 219; good, 59–61, 63–65, 67–68, 80, 89, 109; soul, 69–70; structures, 75, 182, 201; transformation, v, 59, 195
city conversation, 57–58, 69
city leadership, ii, 8, 21–22, 29, 69–70, 146, 179, 186–87, 191, 196, 204; levels, 15, 187; teams, 179, 183
city of God, iii, 11, 15, 25, 58–61, 63, 65, 67, 69–71, 73–74, 80–81, 100–101, 132, 183, 226, 232
citywide, ii–iii, 9–10, 14, 121, 135, 146, 175, 178–79, 183–84, 197, 219
Citywide Transforming Revival, 10, 175, 219
Clancie, Lucy, 212
Clark, Helen, 166, 169, 206
class, 37, 74, 153, 157, 183
CLCA (Christian Life Centre Auckland),

53, 91
Coalition of Concerned Citizens, 171, 173
Colson, Charles, 35, 224
commandments, 165–68, 170, 189, 212
common good, 15, 112, 116
Cone, James, 164, 224
confessional groups, 8, 125, 128, 135, 143, 161
congregations, iv, 42–43, 46–47, 50–51, 54, 136, 139, 144, 148, 184, 196, 221, 239
Conn, Harvey, 13, 19, 37, 67, 90, 222, 224
connectedness, 55, 76
conversation: complexity, 81; conversationalists, 41, 43, 45, 49; conversation space, 73–74, 78–79, 87, 89, 91, 93–95, 109; sources, 213, 221; space, 82, 88, 90–91, 93–94; urban, 10, 23–25, 29
Council: Auckland Regional, 78; Christian Council of Aoteoroa - New Zealand, 202; City, 70; National, 39, 171; World, 33–35, 39, 98, 103, 145, 167, 203, 225
Cox, Harvey, 38, 40, 51–52, 224, 231
creation, 17, 35, 62–66, 100–101, 105, 108–12, 114, 189, 196, 201, 212, 233, 241
creative minorities, 56, 185, 187, 193–94, 219, 239
creativity, 20, 62–63, 67–68, 70, 88, 110–11, 114–15, 170, 212, 219
Cullman, Oscar, 102–3, 224
Curnow, Steve, 51, 223

D

Darragh, Neil, 50, 65, 75, 109, 111, 224
David, Allis, 221
Davidson, Allan, 39, 124–25, 127, 225
Davies, Paul, 88
Dawson, John, 142, 146, 191, 218, 225
Dawson, Rodney, 214–15
deliverance, 8, 150, 158–59

Democrats, Christian, 206
Derrida, Jacques, 86–87, 97, 237
Dickie, Hugh, 48, 51, 225
discipleship, 38, 105–8, 110, 112, 114–15, 119, 198; disciple, 75, 94, 105, 108, 113, 115, 138, 148, 151, 191, 228; discipling, 108, 116, 147, 156–57, 200–201, 224, 227–28; end goal, 106, 109, 112, 114; first step, 107; Kingdom lifestyle, 119; methodology, 107; political, 115; socio-economic, 107–8, 110; work of the Spirit, 115
Dobbins, Dave, 209
Dockery, David S., 98, 225, 228, 235
Donovan, Peter, 73, 223

E

Eagle, Ken, 212
Edwards, Jonathon, 108, 148, 154
Elim, 42, 53, 127
Ellis, David, 140
Ellul, Jacques, 61, 67, 75, 226
empower, 8, 12, 41, 121, 148–50, 154, 158, 160–61, 183–84, 195, 232
engagement, 11, 17, 70, 82, 90, 119, 122, 161, 163–64, 191, 194–95, 200, 202–5, 207, 210
enthusiasm, 32, 135, 231
entrepreneur, 9, 29, 55, 70, 109, 144, 157, 170, 178, 181–84, 195–96, 212, 214, 218, 229
equality, 34, 65–68, 70–71, 106, 151
ethics, Christian, 227, 236
ethnic, 11, 14–15, 37, 42, 44, 46–48, 50–51, 54–56, 69, 71–74, 80, 89, 117, 153, 179, 218–19; church growth, 46, 48, 51, 117; communities, 14, 55, 71–73, 117; congregations, 14, 42, 44, 46–48, 51, 54–56; conversations, 44, 47, 51, 55, 71, 80; diversity, 54, 117; divides, 148, 153; ethnicity, 11, 15, 37, 54, 69, 71–73, 117, 153, 183, 186; integration, 80, 148; lead-

ers, 15, 74, 219; movements, 218; network, 15; origins, 89; politics, 89; sectors, 14; survival, 72; webs, 179
evangelical: theologians, 25–26, 87, 103; theology, 7–8, 26, 78, 98–99, 102, 105, 235
Evans, John, 34, 39, 174

F

Foucault, Michel, 87, 96, 226–27
foundationalism, 26, 96–98
Fox, Matthew, 110, 226
Franklin, Harvey, 74, 232
Fraser, Brooke, 209
Fulford, John, 135
Fuller, Daniel, 102
Fuller Theological Seminary, 235–36, 238–39

G

Galvin, Ray, 206
garden, 62, 64–66, 68
Giddens, Anthony, 84
gift: apostle, 194, 196, 198, 200, 214; discernment, 187; evangelistic, 197; gifted, 56–57; gift in action, 196; higher, 159; leadership, 56, 136, 182, 194, 214; phenomenology, 126; power, 186; primary, 183–84; prophecy, 176, 186–88, 198, 227, 236; sign, 13, 114, 176; speaking in tongues, 158–59; of the Spirit, 110, 114; spiritual, 50, 124–26, 131, 136, 143–44, 158; teacher, administrator, preacher, 141; tongues, 12
Gill, Robin, 53
global culture, 84–85, 92
Gmelch, George, 37, 227, 242
Graham, Billy, 105, 107, 123
Grant, George, 36, 227
Grant, Ian, 208–9
Greenway, Roger, 37, 224
Greenwood, Russell, ii
Grentz, Stanley, 82, 87, 98, 228

Gribben, John, 88
grief, 76, 164, 167, 170, 177, 184
Griffiths, Brian, 36, 78, 228
Grubb, Norman, 155

H

Harley, Rob, 208
Harper, Michael, 125
Hathaway, Brian, 10, 75, 103, 111, 146, 167–68, 229
Haythornthwaite, Peter, 214
healing, 8, 22, 60, 67–68, 105, 114, 131, 135, 150, 152, 188, 190, 210, 225, 229
Heelas, Paul, 95, 224, 229
Heenan, John, 208
hermeneutic, 10, 14, 19–21, 24–25, 29–30, 36, 61, 95, 98, 146, 223, 228, 235
Heschel, Abraham, 62, 189–90, 229
Hessian, Roy, 128, 130–31, 145, 152, 154, 229
Hiebert, Paul, 37, 72, 117, 229–30
holiness, 9, 32, 35, 41, 105, 109, 137–38, 149–50, 182, 219
holistic, 11, 13, 22, 27–28, 37, 39, 96, 102–3, 106–7, 117, 225
holy city, 60, 100
Holy Spirit, 10–14, 17–18, 31–32, 34–35, 39–40, 60, 66–68, 103–5, 109, 124–26, 142–43, 147–53, 156–59, 178–79, 183–84, 186–88; author of history, 60; life-giving, 66; outpouring, 32; work of, 32, 40, 56, 60
hope, 58, 92–93, 98, 100, 105, 115–19, 146, 174, 188, 190, 218–20, 226
Hubbard, Dick, 178, 212
hui, 9–10, 15, 74, 96, 219, 228
humanism, 36, 83, 90, 92, 117, 124, 170–73, 226
humanness, 62, 64–65, 75, 81–82, 92, 94–95, 112–15, 190, 218–19
Hyman, Gavin, 97–98, 230

I

institution, 9, 31, 49, 55–56, 90, 113–14, 126, 128, 132–34, 139, 141, 143, 145, 147, 153, 175–76

J

Jerusalem, 55, 60–61, 89, 100, 153–55, 190–91
Johnson, Bryan, 74
Johnstone, Patrick, 42
Jones: Lindsay, 128; Stanley, 36, 103
Jubilee, 8, 151

K

Kingdom: of God, 8–11, 15, 19, 58, 64, 81, 100–104, 108, 115–16, 119, 132, 146, 152, 174, 218, 222; and Postmodern City, 100; rule, 17, 62, 65, 79, 82, 103–4, 108–9
Kuyper, Abraham, 108, 231

L

Ladd, George Eldon, 231
linkages, 101, 128, 135, 201, 203
Lyotard, Jean-Francois, 87, 90, 97–98, 232

M

Maori, 9, 27, 41, 54-55, 65, 72-74, 80, 89–90, 114, 125, 134, 142, 146–47, 153, 178, 217–18
Masters Institute, 90, 207, 233
metanarrative, 62, 81, 86-93, 95–99, 117, 119
middle axioms, 33-34, 172
Moltmann, Jurgen, i, 35, 39, 101, 115–16, 145, 148–49, 151, 214, 233
movement: AD2000, ii, 11, 38, 146; Anabaptist, 32; apostolic, 194; Brethren, 52, 56, 124, 126; Catholic, 32, 52, 199; cell group, 135; charismatic, 8, 14, 32, 39, 48, 52, 124, 126, 133, 135, 186, 223–24, 242; church, 76, 153, 196; citywide, 179; conciliar, 102; discipling, 147, 157; dynamics, 13, 132-33, 136, 154, 161, 172, 194; ethnic, 179; Evangelical, 44, 46, 57; evangelistic, 208; grassroots, 126; growth, 13-14; holiness, 32, 41; indigenous, 12; Industrial Mission, 199; institutionalisation, 126; integration, 126; Keswick, 42; Kingdom, 119; Lausanne, 11, 35, 173; leadership, 14, 33, 132, 186; narrative theology, 25; national, 127, 201; Navigators, 107; networking, 201; New Age, 56; non-church, 55-56, 198; Pentecostal, 12, 18, 101, 115, 147, 164, 192, 231; people, 48, 156, 178; phenomenology, 147; prayer, 8, 134-35, 201; processes, 15; Promisekeepers, 210; prophetic, 87; religious, 73; renewal, 9, 52, 107, 125, 148, 152, 205; Renovare, 56; revitalization, 133, 185; social, 9, 33, 35-36; social gospel, 116; of the Spirit, 196; structure, 9, 16; student, 172; synergistic, 48, 159, 210; transformation, ii, 11, 202; university, 107; Vineyard, 127, 164; web, 153, 159

N

narrative, 19, 25, 61, 91, 98, 102-3, 215
New Life churches, 112, 126, 140-42, 147, 170, 231
New Zealand Qualifications Authority (NZQA), 130-31, 207
New Zealand Revival, 128-29
Niebuhr, Richard, 103, 166
nodes, 201, 203

O

order, 23, 33-34, 44, 61, 65-66, 70, 78-80, 86, 88-89, 91-92, 106, 116-17, 119, 164, 201, 218-20
Orr, Edwin, i-ii, 33, 41, 123, 134, 145, 147, 150, 153, 163, 177, 210, 235
Otis, George, 8, 179, 235

P

Patrick, Bruce, 40, 131, 225, 228
Peacocke, Dennis, 36, 235
Pentecostal churches, 135-36, 142, 170, 176, 206
periodicity, 134, 154-55
phases, 13, 51, 83-84, 102, 114, 123, 128-29, 131-32, 155, 161, 166, 177-78, 180, 185-87, 193, 217-18
phenomenology, 18, 147-50, 152, 154-56, 159
Pierson, Paul, i-ii, 32, 128, 131-33, 138, 142, 145, 151, 177, 223-24, 236
plurality, 25, 73-74, 82, 117
pneumatology, 10, 18, 20, 24, 30-31, 35, 38-39, 60, 101, 115, 122, 131, 144, 174, 192, 214
populist, 25, 157
postmodern: art, 86; child-raising, 82; church, 56, 89, 115, 138; city, 10-11, 15, 81, 83, 109; city transformation goals, 58; cyborg, 115; discipleship, 111, 113; epistemology, 26; evangelical theology, 96; hermeneutics, 30, 98; humanity, 114-15; liberal theology, 98; music, 208-9; theological method, 95-98; urbanism, 192; urban studies, 37; values consensus, 192
Postmodernism, i, 15, 19, 58, 79, 81-84, 86, 89-92, 94-98, 100, 108, 114, 116-17, 119-20, 218, 228; definition, 81, 84; and Kingdom, 119-20; in philosophy, 86; political and economic, 89; and technology, 94; theology, 95, 97
postmodernity, 20, 40, 87, 97, 112, 117, 119, 224-25, 233
power, 11-13, 31-34, 72-73, 78, 86-87, 94-97, 102-5, 108-9, 117, 142, 144, 149-53, 157-61, 174-76, 186-87, 240-41
Presbyterian, 13, 17, 32, 42, 47, 49-50, 53, 74, 124, 126, 130-31, 138, 155, 182, 197, 240

Prince, Derek, 125
prophetic: prophecy, 17-18, 36, 182-89, 193-94, 197, 200, 202, 212, 214, 236; roles, 123, 185, 188-90, 193
Prophetic, Sources of Transformation in Urban Cultures, 185
public: domain, ii, 11, 117, 171; space, 11, 21, 69, 117, 119, 203; square, 11, 154, 176-77, 182, 184, 189

R

Rauschenbusch, Walter, i, 33, 100, 103, 116-17, 189, 235-36
Ravenhill, Leonard, 145, 236
realism, Christian, 86, 222
redistribution, 111-12, 151, 167-68
reflective-practitioner, ii
reign of God, 100, 103
repentance, 11-12, 128, 130, 138, 145, 149-51, 161, 167, 176, 179-80, 182-83, 187, 189-90
revival: awakening, 152-53, 235; movements, iv, 11, 41, 59, 128, 131, 133, 144-47, 152-53, 155-56, 159-61, 177-79, 183; nature of, iii, 144-45, 147, 149, 151, 153, 155, 157, 159, 161, 240; personal, 161-62; principles, 123, 134, 144, 149, 152, 160, 177, 226; relationship of, 142, 145, 158-59; revivalism, 152, 158; spiritual, 151, 179; sustainable, 133, 145; theology, 10, 14, 41, 148, 159, 210
revival dynamics, 9, 51, 55, 153, 163, 214
righteousness, 94, 109-10, 116, 177, 179, 181, 236
river, 59-60, 66, 124
Robertson: Murray, 126; Peter, 127
Rorty, Richard, 86-87, 236

S

Sax, John, 212, 214
Schaeffer, Francis, 35, 86–87, 172, 237
schooling, Christian, 168, 170, 198, 234
Schwartz, Christian, 50, 55

secular, 7, 14, 33–34, 36, 38, 49–51, 58, 89–90, 92–93, 95–96, 117, 171–73, 183–84, 195–99, 220–21, 224; Secular City, 38, 224; secularization, 49–50, 89–90, 166
Shaw, Colin, 135
Sider, Ron, 35
signs and wonders, 8, 97, 148–49, 156–57, 214
simplicity, 75, 112, 131–32, 142, 167, 197, 218, 228
Skeates, John, 173
small group, 52, 55–56, 71, 93, 125, 127–28, 130–33, 135, 137, 156–57, 161, 197, 200, 203–5, 224
Smith, Milton, 31, 42, 124, 126, 167, 238
Smithies, Ruth, 171, 237
Snyder, Howard A., 32, 114, 128, 130, 132, 136, 145–46, 151–52, 157–58, 161, 237
Sobrino, Jon, 96, 238
social change, 26, 36, 53, 57, 82, 87, 131, 137–38, 159, 164, 179–81, 183–84, 190–92, 195, 219, 229
social gospel, 33–36, 78, 103, 112, 116–17
socialism, 112
social order, 33, 116–17, 164, 201, 239
social sectors, 14–15, 179, 195–96, 200–202, 205
Spirit of God, 8, 31, 60, 63, 70, 75, 78, 101, 109, 150, 152, 217–19, 233
spirituality, v, 7, 13, 38, 40, 56, 73, 75, 90, 92, 98, 107, 110, 136–38, 175, 214
Stark, Rodney, i, 133, 147, 184, 198, 226, 238
Statistics New Zealand, 73, 168, 238
Stenhouse, John, 206, 224–25, 231–32, 238
Sturt, John, 209
Subritsky, Paul, 210; Bill, 126
Sugden, Chris, 103, 105, 225, 238
synergy, 10, 48, 70, 115, 119, 142–43, 155, 157, 159, 172–73, 178–79, 183–84, 201, 210, 218; definition, 178; revival, 48, 70, 115, 179; urban movement, 159

T

Tamaki, Brian, 142, 208, 230
Taylor: Lynne, 128; Steve, 115
Temple, William, 24, 34, 230, 236
Tertiary Students' Christian Fellowship (TSCF), 172
theology: action-reflection, 14, 21, 29, 195; of anointing, 140; anthropological, 37; of the balladeers, 96; of being, 192; biblical, 24, 28; Catholic, 23; charismatic, 137, 159; church growth, 132; of the city, 60–61, 101, 183; of citywide unity, 146; communal, 16, 99; of confessional groups, 125, 128, 130; contextual, ii, 25, 28, 36; conversations, 21, 96; of culture, 172; Death of God, 38; demonization of, 96; diachronic, 28; economic, 167; end of, 97; environmental, 75, 207; ethnotheology, 90; Evangelical, 7–8, 25–26, 98; facilitator, 22; factors preceding revival, 164; global, 22, 183; grassroots, 22, 36; grounded, 145; health and wealth, 140; hermeneutics, 29; historical, 26; indigenous, 22; of justice, 107; Kingdom, 102–3, 108, 116, 174; Kuyper, 108; of land, 64; Latin American, 103; liberal, 26, 34, 37, 49, 94, 130, 136; liberation, 23, 96, 98, 101, 164; methodology, 14, 23; missions, 10, 13, 26, 38, 123; moral, 116; multivariate, 23–24; narrative, 25, 226; nonfoundational, 26; oral, 95; of order, 79; paradigm shift, 125, 128, 132, 143, 161, 177, 184; Pauline, Johanine, 25, 28; Pentecostal, 29, 39, 42, 105; of the people, 13, 16; of periodicity, 154; of place, 64; political, 174; postmodern, 20, 30, 95–98; of power, 78; of property

| 249

and riches, 110; of prophetic, 188; of rage, 164; of reconciliation, 178; of revival, i, 10, 14, 41, 145–48; of revival movements, 147, 152; secular, 50, 90; sloganised, 140; social, 35, 103, 172, 175, 184; of the Spirit, 39, 60, 98, 131, 158, 174, 198; story-telling, 21–23, 25; as structure, 194; synchronic cross-cultural validation, 27; systematic, 22–23, 26, 28–29, 39, 52; theologian, 10, 15, 18, 22, 48, 50, 87, 93, 102; training, 125–26, 128, 130–31, 136–37; transformation, 10, 25, 29, 38–39, 105, 108, 132, 161, 173, 181, 192; of transforming revival, 31, 143, 159, 164, 184; urban, 13, 20–23, 38–39, 61, 228; of urban planning, 65; validity, 26, 138; workplace, 131; Yahwist, Elohist, priestly, Deuteronomic, 28

Thwaites, James, 196
Tillich, Paul, 37, 238
Tippett, Alan, 13, 37, 41, 134, 145, 153, 156, 195, 201, 239
Tonna, Benjamin, 67, 79, 239
Toynbee, Arnold, 155, 185, 239
transform, 7, 9, 184; transformation, 8–11, 15, 31, 35–39, 55–59, 100–101, 105–7, 179, 181, 183–85, 187–89, 199–201, 219–20, 225–28, 237–38; transformational, iii–iv, 10, 14–16, 19–21, 23–25, 27–31, 38–39, 58, 74, 84, 95–99, 108, 117, 183, 191–92, 199–204; transformative, 10, 57; transforming, ii–iv, 10–11, 14–15, 31–34, 116–18, 121–23, 143–44, 161–64, 174–85, 189, 193–97, 201–3, 209–11, 213–15, 219–20, 227–29
transformational conversations, 10, 15, 19–21, 23–25, 27–30, 84, 95–98, 117, 200, 228
Transforming Revival: goals of, 81, 117–18, 121; phases, 180, 185, 189; theology of, 10, 143, 159, 164; theory of, 15, 122, 152, 163, 174, 176
TSCF (Tertiary Students' Christian Fellowship), 172
Turner, Harold, 89–90, 173, 208, 239

U

universities, Christian, 207, 219

V

values, 9–11, 39, 73–74, 84, 86, 110–11, 114–17, 138–40, 166–68, 170, 191–92, 203–5, 207–8, 211–12, 218–19, 241
Values Education, 191, 207–8
Villafañe, Eldon, 39, 63, 175, 192, 240
Vision for Auckland, 9, 14–15, 43, 58, 69, 80, 163, 178, 201, 210, 228
Volf, Miroslav, i, 115, 214, 240
von Rad, Gerhad, 62, 240

W

Wagner, Peter, 53, 127, 146, 191, 195, 200, 240
Wakelin, Bob, 125
Wallace, Anthony, 87, 133, 146–47, 164, 185–86, 240
Wallis: Arthur, 124, 128, 149, 154, 240; Jim, 35
Ward, Kevin, 40, 44, 49, 51, 56, 93, 126, 140, 240
web movement, 145, 153, 155–56, 159, 179; conversion, 195; discipling, 156
web of belief, 23, 26–28, 96, 100, 144, 147, 159, 161–62, 181
Wellington, 40, 70, 146
Wells, David, 84, 241
Wesley: Charles, 187; John, 32, 107, 144, 151, 157, 180, 232, 240
West, 39, 49, 87, 89, 152, 236
Weston, Craig, 212, 215
Wheeler, Rob, 170
Whitefield, George, 32, 36, 48, 144–45,

187, 206, 241
Wilberforce, William, 32, 179, 241
Willems, Emilio, 182, 241
Wilson, Bryan, 42, 49, 241
Wimber, John, 18, 164, 241
Windsor, Paul, 163, 166
Winger, Neville, 124
Winters, Ralph, 153, 198, 222, 241–42
Wishart, Ian, 169, 206, 242
Withy, Alan, 44, 48, 242
Wong, Ben, 135
World Evangelical Fellowship (WEF), 11, 33, 35, 242
worldview, 81–82, 84, 88, 90, 92; Christian, 90, 231, 240

Y
Yaxley, Trevor, vi, 208
Yoder, Howard, 201, 242

www.ingramcontent.com/pod-product-compliance
Lightning Source LLC
Chambersburg PA
CBHW032039150426
43194CB00006B/346